1982

University of St. Francis
GEN 301.31 P274

Responsibilities to future gen

3 0301 00062031 6

D1570083

Responsibilities To Future Generations
Environmental Ethics

Responsibilities To Future Generations
Environmental Ethics

Edited by Ernest Partridge

LIBRARY
College of St. Francis
JOLIET, ILL.

 Prometheus Books
1203 Kensington Avenue
Buffalo, New York 14215

Published 1981 by Prometheus Books
1203 Kensington Avenue, Buffalo, New York 14215

Copyright © 1980 by Ernest Partridge
All rights reserved

Library of Congress Catalog Number: 80-84401
ISBN: 0-87975-142-8

Printed in the United States of America

301.31
P274

Cartoon by Bill Sanders of the Milwaukee Journal. Reprinted with permission of
Mr. Sanders and the Milwaukee Journal.

100,074

CONTENTS

viii   *Contents*

FOREWORD

Because recent ecological insights have thrown somber shadows on the path of history, the idea of earth stewardship and its emphasis on moral obligations owed to future generations has moved into the forefront of world thought. Of course the stewardship concept has ancient origins: it is as old as the Old Testament and was a preoccupation of both husbandmen and prophets in pastoral times.

This book is evidence that this concept is once again becoming a central concern of philosophers and theologians. Seminal thinkers realize already that the vaulting question, "What do we owe posterity?" will haunt humankind as long as men and nations are forced to grapple with the intertwined problems of overpopulation, resource depletion, and ecological exploitation. Even the United States, with its insatiable appetite for resources and its concomitant faith that science and technology will produce substitutes as needed, has felt the shock waves of this new trend.

I recall well the infatuation Americans had with "atomic age" science in the 1960s: we believed implicitly in those days that the energy problem was "solved" (i.e., by nuclear electricity, which would be "so cheap it wouldn't have to be metered") and had a soaring belief that the kinds of minds that had unlocked the secrets of the atom could literally "create" whatever resources we needed from air, sea water, or common rock.

The extent to which this belief captured the imagination of politicians and statesmen in the 1960s was exemplified by this grandiose pronouncement uttered by U Thant, the Secretary-General of the United Nations, in 1967:

> The truth, the central stupendous truth, about developed countries today is that they can have—in anything but the shortest run—the kind and scale of resources they decide to have . . . It is no longer resources that limit decisions. It is the decision that makes the resources. This is the fundamental revolutionary change— perhaps the most revolutionary mankind has ever known.

It goes without saying that this prospect has withered. In the remaining years of this century, we who inhabit this planet will have a preview of the future, as nations are forced to lower their sights and deal with the consequences of resource overutilization.

It is an interesting historical commentary that this book is apparently the first volume ever to collect a broad scope of opinion concerning the moral and ethical questions encompassed by the stewardship idea. Of course the concern for future generations exhibited here is one of the fruits of the ecological revolution, which has been telling us that we are part of a vulnerable natural system and that we are living in a time when no nation, or continent, can sustain itself in isolation from the other parts of the world. It is no wonder this change has put a focus on the future that should make us acutely conscious of our obligations to our children and theirs.

This book is overdue. It should be welcomed by all who are concerned about the tomorrows of the unborn. Stewardship is a *survival* concept. We must nourish it now, before it is too late.

Stewart L. Udall

ACKNOWLEDGMENTS

For several years I have entertained the idea of collecting an anthology of philosophical essays dealing with the moral issue of the duty to posterity. In the fall of 1976, soon after completing my doctoral dissertation (on "Rawls and the Duty to Posterity"), I began exploratory work. In those early days, as the conception of the project was being formulated, I received valuable advice and encouragement from Mike Parsons, Bill Whisner, Peg Batten, and Tom Reed at the University of Utah. While I was in New York City on a National Endowment for the Humanities summer grant, I received useful suggestions from Tom Nagel.

Fortunately, I did *not* bring the project to an immediate conclusion; for, if I had done so, several significant papers included in this collection would not have been completed or published in time for inclusion. Most of the work on the anthology (i.e., selection, editing, and correspondence) was done during the academic year of 1978–79, while I was a Fellow in Environmental Affairs with the Rockefeller Foundation. I am deeply grateful to the Foundation for this assistance, which hastened the completion and enhanced the quality of the anthology. While on leave during that year, I was ably advised and warmly encouraged by Garrett Hardin and Rod Nash at the University of California at Santa Barbara.

Among the contributors to this volume, Thomas Derr, Gregory Kavka, Ruth Macklin, Galen Pletcher, and Annette Baier revised their manuscripts (substantially so, in the latter three cases) for inclusion in this collection. Charles Hartshorne and Holmes Rolston deserve special notice and thanks for submitting original works at my invitation.

The general introduction benefited from the comments and suggestions of Gene Bozniak and Sharon Smock-Hoffman at Weber State College, Garrett Hardin, Rod Nash, and Dan Botkin at the University of California, Santa Barbara, and from those of Holmes Rolston and, above all, Galen Pletcher. Douglas MacLean of the Center for Philosophy and Public Policy offered helpful suggestions for the bibliography. All of these have earned my gratitude

xiv   *Acknowledgments*

for their capable assistance, but none of the blame for errors of content or style that might remain despite their good advice. Karen Miller, also at Weber State College, capably assisted with correspondence and typing, and my brother, Clark, cheerfully offered me the use of his superb office equipment. For their ready and even exuberant assistance with the final proofreading, my thanks go out to Jim Baldwin, Mark Elwell, Fran Fetzer, Kathy Linehan and Laura Siemons. Through it all, Paul Kurtz and Steven Mitchell of Prometheus Books have displayed constant support, confidence, and patience. Above all, I am grateful to my wife, Elinore, for the assistance that she freely and generously gave, even while thoroughly occupied with work on two books of her own. The manuscript was much improved by her efforts and suggestions.

E.D.P.

I

What do we owe posterity? The question is unavoidable, for the course of human events has forced the issue upon us. We of this generation have in our hands unprecedented power to affect the future—forever. And the sciences that have given us this power have also given us an unprecedented ability to foresee the long-term consequences of our acts, our innovations, and our policies. But, while we benefit from the whirlwind of technological innovation, we are not powerless to control it. We can, for instance, choose at last to control world population, or we can tolerate continued growth. We can devote our full attention to the relief of those who are wretched on the earth today, or we can, instead, give additional attention to the problem of mitigating, and even avoiding, the misery of those who are yet to be born. We can continue the current trend of increasing energy consumption supported by massive, resource-depleting, centralized energy technologies, or we can conserve and develop small-scale, diversified, and renewable sources of energy. And there are many other choices of lasting significance that are immediately before us.

The implications for future generations, who at present have no voice in these decisions, are profound beyond comprehension. Consider just a few examples: First, a commitment to develop and utilize nuclear-fission energy on a grand scale will result in the production of vast amounts of highly toxic radioactive materials, some of which will have to be monitored and isolated from the biosphere for hundreds of thousands of years—for all practical purposes, *forever*. Continued development and production of high-altitude supersonic aircraft, along with the continued use of chloro-fluoro-carbons, will continue to erode the ozone layer of the stratosphere, thus increasing the amount of ultraviolet radiation and causing deleterious effects upon crop production and human health.

The response of our political and economic leaders to the current "energy crisis" appears to be "more of the same." Rather than significantly reducing

1

energy consumption, we have accelerated the extraction of coal and oil and have elected to turn to still other fossil fuels, such as tar sands and oil shale. If this policy continues, the increased carbon-dioxide content in the atmosphere could raise the ambient temperature of the earth sufficiently to melt the Greenland and Antarctic ice caps, resulting in the flooding of many major cities of the world and the loss of much prime cropland. Population pressures and the demand for resources are causing an alarming and accelerating destruction of tropical rain forests and, with that depletion, an irreversible loss of exotic species and ecosystems. Tidal marshes and estuaries, the sources of most aquatic nutrients, are being filled and polluted. Continental shelves, the most biologically active areas of the seas, are being contaminated with industrial wastes. The vast ocean itself has been found to be vulnerable to human intervention in its systemic integrity.

While our ability to affect the future is immense, our ability to foresee the results of our environmental interventions is not. But we are not totally blind to the consequences of the technical ventures now at work or contemplated. Our age has witnessed not only a revolution in power but also a revolution in communications and information processing. From satellites and worldwide recording and transmitting stations, we monitor the pulse of the planetary organism: the solar input, the hydrological and nutrient cycles, the climatic changes, the patterns of land use, and so on. We know what is happening; and, with new developments in computer modeling of complex integrated functions, we may be able to discover the graver hazards that lie in the path ahead, both for us and for our posterity. Furthermore, the very enormity of the changes that are projected, or imminent, may render a finely tuned science of forecasting somewhat irrelevant. For whatever their tastes in music and poetry, or whatever their preferences in sports and other amusements, our descendants will need croplands and watersheds to supply their food and water, and they will need to be free of ultraviolet and nuclear radiation. And it is *these* necessities of future life and welfare that are in grave jeopardy *now,* and we know this *now.*

I have suggested that our moral responsibility grows with foresight. And yet, paradoxically, in some cases grave moral responsibility is entailed by the fact of one's ignorance. If the planetary life-support system appears to be complex and mysterious, humble ignorance should indicate respect and restraint. However, as many life scientists have complained, these virtues have not been apparent in this generation. Instead, they point out, we have boldly marched ahead, shredding delicate ecosystems and obliterating countless species, and with them the unique genetic codes that evolved through millions of years. We have altered the climate and even the chemistry of the atmosphere, and, as a result of all this — *what?* A few "results" are immediately to our benefit: more energy, more mineral resources, more cropland, convenient waste disposal. Indeed, these short-term payoffs have motivated us to alter our natural environment. But by far the larger and more significant results, the permanent results, are unknown and perhaps unknowable. Nature, says poet Nancy Newhall, "holds answers to more questions than we know how to ask." And we have scarcely bothered to ask. Year by year, the natural habitats diminish and the species disappear, and thus our planetary ecosystem (literally, our "household") is forever impoverished. The immediacy and urgency of this biotic loss was emphasized in the recently released report of the Council on Environmental Quality, *Global 2000,* which predicted that "perhaps as many as 20 percent of all species on earth will be irretrievably lost as their habitats vanish, especially in tropical forests." In a recent issue of *Harvard* magazine, E. O. Wilson, Baird Professor of Science at Harvard University, reflected that posterity may find us least forgivable for this "loss of genetic and species diversity by the destruction of natural habitats."

Compensating notice should be made of the benefits afforded the future by the accomplishments of our scientific-industrial civilization. Because of our deliberate efforts, no future generations will ever again suffer the scourge of smallpox. The ability to control malaria and yellow fever, developed by this and immediately preceding generations, will benefit posterity into the far future. We have learned to identify some genetic diseases, and thus (if we choose) to control and diminish their transmission, and "genetic engineering" promises still more significant advances in this field of applied science, with implications for the future that are as apparent as they are beneficial. Finally, the very scientific and technical knowledge that has led to the profligate use of energy and resources in our generation *may,* if we are sufficiently provident and prudent, permit us to develop alternative energy and material resources for the future. But such provision, of course, calls for more than science and technology, however necessary they may be. It also calls for a willingness to care, sacrifice, and provide for the future.

We are, in an important sense, "hooked" on science and technology. Despite the urgings of the neo-romantics and the neo-Luddites, we simply cannot return easily and effortlessly to a pre-industrial mode of life. Our physical sustenance depends upon intensive industrial agriculture and upon high energy consumption. As John Passmore and many others have observed, the remedy for the failings of science is more and better science, augmented, to be sure, by a moral vision and commitment that is excluded from science by reason of its very logical structure. As a method and an activity, modern science is a magnificent cultural achievement. But it is a fundamental paradox of our age that scientific knowledge and discipline, supplemented by critical moral sense and passionate moral purpose, will be needed to save the future from the excesses and the perils brought about by a careless, short-sighted application of a scientific knowledge and technological capability that perhaps has developed too fast and affected the earth too much for our own good and for the good of our successors.

If these reflections upon the present human condition and prospect are essentially correct, it then appears that we are not morally permitted simply to let the future be, for our responsibility is forced upon us. We cannot carry on now with "business as usual," for the resulting resource depletion and the accumulating effects of our alterations upon the natural environment force changes upon us. The business of the immediate future, of necessity, will not be "usual," to say the least of it; the immediate future will require us to make momentous and unprecedented decisions, as has the immediate past. So we must decide: Will we have nuclear power and synfuels or renewable solar and biomass energy? The age of abundant, cheap fossil fuels ("as usual") is over forever. Shall we take drastic steps to curb population growth, or shall we not? If not, mankind will have to do without wilderness, tropical rain forests, and many tropical species, and civilized societies will have to manage with a reduced supply of vital, imported raw materials. Shall we reconstruct national and global political and economic structures, or will we just try to muddle through with existing eighteenth- and nineteenth-century institutions? "To do nothing is to do something." We cannot escape our responsibility.

The claim that this generation has an unprecedented responsibility to the future has often been voiced and written recently. That claim will be repeated several times in this anthology. One rarely encounters, however, the suggestion that this burden of responsibility may now be at a peak and that no generation in the foreseeable future will have an equivalent degree of opportunity to affect the future. And yet this may well be the case. For many of the same massive and portentous interventions in nature that are now contemplated, and even underway, cannot be undone. We cannot replace lost species or restore lost ecosystems. Once we commit ourselves to full-scale reliance upon nuclear power, as we likely shall within the coming decade, retreat will be politically and economically impossible, and future generations will face the choice either of permanent surveillance of the wastes or (and more likely) of lapsing into indifference and neglect and ultimately facing biological catastrophe. Nuclear power is but one of many technological "fixes" we have acquired. Energy-intensive mechanized agriculture is another. Many have forgotten that the term *fix,* in the fashionable phrase *technological fix,* might be interpreted to refer, not to "repair," but to "addiction."

Rising population combined with depleting resources adds up to diminished expectations and diminished capacity to act in behalf of the long-term future, a point that Garrett Hardin stresses in this anthology. And so, as food, resources, and energy become increasingly scarce and costly, capital and labor surplus will diminish. (This will be especially so if we continue on our course of developing capital-intensive "hard" sources of energy.) "Nonessential" activities and professions will be more difficult to support, and among the endangered "nonessential" professions will be the arts and letters, leisurely reflection on the human condition and prospect, futures forecasting, and even research and development in the "pure" (nonapplied) sciences. (The reader who doubts this dismal prognosis might contemplate recent trends in higher education, particularly the state of the "academic job market".) As the scope of urgent needs contract to the here and now, so too will the scope of foresight and action. Posterity's chance to be saved from our folly may even now be nearly lost.

II

The foregoing survey indicates that we now possess the *capability,* the *knowledge,* and the *options* to affect variously and profoundly the *welfare* of our successors (and, to be sure, of our contemporaries as well). If these factors correctly *describe* our present circumstances, then they also *define* these circumstances as "morally significant." They also help us to define the scope of our topic: "the duty to posterity." As suggested above, to say that an agent has a "moral duty" to perform an act implies (*a*) that the act is the most morally valuable of the available acts. By "morally valuable" I mean either that the act best exemplifies respect for the rights of affected beings ("deontological value") or that the act optimally affects the welfare of beings with interests — that is, beings who can be benefited or harmed ("teleological value"). "Moral duty" also implies (*b*) that one knows, or that it is one's responsibility to know, that the act is morally valuable in one of the senses defined above; (*c*) that one is capable of performing that act; and (*d*) that one can deliberately choose either to perform the act or not to perform it. ("Moral action" is here interpreted with sufficient generality to include *forebearances* — that is, "acts" of choosing *not* to perform morally undesirable acts.) In strong formulations of the concept of duty, the beneficiaries of the duties are identified as holders of correlative *rights.* This last qualification, however, is controversial, and I will not insist upon it in order to permit the adoption of a broad sense of "duty." In the sense I intend, "duty" is roughly synonymous with a "requirement" or a "responsibility" to act knowledgeably, capably, and freely when faced with morally significant options.

I have attempted here to offer only the beginning of an analysis of the concept of duty. Much more needs to be explicated if we are to distinguish the concept of a "morally dutiful act" from bordering concepts such as a "morally permitted act" (favoring the interests of oneself or of one's family, friends, or kind) and a "supererogatory act" (such as the act of a saint or a hero on behalf of others or on behalf of institutions or ideals). However, since such additional attempts at clarification would introduce considerable controversy, I will carry this analysis no further. Our purposes will have been sufficiently served if I have succeeded in indicating that the concept of "moral duty" entails, at the minimum, (*a*) moral significance, (*b*) knowledge, (*c*) capacity, and (*d*) choice.

Like R. B. Brandt, H. L. A. Hart, John Rawls, and many other moral philosophers, I prefer to interpret the word *obligation* as referring to voluntary, mutually acknowledged commitments to, or between, identifiable persons (Partridge, 1976, p. 28).* Accordingly, while we might properly speak of

---

* In this Introduction, as well as in editorial comments throughout the book, in-text citations such as this will refer to items listed in the Bibliography to this anthology. The Bibliography is in two parts ("I. The Duty to Posterity," and "II. Population Policy"). The context of the citation will usually indicate the list to be consulted. If not, both lists should be searched. Published material will be cited by author and date. Unpublished or pending material will be identified by author and abbreviated title.

"duties" to future persons, it would be inappropriate to speak of "obligations to future persons." A glance at the table of contents in this anthology will indicate that the editor's linguistic preference has been overruled by at least six of the contributors. These writers, and many others, understand that, with reference to posterity, "obligation" is to be interpreted broadly, perhaps even synonymously with "duty" or "responsibility." While I will personally favor the word "duty," I will understand that this word may be interchangeable with others' use of "obligation."

So much for "duty." What of "posterity"? The editor and most of the writers will interpret "posterity" to mean, in Martin P. Golding's words, "[future] generations with which the possessors of the obligations cannot expect in a literal sense to share a common life." (This collection, pp. 61–62.) We are thus able to treat such "obligations" apart from the obligations that bind parents and children and from those that otherwise obtain between adjacent generations.

One final clarification is in order if we are to place our topic in focus. By "duty to posterity," we are to understand "duties to persons *who may be assumed to exist in the future.*" This apparently arbitrary qualification is introduced to allow us to distinguish between "duty to posterity" and the related question of "population policy," namely, "What moral duties (and permissions) do we have to produce, or to refrain from producing, future persons?" The astute reader will immediately perceive that the questions are more readily distinguished by explication than they are separable in moral deliberation. After all, those who "may be assumed to exist" will be affected by our past reproductive decisions. (Indeed, as Derek Parfit ["Energy Policy . . ."] and Thomas Schwartz [1978] point out, our reproductive decisions will, in effect, totally "repopulate" the future with different persons from those who would have otherwise existed.) Conversely, morally responsible procreative decisions should take into account the anticipated life-conditions of future generations.

The distinction between the issues of "duty to posterity" and "population policy" is admittedly somewhat artificial. Still, it is very useful to an editor who is anxious to contain his topic. And, though the two issues cannot be neatly isolated in a logical sense, it is not difficult to utilize the distinction to separate philosophical papers according to emphasis upon one issue or the other. Of the two topics, population policy has probably received more attention in the recent philosophical literature, and two fine anthologies (by Bayles in 1976 and Sikora and Barry in 1978) are available that devote considerable attention to that topic. However, the following anthology is probably the only collection of philosophical papers now in print that devotes almost complete attention to the topic of the duty to posterity. But while I have selected papers that emphasize the posterity issue, I have also chosen two papers (i.e., one by Hardy Jones and one by Mary Anne Warren) that are well suited to "bridge" the two issues. (For more about this distinction, see the bibliographical note at the end of this anthology.)

Within the scope of the issue of the duty to posterity, several controversial issues arise. Two in particular are significant enough to merit separate sections of the anthology. The first question (examined in Part 3) concerns the purported *rights* of future persons. Many philosophers who readily concede that the living have duties to posterity will balk at the suggestion that these duties are entailed by corresponding *rights* of those who are yet to be. The question may be quite significant, since duties derived from *rights* may require more of the living in terms of sacrifices and forebearances. The second question deals with moral psychology. Duties, we will recall, presuppose a *capacity* to act. But might not human beings be psychologically incapable of acting in behalf of the remote future? And if so, might they not thus be absolved of moral responsibility to so act? The question of the capacity, even the need, to care for the future is examined in the fourth part of this anthology.

III

Several arguments might be raised against the claim that the living have duties to posterity (or, more stringently, that future generations have rights-claims against the living). Some of these arguments are examined in the papers that follow. Not included among the criticisms of the duty to posterity is the "argument from moral nihilism"—that is to say, the claim that there are no such things as rights and duties *at all,* and therefore no rights and duties between present and future generations. Such an argument, however, belongs to general ethical theory. If we were to examine it seriously, it would be difficult to depart from this general theoretical dispute and return to the subsidiary question of the duty to posterity.

Instead, the editor and the contributors all seem to agree that the concepts of "duties" and "rights" are, in some cases at least, meaningful, coherent, and applicable among contemporaries. The issue, then, is simply this: Are there any identifiable features of "futurity" *as such* that are sufficient to disallow any claim of moral duty to future persons? Several features have been suggested. Among them:

- The further we project into the future, the less probability we can assign to certain events and circumstances.
- We are unable to predict the course of the future.
- We are unable to alter the course of the future.
- Future persons are indeterminate (that is, unknowable to us as individuals).
- Future persons are contingent, not actual.
- We are ignorant of the needs, desires or tastes of future people.
- We are ignorant of the *number* of future people (and thus, for example, unable to make utility calculations regarding them).
- We are unable to determine whether, or how many, future generations will "share our social ideal" and thus be members of our "moral community." (Cf. Golding, in this anthology.)

In reply, defenders of the duty to posterity (or, more rigorously, of posterity's *rights*) have argued that these are not features that are essential to "futurity," since some of these claims are false (for example, the claim that we cannot predict or affect the future), and several of these features apply to cases that are both contemporary and morally significant (i.e., such features as unidentifiability, improbability, ignorance of number, ignorance of tastes and desires, and so on). Thus, for example, a defender of the duty to posterity would insist that if it is morally improper to place an unknown *living* person in possible jeopardy (the "unidentifiability" and "probability" features), there appears to be no reason for future "indeterminates," *qua* future, being any less deserving of our protection, *all other factors being equal.*

Those who feel that futurity as such makes a difference to the value of a benefit or a cost will support a policy of "discounting the future." Accordingly, a given value in "present-time equivalents" (say, in dollars), decreases as it is projected further into the future. (Thus, at a discount rate of 6 percent per annum, $100 in ten years is worth $55.84 today, in constant dollars. See Garrett Hardin, this anthology, p. 223.) On the other hand, those who deny this axiom of "pure time preference" (e.g., John Rawls, 1971, §45) hold that "a value is a value," regardless of the time of its realization. The concept of "discounting the future" is a point of fundamental contention between economists and moral philosophers. To economists, the concept is virtually axiomatic and thus beyond dispute. To many philosophers, the notion is, at best, arbitrary and unproved and, at worst, absurd. In this anthology, the policy of "discounting the future" is discussed and debated by Passmore, Golding, Hardin, and the Routleys. (The controversy will be further discussed in Brown and MacLean's forthcoming anthology, *Energy Policy and Future Generations.*)

We are prepared, at last, to list some of the fundamental and persistent questions that have been raised with regard to the duty to posterity. These questions appear, time and again, implicitly and explicitly, in philosophical discussions and publications devoted to the issue. Indeed, many have appeared earlier in this Introduction. The questions are grouped in the following list according to these categories: (*a*) *Metaethics* (questions *about* moral philosophy as it is applied to the future, for instance, explications of moral concepts and analyses of methods of moral justification). (*b*) *Normative ethics* (questions directly addressed to matters of duty, obligation, and moral worth, for example, "What should be done?" "What is worthwhile?" "What acts and policies are most praiseworthy?"). (*c*) *Empirical and practical considerations* (questions about matters of fact; in general, these include: "What do we, and can we, know about the future?" "What will be the effects of present technological innovation and environmental impacts upon the remote future?" "What capacities do we have to affect the future?" "What needs and capacities do human beings have to care about the future?").

Metaethical Questions

— What moral categories apply, or do not apply, to our relationship to posterity? Rights? Obligations? Duties? Responsibilities? Other categories? On what grounds might such applications or exclusions be based? Nonactuality? Nonconcurrence? Indeterminacy? Other grounds?

—To what degree are our responsibilities to the future contingent upon our knowledge of the needs, values, and tastes of future persons?

—Are future persons members of our "moral community"? What characteristics would qualify or disqualify them?

—What constitutes a justification or validation of a putative "duty to posterity"?

Normative Questions

—What *kinds* of future beings may, or may not, have duty claims upon living persons? What interests might they have that would entail duties on the part of their predecessors?

—What environments and circumstances should we most desire to preserve and create for future generations? Why? What can we do in behalf of posterity that is *most* in our power to do? In what sense would these results be "good for" future people?

—What are the moral implications of our ability to *affect* the life conditions of future persons and of our ability to *foresee* the results of our present technologies and policies?

—How might the duties to posterity best be characterized? As "just savings" of capital, resources, cultural values, and just institutions? (Cf. Rawls, 1971.) As forebearances from harmful activities? As the promotion of benefits? As restitution for prior damages (e.g., to the natural environment)? As a broadening of the ability to anticipate future impacts of present policies?

—What *weight* does the duty to posterity have when in conflict with short-term benefits? (For example, have we a duty to keep some resources "in reserve"? At what point of scarcity is this duty overridden?) How might such priorities be assessed?

—To what degree might living persons *need* to feel a sense of duty to future persons? Is a sense of duty to posterity a necessary ingredient of a functioning moral sense, or even of an integrated, well-functioning, personality?

—Does an understanding of the past illuminate a responsibility to the future?

—Do "potential persons" have a "right" to be brought into existence?

Empirical and Practical Questions

—Are we able adequately to predict the future so as to make proper provision for the needs of posterity? That is to say, have we *both* the knowledge and the power to do so?

—Can we anticipate the interests, needs, and tastes of posterity? Will our descendants want what we preserve and prepare for them?

—Will posterity miss what it has never known (e.g., wildlife, wilderness, and so on)?

—Are we able to plan and act appropriately to bring about desired results or to avoid projected problems?

—Might not the political, social, economic, psychological, and aesthetic costs of significant improvement of posterity's prospects simply be beyond what our generation should reasonably be called upon to bear?

—Will not the poor and disadvantaged members of present generations be called upon to bear a disproportionate share of the cost of benefiting those who are yet unborn?

—Does posterity need our care? Can't future generations take care of themselves so long as we turn over our scientific and technological knowledge and techniques? Won't they find adequate resources and solutions on their own?

—What prospects are there for *educating* and *motivating* members of the present generation to fulfill these duties to posterity?

The list, however long, is only partial, and the reader should be able to add to it with little difficulty. It will soon be apparent to the reader that the issues discussed in this collection are more "philosophical" (that is to say, metaethical and normative) than empirical. This emphasis is deliberate and follows from the editor's conviction that most empirical analyses of long-term effects upon the future (namely, "cost-benefit studies," "environmental impact studies," "policy analyses," "alternative futures forecasting," and so on) are long on data and short on evaluative concepts, techniques, and norms. In short, we have an abundance of "facts" but are ill equipped to make moral sense of it all. In this collection I have attempted to bring together the best insights of contemporary moral philosophers; those whose business it is to make "moral sense" of the empirical trends and data of our time.

IV

The published and invited papers selected for this collection are all, I believe, of high philosophical quality. The high quality of some papers not included and of portions of papers that had to be deleted for space requirements testifies to the merit of the final collection. These exclusions and abridgements were often made with great reluctance. And yet these papers, for all their value, were not drawn from a large pool of works; the question of the duty to posterity, for all its significance and urgency, has not elicited widespread interest and response from the philosophical profession. In the first footnote of his 1972 paper, "Obligations to Future Generations" (in this anthology), Martin P. Golding writes, "I know of no other explicit discussion of the topic." Golding was unfamiliar with "other discussions" for the justifiable reason that there were very few philosophical papers on the topic that were available as recently as a decade ago, as a glance at the Bibliography of this book will indicate. (Complaints and remarks about this shortage appear throughout this anthology.) The lack of manifest philosophical interest in the topic is further indicated by the fact that of the almost 700,000 doctoral dissertations on file at University Microfilms in Ann Arbor, Michigan, only one has in its title either the words "posterity," "future generations," or "unborn generations." (The dissertation in question is the editor's "Rawls and the Duty to Posterity." This information was determined by a computer scan of Dissertation Abstracts on February 14, 1980.)

This regrettable history of neglect by the philosophical profession appears, at last, to be coming to an end. Again, the Bibliography of this anthology supplies evidence in support of this claim. There we shall find that the number of philosophical publications devoted to the topic of future generations is increasing each year, reflecting the remarkable and widespread renewal of interest by the profession in moral, social, and public issues. The editor, the publisher, and the contributors of this collection hope that this effort will further stimulate active and public debate and scholarly research into this crucial question of the moral duties of the living to their successors.

Philosophical quality, as I have noted, has been a primary criterion in the selection of these papers. But I have also endeavored to include papers that were accessible to the general reader. Although many of these papers will be more readily understood by a student of moral philosophy, such a background is by no means prerequisite. And while a few technical papers of manifest philosophical merit (listed in the Bibliography) were screened out by this criterion, there were not many of these. The best and most influential papers passed that test of "accessibility" to the layman and are included here. Three papers in Sikora and Barry's collection (1978), those by Thomas Schwartz, Mary B. Williams and Brian Barry, were eminently suitable for this anthology and are highly recommended to the reader. However, since two other essays from that book were selected (namely, those by Kavka and Warren), clearly the adoption of additional material would have been excessive and unfair to the publisher, Temple University Press, and the editors.

The scope of a project is defined by its exclusions as well as its inclusions. Some of the exclusions have already been noted, such as papers devoted primarily to "population policy" and a detailed, technical discussion of the policy of "discounting the future" (although, again, the issue appears in several of the papers herein). Both topics are treated in other anthologies, either in print or forthcoming (Bayles, 1976; Sikora and Barry, 1978; Brown and MacLean, forthcoming).

The work of John Rawls is conspicuously absent from this collection. Surely, Rawls's examination of "Justice Between Generations" and "Time Preference" (§§44–45 of his splendid work, *A Theory of Justice,* 1971) is one of the most significant recent philosophical discussions of the posterity question. Moreover, at fifteen pages, these particular sections of his book are of suitable size for inclusion. Unfortunately, these sections appear midway through a long, complex, profoundly original philosophical work. Because Rawls's treatment of "justice between generations" presupposes an understanding of his general moral concepts and theories, those sections cannot effectively be excised from the content of the book—not, at least, without considerable effort and space being devoted to an attempt to explicate the missing or presupposed concepts and principles. The regrettable exclusion of Rawls from this collection is somewhat mitigated by Passmore's and Green's papers. Passmore gives explicit attention to Rawls's ideas, and Green presents and defends his position from a point of view that is closely reminiscent of Rawls.

The papers in this collection were chosen on the basis of their philosophical merit and on the basis of their relevance to the fundamental question, "What moral responsibilities do the living have to future generations?" Understandably, as it turns out, most of the papers have been written by professional philosophers (the exceptions being Robert Heilbroner, an economist, Garrett Hardin, a biologist, and presumably the anonymous author of the *New Yorker* feature). Following their selection on the basis of merit and relevance, other characteristics, not deliberately sought, became apparent. First of all, it turns out that all but two of the papers were either written or published within the past decade (the exceptions being the one-page "Postscript" by Hardin, published in 1968, and "Love of the Remote" by Hartmann, first published in English in 1932). In addition, the reader will discover that most of the papers do not fit neatly into a single section category. (This is especially the case with the papers in Parts 1, 2, and 5.) "Issues" papers reflect "Perspectives," and "Perspectives" papers raise "Issues." "Rights" and "Motives" are widely discussed outside the "appropriate" sections. The papers have been grouped, perhaps somewhat arbitrarily in some cases, according to their emphases. While this circumstance is disconcerting to an editor, it is not a serious problem. Rather, it reflects the fact that the posterity question raises a number of subsidiary issues and problems, most of which are interrelated. These topics, issues, and questions tie together and "spill over" because, due to the nature of the posterity problem, they *should* do so.

V

This anthology is intended to serve as a prologue, as a stimulus to thought, research, discussion and action, by philosophers, behavioral scientists, life and physical scientists, policy-makers, administrators, legislators, and concerned citizens. Included in these nontechnical papers are appeals for responsible reflection and concern and for thoughtful and resolute action. The appeals are directed to us all: to students, to scholars, to professionals, to practitioners. The call to reflection and action is urgent, but it is neither clear nor unambiguous. Few of the issues are sharply defined, and many of the moral imperatives are confused, conflicting, and uncoordinated. We bear a burden of incalculable responsibility. And yet we find that we must clarify the issues, analyze the concepts, defend the moral principles, and assess the implications, even as we attempt appropriate action in behalf of our successors. In short, the task before us is not only political, economic, and technological. It is also profoundly, and even inescapably, *philosophical.* What, then, are we to do?

The metaethical task of explicating the moral concepts that may apply to the posterity question and defining the rules for justifying claims of responsibility to the future falls to the moral philosopher, who also has the normative task of articulating moral principles of duty to future generations. And yet, while occupied with these abstract and theoretical questions, the moral philosopher must endeavor, with deliberate haste, to bridge the gap between concepts, principles, and theories, on the one hand, and working policies and practical moral judgments on the other. The issues are urgent and momentous, and the political and economic conditions of our time are forcing us to make immediate decisions of permanent significance and consequence for the future.

The events of the day will not await clear articulations and prolonged deliberations by the philosophers. Once again, we find that history has not well accommodated our needs and comforts. Time is needed to effect clarification and explication of the moral issues that we face, and time is what we do not have. The best that we can hope for is more philosophers to engage in better philosophizing. And much of that philosophizing will have to be done outside of academic departments of philosophy. Some philosophers have responded to this challenge, but that response has, to this date, been too little and possibly too late. For all the recent and accelerating philosophical discussion and publication on the issue, the posterity question remains a matter of minor interest and attention among contemporary moral philosophers. This should not and need not be the case; for here is a topic well suited to excite the young philosophers who, in their student days a decade ago, clamored for academic "relevance" and professional involvement with the moral and social issues of our time.

There are also urgent questions to be addressed by researchers in moral philosophy. Among these questions are the following: Can we and should we care about the remote future? What basic human capacities, needs, and motives, if any, are involved in transpersonal concern for the future? Do we, in some significant psychological sense, need the future *now?* That is to say, do we need to hope and work for the welfare of those who will never share our lives? Perhaps not. But, if not, we should know this. If, on the other hand, we have such capacities, needs, and motives, how might they be evoked, nurtured, and enlisted in behalf of our posterity and, at the same time, in behalf of our *own* needs for self-transcending moral commitment and activity? Once they discover and articulate answers to these crucial questions, the moral psychologists have the task of translating those answers into effective procedures and methods of moral education and activism.

Psychologists, sociologists, and anthropologists have a further task to perform in behalf of posterity. We urgently need to know what future human beings will need *just because they will be human beings.* Consider one timely example: We may soon be destroying the last of the unspoiled natural wilderness. Will this be a loss to future generations, or are human beings sufficiently adaptable that they will manage quite well, say, with astroturf lawns and plastic trees in lieu of wilderness — or even with no turf or trees at all? Some biologists and psychologists believe that man cannot adapt well to a totally artificial world, that man needs the environment in which he evolved as a species simply because that need is in his *genes*. Is this so? We need to know this, and soon, while there is still a natural environment to be preserved. Otherwise, our successors may be permanently impoverished.

If the philosophers define the concepts and prescribe the principles of duty to the future, and if the psychologists and the biologists determine the fundamental needs of future human beings, what then? Then we turn to the life scientists and the physical scientists. We will turn to them for projections and sketches of alternative futures. We will rely on them to forecast the short- and long-term effects of our various choices. We will need them to guide us in our attempts to fulfill our duties to the future, in our attempts to avoid harm and promote benefits for those who will follow us. And we need the sciences not only for knowledge but also for *capacity* and *action*. We must act, and act effectively and soon, but we must also act prudently and cautiously. For while we have, in the past, both benefited enormously from our technological advances and paid heavily for our technological miscalculations, now the stakes are much higher. For now our brain cells, our germ plasm, and our supporting planetary atmosphere and life communities are all in our own, often careless, hands. We cannot afford more sudden, catastrophic surprises. Our successors will need energy, basic resources, and a life-supporting eco-system. We should thus endeavor to develop new and benign technologies that will supply these needs without exacting the ruinous long-term costs that we have heretofore assessed to the future and, to some degree, to ourselves. Thus do the scientists, the technologists, and the industrialists share in a responsibility to the future.

The conditions of future life are contingent not only upon the scientific knowledge and capabilities available to this generation but also upon the moral presuppositions and the motives that underlie and direct the selection and evaluation of this information and capability in the formulation of policy, and the consequent investment, implementation, and regulation of technology. Accordingly, in addition to the data and projections of the scientists and technologists, the judgments of the philosophers and the psychologists should be made available to policy-makers, administrators, and legislators, whose difficult and awesome task it is to interpret and integrate this mass of information and opinion, to assess and weigh options, and finally to select specific courses of action and to enact particular items of regulation and legislation.

Clearly we haven't the space even to begin a discussion of the difficult issue of "policy analysis." Let it suffice for us to note that the insights of the moral philosophers are needed as policy-makers attempt, as they must, to clarify the moral assumptions, implications, and constraints that are to guide their decision-making. Decisions of enduring moral significance are being made in our generation because they must be made. We cannot avoid our responsibility, since postponement and evasion of many moral decisions may prove to be ultimately irresponsible. "Not to decide is to decide," that is, to decide in favor of the status quo (which, as we have noted, is *not* "static"). And so, in the face of forced moral decisions of transcending and permanent significance, policy-makers have the responsibility to consult the experts, the moral philosophers, for clarification of moral issues and for guidance in moral judgments. Conversely, the philosophers (or at least an appreciable number of them) should conduct their research with an eye toward application. "Applied philosophy" need not and should not be regarded in the profession as second-rate work—as a sell-out or a compromise of academic purity and abstraction. Like it or not, "men of affairs" in government and business hold the future hostage to their decisions. Philosophers, of various persuasions, can and should have a voice in these decisions. If not, generations yet unborn will justly regard the profession to have been in default of its moral responsibility.

The need for an involvement of the philosophical profession in policy analysis seems especially acute when one reviews the practices and assumptions that are regarded as virtually axiomatic among many policy-makers today. In a deliberate attempt both to avoid ideological bias and to obtain precision, policy-makers have generally adopted the economist's methodology of "value-free, cost-benefit analysis" and the economist's habit of substituting measurable market *costs* for "qualitative" and "subjective" *values*. This philosopher might object that, despite deliberate efforts to avoid bias, such methods and assumptions *are* biased and that they are biased toward a highly controversial ethical theory, namely, *utilitarianism*. Not only that, but the "market value" criterion of cost and benefit assessment leads directly to the policy of "discounting the future"—a policy based upon the assumption that the value of future costs and benefits is directly proportional to their *proximity* in the future. (Thus, according to this "social discount theory," at a per-annum discount rate of 5 percent, one death a year is equivalent to over two million deaths three-hundred years in the future.) This conclusion is repugnant even to utilitarians (such as Henry Sidgwick) who generally argue that time, per se, is not relevant to value assessments. Another remarkable assumption, uncritically borrowed from prevailing economic theory, is that public policy is to be regarded as similar in kind to private or corporate policy, though different in degree, and that "society," in other words, is to be regarded as the *sum* of its individual decision-making parts.

Are the current presuppositions and procedures of policy analysis correct or are they not? I do not propose to answer that question here. Perhaps the economic approach to policy analysis is valid. But, if it is, the validity of this approach, and of the fundamental presuppositions upon which it is based, should be articulated and justified, and not merely assumed by government administrators and legislators. However, if the economic approach to policy analysis is inappropriate, then the foundation of much, if not most, of our traditional policy analysis is untenable, and many decisions of lasting importance to future generations may be fundamentally misguided. Our whole structure of policy theory and application should be reviewed and assessed, and philosophers should have an important role in this work.

Ultimately, posterity will not be cared for unless the citizens care enough. There are many temptations before us to rob the future for the sake of the present. And posterity has no retaliation for such villainy, except, abstractly, through our consciences. All our power, knowledge, and good intentions will fail to serve the future if we lack collective will. And that means *political* will. Thus the responsibility ultimately resides in the citizens. In particular, the citizen's duty to posterity translates into a responsibility to be informed of the threats we pose and the opportunities we promise for the future. It also translates into a responsibility to develop and to sustain, through reflection and practice, a sound moral sense and judgment. This means that the citizen must also expand his time sense so that he might perceive himself and his generation as part of an ongoing historical adventure. Thus our duty to generations past and future requires us to acquire a historical consciousness and to reflect and act from the broad perspective of such a consciousness. In acquiring, reflecting, and acting with historical consciousness and conscience, we may favor ourselves with a sense of transcending involvement and worth. And, finally, with this knowledge, this perspective, and this commitment and conscience, the citizen has a duty to insist that his political leaders count, as constituents, the "silent majority" of the yet to be born. And if the leaders do not, it is the citizen's duty, in behalf of posterity, to select and to install new leaders.

In 1862, Abraham Lincoln said:

> We cannot escape history. We . . . will be remembered in spite of ourselves. No personal significance or insignificance can spare one or another of us. The fiery trial through which we pass will light us down in honor or dishonor to the latest generation. . . . We, even we here, hold the power and bear the responsibility.

When he spoke those words, Lincoln was addressing the Congress of the United States. Today, more than ever before, and possibly more than ever again, those words apply to an entire generation—to *our* generation. But before we can act responsibly we must recognize and acknowledge our responsibility. These papers have been collected and published here to serve that purpose.

Ernest Partridge

Santa Barbara
October 1980

PART ONE

The Duty to Posterity
The Issues

Part 1. The Duty to Posterity
The Issues

Introduction

In choosing the selections for this first section, the guiding purpose was, quite appropriately, to locate papers that would vividly introduce the topic of the duty to posterity to the reader. In particular, I have endeavored in this section to display (*a*) how the posterity question is viewed from several differing philosophical and ideological perspectives, (*b*) the basic and recurring moral issues that are associated with, and which follow from, this question, and (*c*) the pertinence of this moral issue in the context of the social, cultural, and psychological conditions of our time.

The anonymous author of the *New Yorker* feature that opens the book presents a vigorous and eloquent statement of the moral significance, even the *arrogance,* of our interventions in nature and of the insensitivity of our contemporaries to the moral implications of these interventions. Our responsibility to the future, the writer observes, is of unprecedented portent and gravity; our response thereto has, to this date, been wholly inappropriate and inadequate.

Responsibility is also the theme of the essay by Hans Jonas. Jonas agrees that the responsibility of this generation to the future is unprecedented. The source of this new responsibility, he points out, is the foresight and the power that have come with our scientific knowledge and with our technology. In view of this new knowledge and power, Jonas calls for a reconstruction of moral philosophy.

Thomas Derr offers further clarification of the issues and problems generated by the question of the duty to posterity. However, unlike most of the other writers represented in this collection, Derr feels that the case for such a duty may be significantly enhanced by viewing the human condition from "the transcendent perspective which the religious imagination affords."

John Passmore's perspective and approach is secular. An eminent historian of thought and a commentator upon current philosophical trends, Passmore reviews several prominent philosophical responses, both past and present, to the posterity issue. His discussion is illuminated by a wealth of examples and

19

citations from such diverse fields as economics, politics, engineering, and the sciences. This impressive display of scholarship and erudition is assembled in search of an answer to the fundamental questions: (*a*) *Can* we wisely and effectively provide for posterity, and (*b*) If so, *should* we do so? After sensitively considering some negative responses to these questions, Passmore concludes that we can and should provide for the future (with certain constraints, such as competing present obligations and imperfect knowledge of the future) and that our care for the future might best be based upon our concern for institutions, places, activities, and ideals that we love, respect, and cherish now.

Martin Golding's paper, "Obligations to Future Generations," deserves its early and prominent place in this collection in view of the widespread and appropriate attention it has received. (In fact, this paper seems to be the one most cited by the *other* authors in this anthology.) Early in this paper, Golding asks: "(1) Who are the individuals in whose regard it is maintained that we have such obligations, to whom do we owe such obligations? (2) What, essentially, do obligations to future generations oblige us to do, what are they aimed at? and (3) To what class of obligation do such obligations belong, what kind of obligations are they?" These questions reappear throughout the philosophical literature devoted to this question (and throughout this book), although many subsequent papers have taken strong exception to Golding's own answers to these questions. It is remarkable that this influential, provocative, and oft-cited piece was published as recently as January, 1972. Its influence in so brief a time testifies to the vitality and currency of interest in the question of "Obligations to Future Generations."

Daniel Callahan's paper is an early critical response to Golding's essay. (So early, in fact, that Callahan's piece was published before Golding's.) Like so many contributors to this anthology (not to mention many others who have written on the topic of the duty to future generations), Callahan is alarmed at the enormity of our capability to affect, for good or ill, the conditions of life in the future. He reminds us that we cannot escape our responsibility to the future, least of all by ignoring it. He closes his paper with a list of four ethical norms that might guide the "behavior of our present generation which has implications for the lives of future generations." While both Golding and Callahan affirm that we have obligations to our successors, there are significant differences in their views. In the first place, Callahan is more concerned with avoiding or minimizing future harm, while Golding writes of "an obligation to produce—or attempt to produce"—future benefits. Furthermore, Callahan's sense of obligation to the future is more inclusive and extensive; for, unlike Golding, he believes that we are morally responsible to future persons who might not be members of our "moral community" (that is, who will not "share our social ideal"). Accordingly, in Callahan's view, our responsibility to the future will extend much further *into* the future.

The New Yorker

Concerning *Conservation* and *Conservatism*

. . . It strikes us that the dominant note in any sane contemporary political philosophy should be a spirit of conservatism. A conservative is someone who cherishes and wants to protect a people's inheritance, so that it can be passed on undamaged to new generations. In the past, this inheritance was seen, in large part, as consisting of the established political order. In an awed and awesome tribute to the English polity in "Reflections on the Revolution in France," the conservative Edmund Burke wrote, "The people of England well know that the idea of inheritance furnishes a sure principle of conservation, and a sure principle of transmission, without at all excluding a principle of improvement. . . . By a constitutional policy, working after the pattern of nature, we receive, we hold, we transmit our property and our privileges in the same manner in which we transmit our property and our lives. The institutions of policy, the goods of fortune, the gifts of providence are handed down to us, and from us, in the same course and order. Our political system is placed in a just correspondence and symmetry with the order of the world and with the mode of existence decreed to a permanent body composed of transitory parts, wherein, by the disposition of a stupendous wisdom, molding together the great mysterious incorporation of the human race, the whole, at one time, is never old or middle-aged or young, but, in a condition of unchangeable constancy, moves on through the varied tenor or perpetual decay, fall, renovation, and progression." But today's conservatives should give their primary allegiance to the establishment much more ancient, more majestic, and more fundamental than a government. They should give it directly to nature herself. Burke himself paid his respects to nature by envisioning society as patterned after it, but he doubtless never dreamed that nature — the pattern itself — could be threatened. Today, however, we hold a dagger to the very heart of life.

From "Notes and Comment" in *The New Yorker,* May 13, 1972. Reprinted by permission; © 1972 The New Yorker Magazine, Inc. Since the original was untitled, the title above was supplied by the editor. In conformity with *New Yorker* policy, the identity of the author of this "Notes and Comment" feature has not been disclosed.

21

A conservative in our time should first of all learn to cherish and protect nature within us, which is to say, our human nature. It is threatened by radiation, which can corrupt the gene pool and destroy the very frame of man, and it is threatened, of course, by the sheer explosive force of nuclear weapons, which, if they were used, would be great enough to kill every human being. Conservatives should also learn to cherish and protect nature outside us — the land, the sea, the air, our plants and animals, or what we call the ecosystem — from industrial pollution and, again, from nuclear war. As Burke saw things, it was an act of intolerable presumption and imprudence for any single generation to destroy, by a revolution, an ancient, established order that embodied the accretive wisdom of countless generations and to replace it with a political order based on new and untested ideas of its own. It was to rob one's heirs of their inheritance. But how much more presumptuous he would have found it for a single generation, such as our own, to imagine that its wants and its political causes might conceivably justify our jeopardizing not just our inheritance, political and otherwise, but our inheritors as well — our sons and grandsons and the myriad unborn generations whose hopes and achievements we cannot know. This takes truly colossal arrogance. Is it possible that our generation thinks its own transient conflicts more weighty than the infinity of the human future? . . .

It should be plain that a true conservatism today would have nothing to do with what now passes for conservatism in the United States. Our "conservatives" follow Burke in respecting the established *political* order but part ways with him in the deeper matters of respecting the *natural* order. And our political order is not in a just correspondence and a symmetry with the order of the world. Far from it. Burke knew that there was something in the natural world, in society and also in ourselves, that was best left to unfold and change of its own accord, without our deliberate intervention. Perhaps this is what he meant by nature. But today we rush in everywhere with schemes of destruction and presumed improvement. With respect to the natural order, we are blind wreckers who have nothing to offer in place of what we tear down. Our most powerful institutions of production and war — and the "conservatives" who give them unquestioning support — are forces of extreme radicalism. They have taken it upon themselves to remake, and perhaps destroy, the legacy not just of generations but of all time. Burke advised his countrymen to "approach to the faults of the state as to the wounds of a father, with pious awe and trembling solicitude," and to "look with horror on those children of their country who are prompt rashly to hack that ancient parent to pieces." Today, a true conservatism, rooted in a new-found reverence not just for the political, or even the social, order but for an inheritance so great that we have scarcely noticed it until recently — an inheritance that is all around us, and is, in fact, us — would ask the state and all other human institutions to approach the whole of creation with the same awe and solicitude.

Hans Jonas

Technology and Responsibility: The Ethics of an Endangered Future

All previous ethics — whether in the form of issuing direct enjoinders to do and not to do certain things, or in the form of defining principles for such enjoinders, or in the form of establishing the ground of obligation for obeying such principles — had these interconnected tacit premises in common: that the human condition, determined by the nature of man and the nature of things, was given once for all; that the human good on that basis was readily determinable; and that the range of human action and therefore responsibility was narrowly circumscribed. It will be the burden of my argument to show that these premises no longer hold, and to reflect on the meaning of this fact for our moral condition. More specifically, it will be my contention that with certain developments of our powers the *nature of human action* has changed, and since ethics is concerned with action, it should follow that the changed nature of human action calls for a change in ethics as well: this not merely in the sense that new objects of action have added to the case material on which received rules of conduct are to be applied, but in the more radical sense that the qualitatively novel nature of certain of our actions has opened up a whole new dimension of ethical relevance for which there is no precedent in the standards and canons of traditional ethics.

I

The novel powers I have in mind are, of course, those of modern *technology*. My first point, accordingly, is to ask how this technology affects the nature of our acting, in what ways it makes acting under its dominion *different* from what it has been through the ages. Since throughout those ages man was never

Originally presented as a plenary address to the International Congress of Learned Societies in the Field of Religion held in Los Angeles, September 1972, and included in *Religion and the Humanizing of Man,* ed. by James M. Robinson, 2nd ed. (Waterloo, Ontario: Council on the Study of Religion, 1973). Reprinted with the permission of the publisher and author. Copyright by Hans Jonas.

without technology, the question involves the human difference of *modern* from previous technology. Let us start with an ancient voice on man's powers and deeds which in an archetypal sense itself strikes, as it were, a technological note—the famous Chorus from Sophocles' *Antigone.*

> Many the wonders but nothing more wondrous than man.
> This thing crosses the sea in the winter's storm,
> making his path through the roaring waves.
> And she, the greatest of gods, the Earth—
> deathless she is, and unwearied—he wears her away
> as the ploughs go up and down from year to year
> and his mules turn up the soil.
>
> The tribes of the lighthearted birds he ensnares, and the races
> of all the wild beasts and the salty brood of the sea,
> with the twisted mesh of his nets, he leads captive, this clever man.
> He controls with craft the beasts of the open air,
> who roam the hills. The horse with his shaggy mane
> he holds and harnesses, yoked about the neck,
> and the strong bull of the mountain.
>
> Speech and thought like the wind
> and the feelings that make the town,
> he has taught himself, and shelter against the cold,
> refuge from rain. Ever resourceful is he.
> He faces no future helpless. Only against death
> shall he call for aid in vain. But from baffling maladies
> has he contrived escape.
>
> Clever beyond all dreams
> the inventive craft that he has
> which may drive him one time or another to well or ill.
> When he honors the laws of the land and the gods' sworn right
> high indeed is his city; but stateless the man
> who dares to do what is shameful.

(lines 335–370)

This awestruck homage to man's powers tells of his violent and violating irruption into the cosmic order, the self-assertive invasion of nature's various domains by his restless cleverness; but also of his building—through the self-taught powers of speech and thought and social sentiment—the home for his very humanity, the artifact of the city. The raping of nature and the civilizing of himself go hand in hand. Both are in defiance of the elements, the one by venturing into them and overpowering their creatures, the other by securing an enclave against them in the shelter of the city and its laws. Man is the maker of his life *qua* human, bending circumstances to his will and needs, and except against death he is never helpless.

Yet there is a subdued and even anxious quality about this appraisal of the marvel that is man, and nobody can mistake it for immodest bragging. With all his boundless resourcefulness, man is still small by the measure of the elements: precisely this makes his sallies into them so daring and allows those elements to tolerate his forwardness. Making free with the denizens of land and sea and air, he yet leaves the encompassing nature of those elements unchanged, and their generative powers undiminished. Them he cannot harm by carving out his little dominion from theirs. They last, while his schemes have their shortlived way. Much as he harries Earth, the greatest of gods, year after year with his plough—she is ageless and unwearied; her enduring patience he must and can trust, and to her cycle he must conform. And just as ageless is the sea. With all his netting of the salty brood, the spawning ocean is inexhaustible. Nor is it hurt by the plying of ships, nor sullied by what is jettisoned into its deeps. And no matter how many illnesses he contrives to cure, mortality does not bow to his cunning.

All this holds because man's inroads into nature, as seen by himself, were essentially superficial, and powerless to upset its appointed balance. Nor is there a hint, in the *Antigone* chorus or anywhere else, that this is only a beginning and that greater things of artifice and power are yet to come—that man is embarked on an endless course of conquest. He had gone thus far in reducing necessity, had learned by his wits to wrest that much from it for the humanity of his life, and there he could stop. The room he had thus made was filled by the city of men—meant to enclose, and not to expand—and thereby a new balance was struck within the larger balance of the whole. All the well or ill to which man's inventive craft may drive him one time or another is inside the human enclave and does not touch the nature of things.

The immunity of the whole, untroubled in its depth by the importunities of man, that is, the essential immutability of Nature as the cosmic order, was indeed the backdrop to all of mortal man's enterprises, including his intrusions into that order itself. Man's life was played out between the abiding and the changing: the abiding was Nature, the changing his own works. The greatest of all these works was the city, and on it he could confer some measure of abidingness by the laws he made for it and undertook to honor. But no long-range certainty pertained to this contrived abidingness. As a precarious artifact, it can lapse or go astray. Not even within its artificial space, with all the freedom it gives to man's determination of self, can the arbitrary ever supersede the basic terms of his being. The very inconstancy of human fortunes assures the constancy of the human condition. Chance and luck and folly, the great equalizers in human affairs, act like an entropy of sorts and make all definite designs in the long run revert to the perennial norm. Cities rise and fall, rules come and go, families prosper and decline; no change is there to stay, and in the end, with all the temporary deflections balancing each other out, the state of man is as it always was. So here too, in his very own artifact, man's control is small and his abiding nature prevails.

Still, in this citadel of his own making, clearly set off from the rest of things and entrusted to him, was the whole and sole domain of man's

College of St. Francis Library

100, 074

responsible action. Nature was not an object of human responsibility—she taking care of herself and, with some coaxing and worrying, also of man: not ethics, only cleverness applied to her. But in the city, where men deal with men, cleverness must be wedded to morality, for this is the soul of its being. In this intra-human frame dwells all traditional ethics and matches the nature of action delimited by this frame.

II

Let us extract from the preceding those characteristics of human action which are relevant for a comparison with the state of things today.

1. All dealing with the non-human world, i.e., the whole realm of *techne* (with the exception of medicine), was ethically neutral—in respect both of the object and the subject of such action: in respect of the object, because it impinged but little on the self-sustaining nature of things and thus raised no question of permanent injury to the integrity of its object, the natural order as a whole; and in respect of the agent subject it was ethically neutral because *techne* as an activity conceived itself as a determinate tribute to necessity and not as an indefinite, self-validating advance to mankind's major goal, claiming in its pursuit man's ultimate effort and concern. The real vocation of man lay elsewhere. In brief, action on non-human things did not constitute a sphere of authentic ethical significance.

2. Ethical significance belonged to the direct dealing of man with man, including the dealing with himself: all traditional ethics is *anthropocentric*.

3. For action in this domain, the entity "man" and his basic condition were considered constant in essence and not itself an object of reshaping *techne*.

4. The good and evil about which action had to care lay close to the act, either in the praxis itself or in its immediate reach, and were not a matter for remote planning. This proximity of ends pertained to time as well as space. The effective range of action was small, the time-span of foresight, goal-setting and accountability was short, control of circumstances limited. Proper conduct had its immediate criteria and almost immediate consummation. The long run of consequences beyond was left to chance, fate or providence. Ethics accordingly was of the here and now, of occasions as they arise between men, of the recurrent, typical situations of private and public life. The good man was he who met these contingencies with virtue and wisdom, cultivating these powers in himself, and for the rest resigning himself to the unknown.

All enjoinders and maxims of traditional ethics, materially different as they may be, show this confinement to the immediate setting of the action. "Love thy neighbor as thyself"; "Do unto others as you would wish them to do unto you"; "Instruct your child in the way of truth"; "Strive for excellence by developing and actualizing the best potentialities of your being *qua* man"; "Subordinate your individual good to the common good"; "Never treat your fellow man as a means only but always *also* as an end in himself"—and so on. Note that in all these maxims the agent and the "other" of his action are sharers of a common present. It is those alive now and in some commerce with me that have a claim on my conduct as it affects them by deed or omission. The ethical universe is composed of contemporaries, and its horizon to the future is confined by the foreseeable span of their lives. Similarly confined is its horizon of place, within which the agent and the other meet as neighbor, friend or foe, as superior and subordinate, weaker and stronger, and in all the other roles in which humans interact with one another. To this proximate range of action all morality was geared.

III

It follows that the *knowledge* that is required — besides the moral will — to assure the morality of action, fitted these limited terms; it was not the knowledge of the scientist or the expert, but knowledge of a kind readily available to all men of good will. Kant went so far as to say that "human reason can, in matters of morality, be easily brought to a high degree of accuracy and completeness even in the most ordinary intelligence";[1] that "there is no need of science or philosophy for knowing what man has to do in order to be honest and good, and indeed to be wise and virtuous. . . . [Ordinary intelligence] can have as good hope of hitting the mark as any philosopher can promise himself";[2] and again: "I need no elaborate acuteness to find out what I have to do so that my willing be morally good. Inexperienced regarding the course of the world, unable to anticipate all the contingencies that happen in it, I can yet know how to act in accordance with the moral law."[3]

Not every thinker in ethics, it is true, went so far in discounting the cognitive side of moral action. But even when it received much greater emphasis, as in Aristotle, where the discernment of the situation and what is fitting for it makes considerable demands on experience and judgment, such knowledge has nothing to do with the science of things. It implies, of course, a general conception of the human good as such, a conception predicated on the presumed invariables of man's nature and condition, which may or may not find expression in a theory of its own. But its translation into practice requires a knowledge of the here and now, and this is entirely non-theoretical. This "knowledge" proper to virtue (of the "where, when, to whom, and how") stays with the immediate issue, in whose defined context the action *as the agent's own* takes its course and within which it terminates. The good or bad of the action is wholly decided wtihin that short-term context. Its moral quality shines forth from it, visible to its witnesses. No one was held responsible for the unintended later effects of his well-intentioned, well-considered, and well-performed act. The short arm of human power did not call for a long arm of predictive knowledge; the shortness of the one is as little culpable as that of the other. Precisely because the human good, known in its generality, is the same for all time, its realization or violation takes place at each time, and its complete locus is always the present.

IV

All this has decisively changed. Modern technology has introduced actions of such novel scale, objects, and consequences that the framework of former ethics can no longer contain them. The *Antigone* chorus on the *deinotes,* the wondrous power, of man would have to read differently now; and its admonition to the individual to honor the laws of the land would no longer be enough. To be sure, the old prescriptions of the "neighbor" ethics — of justice, charity, honesty, and so on — still hold in their intimate immediacy for the nearest, day by day sphere of human interaction. But this sphere is overshadowed by a growing realm of collective action where doer, deed, and effect are no longer the same as they were in the proximate sphere, and which by the enormity of its power forces upon ethics a new dimension of responsibility never dreamt of before.

Take, for instance, as the first major change in the inherited picture, the critical *vulnerability* of nature to man's technological intervention — unsuspected before it began to show itself in damage already done. This discovery, whose shock led to the concept and nascent science of ecology, alters the very concept of ourselves as a causal agency in the larger scheme of things. It brings to light, through the effects, that the nature of human action has *de facto* changed, and that an object of an entirely new order — no less than the whole biosphere of the planet — has been added to what we must be responsible for because of our power over it. And of what surpassing importance an object, dwarfing all previous objects of active man! Nature as a human responsibility is surely a *novum* to be pondered in ethical theory. What kind of obligation is operative in it? Is it more than a utilitarian concern? Is it just prudence that bids us not to kill the goose that lays the golden eggs, or saw off the branch on which we sit? But the "we" that here sits and may fall into the abyss is all future mankind, and the survival of the species is more than a prudential duty of its present members. Insofar as it is the fate of *man,* as affected by the condition of nature, which makes us care about the preservation of nature, such care admittedly still retains the anthropocentric focus of all classical ethics. Even so, the difference is great. The containment of nearness and contemporaneity is gone, swept away by the spatial spread and time-span of the cause-effect trains which technological practice sets afoot, even when undertaken for proximate ends. Their irreversibility conjoined to their aggregate magnitude injects another novel factor into the moral equation. To this take their cumulative character: their effects add themselves to one another, and the situation for later acting and being becomes increasingly different from what it was for the initial agent. The cumulative self-propagation of the technological change of the world thus constantly overtakes the conditions of its contributing acts and moves through none but unprecedented situations, for which the lessons of experience are powerless. And not even content with changing its beginning to the point of unrecognizability, the cumulation as such may consume the basis of the whole series, the very condition of itself. All this would have to be co-intended in the will of the single action if this is to be a morally responsible one. Ignorance no longer provides it with an alibi.

Knowledge, under these circumstances, becomes a prime duty beyond anything claimed for it heretofore, and the knowledge must be commensurate with the causal scale of our action. The fact that it cannot really be thus commensurate, i.e., that the predictive knowledge falls behind the technical knowledge which nourishes our power to act, itself assumes ethical importance. Recognition of ignorance becomes the obverse of the duty to know and thus part of the ethics which must govern the ever more necessary self-policing of our out-sized might. No previous ethics had to consider the global condition of human life and the far-off future, even existence, of the race. Their now being an issue demands, in brief, a new concept of duties and rights, for which previous ethics and metaphysics provide not even the principles, let alone a ready doctrine.

And what if the new kind of human action would mean that more than the interest of man alone is to be considered — that our duty extends farther and the anthropocentric confinement of former ethics no longer holds? It is at least not senseless anymore to ask whether the condition of extra-human nature, the biosphere as a whole and in its parts, now subject to our power, has become a human trust and has something of a moral claim on us not only for our ulterior sake but for its own and in its own right. If this were the case it would require quite some rethinking in basic principles of ethics. It would mean to seek not only the human good, but also the good of things extra-human, that is, to extend the recognition of "ends in themselves" beyond the sphere of man and make the human good include the care for them. For such a role of stewardship no previous ethics has prepared us — and the dominant, scientific view of *Nature* even less. Indeed, the latter emphatically denies us all conceptual means to think of Nature as something to be honored, having reduced it to the indifference of necessity and accident, and divested it of any dignity of ends. But still, a silent plea for sparing its integrity seems to issue from the threatened plenitude of the living world. Should we heed this plea, should we grant its claim as sanctioned by the nature of things, or dismiss it as a mere sentiment on our part, which we may indulge as far as we wish and can afford to do? If the former, it would (if taken seriously in its theoretical implications) push the necessary rethinking beyond the doctrine of action, i.e., ethics, into the doctrine of being, i.e., metaphysics, in which all ethics must ultimately be grounded. On this speculative subject I will here say no more than that we should keep ourselves open to the thought that natural science may not tell the whole story about Nature.

V

Returning to strictly intra-human considerations, there is another ethical aspect to the growth of *techne* as a pursuit beyond the pragmatically limited terms of former times. Then, so we found, *techne* was a measured tribute to necessity, not the road to mankind's chosen goal — a means with a finite measure of adequacy to well-defined proximate ends. Now, *techne* in the form of modern technology has turned into an infinite forward-thrust of the race, its most significant enterprise, in whose permanent, self-transcending advance to ever greater things the vocation of man tends to be seen, and whose success of maximal control over things and himself appears as the consummation of his destiny. Thus the triumph of *homo faber* over his external object means also his triumph in the internal constitution of *homo sapiens,* of whom he used to be a subsidiary part. In other words, technology, apart from its objective works, assumes ethical significance by the central place it now occupies in human purpose. Its cumulative creation, the expanding artificial environment, continuously reinforces the particular powers in man that created it, by compelling their unceasing inventive employment in its management and further advance, and by rewarding them with additional success — which only adds to the relentless claim. This positive feedback of functional necessity and reward — in whose dynamics pride of achievement must not be forgotten — assures the growing ascendancy of one side of man's nature over all the others, and inevitably at their expense. If nothing succeeds like success, nothing also entraps like success. Outshining in prestige and starving in resources whatever else belongs to the fullness of man, the expansion of his power is accompanied by a contraction of his self-conception and being. In the image he entertains of himself — the potent self-formula which determines his actual being as much as it reflects it — man now is evermore the maker of what he has made and the doer of what he can do, and most of all the preparer of what he will be able to do next. But not you or I: it is the aggregate, not the individual doer or deed that matters here; and the indefinite future, rather than the contemporary context of the action, constitutes the relevant horizon of responsibility. This requires imperatives of a new sort. If the realm of making has invaded the space of essential action, then morality must invade the realm of making, from which it had formerly stayed aloof, and must do so in the form of public policy. With issues of such inclusiveness and such lengths of anticipation public policy has never had to deal before. In fact, the changed nature of human action changes the very nature of politics.

For the boundary between "city" and "nature" has been obliterated: the city of men, once an enclave in the non-human world, spreads over the whole of terrestrial nature and usurps its place. The difference between the artificial and the natural has vanished, the natural is swallowed up in the sphere of the artificial, and at the same time the total artifact, the works of man working on and through himself, generates a "nature" of its own, i.e., a necessity with which human freedom has to cope in an entirely new sense. Once it could be said *Fiat justitia, pereat mundus,* "Let justice be done, and may the world perish" — where "world," of course, meant the renewable enclave in the imperishable whole. Not even rhetorically can the like be said anymore when the perishing of the whole through the doings of man — be they just or unjust — has become a real possibility. Issues never legislated on come into the purview of the laws which the total city must give itself so that there will be a world for the generations of man to come.

That there *ought* to be through all future time such a world fit for human habitation, and that it ought in all future time to be inhabited by a mankind worthy of the human name, will be readily affirmed as a general axiom or a persuasive desirability of speculative imagination (as persuasive and undemonstrable as the proposition that there being a world at all is "better" than there being none): but as a *moral* proposition, namely, a practical *obligation* toward the posterity of a distant future, and a principle of decision in present action, it is quite different from the imperatives of the previous ethics of contemporaneity; and it has entered the moral scene only with our novel powers and range of prescience.

The *presence of man in the world* had been a first and unquestionable given, from which all idea of obligation in human conduct started out. Now it has itself become an *object* of obligation—the obligation namely to ensure the very premise of all obligation, i.e., the *foothold* for a moral universe in the physical world—the existence of mere *candidates* for a moral order. . . .

VII

. . . The new order of human action requires a commensurate ethics of foresight and responsibility, which is as new as are the issues with which it has to deal. We have seen that these are the issues posed by the works of *homo faber* in the age of technology. But among those novel works we haven't mentioned yet the potentially most ominous class. We have considered *techne* only as applied to the non-human realm. But man himself has been added to the objects of technology. *Homo faber* is turning upon himself and gets ready to make over the maker of all the rest. This consummation of his power, which may well portend the overpowering of man, this final imposition of art on nature, calls upon the utter resources of ethical thought, which never before has been faced with elective alternatives to what were considered the definite terms of the human condition.

a. Take, for instance, the most basic of these "givens," man's mortality. Who ever before had to make up his mind on its desirable and *eligible* measure? There was nothing to choose about the upper limit, the "threescore years and ten, or by reason of strength fourscore." Its inexorable rule was the subject of lament, submission, or vain (not to say foolish) wish-dreams about possible exceptions—strangely enough, almost never of affirmation. The intellectual imagination of a George Bernard Shaw and a Jonathan Swift speculated on the privilege of not having to die, or the curse of not being able to die. (Swift with the latter was the more perspicacious of the two.) Myth and legend toyed with such themes against the acknowledged background of the unalterable, which made the earnest man rather pray "teach us to number our days that we may get a heart of wisdom" (Psalm 90). Nothing of this was in the realm of doing and effective decision. The question was only how to relate to the stubborn fact.

But lately, the dark cloud of inevitability seems to lift. A practical hope is held out by certain advances in cell biology to prolong, perhaps indefinitely extend, the span of life by counteracting biochemical processes of aging. Death no longer appears as a necessity belonging to the nature of life, but as an avoidable, at least in principle tractable and long-delayable, organic malfunction. A perennial yearning of mortal man seems to come nearer fulfillment. And for the first time we have in earnest to ask the question "How desirable is this? How desirable for the individual, and how for the species?" These questions involve the very meaning of our finitude, the attitude toward death, and the general biological significance of the balance of death and procreation. Even prior to such ultimate questions are the more pragmatic ones of who should be eligible for the boon: persons of particular quality and merit? of social eminence? those that can pay for it? everybody? The last would seem the only just course. But it would have to be paid for at the opposite end, at the source. For clearly, on a population-wide scale, the price of extended age must be a proportional slowing of replacement, i.e., a diminished access of new life. The result would be a decreasing proportion of youth in an increasingly aged population. How good or bad would that be for the general condition of man? Would the species gain or lose? And how *right* would it be to preempt the place of youth? Having to die is bound up with having been born: mortality is but the other side of the perennial spring of "natality" (to use Hannah Arendt's term). This had always been ordained; now its meaning has to be pondered in the sphere of decision.

To take the extreme (not that it will ever be obtained): if we abolish death, we must abolish procreation as well, for the latter is life's answer to the former, and so we would have a world of old age with no youth, and of known individuals with no surprises of such that had never been before. But this perhaps is precisely the wisdom in the harsh dispensation of our mortality: that it grants us the eternally renewed promise of the freshness, immediacy and eagerness of youth, together with the supply of otherness as such. There is no substitute for this in the greater accumulation of prolonged experience: it can never recapture the unique privilege of seeing the world for the first time and with new eyes, never relive the wonder which, according to Plato, is the beginning of philosophy, never the curiosity of the child, which rarely enough lives on as thirst for knowledge in the adult, until it wanes there too. This ever renewed beginning, which is only to be had at the price of ever repeated ending, may well be mankind's hope, its safeguard against lapsing into boredom and routine, its chance of retaining the spontaneity of life. Also, the role of the *memento mori* in the individual's life must be considered, and what its attenuation to indefiniteness may do to it. Perhaps a nonnegotiable limit to our expected time is necessary for each of us as the incentive to number our days and make them count.

So it could be that what by intent is a philanthropic gift of science to man, the partial granting of his oldest wish — to escape the curse of mortality — turns out to be to the detriment of man. I am not indulging in prediction and, in spite of my noticeable bias, not even in valuation. My point is that already the promised gift raises questions that had never to be asked before in terms of practical choice, and that no principle of former ethics, which took the human constants for granted, is competent to deal with them. And yet they must be dealt with ethically and by principle and not merely by the pressure of interest.

b. It is similar with all the other, quasi-utopian powers about to be made available by the advances of biomedical science as they are translated into technology. Of these, *behavior control* is much nearer to practical readiness than the still hypothetical prospect I have just been discussing, and the ethical questions it raises are less profound but have a more direct bearing on the moral conception of man. Here again, the new kind of intervention exceeds the old ethical categories. They have not equipped us to rule, for example, on mental control by chemical means or by direct electrical action on the brain via implanted electrodes—undertaken, let us assume, for defensible and even laudable ends. The mixture of beneficial and dangerous potentials is obvious, but the lines are not easy to draw. Relief of mental patients from distressing and disabling symptoms seems unequivocally beneficial. But from the relief of the *patient,* a goal entirely in the tradition of the medical art, there is an easy passage to the relief of *society* from the inconvenience of difficult individual behavior among its members; that is, the passage from medical to social application; and this opens up an indefinite field with grave potentials. The troublesome problems of rule and unruliness in modern mass society make the extension of such control methods to non-medical categories extremely tempting for social management. Numerous questions of human rights and dignity arise. The difficult question of preempting care versus enabling care insists on concrete answers. Shall we induce learning attitudes in school children by the mass administration of drugs, circumventing the appeal to autonomous motivation? Shall we overcome aggression by electronic pacification of brain areas? Shall we generate sensations of happiness or pleasure or at least contentment through independent stimulation (or tranquilizing) of the appropriate centers—independent, that is, of the objects of happiness, pleasure, or content and their attainment in personal living and achieving? Candidacies could be multiplied. Business firms might become interested in some of these techniques for performance-increase among their employees.

Regardless of the question of compulsion or consent, and regardless also of the question of undesirable side-effects, each time we thus bypass the human way of dealing with human problems, short-circuiting it by an impersonal mechanism, we have taken away something from the dignity of personal selfhood and advanced a further step on the road from responsible subjects to programmed behavior systems. Social functionalism, important as it is, is only one side of the question. Decisive is the question of what kind of individuals the society is composed of—to make its existence valuable as a whole. Somewhere along the line of increasing social manageability at the price of individual autonomy, the question of the worthwhileness of the human enterprise must pose itself. Answering it involves the image of man we entertain. We must think it anew in light of the things we can do to it now and could never do before.

c. This holds even more with respect to the last object of a technology applied on man himself — the genetic control of future men. This is too wide a subject for cursory treatment. Here I merely point to this most ambitious dream of *homo faber,* summed up in the phrase that man will take his own evolution in hand, with the aim of not just preserving the integrity of the species but of modifying it by improvements of his own design. Whether we have the right to do it, whether we are qualified for that creative role, is the most serious question that can be posed to man finding himself suddenly in possession of such fateful powers. Who will be the image-makers, by what standards, and on the basis of what knowledge? Also, the question of the moral right to experiment on future human beings must be asked. These and similar questions, which demand an answer before we embark on a journey into the unknown, show most vividly how far our powers to act are pushing us beyond the terms of all former ethics.

VIII

The ethically relevant common feature in all the examples adduced is what I like to call the inherently "utopian" drift of our actions under the conditions of modern technology, whether it works on non-human or on human nature, and whether the "utopia" at the end of the road be planned or unplanned. By the kind and size of its snowballing effects, technological power propels us into goals of a type that was formerly the preserve of Utopias. To put it differently, technological power has turned what used and ought to be tentative, perhaps enlightening, plays of speculative reason into competing blueprints for projects, and in choosing between them we have to choose between extremes of remote effects. The one thing we can really know of them is their extremism as such — that they concern the total condition of nature on our globe and the very kind of creatures that shall, or shall not, populate it. In consequence of the inevitably "utopian" scale of modern technology, the salutary gap between everyday and ultimate issues, between occasions for common prudence and occasions for illuminated wisdom, is steadily closing. Living now constantly in the shadow of unwanted, built-in, automatic utopianism, we are constantly confronted with issues whose positive choice requires supreme wisdom — an impossible situation for man in general, because he does not possess that wisdom, and in particular for contemporary man, who denies the very existence of its object: viz., objective value and truth. We need wisdom most when we believe in it least.

If the new nature of our acting then calls for a new ethics of long-range responsibility, coextensive with the range of our power, it calls in the name of that very responsibility also for a new kind of humility — a humility not like former humility, i.e., owing to the littleness, but owing to the excessive magnitude of our power, which is the excess of our power to act over our power to foresee and our power to evaluate and to judge. In the face of the quasi-eschatological potentials of our technological processes, ignorance of the ultimate implications becomes itself a reason for responsible restraint — as the second best to the possession of wisdom itself.

One other aspect of the required new ethics of responsibility for and to a distant future is worth mentioning: the insufficiency of representative government to meet the new demands on its normal principles and by its normal mechanics. For according to these, only *present* interests make themselves heard and felt and enforce their consideration. It is to them that public agencies are accountable, and this is the way in which concretely the respecting of rights comes about (as distinct from their abstract acknowledgment). But the *future* is not represented, it is not a force that can throw its weight into the scales. The non-existent has no lobby, and the unborn are powerless. Thus accountability to them has no political reality behind it yet in present decision-making, and when they can make their complaint, then we, the culprits, will no longer be there.

This raises to an ultimate pitch the old question of the power of the wise, or the force of ideas not allied to self-interest, in the body politic. What *force* shall represent the future in the present? However, before *this* question can become earnest in practical terms, the new ethics must find its theory, on which do's and don'ts can be based. That is: before the question of what *force,* comes the question of what *insight* or value-knowledge shall represent the future in the present.

IX

And here is where I get stuck, and where we all get stuck. For the very same movement which puts us in possession of the powers that have now to be regulated by norms — the movement of modern knowledge called science — has by a necessary complementarity eroded the foundations from which norms could be derived; it has destroyed the very idea of norm as such. Not, fortunately, the feeling for norm and even for particular norms. But this feeling becomes uncertain of itself when contradicted by alleged knowledge or at least denied all sanction by it. Anyway and always does it have a difficult enough time against the loud clamors of greed and fear. Now it must in addition blush before the frown of superior knowledge, as unfounded and incapable of foundation. First, Nature had been "neutralized" with respect to value, then man himself. Now we shiver in the nakedness of a nihilism in which near-omnipotence is paired with near-emptiness, greatest capacity with knowing least what for. With the apocalyptic pregnancy of our actions, that very knowledge which we lack has become more urgently needed than at any other stage in the adventure of mankind. Alas, urgency is no promise of success. On the contrary, it must be avowed that to seek for wisdom today requires a good measure of unwisdom. The very nature of the age which cries out for an ethical theory makes it suspiciously look like a fool's errand. Yet we have no choice in the matter but to try.

It is a question whether without restoring the category of the sacred, the category most thoroughly destroyed by the scientific enlightenment, we can have an ethics able to cope with the extreme powers which we possess today and constantly increase and are almost compelled to use. Regarding those consequences imminent enough still to hit ourselves, fear can do the job—so often the best substitute for genuine virtue or wisdcm. But this means fails us towards the more distant prospects, which here matter the most, especially as the beginnings seem mostly innocent in their smallness. Only awe of the sacred with its unqualified veto is independent of the computations of mundane fear and the solace of uncertainty about distant consequences. But religion as a soul-determining force is no longer there to be summoned to the aid of ethics. The latter must stand on its worldly feet—that is, on reason and its fitness for philosophy. And while of faith it can be said that it either is there or is not, of ethics it holds that it must be there.

It must be there because men act, and ethics is for the ordering of actions and for regulating the power to act. It must be there all the more, then, the greater the powers of acting that are to be regulated; and with their size, the ordering principle must also fit their kind. Thus, novel powers to act require novel ethical rules and perhaps even a new ethics.

"Thou shalt not kill" was enunciated because man has the power to kill and often the occasion and even inclination for it—in short, because killing is actually done. It is only under the *pressure* of real habits of action, and generally of the fact that always action already takes place, without *this* having to be commanded first, that ethics as the ruling of such acting under the standard of the good or the permitted enters the stage. Such a *pressure* emanates from the novel technological powers of man, whose exercise is given with their existence. *If* they really are as novel in kind as here contended, and if by the kind of their potential consequences they really have abolished the moral neutrality which the technical commerce with matter hitherto enjoyed—then their pressure bids to seek for new prescriptions in ethics which are competent to assume their guidance, but which first of all can hold their own theoretically against that very pressure. To the demonstration of those premises this paper was devoted. If they are accepted, then we who make thinking our business have a task to last us for our time. We must do it in time, for since we act anyway we shall have some ethic or other in any case, and without a supreme effort to determine the right one, we may be left with a wrong one by default.

NOTES

1. Immanuel Kant, *Groundwork of the Metaphysics of Morals,* Preface.
2. Ibid., chapter 1.
3. Ibid. (I have followed H. J. Paton's translation with some changes.)

Thomas Sieger Derr

The Obligation to the Future

Generations Yet Unborn

To speak of man's shaping his destiny is to talk in terms of human continuity across generations. It is to set forth the obligation of those now alive to build for the sake of those to come. Ecologically-minded persons all *assume* this obligation to exist, and in fact their argument and concern are unintelligible without the sense that present practices are mortgaging the future. Of course they are right. It is easy to see how depleting resources, damaging the biosphere, and running up the population count are ways of sowing the wind for tomorrow's children to reap as the whirlwind. Conceivably, too, we could institute programs that would improve conditions of life for the next three or four generations, yet prove fatal to mankind after that. In the protection of the environment, long-range policies are crucial. In order to avoid disaster by postponement of consequences, our notion of the proper care of the earth has to reach imaginatively into the far future.

Standard ecological rhetoric always speaks of present restraint for the sake of future life and happiness, thus taking for granted the claims of coming generations against us. And yet surprisingly little systematic thinking has been done about this indispensable assumption.

When I first wrote this essay, in 1972, I found that virtually *nothing* had been written about the basis of this obligation to our descendants in managing our environment. It is only since that time that the subject has begun to receive its due notice.

Perhaps the reason for the long lack of interest is that we do not find it easy to extend the horizons of our social responsibility very far in either space or time. It is hard enough in spacial conception, where our concerns tend to be

From *Ecology and Human Need,* by Thomas Sieger Derr. Copyright © 1973 and 1975 by Thomas Sieger Derr. Published by The Westminster Press (1975) and the World Council of Churches (in 1973, as *Ecology and Human Liberation*). Used with permission.

limited to our own group. We can perhaps widen the circle of our care from family to community, even as far as our nation, but beyond that point the going is difficult and our sympathetic resources weak. Responsibility in temporal extent is in some ways even harder to conceive. We care for our children and grandchildren, and maybe our imaginations can grasp the needs also of our great-grandchildren; but after them the picture becomes very fuzzy. Planning commissions tend to focus on the year 2000 as a nice round figure and suitably future-sounding. The details fade out when we push our imaginations much farther, though A.D. 2000 is less than a generation away.

People sometimes explain their lack of concern for the future by saying that it is impossible anyway to plan very concretely for the next century, or that we should have confidence in the ability of future generations to manage their own problems. In other words, we do not know what the lives of our descendants will be like, and so we cannot anticipate their needs. The farther that succeeding generations are from us, the less likely they are to share a common life with us, just as we have little sense of a common life with primitive men of the past.[1] Distance cuts our ties to them. We cannot presume to know their values or desires, literally do not know what will be "good" for them. What if they are robots or simpletons or beasts? Will *their* good be like *our* good? And why should we sacrifice now to help those whose good we cannot really know? It is surely absurd to say we should "love" them as we love our children and grandchildren.

These are strong and natural reservations, but a committed ecologist must find some way around them if he is to enlist the popular support his cause requires. Is the appeal to self-interest, perhaps, a possible tool? It does have its uses in extending our sense of ecological responsibility *spatially,* at least. Ecologists have made us understand the interdependent character of human existence around the globe, the threat to all life everywhere posed by damage from any particular local source to the unitary, life-supporting biosphere. If we want clean air over our own land, and clean seas washing our shores, we shall have to play our part in worldwide pollution control. If we want to continue having heat and power and transportation, we shall have to cooperate with other nations in the use of the world's natural resources. If we want to enjoy the enrichments of travel, we shall have to be part of a global effort to preserve the natural reserves and the cultural monuments which are the heritage of all mankind.

But such a global view does not reach very far into the future. It plans rationally and cooperatively for the lifetimes of contemporary men, their children and grandchildren; but beyond that there seems to be no appreciable self-interest at work. Few men can project their personal concerns a century or more ahead. Some statesmen, of course, may be genuinely worried about the way historians of the future will judge them. *Their* self-interest may thus be engaged in long-term environmental management; and they are, after all, in key positions to do something about the problem. But most of us know that we will be anonymous to future generations and have no reputations to protect.

Even the genealogical hobbyists among our descendants will care little about us save our names, dates, birthplaces, family members, and occupations — not much more than can be put on our gravestones. The subtle reaches of our thoughts, our style of life, whether we cared about these future beings and acted with their well-being in mind — all this will be inaccessible to them.

Reciprocity is a feature of obligations based on self-interest. If someone does something for me, such as lending me money, it is in my interest to discharge the obligation this act creates, such as paying back the loan. In so doing, I keep my credit good and preserve my standing as a trustworthy member of society. Or if I am the lender, I create an obligation which I expect will one day be discharged to my advantage. This reasoning, however, can hardly apply to our descendants. They will not be able to do anything for *us*. They may preserve our memory in kindly fashion in return for our leaving them a habitable environment; but that is not much of a favor to us, personally, if we are all dead. Perhaps someone with a whimsical turn of mind will remember that in some cultures the ghosts of the dead, like Hamlet's father, are thought to need comforting by certain actions of the living, which creates the possibility of reciprocity across generations. But such idle thoughts aside, mutuality seems not to be possible between distant generations and ours.

If not by reciprocity, maybe self-interest can be extended into the future by the phenomenon of collective immortality. Seeking a way to overcome the threat of death, a man may identify himself with his group, which will outlive him. So he has a real interest in its future well-being, and acts in his lifetime to ensure its survival far into the future. In fact, he wishes it to survive forever, for it is his immortality. An optimistic ecologist might hope such desire for immortality could be translated from survival of the group to that of the whole human race.

But judging by history, the odds are against this wider identification. Historically the phenomenon appears in tribal, ethnic, or national chauvinism directed *against* other men. It is particular in impact, not general. I will survive only in my country, my race. Others are not my descendants and do not carry me on in eternal human life, so what I do now is meant to benefit only "my kind." Obviously such group idolatry will not help the whole world. It is more likely to pit one people against another in destructive competition than to promote a long-term program of sound international cooperation in environmental defense.

One more possibility for putting self-interest to work in ecological service is to appeal to concern for the future as a sign of *present* health. It is possible to argue that a society which fails to care for the future has lost its sense of purpose and thus its capacity to deal with the present. Social goals have a way of transcending particular generations. While our ideals — let us say, a society of freedom, justice, and happiness — influence, inform, and guide our present actions, they are never fully realized. We are always moving toward them. Our grasp on our own purposes in society, our way of coping with our current problems, carries with it an explicit commitment to the future.

This argument has merit, but there are at least two problems with it. One is that it may credit social ideals with too much power over current behavior when sacrifices are demanded in their name, especially sacrifices of the magnitude that good environmental care may require. The political difficulty in imposing such restraints is enormous. It is easier to postpone, redefine, or simply ignore inconvenient ideals. The other fault with the argument is that its reach is too short. Even if we were to act consistently on the basis of our social goals, we would be thinking of the society we aim to have in a generation or two. This reasoning does not get us much beyond the generation of our grandchildren, whereas environmental planning asks us to leap far ahead of that. In short, here, as in the preceding argument, we reach all too soon the limits of self-interest as a viable motive in establishing an ecological responsibility to future generations.

Breaking the Bonds of Self-Concern

If self-interest is not the key to the problem, perhaps it lies in the moral instinct which seems to tell us that we are responsible to coming generations. The unborn have rights in law, for example, as when trusts are created on behalf of possible descendants and the money withheld from living claimants. In certain circumstances we do recognize that the living may be deprived for the sake of those to come.

We also seem to be intuitively aware of the wrong in imposing the bad consequences of our acts on others without their acquiescence. As we now know for certain that the ecological results of many of our current habits will be visited, unwanted, on future generations, it seems congruent with our moral intuitions to say we ought to change our ways to spare our descendants. The word "responsibility" itself means that we must "answer" to someone for our acts after we commit them. If our death should intervene, that does not really wipe the slate clean, just because we cannot from the grave literally "answer" to the living for our deeds. We are still guilty. To use a legal example again, the estate of a deceased person is liable for the debts he incurred while alive. None of us really believes that we are relieved of responsibility for our works just because we will not be around to face the victims.

There is some logic behind these moral intuitions. The generations of man are obviously linked together tightly in a cause-and-effect chain. What we are today we owe to what our predecessors have left us, and what our descendants will be depends on what we bequeath to them. Of course we must care for those progenitors still alive, the aged among us. But our more remote ancestors, to whom we also owe much, are dead; and so, for their sake, we pay our descendants. We bequeath good to the future as a way of affirming our thankfulness for our own lives. It should be noted, however, that this is a gesture of gratitude, like building a monument, and not, strictly speaking, an obligation. If I owe A a debt, I do not discharge it by paying B, unless A has prearranged this transfer.

As for the argument that we cannot presume any definition of "good" for our distant successors which would govern our actions today,[2] it may be replied that for as far into the future as we can reasonably foresee, the similarities between their life and ours will greatly outweigh the differences. It is too easy to exaggerate the changes as an excuse for our indifference to their fate. We can presume their basic needs for air, water, space, food, and shelter, by whatever technology they will secure these things. The continuity between their needs and ours is real. What we do now will certainly affect them — think of our rate of reproduction, for instance — and, thanks to ecological studies, we have a fair knowledge of these effects. These people *will* one day be alive; as their existence is not just hypothetical, they will actually experience the consequences of our acts. Despite their differences from us, they will, to our certain knowledge, appear one day as claimants to challenge us, the deceased ancestors, for what we have done. It really would be "irresponsible" of us not to consider them.

To these arguments, with their varied strengths and limitations, we may add another group drawn from specifically religious sources. The claim that our accountability to others, our obligation to love our neighbors, means not only our contemporaries but those who come long after us may be strengthened considerably where people view their lives in the transcendent perspective which the religious imagination affords. If we feel that our answerability is to a God who stands outside the processes of nature and the course of history, our responsibility in our actions has to extend forward in time as far as those actions have consequences. We are part of a cosmic process whose purposes reach far beyond our personal lives. Generations past and unborn are all part of this providence. To love such a God moves us powerfully to serve our future fellow humans, more powerfully, it may be, than any merely rational reflection on the inherent nature of debt and repayment, or any direct reliance on our moral intuitions. Religious motivation can be very strong motivation indeed, with effects usually wider-reaching than secular systems, whatever the merit of the latter.

In the classic Western religious tradition, biblical theology makes explicit the sense of future obligation implied in its doctrine of divine creation and governance of the universe. One of its master images is the covenant, made between God and His people at a point in time, maintained and renewed from generation to generation as a sign of God's faithfulness and men's continuing duty. To Noah, to Abraham, to Isaac, to Jacob, God promises His blessing forever, not only to the particular patriarch but also to his descendants. The idea is constantly repeated, the divine gift and the human response which establish a network of obligation reaching forward as far as the mind can imagine. Consequences of acts do descend to posterity, and the inheritance has moral significance.

There is also a negative form of this intergenerational responsibility, the fear that the God of history will punish future generations for the mistakes of the present. And even though this particular formulation belongs to a passing phase of Hebrew religion, and the convenant responsibility is individualized by later prophets, there remains the solidarity of the generations, the responsibility of each to accept appropriately what its predecessors have done for it, and to pass on the gift, unsullied, to those following.

Christian thought inherited the Hebrew sense of historical responsibility, and at first differed principally in believing that the course of history would very soon reach its end, with the imminent return of Christ. But with the rapid passing of the apocalyptic expectation, and the reduction of millennialism to a minor and off-beat note in Christian thought, there remained the Hebrew inheritance that history is a drama of salvation in which all the parts, in all ages, are relevant. The unity of the generations in mutual care and concern receives additional expression in the Christian doctrine of the communion of saints, where the faithful, dead and alive, are virtually present to each other in living relation. So also the faithful of the future will be part of us, and we of them. Furthermore, Christian *love* is the divine *agape* which applies not just to people with whom we share values, to "our group," or "our generation," but to all people in all time, all the household of God, all the Father's children. This idea, too, establishes an obligation to future generations.

Finally, for the whole of Judeo-Christian thought, the concept of obligation to our descendants is powerfully undergirded by the Bible's linear sense of time, where actions affect and permanently alter the future, and where no eternal cycle of recurrence robs us of our sense of purpose and responsibility. The historical sense is critical. Although my examples here are drawn from Western religious thought, there may well be points in other religious systems which also promote an obligation to the future — provided, however, that these other religions are not ahistorical or world-denying.

This brief review suggests that an obligation to posterity may be established in a variety of ways, some more compelling, no doubt, than others, depending on one's sensitivities. It is, however, quite possible to imagine situations where the legitimate claims of present and future conflict, and where the choice must be made between them. Perhaps we must commit nonrenewable phosphate to current use as fertilizer to feed today's hungry masses, thus severely limiting our food technology options in years to come. Perhaps we must either make a total effort to spare the world's present population from premature death, thus ultimately increasing the global census to a dangerously high level, or let large numbers die early by neglecting the great efforts that might save them, thus leaving a smaller and more manageable population level to the future. How shall we choose between the obligation to the present and to the future in such cases?

There are ecologists who would frankly opt for the future in these dilemmas. Their commitment is to the long-term, and they are willing to accept the death of many contemporaries to make a better future possible, or as they would say, to make *any* future possible. Perhaps their policy might be justified in the language of general utilitarianism as serving the greatest good of the greatest number, where the greatest number obviously means future generations, who in the aggregate will infinitely outnumber us, the living. But of course such ecologists would not accept their own death to bring about this future, and that is the rub. The intended victims are the poor and powerless, already the wretched of the earth — and they are not interested in dying miserably so that future unknowns may live happily. Asian, African, and Latin-American participants in the international and ecumenical study conferences quite understandably showed considerable hesitation in accepting the idea of future obligation when they saw the concept being used against the lives of their own countrymen.

I would say plainly that when future-mindedness is used to condemn present people to early deaths, it is grossly misused. Such talk serves to distract us from our obligations to our hungry and sick neighbors today. It is diversionary chatter which helps the malingerers among us to avoid their responsibilities to the present by assuring them they are serving the future well.[3] Many of the arguments for future obligation lose their force when they are used this way. For example, in spite of the support in biblical theology for solidarity across the generations, it would be impossible to use the Christian ethic, with its spontaneity and immediacy in assessing human need, *against* the miserable of our day. No Christian could ever say that he was not called to feed the hungry and clothe the naked.

If, then, we admit that the obligation to the future, real and binding though it is, is less compelling than that we owe to the present, how can we justify this difference in value? I suggest that our decision is made this way because the harm we do to future generations, certain though it is, is hard to know with precision, while the harm we do to the present is quite tangible and measurable. We do know that we will hurt people to come, but we know this in a comparatively general way. The details are partly conjecture, and the amount of guesswork increases the more distant the future considered. But present suffering is obvious, a known quantity. The best course for the sensitive conscience would seem to be first the elimination of those evils which are certain and currently experienced, and then management of the longer-term consequences as well as possible. Such a policy has obvious faults. The situation is a genuine dilemma, and dilemmas by definition have no satisfactory solution. "Priority to the present" is not an ethically pure directive, but it is better than the arrogance of claiming the right to choose other people to be martyrs to the future.

Yet even in such a dilemma, the idea of an obligation to posterity does not lose its force. We may not be able to sacrifice the living for the unborn, but neither can we defend the life-style of the currently affluent where it robs future generations of basic necessities. Given the *fact* of an obligation to the future, we have the problem of applying it. We have to decide what current needs have priority over the future, and when, on the contrary, the future's claim against the present must be honored. Such decisions will require us to determine what people really need, what is a responsible use of property and resources, what is an adequate level of life.

NOTES

1. In Geneva, I once heard a woman of that city tell a group of foreign residents that local archaeologists had found in nearby Stone Age remains small stones not native to the region, but originating in Lyon, a fair distance away. Apparently they were used in trade. Thus, she said, it seems that "we" were in commerce as early as Neolithic times. But this is an astonishing and rare identification of generations across the centuries. Most of us, I am sure, would refer to the Stone Age inhabitants of our region as "they," not "we."

2. This issue is discussed by Martin P. Golding in "Obligations to Future Generations," reprinted in this anthology. — Ed.

3. For a differing view of this dilemma, see Garrett Hardin's "Who Cares About Posterity" in this anthology, pp. 221-34, and also Hardin's "Living in a Lifeboat," *BioScience* (October 1974). — Ed.

John Passmore

Conservation

To conserve is to save, and the word "conservation" is sometimes so used as to include every form of saving, the saving of species from extinction or of wildernesses from land-developers as much as the saving of fossil fuels or metals for future use. Such organisations as the Australian Conservation Society, indeed, focus their attention on kangaroos and the Barrier Reef, not on Australia's reserves of oil and fuel. In accordance with what is coming to be the common practice, however, I shall use the word to cover only the saving of natural resources for later consumption. Where the saving is primarily a saving *from* rather than a saving *for,* the saving of species and wildernesses from damage or destruction, I shall speak, rather, of "preservation." My [present] concern . . . is solely with conservation, in the sense in which I have just defined it. [1]

. . . The conservationist programme confronts us with a fundamental moral issue: ought we to pay any attention to the needs of posterity? To answer this question affirmatively is to make two assumptions: first, that posterity will suffer unless we do so; secondly that if it will suffer, it is our duty so to act as to prevent or mitigate its sufferings. Both assumptions can be, and have been, denied. To accept them does not, of course, do anything to solve the problem of conservation, but to reject them is to deny that there is any such problem, to deny that our society would be a better one—morally better if it were to halt the rate at which it is at present exhausting its resources. Or it is to deny this, at least, in so far as the arguments in favor of slowing down are purely conservationist in character—ignoring for the moment, that is, such facts as that the lowering of the consumption rate is one way of reducing the incidence of pollution and that a high rate of consumption of metals and fossil fuels makes it impossible to preserve untouched the wildernesses in which they are so often located.

Used by permission of Charles Scribner's Sons and Gerald Duckworth and Co., Ltd., from *Man's Responsibility for Nature* by John Passmore. Copyright 1974 by John Passmore.

To begin with the assumption that posterity will suffer unless we alter our ways, it is still often suggested that, on the contrary, posterity can safely be left to look after itself, provided only that science and technology continue to flourish. This optimistic interpretation of the situation comes especially from economists and from nuclear physicists. . . .

Very many scientists, of course, take the opposite view, especially if they are biologists. Expert committees set up by such scientific bodies as the American National Academy of Sciences have, in fact, been prepared to commit themselves to definite estimates of the dates at which this resource or that will be exhausted.[2] . . .

The possibility that substitute [resources] will be discovered introduces a note of uncertainty into the whole discussion, an uncertainty which cannot be simply set aside as irrelevant to our moral and political decisions about conservation, which it inevitably and properly influences. At the moment, for example, the prospect of developing a fuel-cell to serve as a substitute for petrol is anything but bright; confident predictions that by 1972 nuclear fusion would be available as an energy source have proved to be unrealistic. But who can say what the situation will be in twenty years time?[3] The now commonplace comparison of earth to a space-ship is thus far misleading: the space-ship astronaut does not have the facilities to invent new techniques, nor can he fundamentally modify his habits of consumption. Any adequate extrapolation would also have to extrapolate technological advances. But by the nature of the case—although technologists have a bad habit of trying to persuade us otherwise—we cannot be at all certain when and whether those advances will take place, or what form they will assume, especially when, unlike the moonshots, they involve fundamental technological innovations such as the containing of nuclear fusion within a magnetic field. . . .

Let us begin by supposing, for the sake of argument, that the optimists[4] are right, that we have no good ground for believing that any particular resource will still be in demand at any particular time in the future, that all we can say with certainty is that sooner or later, at some very remote epoch, civilisation will run out of resources. That is as far as the space-ship analogy can carry us. Should we then set aside "the problem of resource depletion" as a mere pseudo-problem, on the ground that so distant a posterity is no concern of ours?

Kant thought it was *impossible* for us to do so. "Human nature," he once wrote, "is such that it cannot be indifferent even to the most remote epoch which may eventually affect our species, so long as this epoch can be expected with certainty."[5] And other philosophers have demonstrated a similar concern for their most distant descendants. That "the Universe is running down," as the theory of entropy was at one time interpreted as demonstrating, is a conclusion William James found intolerable; only a faith in God, he thought could deliver men from "the nightmare of entropy."[6] . . . But for myself, I more than doubt whether a concern for the ultimate future of the human race forms an essential part of human nature. Kant notwithstanding, a man is not a *lusus naturae* or a moral monster because his sleep is undisturbed by the prospect that human beings will at some infinitely remote date run out of resources or that, however they behave, they will eventually be destroyed by cosmological convulsions.

But even if this is not so, even if men are inevitably perturbed by the reflection that in some remote epoch their race will be extinct, their perturbation does not, of itself, generate any sort of responsibility towards a posterity whose fate they may lament but cannot prevent. The case is no doubt rather different when what is involved is the long-term exhaustion of resources rather than what James had in mind—the "running down of the Universe." For men can, in principle, so act as to delay that exhaustion whereas they cannot delay the earth's cosmological destruction. But if all that can be predicted—the hypothesis I have for the moment adopted—is a very long-term exhaustion of resources, no *immediate* action on our part seems to be called for. Anything we can do would, over millions of years, be infinitesimal in its effects; not even by reducing our consumption of petrol to a thimbleful apiece could we ensure the availability of a similar quantity to our remotest descendants.

If the exhaustion of resources is really, as the more optimistic scientists assert, a problem only for a future so distant as to be scarcely imaginable, then I do not think there is any good reason for our troubling our heads about it.

Should we, then, move to the opposite extreme and leave the future to look after itself, concentrating all our efforts on making the best we can of today? . . . We are confronted, in the present, by evils of every kind: in some of the developing countries by precisely the starvation, the illiteracy, the abysmal housing, the filth and disease which we fear for posterity; in many of our own cities by urban decay, impoverished schools, rising tides of crime and violence. It might well seem odd that the conservationist—and this is an argument not uncommonly directed against him—is so confident that he knows how to save posterity when he cannot even save his own contemporaries. Over a large part of the globe, too, the "needs of posterity" are already being used to justify not only tyranny but a conspicuous failure to meet the needs of the present. One can easily be led to the conclusion that it would be better to let the morrow look after itself and to concentrate, as more than sufficient, upon the evils of our own time. . . .

. . . Had Western man been able to continue to believe either that the future of the world lies in the hands of Providence or that progress is inevitable he would not feel his present qualms about the future; the problem of conservation would not exist for him. But while a belief in the inevitability of progress still affects the thinking of a great many of the world's inhabitants—not only, but most obviously, in Marxist countries—amongst Western intellectuals it tends now to be replaced by the quite opposite view that unless men change their ways, catastrophe is inevitable. Such prophecies are often conjoined with the assumption that simply by *deciding* to change their ways men can create a better world. This is the fullest expression of the activist side of the Western tradition, its Pelagianism, what its nineteenth-century critics called its "voluntarism."

Men are now being called upon, entirely without help, to save the future. The future, it is presumed, lies entirely in their hands; tomorrow *cannot* take thought of itself; it is they, now, who have to save tomorrow, without any help either from Providence or from History. No previous generation has thought of itself as being confronted by so Herculean a task.

How far is such a picture of man's relation to the future acceptable? Obviously, this is a highly controversial matter, entangled, in the last resort, in the old dispute between determinism and free-will. For my part, I am perfectly willing to accept what is negative in it: there is no guiding hand, secular or supernatural, which will ensure that man is bound to flourish, let alone survive. But it is a different matter to suppose that the future lies entirely in men's own hands, if this is taken to imply that, given sufficient goodwill, men need not fear for the future—or, more generally, that once men decide what they want the future to be like they can bring it to pass.

Some of the difficulties in this view emerge from the simulation studies of Jay Forrester and his associates.[7] Supporting his case by reference to the dismal record of good intentions in the field of urban renewal Forrester argues that what happens in society as a result of man's deliberate intervention is counter-intuitive. With great goodwill, men may conserve resources for posterity only to leave it worse off, in respect to both pollution and excessive population and so in the long run to resources, than it would have been had they been less generous. Forrester nevertheless extracts a programme for the future from his simulation-models. The computer can, he thinks, do what unaided intuition cannot; it can calculate the consequences of social actions. The present generation can save mankind from calamity, he suggests, by simultaneously and substantially reducing its capital investment, the birth rate, the generation of pollution, while holding the standard of living to a point not higher than its present level.

These predictions depend, however, on a number of assumptions. It has to be presumed, for example, that the *direction* of investment will remain constant, that individual preference scales will not profoundly alter, so that peace and quiet, or freedom from pollution, come to be more highly valued than the possession of consumer goods. But an even more serious point—for this presumption is not totally implausible—is that Forrester does not consider whether the policies he suggests could be implemented without social and political disruption, including the risk of civil and nuclear war. Relationships between economic restraints and war are not sufficiently precise to be fed into his model. At best, his policies would be effective only in an industrial community hermetically sealed off from the rest of the world.

But even if, for such reasons, we can be more than doubtful about the policies he advocates, Forrester's analysis helps us to see first, that goodwill is not enough and, secondly, that men cannot, in the social any more than in the ecological sphere, do one thing at a time, that their actions have consequences which flow from the character of their society and which operate quite independently of their wishes. It is scarcely a modern discovery, of course, that the road to hell is paved with good intentions. Both Kant and Hegel drew forcible attention to the fact that men's vices, their greed, their ferocity, what Kant calls their "unsociableness," have as a matter of history done more to advance civilisation, however unintentionally, than their sacrificial virtues. And Marx long ago rejected as "Utopianism" the supposition that good intentions are either necessary or sufficient to bring about desirable social changes.

The supposition, indeed, that history lies entirely in man's hands, that men can deliberately create the world of their choice, will not stand up to historical scrutiny. The Soviet Union and the United States are both of them sad reminders of that fact. Nor can it truly be replied that now we know better. Our knowledge of the social consequences of even so limited a form of action as the devaluation of a currency is extremely imperfect; an arms agreement, a rapprochement, plunge us into a sea of uncertainty. Against this background, it might be argued, to trouble ourselves about the needs of even a relatively near posterity is wholly absurd. Our ignorance is too great, our capacity is too limited.

We know at least this much, however. Men will need the biosphere. And it is sometimes suggested that our present level of industrial activity is so heating up the atmosphere that large parts of the earth's surface will — as a result of the melting of polar ice — eventually be rendered uninhabitable. So, it is concluded, we ought at once, for the sake of posterity, to reduce the level of that activity. Once again, of course, the facts are in dispute. The Royal Commission on Environmental Pollution concluded that "such eventualities are not only remote: they are conjectural."[8] But this case serves as a sort of touchstone, an example extreme both in its uncertainty and in the disastrousness of the consequences it envisages, were they to eventuate.

Let us now approach our problem from the opposite point of view. What positive arguments are there to justify the conclusion, so often taken for granted, that we ought to be prepared to make sacrifices for posterity, that we ought to take thought for posterity's tomorrow? It is sometimes suggested, as by Montefiore, that "until men come to believe in their hearts that all life is held in trust from God, there can be no valid ethical reason why we should owe a duty to posterity."[9] If Montefiore is right, this would certainly be unfortunate, since the greater part of the human race does not "believe in its heart" that it is a trustee of God. . . .

But what are the alternatives? How can men justify their concern for posterity, if not on the ground that it arises out of a duty imposed upon them by God?

This is a question that has seldom been asked. For the common assumption has been . . . that what happens to posterity will depend scarcely at all on how men choose to act. Only very recently, indeed, have men thought it possible to engage in any kind of economic or social planning. But although Kant, for example, is mainly concerned to find good reasons for believing that the world, however men behave, is bound someday to be a better place than it now is, we can construct out of his political writings an important argument for thinking of ourselves as having a duty to posterity. It would run thus: men have not yet achieved all that they have it in them to achieve. They live in a society which is far from ideal. But they are capable of something much better than this. Their reaction to the French Revolution—their open expression of universal but disinterested sympathy when the expression of that sympathy involved them in considerable risk—was sufficient to demonstrate, Kant thought, that men possess a moral enthusiasm for the ideal, however greedy and violent their history might show them to be.[10] They have a duty to posterity simply because only posterity can realise that ideal.

This argument, as will at once be obvious, treats man's duty to posterity as an instance of his more general duty to sacrifice himself in the attempt to construct an ideal society—a duty which, Kant thought, survives the discovery that in trying to construct such a society the well-intentioned man will almost certainly do the wrong thing, whereas the greedy and the violent, as a result of what Hegel was to call "the cunning of history" may well, however unwillingly and unwittingly, act as the agents of progress. Fichte, equally convinced on this point, offers, as Kant does not, the well-intentioned sacrificer a solace; he will go to heaven for *trying* to do the right thing even if, objectively considered, it is quite the wrong thing to do—so that, to return to Forrester's analysis, the anti-pollution campaigner will go to heaven even if by fighting for anti-pollution measures he is working against, rather than for, a better future.[11] That large segment of the world, however, which does not believe in supernatural rewards, has simply to recognise, on the Kant-Fichte view, that it is its duty to try to work for a better society—in the long run for an ideal society—even when it has become conscious that the actual effects of its actions may well be to hinder rather than to advance the emergence of such a society. This is not a very encouraging line of reasoning. Yet perhaps in the long run we shall not be able to come up with anything much more attractive. It is at least realistic, firmly based on human history, in its recognition that the unintended consequences of men's actions are more important, for the most part, than the consequences they intend.

Another possible line of argument is utilitarian. If, as Bentham tells us, in deciding how to act men ought to take account of the effects of their action upon every sentient being, they obviously ought to take account of the pleasures and pains of the as yet unborn. Sidgwick, writing in this same utilitarian tradition, explicitly formulates a principle of impartiality: "Hereafter *as such* is to be regarded neither less nor more than Now."[12]

In general terms, this seems sound enough. If the general maxim is that I ought not to act in a way which will do more harm than good, then the question whether the person I am harming or benefiting is yet alive is, on the face of it, morally irrelevant. Notice, however, Sidgwick's phrase "hereafter *as such*." If we were to adopt the principle never to act until we were quite sure that in so acting we would not do more harm than good, we could never act at all. We cannot be *quite* sure that a beggar will not choke on the bread we offer him. Obviously, we have to think in terms of probabilities. Bentham and Sidgwick after him were fully prepared to admit that we ought to take into account both the probability of the effects of our actions and also their remoteness; in general we should place the greater emphasis on effects which are near at hand. Although the hereafter *as such* has the same moral importance as the *now,* this is not true when account is taken of its uncertainty. As Sidgwick sums up: "It seems clear that the time at which a man exists cannot affect the value of his happiness from a universal point of view; and that the interests of posterity must concern a Utilitarian . . . *except in so far as the effect of his actions on posterity — and even the existence of human beings to be affected — must necessarily be more uncertain.*"[13] A more recent utilitarian, T. L. Sprigge, makes the same point: the happiness we ought to take into account in determining how to act must be reasonably predictable and "has a weight according to its degree of probability."[14]

In the present case, this is a large part of the difficulty. As we have already seen, we cannot be at all certain that posterity will need the resources we propose to save for them more badly than they are needed now. Nor do we find it easy to assign probabilities. How probable is it that the more optimistic nuclear physicists are right in their estimate of the probability that in twenty years time nuclear fission, or solar energy, will be mastered? Or even accepting the argument put forward in *Limits to Growth* that the discovery of new energy sources would not solve posterity's problems, how confident can we be that in attempting to cut down on growth in order to save the biosphere we would not provoke social and political upheavals of the first order, upheavals culminating, perhaps, in the setting up of a rigidly totalitarian state?

So even if we accept the principle of impartiality and the utilitarian framework in which it is embedded, even if we accept the view that we ought not so to act as *certainly* to harm posterity, this does not appear to be a principle strong enough to justify the kinds of sacrifice some conservationists now call upon us to make. The uncertainty of the harms we are hoping to prevent would, in general, entitle us to ignore them, especially if we have good grounds for believing that the harm we could do to ourselves in trying to prevent them is considerable. We might be able to use possible damage to the biosphere as an additional argument against flying supersonic planes, when the benefits are minimal and the present damage considerable. But utilitarian principles are not strong enough to justify the cutting down of industrial growth merely *in case* posterity should run out of petrol, or merely because industrial growth *might* be heating up the atmosphere.

A general consequence of this analysis is that it would be useless to rely upon the market as an agent of conservation. We cannot assume that increases in prices, with rising demand, will suffice adequately to conserve resources. The market acts on principles even more restricted than Bentham's; each operator in the market is interested only in his personal gains, not in the greatest happiness of the greatest number. But, like Bentham, the market places great emphasis on certainty and propinquity. Demand for it means *present* demand; supply *present* supply. (Or if this is not quite true, at least it does not look far ahead—only reluctantly so far as to supply capital for, say, afforestation.) That is why although the total volume of the earth's resources—as distinct from the total volume of resources available at a particular time—is obviously diminishing, up till now their cost has for the most part declined.[15] . . .

. . . A somewhat different line of argument—which takes justice rather than happiness as its starting point—has been put forward by John Rawls. He does not so much as mention the saving of natural resources. (How rare it is for moral philosophers to pay any attention to the world around them!) But he has a good deal to say about the general concept of saving for posterity; that we ought to save for posterity, he in general argues, is a consequence of the fact that we ought to act justly, to posterity as to our contemporaries. The utilitarian principle of impartiality, taken literally, demands too much from us; we cannot reasonably be expected to share our resources between ourselves and the whole of posterity. What we can reasonably be expected to do is to hand on to our immediate posterity a rather better situation than we have ourselves inherited. Anything less than this would be unfair to them, anything more would be unfair to the present generation. Rawls is Kantian in so far as he presumes that the final aim of our efforts is an ideal society we shall not live to see realised. But he so far compromises with such of Kant's critics as Herder and Herzen as to argue that we can best work towards that society by improving the conditions of life *now* and passing on the results to our immediate descendants, for them to do likewise. Exactly to what degree we should save for posterity, it is not possible, he admits, accurately to determine. But about the general character of what we ought to do he has no doubts. "Each generation," he writes, "must not only preserve the gains of culture and civilisation, and maintain intact those just institutions that have been established, but it must also put aside in each period of time a suitable amount of real capital accumulation.[16] The "capital accumulation" may take various forms—investment in learning and education as well as in machinery, factories, agriculture.

Note that, as Rawls see the situation, we have a threefold task: first to "preserve the gains of our civilisation"; secondly to "maintain intact" our "just institutions"; thirdly to hand over to posterity an accumulation of capital greater than we received from our ancestors. Many nowadays would, of course, challenge the assumptions inherent in this conception of our task. What we have been accustomed to call "gains," they would argue, are not really such; none of our institutions are just; we should be doing no kindness to posterity by handing over to them a greater capital accumulation. But for my part, I am prepared to accept the view, at least, that if our situation were a normal one, Rawls has accurately described what posterity would expect, and all it could properly expect, from us. So far, so good. But it is not very far.

Each generation, Rawls is suggesting, should decide what it ought to save for posterity by answering in particular terms a general question: what is it reasonable for a society to expect, at the stage of development it has reached, from its predecessor? If it then acts upon the answer at which it arrives, each generation will be better off than its predecessor but no generation will be called upon to make an exceptional sacrifice. This is as far as we can go, I should agree, if our relationship with succeeding generations is to be governed by the principle of justice. The consequence is that each generation is concerned, when it is considering what sacrifices it should make, only with the next succeeding generation, not with some remote posterity. And this, as contrasted with classical utilitarianism, presents it with an easier set of calculations to make, difficult although they still are.

But although this means that, up to a point, each generation is in a unique position, unique in respect both to exactly what it inherits and to exactly what it has a duty to hand on, it does not allow for the position of a generation which is unique in a quite different sense: it cannot calculate what it should do for posterity by reflecting on what its predecessors did for it. The sacrifice required of such a generation may be heroic, and Rawls's theory is based on the concept of justice, fairness, equal shares; it leaves no room for the heroic sacrifice. Yet if the conservationists are right it is precisely such a heroic sacrifice we are now called upon to make, a sacrifice far beyond anything our ancestors had to make. And this transforms the situation.

Now, in fact, men quite often do make heroic sacrifices. They make them out of love. It is as lovers that they make sacrifices for the future more extensive than any a Benthamite calculus would admit to be rational. When men act for the sake of a future they will not live to see, it is for the most part out of love for persons, places and forms of activity, a cherishing of them, nothing more grandiose. It is indeed self-contradictory to say: "I love him or her or that place or that institution or that activity, but I don't care what happens to it after my death." To love is, amongst other things, to care about the future of what we love.[17] (Of course, the word "love" is used in many different ways. I have in mind the sense in which to love is to cherish. I can "love ice-cream" without caring about what happens to it after I die.) This is most obvious when we love our wife, our children, our grand-children. But it is also true in the case of our more impersonal loves: our love for places, institutions and forms of activity. To love philosophy – to philosophize with joy – is to care about its future as a form of activity: to maintain that what happens to it after our death is of no consequence would be a clear indication that our "love of philosophy" is nothing more than a form of self-love. The tourist who writes his name on a tree or rock-face in a "beloved beauty spot" makes it only too clear what *he* loves. To love a place is to wish it to survive unspoiled.

Sometimes, one must grant to the Augustinian moralist, what is involved in a concern for posterity is a form of self-love, the desire to win "immortality." An institution, a person, is then thought of as carrying forward into the future at least one's name and perhaps some dim memory of one's character and achievements. So a grandfather may wish to have a grandchild named after him, or a municipal councillor a street or park. An author may be content to have his name inscribed on a catalogue card in the British Museum; an Ozymandias may have his statue set up for the admiration of all who pass by. In a way this is pitiable, as Shelley saw, but perhaps it is essential to the continuance of civilisation. That "love of literary fame" with which Hume, he tells us, was consumed is at worst harmless, and at best can help men to write great works. It is only when self-love is substituted for love for an object, as distinct from being conjoined with it, that it is destructive.

Love, no doubt, extends only for a limited distance in time. Men do not love their grand-children's grand-children. They cannot love what they do not know. But in loving their grand-children – a love which already carries them a not inconsiderable distance into the future – they hope that those grand-children, too, will have grand-children to love. They are *concerned,* to that degree, about their grand-children's grand-children. "For myself," writes Macfarlane Burnet, "I want to spare my grand-children from chaos and to hope that they will live to see *their* grand-children getting ready to bring a stable ecosystem into being."[18] Such a degree of concern for one's grand-children's grand-children is a natural consequence of one's love for one's grand-children; it is, as it were, an anticipation of *their* love. And so is a concern for the future of art, of science, of one's own town or country or university. By this means there is established a chain of love and concern running throughout the remote future.

Of course, a particular chain may be broken; not every parent loves his children, not every pupil of a philosopher loves philosophy. But such links are sufficiently common and persistent to lend continuity to a civilisation. They serve to explain sacrifices beyond the call of a Benthamite calculation or a sense of justice. There is, then, no novelty in a concern for posterity, when posterity is thought of not abstractly – as "the future of mankind" – but as a world inhabited by individuals we love or feel a special interest in, a world containing institutions, social movements, forms of life to which we are devoted – or, even, a world made up of persons some of whom might admire us.

No doubt, this concern has often been made worthless by ignorance or outweighed by greed. But the new settlers in America or in Australia were not, for the most part, *deliberately* disregarding, when they destroyed the countryside, the interests of posterity. Many of them believed that the resources of the new countries were endless. . . . The best of the new settlers – others, of course, were obsessed by greed – were convinced that they were building a better country for posterity to inherit. Total indifference to posterity has not been a leading characteristic of Western civilisation over the last few centuries; much of what has been most devastating has been sincerely done for posterity's sake. . . .

I admitted, however, that chains of love might be disrupted. What is usually called the "generation gap" is often not so much a "gap" as an active hostility, a form of hatred, a kind of civil war. It is easy to imagine it accentuated, so that parents ceased, in general, to love their children. Then, too, it is often suggested that we are approaching a period in which the major activities and institutions we have learned to love will perish. "It seems clear," writes Harrison Brown, "that the first major penalty man will have to pay for his rapid consumption of the earth's non-renewable resources will be that of having to live in a world where his thoughts and actions are ever more strongly limited, where social organisation has become all-pervasive, complex, and inflexible and where the state completely dominates the actions of the individual."[19] One hopes he is wrong; one fears that he might be right. Suppose we accept his view and push it a little further, to its gloomiest extremes. For, on the face of it, this possibility greatly affects the kind and the degree of sacrifice we ought to be prepared to make. . . .

. . . Obligations deriving from loves relate us to posterity just in so far as we have some grounds for believing that the future will contain what we love. But love, we also suggested, carries us beyond "good grounds," at least in the most calculating sense of that phrase. It is certainly not possible to *demonstrate* that the kind of society, the kind of human being, both Golding[20] and I dread will in fact come into existence. And so long as the possibility remains that men will continue to be what they have been in the past — cruel but gentle, destructive but creative, hating but loving — and will continue to carry on the activities we love, we shall not wish to take the risk that by failing to make sufficient sacrifices now we shall jeopardise their survival. This is so even when the risk is a slight one.

But what sort of sacrifices ought we to make? It follows from what I have already said that we ought not to be prepared, in the supposed interests of posterity, to surrender our loves or the freedom which makes their exercise possible, to give up art, or philosophy, or science, or personal relationships, in order to conserve resources for posterity. Posterity will need our loves as much as we need them; it needs chains of love running to and through it. (Developing these loves will also necessarily involve, of course, developing *in those we love* the idea of a duty to posterity.) So far Herder was right to rebel against Kant's emphasis on sacrifices for posterity, right in arguing that the greatest service we can perform for posterity is to do what we can to make the world a better place *now*. And that, as we saw, is substantially the conclusion both Rawls and Golding also come to. Those who urge us to surrender our freedom and to abandon our loves so that posterity can enjoy a "true freedom" and a "true love" ought never to be trusted. No doubt, as individuals, we might sometimes have to sacrifice our freedom or certain of our loves. But only to ensure their maintenance and development by others. And this is true, I should argue, even if they can be maintained only at the cost of human suffering — although there is in fact no evidence to suggest that we shall save posterity from suffering by surrendering our freedoms.

The surrender of forms of enjoyment is a different matter. What we would be called upon to do, at this level, is to reduce the consumption of certain goods — those which depend on raw materials which cannot be effectively recycled — and to recycle whenever that is possible, even although the costs of doing so would involve the sacrifice of other goods. That is the kind of sacrifice we ought to be prepared to make, if there is a real risk that it is essential for the continued existence of a posterity able to carry on the activities we love. It is, indeed, the kind of sacrifice we are quite accustomed to making, the deferring of consumption for the sake of the future of our children or of our impersonal loves. Nor does it rest on a concern for a remote posterity, with unguessable needs and resources: it is our grand-children who will have to make their way in a world, if the forecasters are correct, denuded of resources. A Benthamite might be prepared to take that risk; a lover will not.

Now to sum up. Whether there is a problem of conservation is warmly disputed; our conclusion on that point will depend on whether or not we are convinced that certain technological devices will be available for use in the very near future. And the grounds on which most of us have to come to a decision on this point are anything but adequate. We cannot be certain that posterity will need what we save — or on the other side that it will not need what we should not think of saving. There is always the risk, too, that our well-intentioned sacrifices will have the long-term effect of making the situation of posterity worse than it would otherwise be. That is the case for simply ignoring posterity, and doing what we can to repair present evils.

On the other side, this is not our ordinary moral practice. We love, and in virtue of that fact we are prepared to make sacrifices for the future and are not prepared to take risks, arising out of uncertainties, which would otherwise strike us as being rational. No doubt, we often make the wrong decisions; trying to protect what we love we in fact destroy it. Over-protection can be as damaging as neglect. But these uncertainties do not justify negligence. Furthermore, we now stand, if the more pessimistic scientists are right, in a special relationship to the future; unless we act, posterity will be helpless to do so. This imposes duties on us which would not otherwise fall to our lot.

But granted that it ought to do so, is any democratic-capitalist state likely to introduce effective measures to conserve resources? Conservation has not the same popular appeal as pollution; especially when it involves genuine sacrifices. Even those who are in favour of it in principle may still find it hard to accept the view that they must, for example, reduce the level of winter heating to which they have been accustomed. Indeed, if conservation were an isolated issue, one might be inclined to doubt whether the conservationist programme would ever win widespread support. Admittedly it has already had its successes. Afforestation and the control of soil erosion were both of them conservationist programmes which have more than occasionally, if by no means universally, been implemented. But they involve far less, and less widespread, sacrifice than would the adoption of a policy of conserving fossil fuels. Furthermore, they were often accompanied by a degree of subsidisation which more than compensated for temporary losses and which could not be matched in a thoroughgoing conservationist programme.

The fact is, however, that conservationism is not an isolated issue. By "doing what is just in the present," we may be doing what is best for posterity to a degree somewhat greater than is ordinarily allowed. If we were to concentrate on improving public facilities as distinct from private wealth, on diminishing noise and air pollution by substantially reducing automobile traffic, we might find that we have in the process decreased the level of industrial activity to a relatively harmless point. In general, people do not seem to find their present mode of life particularly enjoyable; we certainly need to experiment with alternatives which are at the same time less polluting and less wasteful of resources. The recycling of resources both benefits us, as helping to solve the problem of wastes, and would, we hope, also benefit posterity. The extension of public transport will help our cities as well as reducing the use of fossil fuels. Education, which certainly needs improvement, is not a great polluter, or a great user of scarce resources. In the uncertainties in which we find ourselves, it is perhaps on these double-benefit forms of action that we should concentrate our principal efforts. Certainly we shall have set up objectives which are hard enough to realise, but the benefits of which are immediately obvious — or obvious to those who are not enamoured of squalor, decaying schools, over-crowded cities, inadequate hospitals and nursing homes, crime or official violence. If they are hard to realise, it is because the ownership of commodities, private affluence, is in fact generally preferred, when the crunch comes, to the improvement of the public conditions of life.

There is also the question of time. The degree of urgency, on the views of some scientists, is very great; political action is generally speaking slow, and in this case is subjected to an enormous range of special interests. In these circumstances there is a strong temptation to fall back on the ideal of the strong man, who could conserve by the direct exercise of coercion. I have refused to accept this as a "solution" for the conservation problem, partly because I do not think there is any good reason for believing that any "strong man" who is likely to emerge after the collapse of democracy would be primarily concerned with conservation and partly because I do not believe this to be the kind of cost we ought to be prepared to meet, for posterity's sake as well as our own. Much the same is true of the suggestion that what we should work for is the collapse, as rapidly as possible, of our entire civilisation, as the only way of conserving resources. The cost would be enormous; the benefit more than dubious.

My conclusions are limited and uncertain. That is how it should be; as Socrates liked to point out, confidence based on ignorance is not a virtue. Nor is there any point in turning to religion in an attempt to bolster up our confidence. Men do not need religion, or so I have argued against Montefiore, to justify their concern for the future. That concern arises out of their character as loving human beings; religion, indeed, often tells its adherents — whether in the accents of the East or of the West — to set such concern aside, to "take no thought of the morrow." If Allah, as the proponents of stewardship now like to emphasise, is represented in the Koran as setting up men on earth as his "deputy," it by no means follows that a Muslim ruler can be rebuked for heresy when he sells off the oil which Allah has hidden beneath the desert sands. In short, the faithful cannot hope by recourse to Revelation, Christian or Muslim, to solve the problems which now confront them. Nor will mysticism help them. There is no substitute for hard thinking, thinking which cuts clean across the traditional disciplines. But intellectuals, no less than the religious, have their delusions of grandeur. Society, as much as nature, resists men's plans; it is not wax at the hands of the scientist, the planner, the legislator. To forget that fact, as a result of conservationist enthusiasm, is to provoke rather than to forestall disaster.

NOTES

1. The preceding constitutes about half of the fourth chapter of Passmore's book, *Man's Responsibility for Nature* (New York: Scribner, 1974). The excluded portion of the chapter contains a wealth of illustrations of Passmore's main points and also deals perceptively with the political, economic and historical aspects of the posterity issue. The chapter that follows in the book deals with the separate but related issue of "preservation" (e.g., of species and wilderness). These two chapters deserve the thoughtful attention of the student and scholar desiring to read further into the question of the duty to posterity. Indeed, the entire book deserves such attention, although many environmental philosophers (including this editor) are in substantial disagreement with some of Professor Passmore's assumptions and conclusions. (See especially the Routleys' criticism of Passmore [1978] in a portion of their paper *not* reprinted in this anthology). —ED.

2. See "The Energy Crisis," pts. 1 and 2, in *Science and Public Affairs: Bulletin of the Atomic Scientists,* 27 (September–October 1971):8-9.

3. See M. K. Hubbert, "Energy Resources," in M. K. Hubbert, *Resources and Man* (San Francisco: W. H. Freeman, 1969).

4. "Optimists," if all we take into account is the depletion of resources. From a broader point of view, of course, the depletion of resources might be the only thing that can save the world from dying either from overpopulation or from pollution.

5. Immanuel Kant, "Idea For a Universal History With a Cosmopolitan Purpose," Proposition 8, in *Kant's Political Writings,* ed. H. Reiss, trans. H. B. Nisbet (Cambridge: Cambridge University Press, 1970), p. 50.

6. William James, *Pragmatism* (London: Longmans Green, 1908), ch. 3.

7. Jay Forrester, *World Dynamics* (Cambridge, Mass.: M.I.T. Press, 1971). He gives a brief account of his work in two articles in *Ecologist,* "Alternatives to Catastrophe," 1 (August–September 1971), and in "Counterintuitive Behavior of Social Systems," *Theory and Decision,* 2 (December 1971). Large-scale simulation studies are also being conducted at the University of British Columbia, Vancouver.

8. First Report of the *Royal Commission on Environmental Pollution,* Chairman: Sir Eric Ashby (London, 1971), pp. 38, 41. For a brief account of the argument on the other side, see David Gates, "Weather Modification in the Service of Mankind: Promise or Peril?" in H. W. Helfrich, ed., *The Environmental Crisis* (New Haven: Yale University Press, 1970).

9. Hugh Montefiore: *Can Man Survive?, * p. 55.

10. *The Contest of Faculties,* 6, trans. H. B. Nisbet, p. 182.

11. For Fichte, and for detailed references, see John Passmore, *The Perfectability of Man* (New York: Scribner, 1970), pp. 231-32.

12. Henry Sidgwick, *The Methods of Ethics* (7th ed., London, 1907; reissued 1962), bk. 3, ch. 13, p. 381.

13. *Ibid.,* bk. 4, ch. 1, p. 414 [my italics].

14. T. L. S. Sprigge, "A Utilitarian Reply to Dr. McCloskey," in M. D. Bayles, ed., *Contemporary Utilitarianism* (New York: Peter Smith, 1968), p. 263.

15. Economists, quite unlike biologists, inevitably think in short terms. This is one reason why, in debates about the need for conserving raw materials, they so often sound optimistic. From their point of view it is quite absurd to worry about what may happen thirty years hence. An economist, indeed, thinks of himself as soothing our conservationist qualms if he tells us that supplies of a particular mineral will last until the year 2000 — less than thirty years off!

16. John Rawls, *A Theory of Justice* (Cambridge, Mass.: Harvard University Press, 1971), p. 285.

17. On this general theme see John Passmore, *The Perfectibility of Man,* pp. 299–302 and 323–325.

18. Macfarland Burnet, *Dominant Mammal* (Melbourne: Heinemann, 1970), ch. 9; Pelican ed. (Harmondsworth, 1971), p. 182.

19. Harrison Brown, *The Challenge of Man's Future* (London, 1954), p. 219.

20. Passmore is referring here to Martin P. Golding's paper, "Obligations to Future Generations," which follows immediately in this anthology. — ED.

Martin P. Golding

Obligations to Future Generations

The purpose of this note[1] is to examine the notion of obligations to future generations, a notion that finds increasing use in discussions of social policies and programs, particularly as concerns population distribution and control and environment control. Thus, it may be claimed, the solution of problems in these areas is not merely a matter of enhancing our own good, improving our own conditions of life, but is also a matter of discharging an obligation to future generations.

Before I turn to the question of the basis of such obligations — the necessity of the plural is actually doubtful — there are three general points to be considered: (1) Who are the individuals in whose regard it is maintained that we have such obligations, to whom do we owe such obligations? (2) What, essentially, do obligations to future generations oblige us to do, what are they aimed at? and (3), To what class of obligation do such obligations belong, what kind of obligation are they? Needless to say, in examining a notion of this sort, which is used in everyday discussion and polemic, one must be mindful of the danger of taking it — or making it out — to be more precise than it is in reality.

This cautionary remark seems especially appropriate in connection with the first of the above points. But the determination of the purview of obligations to future generations is both ethically and practically significant. It seems clear, at least, who does not come within their purview. Obligations to future generations are distinct from the obligations we have to our presently living fellows, who are therefore excluded from the purview of the former, although it might well be the case that *what* we owe to future generations is identical with (or overlaps) what we owe to the present generation. However, I think we may go further than this and also exclude our most immediate descendants, our children, grandchildren and great-grandchildren, perhaps. What is distinctive about the notion of obligations to future generations is, I think, that it

Reprinted from *The Monist,* 56 (January 1972), with the permission of the author and the publisher.

refers to generations with which the possessors of the obligations cannot expect in a literal sense to share a common life. (Of course, if we have obligations to future generations, understood in this way, we *a fortiori* have obligations to immediate posterity.) This, at any rate, is how I shall construe the reference of such obligations; neither our present fellows nor our immediate posterity come within their purview. What can be the basis of our obligations toward individuals with whom we cannot expect to share a common life is a question I shall consider shortly.

But if their inner boundary be drawn in this way, what can we say about their outer limits? Is there a cut-off point for the individuals in whose regard we have such obligations? Here, it seems, there are two alternatives. First, we can flatly say that there are no outer limits to their purview: all future generations come within their province. A second and more modest answer would be that we do not have such obligations towards any assignable future generation. In either case the referent is a broad and unspecified community of the future, and I think it can be shown that we run into difficulties unless certain qualifications are taken into account.

Our second point concerns the question of what it is that obligations to future generations oblige us to do. The short answer is that they oblige us to do many things. But an intervening step is required here, for obligations to future generations are distinct from general duties to perform acts which are in themselves intrinsically right, although such obligations give rise to duties to perform specific acts. Obligations to future generations are essentially an obligation to produce — or to attempt to produce — a desirable state of affairs *for* the community of the future, to promote conditions of good living for future generations. The many things that we are obliged to do are founded upon this obligation (which is why I earlier questioned the necessity of the plural). If we think we have an obligation to transmit our cultural heritage to future generations it is because we think that our cultural heritage promotes, or perhaps even embodies, good living. In so doing we would hardly wish to falsify the records of our civilization, for future generations must also have, as a condition of good living, the opportunity to learn from the mistakes of the past. If, in addition, we believe lying to be intrinsically wrong we would also refrain from falsifying the records; but this would not be because we think we have any special duty to tell the truth to future generations.

To come closer to contemporary discussion, consider, for example, population control, which is often grounded upon an obligation to future generations. It is not maintained that population control is intrinsically right — although the rhetoric frequently seems to approach such a claim — but rather that it will contribute towards a better life for future generations, and perhaps immediate posterity as well. (If population control were intrinsically anything, I would incline to thinking it intrinsically wrong.) On the other hand, consider the elimination of water and air pollution. Here it might be maintained that we have a definite duty to cease polluting the environment on the grounds that such pollution is intrinsically bad[2] or that it violates a Divine command. Given the current mood of neopaganism, even secularists speak of the despoilment of the environment as a sacrilege of sorts. When the building of a new dam upsets the ecological balance and puts the wildlife under a threat, we react negatively and feel that something bad has resulted. And this is not because we necessarily believe that our own interests or those of future generations have been undermined. Both views, but especially the latter (Divine command), represent men as holding sovereignty over nature only as trustees to whom not everything is permitted. Nevertheless, these ways of grounding the duty to care for the environment are distinguishable from a grounding of the duty upon an obligation to future generations, although one who acknowledges such an obligation will also properly regard himself as a trustee to whom not everything is permitted. Caring for the environment is presumably among the many things that the obligation to future generations obliges us to do because we thereby presumably promote conditions of good living for the community of the future.

The obligation—dropping the plural again for a moment—to future generations, then, is not an immediate catalogue of specific duties. It is in this respect rather like the responsibility that a parent has to see to the welfare of his child. Discharging one's parental responsibility requires concern, seeking, and active effort to promote the good *of* the child, which is the central obligation of the parent and out of which grows the specific parental obligations and duties. The use of the term "responsibility" to characterize the parent's obligation connotes, in part, the element of discretion and flexibility which is requisite to the discharging of the obligation in a variety of antecedently unforseeable situations. Determination of the specific duty is often quite problematic even—and sometimes especially—for the conscientious parent who is anxious to do what is good for his child. And, anticipation my later discussion, this also holds for obligations to future generations. There are, of course, differences, too. Parental responsibility is enriched and reinforced by love, which can hardly obtain between us and future generations.[3] (Still, the very fact that the responsibility to promote the child's good is an obligation means that it is expected to operate even in the absence of love.) Secondly, the parental obligation is always towards assignable individuals, which is not the case with obligations to future generations. There is, however, an additional feature of likeness between the two obligations which I shall mention shortly.

The third point about obligations to future generations—to what class of obligation do they belong?—is that they are *owed,* albeit owed to an unspecified, and perhaps unspecifiable, community of the future. Obligations to future generations, therefore, are distinct from a general duty, when presented with alternatives for action, to choose the act which produces the greatest good. Such a duty is not owed to anyone, and the beneficiaries of my fulfilling a duty to promote the greatest good are not necessarily individuals to whom I stand in the moral relation of having an obligation that is owed. But when I owe it to someone to promote his good, he is never, to this extent, merely an incidental beneficiary of my effort to fulfill the obligation. He has a presumptive *right* to it and can assert a claim against me for it. Obligations to future generations are of this kind. There is something which is due to the community of the future from us. The moral relation between us and future generations is one in which they have a claim against us to promote their good. Future generations are, thus, possessors of presumptive rights.

This conclusion is surely odd. How can future generations – the not-yet-born – *now* have claims against us? This question serves to turn us finally to consider the basis of our obligations to future generations. I think it useful to begin by discussing and removing one source of the oddity.

It should first be noticed that there is no oddity in investing present effort in order to promote a future state of affairs or in having an owed obligation to do so. The oddity arises only on a theory of obligations and claims (and, hence, of rights) that virtually identifies them with acts of willing, with the exercise of sovereignty of one over another, with the pressing of demands – in a word, with *making* claims. But, clearly, future generations are not now engaged in acts of willing, are not now exercising sovereignty over us, and are not now pressing their demands. Future generations are not now making claims against us, nor will it be *possible* for them to do so. (Our immediate posterity are in this last respect in a different case.) However, the identification of claims with making claims, demanding, is plausible within the field of rights and obligations because the content of a system of rights is historically conditioned by the making of claims. Individuals and groups put forward their claims to the goods of life, demand them as their right; and in this way the content is increasingly expanded towards the inclusion of more of these goods.

Nevertheless, as suggestive a clue as this fact is for the development of a theory of rights, there is a distinction to be drawn between *having* claims and *making* claims. The mere fact that someone claims something from me is not sufficient to establish it as his right, or that he has a claim relative to me. On the other hand, someone may have a claim relative to me whether or not he makes the claim, demands, or is even able to make a claim. (This is not to deny that claiming plays a role in the theory of rights.) Two points require attention here. First, some claims are frivolous. What is demanded cannot really be claimed as a matter of right. The crucial factor in determining this is the *social ideal,* which we may provisionally define as a conception of the good life for man. It serves as the yardstick by which demands, current and potential, are measured.[4] Secondly, whether someone's claim confers an entitlement upon him to receive what is claimed *from me* depends upon my moral relation to him, on whether he is a member of my *moral community.* It is these factors, rather than any actual demanding, which establish whether someone has a claim relative to me. (I should like to emphasize that I am not necessarily maintaining that the concepts of a social ideal and a moral community are involved in a theory of every kind of obligation, but, rather, that they are required by the kind of obligation being considered here.)

The concepts of a social ideal and a moral community are clearly in need of further explanation, yet as they stand the above considerations should serve to relieve a good deal of the oddity that is felt in the assertion that future generations now have claims against us and that they are possessors of presumptive rights. There is, however, a residual sense of peculiarity in the assertion because it still remains to be shown whether future generations are members of our moral community. A discussion of the question of membership in a moral community will, I think, shed light on these subjects.

Who are the members of my moral community? (Who is my neighbor?) The fact is that I am a member of more than one moral community, for I belong to a variety of groups whose members owe obligations to one another. And many of the particular obligations that are owed vary from group to group. As a result my obligations are often in conflict and I experience a fragmentation of energy and responsibility in attempting to meet my obligations. What I ought to desire for the members of one of these groups is frequently in opposition to what I ought to desire for the members of another of these groups. Moral communities are constituted, or generated, in a number of ways, one of which is especially relevant to our problem. Yet these ways are not mutually exclusive, and they can be mutually reenforcing. This is a large topic and I cannot go into its details here. It is sufficient for our purpose to take brief notice of two possible ways of generating a moral community so as to set in relief the particular kind of moral community that is requisite for obligations to future generations.

A moral community may be constituted by an explicit contract between its members. In this case the particular obligations which the members have towards each other are fixed by the terms of their bargain. Secondly, a moral community may be generated out of a social arrangement in which each member derives benefits from the efforts of other members. As a result a member acquires an obligation to share the burden of sustaining the social arrangement. Both of these are communities in which entrance and participation are fundamentally a matter of self-interest, and only rarely will there be an obligation of the sort that was discussed earlier, that is, a responsibility to secure the good of the members. In general the obligations will be of more specialized kinds. It is also apparent that obligations acquired in these ways can easily come into conflict with other obligations that one may have. Clearly, a moral community comprised of present and future generations cannot arise from either of these sources. We cannot enter into an explicit contract with the community of the future. And although future generations might derive benefits from us, these benefits cannot be reciprocated. (It is possible that the [biologically] dead do derive *some* benefits from the living, but I do not think that this possibility is crucial. Incidentally, just as the living could have obligations to the distant unborn, the living also have obligations to the dead. If obligation to the past is a superstition, then so is obligation to the future.)[5] Our immediate posterity, who will share a common life with us, are in a better position in this respect; so that obligations towards our children, born and unborn, conceivably *could* be generated from participation in a mutually beneficial social arrangement. This, however, would be misleading.

It seems, then, that communities in which entrance and participation are fundamentally matters of self-interest, do not fit our specifications. As an alternative let us consider communities based upon altruistic impulses and fellow-feeling. This, too, is in itself a large topic, and I refer to it only in order to develop a single point.

The question I began with was: Who are the members of my moral community? Now it is true that there are at least a few people towards whom I have the sentiments that are identified with altruism and sympathetic concern. But are these sentiments enough to establish for me the moral relationship of owing them an obligation? Are these enough to generate a moral community? The answer, I think, must be in the negative so long as these affections towards others remain at the level of animal feeling. The ancient distinction between mere affection, mere liking, and conscious desire is fundamental here. Genuine concern and interest in the well-being of another must be conscious concern. My desire for another's good must in this event be more than impulsive, and presupposes, rather, that I have a *conception* of his good. This conception, which cannot be a bare concept of what is incidentally a good but which is rather a conception of the good *for* him, further involves that he not be a mere blank to me but that he is characterized or described in some way in my consciousness. It is perhaps unnecessary to add that there is never any absolute guarantee that such a conceived good is not, in some sense, false or fragmentary. Nevertheless, an altruism that is literally mindless—if it can be called "altruism" at all—cannot be the basis of moral community.

But even if it be granted that I have a conception of another's good, I have not yet reached the stage of obligation towards him. We are all familiar with the kind of "taking an interest in the welfare of another" that is gracious and gift-like, a matter of *noblesse oblige*. It is not so much that this type of interest-taking tends to be casual, fleeting and fragmentary—*"cette charité froide qui on nomme altruisme"*—and stands in contrast to interest-taking that is constant, penetrating and concerned with the other's total good. It is, rather, a form of interest-taking, however "conceptual," that is a manifestation of an unreadiness or even an unwillingness to recognize the other's claim (as distinct, of course, from his claiming), the other's entitlement, to receive his good from me. An additional step is, therefore, required, and I think it consists in this: that I acknowledge this good as a good, that his good is good-to-me. Once I have made this step, I cannot in conscience deny the pertinence of his demand, if he makes one, although whether I should now act so as to promote his good is of course dependent on a host of factors. (Among these factors are moral considerations that determine the permissibility of various courses of action and priorities of duty.) The basis of the obligation is nevertheless secured.

This conclusion, it should be clear, does not entail that I am required to concede the status of an entitlement to every demand that is made by someone in whose well-being I have an interest. Some claims (claimings), as remarked above, are frivolous. The test of this, in the case we have been considering, is my conception of the other's good. This conception is a model in miniature of

what I earlier called a *social ideal*. However, the provisional definition of it —
a conception of the good life for man — was unnecessarily broad. In using this
term, I mean, first of all, to contrast the ideal with a personal ideal of the good
life. A personal ideal of the good life is an ideal that is not necessarily maintained as desirable for others to seek to achieve. It is what an individual, given
his unique interests and idiosyncrasies, sees as the private end of his striving;
while it does not necessarily exclude elements of sociality, it is not social in its
purview. By the term "social ideal," however, I mean primarily a conception of
the good life for individuals under some general characterization and which
can be maintained by them as good for them in virtue of this characterization.
The term covers the possibility of a social ideal that is a conception of the good
life for individuals characterized in the broadest terms, namely, as human. But
a social ideal may be narrower in its scope. For example, one may have a conception of the good life for the city-dweller or for the outdoors type. Since it is
possible for me to maintain as good-to-me a variety of ideals bearing upon
groups of individuals characterized in different ways, it is possible for me to be
a member of more than one moral community. It is in such circumstances, as
mentioned earlier, that I will experience the conflicting pulls of obligation and
competing claims upon my energy and effort.

(There is admittedly much more to be said in explanation of the nature of
social ideals, for they need not be static. The implications of our ideals are not
always immediately available, and they are enriched and clarified through
experience. They are adaptable to new life-circumstances. And they can also
become impoverished. Just as ideals are not static, neither are the characteriza-
tions of the individuals to whom the ideals are meant to apply. Another topic
that requires further study is the "logic" of the ideal-claim relationship, a study
of the ways in which ideals confer entitlements upon claims. Questions also
arise concerning justice and reciprocity. This list could be extended; it is only
meant to be suggestive. I make no pretence that I am able to solve these problems at this time.)

So far, in the above account of the generation of my moral community, the
question of membership has been discussed solely in reference to those
towards whom I initially have the sentiments that are identified with fellow-
feeling. But we can go beyond this. Again we take our clue from the history of
the development of rights. For just as the content of a system of rights that are
possessed by the members of a moral community is enlarged over time by the
pressing of claims, demanding, so also is the moral community enlarged by the
pressing of claims by individuals who have been hitherto excluded. The claiming is not only a claim for something, but may also be an assertion: "Here I
am, I count too." The struggle for rights has also been a counter-struggle. The
widening of moral communities has been accompanied by attempts at exclusion. It is important for us to take note of one feature of this situation.

The structure of the situation is highlighted when a stranger puts forward
his demand. The question immediately arises, shall his claim be recognized as a
matter of right?[6] Initially I have no affection for him. But is this crucial in

determining whether he ought to count as a member of my moral community? The determination depends, rather, on what he is like and what are the conditions of his life. One's obligations to a stranger are never immediately clear. If a visitor from Mars or Venus were to appear, I would not know what to desire for him. I would not know whether my conception of the good life is relevant to him and to his conditions of life. The good that I acknowledge might not be good for him. Humans, of course, are in a better case than Martians or Venusians. Still, since the stranger appears as strange, different, what I maintain in my attempt to exclude him is that my conception of the good is not relevant to him, that "his kind" do not count. He, on the other hand, is in effect saying to me: Given your social ideal, you must acknowledge my claim, for it *is* relevant to me given what I am; your good is my good, also.[7] If I should finally come to concede this, the full force of my obligation to him will be manifest to me quite independently of any fellow-feeling that might or might not be aroused. The *involuntary* character of the obligation will be clear to me, as it probably never is in the case of individuals who command one's sympathy. And once I admit him as a member of my moral community, I will also acknowledge my responsibility to secure this good for him even in the absence of any future claiming on his part.

With this we have completed the account of the constitution of the type of moral community that is required for obligations to future generations. I shall not recapitulate its elements. The step that incorporates future generations into our moral community is small and obvious. Future generations are members of our moral community because, and insofar as, our social ideal is relevant to them, given what they are and their conditions of life. I believe that this account applies also to obligations towards our immediate posterity. However, the responsibility that one has to see to the welfare of his children is in addition buttressed and qualified by social understandings concerning the division of moral labor and by natural affection. The basis of the obligations is nevertheless the same in both instances.[8] Underlying this account is the important fact that such obligations fall into the area of the moral life which is independent of considerations of explicit contract and personal advantage. Moral duty and virtue also fall into this area. But I should like to emphasize again that I do not wish to be understood as putting this account forward as an analysis of moral virtue and duty in general.

As we turn at long last specifically to our obligations to future generations, it is worth noticing that the term "contract" has been used to cover the kind of moral community that I have been discussing. It occurs in a famous passage in Burke's *Reflections on the Revolution in France:*

> Society is indeed a contract. Subordinate contracts for objects of mere occasional interest may be dissolved at pleasure—but the state ought not to be considered as nothing better than a partnership agreement in a trade of pepper and coffee, calico or tobacco, or some other such low concern, to be taken up for a little temporary interest, and to be dissolved by the fancy of the parties. It is to be looked

upon with other reverence; because it is not a partnership in things subservient only to the gross animal existence of a temporary and perishable nature.

It is a partnership in all science; a partnership in all art; a partnership in every virtue, and in all perfection. As the ends of such a partnership cannot be obtained in many generations, it becomes a partnership not only between those who are living, but between those who are living, those who are dead and those who are to be born.

Each contract of each particular state is but a clause in the great primaeval contract of eternal society, linking the lower with the higher natures, connecting the visible and invisible world, according to a fixed compact sanctioned by the inviolable oath which holds all physical and all moral natures, each in their appointed place.[9]

The contract Burke has in mind is hardly an explicit contract, for it is "between those who are living, those who are dead and those who are to be born." He implicitly affirms, I think, obligations to future generations. In speaking of the "ends of such a partnership," Burke intends a conception of the good life for man—a social ideal. And, if I do not misinterpret him, I think it also plain that Burke assumes that it is relatively the same conception of the good life whose realization is the object of the efforts of the living, the dead, and the unborn. They all revere the same social ideal. Moreover, he seems to assume that the conditions of life of the three groups are more or less the same. And, finally, he seems to assume that the same general characterization is true of these groups ("all physical and moral natures, each in their appointed place").

Now I think that Burke is correct in making assumptions of these sorts if we are to have obligations to future generations. However, it is precisely with such assumptions that the notion of obligation to future generations begins to run into difficulties. My discussion, until this point, has proceeded on the view that we *have* obligations to future generations. But do we? I am not sure that the question can be answered in the affirmative with any certainty. I shall conclude this note with a very brief discussion of some of the difficulties. They may be summed up in the question: Is our conception—"conceptions" might be a more accurate word—of the good life for man relevant to future generations?

It will be recalled that I began by stressing the importance of fixing the purview of obligations to future generations. They comprise the community of the future, a community with which we cannot expect to share a common life. It appears to me that the more *remote* the members of this community are, the more problematic our obligations to them become. That they are members of our moral community is highly doubtful, for we probably do not know what to desire for them.

Let us consider a concrete example, namely, that of the maintenance of genetic quality. Sir Julian Huxley has stated:

[I]f we don't do something about controlling our genetic inheritance, we are going to degenerate. Without selection, bad mutations inevitably tend to accumulate; *in the long run, perhaps 5,000 to 10,000 years from now,* we [sic] shall certainly have to do something about it. . . . Most mutations are deleterious, but we now keep many of them going that would otherwise have died out. If this continues indefinitely . . . then the whole genetic capacity of man will be much weakened.[10]

This statement, and others like it, raise many issues. As I have elsewhere (see footnote 1) discussed the problems connected with eugenic programs, positive and negative, I shall not go into details here. The point I would make is this: given that we do not know the conditions of life of the very distant future generations, we do not know what we ought to desire for them even on such matters as genic constitution. The chromosome is "deleterious" or "advantageous" only relative to given circumstances. And the same argument applies against those who would promote certain social traits by means of genetic engineering (assuming that social traits are heritable). Even such a trait as intelligence does not escape immune. (There are also problems in eugenic programs having nothing to do with remoteness.) One might go so far as to say that if we have an obligation to distant future generations it is an obligation not to plan for them. Not only do we not know their conditions of life, we also do not know whether they will maintain the same (or a similar) conception of the good life for man as we do. Can we even be fairly sure that the same general characterization is true both of them and us?

The moral to be drawn from this rather extreme example is that the more distant the generation we focus upon, the less likely it is that we have an obligation to promote its good. We would be both ethically and practically well-advised to set our sights on more immediate generations and, perhaps, solely upon our immediate posterity. After all, even if we do have obligations to future generations, our obligations to immediate posterity are undoubtedly much clearer. The nearer the generations are to us, the more likely it is that our conception of the good life is relevant to them. There is certainly enough work for us to do in discharging our responsibility to promote a good life for them. But it would be unwise, both from an ethical and a practical perspective, to seek to promote the good of the very distant.

And it could also be *wrong,* if it be granted—as I think it must—that our obligations towards (and hence the rights relative to us of) near future generations and especially our immediate posterity are clearer than those of more distant generations. By "more distant" I do not necessarily mean "very distant." We shall have to be highly scrupulous in regard to anything we do for any future generation that also could adversely affect the rights of an intervening generation. Anything else would be "gambling in futures." We should, therefore, be hesitant to act on the dire predictions of certain extreme "crisis ecologists" and on the proposals of those who would have us plan for mere survival. In the main, we would be ethically well-advised to confine ourselves to removing the obstacles that stand in the way of immediate posterity's realizing the social ideal. This involves not only the active task of cleaning up the environment and making our cities more habitable, but also implies restraints upon us. Obviously, the specific obligations that we have cannot be determined in the abstract. This article is not the place for an evaluation of concrete proposals that have been made. I would only add that population limitation schemes seem rather dubious to me. I find it inherently paradoxical that we should have an obligation to future generations (near and distant) to determine in effect the very membership of those generations.[11]

A final point. If certain trends now apparent in our biological technology continue, it is doubtful that we should regard ourselves as being under an obligation to future generations. It seems likely that the man — humanoid(?) — of the future will be Programmed Man, fabricated to order, with his finger constantly on the Delgado button that stimulates the pleasure centers of the brain. I, for one, cannot see myself as regarding the good for Programmed Man as a good-to-me. That we should do so, however, is a necessary condition of his membership in our moral community, as I have argued above. The course of these trends may very well be determined by whether we believe that we are, in the words of Burke, "but a clause in the great primaeval contract of eternal society, linking the lower with the higher natures, connecting the visible and invisible world, according to a fixed compact sanctioned by the inviolable oath which holds all physical and all moral natures, each in their appointed place." We cannot yet pretend to know the outcome of these trends. It appears that whether we have obligations to future generations in part depends on what we do for the present.

NOTES

1. This paper is highly speculative, and it is put forward with hesitation. It is an attempt to extend a position developed in my article "Towards a Theory of Human Rights," *The Monist,* 52, No. 4 (1968), 521–549, wherein I also discuss some of the classical and contemporary literature on Rights. See also my paper "Ethical Issues in Biological Engineering," *UCLA Law Review,* 15 (1968), 443–479, esp. 451–463, wherein I discuss obligations to future generations and some of the problems they provoke. I know of no other explicit discussion of the topic. The author wishes to thank the Institute of Society, Ethics, and the Life Sciences (Hastings-on-Hudson, New York) for its support.

2. See the remarks of Russell E. Train (chairman of the Council on Environmental Quality), quoted in *National Geographic,* 138 (1970), 780. "If we're to be responsible we must accept the fact that we owe a massive debt to our environment. It won't be settled in a matter of months, and it won't be forgiven us."

3. Cf. the discussion of "Fernstenliebe" [Love of the remotest] in Nicolai Hartmann, *Ethics,* trans. by Coit, II (New York: Macmillan, 1932), 317 ff. [Portions reprinted in the "Afterword" to this anthology.]

4. There is also another factor relevant to determining whether what is demanded can be claimed as a matter of right, namely, the availability of resources of goods. But I am suppressing this for purposes of this discussion.

5. Paraphrasing C. S. Lewis, *The Abolition of Man* (New York: Macmillan, paperback ed., 1969), p. 56: "If my duty to my parents is a superstition, then so is my duty to posterity."

6. When Sarah died, Abraham "approached the children of Heth, saying: I am a stranger and a sojourner with you; give me a possession of a burying-place with you, that I may bury my dead out of my sight" (Gen. 23:3, 4). A classical commentary remarks that Abraham is saying: If I am a stranger I will purchase it, but if I am a sojourner it is mine as a matter of right.

7. Cf. T. H. Green, *Lectures on the Principles of Political Obligation* (New York and London: Longman's, 1959; Ann Arbor: University of Michigan Press, 1967), Sec. 140. I here acknowledge my debt to Green, in which acknowledgment I was remiss in my article on Human Rights.

8. I think it an interesting commentary on our times that the rhetoric of obligation to future generations is so much used just when the family bond has become progressively tenuous.

9. *Reflections on the Revolution in France* (London: Dent, 1910), pp. 93–94.

10. In *Evolution after Darwin,* ed. by S. Tax III (Chicago: University of Chicago Press, 1960), p. 61. Emphasis added.

11. On this and other arguments relating to the problem, see Martin P. Golding and Naomi H. Golding, "Ethical and Value Issues in Population Limitation and Distribution in the United States," *Vanderbilt Law Review,* 24 (1971), 495–523.

Daniel Callahan

What Obligations Do We Have to Future Generations?

The problem which this paper poses immediately raises some questions. How can we say anything at all about our obligations to future generations, those generations yet-to-be-born? Is it not the case, precisely because they do not yet exist, that it becomes meaningless to even conceive of obligations toward them? Since the future does not exist, and is in that respect nothingness, how can we possibly have obligations toward it? Moreover, since it is possible that a contemplation of our obligations to future generations may result in posing moral dilemmas for those of us already alive—what if we have to give up something in their behalf?—is it not just a way of asking for trouble to raise the question at all?

Let me attempt an answer to the first question. If future generations do not exist for us, we can, nonetheless, be certain that we *will have existed for them*— as part of their heritage, some marks of which are bound to still be around even thousands of years in the future. This is only to say that just as we now exist, they will also exist—the nothingness of future generations is a pregnant nothingness, needing only time to come to birth. As for a contemplation of our obligation toward future generations being understood as an evasion of obligations to present lives, there are some senses in which this could well be true. In particular, when it is said that we should immediately introduce coercive population control for the sake of the unborn, at the price of a loss of freedom and the likelihood of injustice for those already born, one can only wonder about the priorities of human life thus expressed. This is a point to which I shall return.

The most obvious reason for raising the question about our obligations to future generations stems from a simple perception: that what we do now will have consequences, good or ill, for those who come after us. Just as the actions, choices and thinking of our ancestors, close and distant, influence the

Reprinted from the *American Ecclesiastical Review* (The Catholic University of America Press), 164 (April 1971), 265–80, with permission of the publisher and author.

way we live our lives, what we do will influence the lives of those for whom we will be ancestors. That we do not know how or by what particular chain of events this influence will exert or express itself a hundred, or a thousand or ten thousand years from now is beside the point for the moment. What matters at the outset is to recognize that there will be some influence. Just as we can trace the roots of our culture back at least 3,000 years, future generations will be able to trace theirs. To proceed as if there will be no relationship between the now and the then would be, at the very least, silly; there is no reason to presume a complete break in the chain of generations and the continuing transmission of everything from genes, to ideas, to cultures. More critically, to act as if future generations will not exist and will not be the heirs of what we do could be to act in a most irresponsible way. Modern technology, weaponry and pollution have given mankind an unprecedented power to influence the lives of those who will live in the future. It may be optimistic to think that this power will be used for good, or even that it can be; but it is only realistic to think that it can be used for evil, that we already have the power to exert a very baneful influence on the lives of those who will follow us.

Let me briefly sketch some of the more unpleasant possibilities. If we choose to take seriously the demographers, we have to recognize that present rates of population growth will, unless checked, produce a vastly more crowded world for our children and grandchildren than we now live in. The present doubling time for world population is 37 years. We may be as hopeful as we like about agricultural miracles, better systems of population distribution, and more ingenious technologies of production, consumption and reclamation—in short, we may argue that the world can cope with 7 to 10 to 20 billion people. But even if we are all that hopeful we should admit that life a few generations hence will be different; perhaps no worse, but still different. And it will be our actions today which will in many critical ways make that difference. For it is we who by our rate of reproducing are preparing the demographic base from which future generations will proceed. We can proclaim ourselves innocent and non-responsible for the present state of affairs. After all, in reproducing we are doing nothing different from what our ancestors did; and after all as well, if we are going to hold any generation responsible for the population problems being stored up for future generations, why not point the finger at our parents' generation, or at our grandparents', and so on, well back into the past? Just as we have had to take our chances with the population size our ancestors gave us, why should not future generations have to take their chances with the size we bequeath to them?

I do not think it quite so easy to wash our hands of the matter. There is one difference between our generation and those which went before. We *know* there is a certain rate of population growth at present, and we can see its implications; that cannot be said for earlier generations, Malthus notwithstanding. Moreover, we know why it is growing so rapidly: better nutrition, reduced infant mortality rates, longer life-spans.

The possibility of genetic engineering provides another example. It has been contended, with considerable plausibility, that we will soon be able to clone genetically identical human beings; that we will be able to perform genetic surgery for the correction of defects and the changing of phenotypes; that we will be able to engage in positive eugenics, that is, the production, by rational design, of those types of human beings thought genetically desirable. The list could be extended. Some of these developments may never be achieved; others could take decades. But the point is that if they are developed, man will have in his hands a powerful instrument for determining the future of his own biological nature. And one can be sure that, whatever the consequences for the generation which introduces these things, they will be relatively slight in comparison with their implications for future generations. Indeed, a major motivation behind the efforts of some of those trying for the biomedical leaps is to change the quality of the lives of future generations.

A few more examples. If the ecologists are correct, what we are now doing to our natural resources and our environment may well be irreparably harmful. It is not just that we may be ruining things for ourselves; we may be ruining things for all of those who follow us. The animals we poison into extinction will not exist in the future; that is what extinction means. The lands we ruin will not bear fruit for our heirs. The lakes we pollute will not be available for our children, or for theirs. To take another type of example, the cities we plan now will be lived in by future generations; the technologies we devise will condition the ways and meaning of life of those who proceed from us.

One can go on in this vein, but what are the essential issues? I would like to deal with three of them here. First, the problem of the nature of the obligation we owe to future generations. Second, the relationship between our obligations to the present generation and our obligations to future generations. Third, the problem of developing some appropriate norms for our present behavior where that behavior has implications for the lives of the unborn.

1. *What is the nature of the obligation we owe to future generations?* Professor Martin P. Golding, the only person I know of who has recently written on this subject, has argued cogently that what is distinctive about

> the notion of the obligation to future generations is . . . that it refers to generations with which the possessors . . . cannot expect in a literal sense to share a common life.[1]

In this respect, he is making a distinction between our immediate descendants, with whom our own generation will overlap, and our far-distant descendants. The question he poses is how we can have obligations toward those with whom we will not share a common life—who will not, as he puts it, apparently be part of our own moral community, as those living now are. If future generations are to have a claim on us, if they are able in a sense to make demands upon us, need we take these claims seriously, as a matter of rights? For Golding, the solution to this question depends on whether the claim can be seen as part of our present "social ideal," that is, our present conception of the "good life for man." It also depends on whether we are to see future generations as part of our own moral community. Golding argues, in response to these quandaries, that in order for us to recognize an obligation toward the unborn, it is necessary that I acknowledge his human good as a "good-to-me." This can happen if, in turn, I recognize that my conception of the other's good is a part of my social ideal, that is, my conception of the good life for individuals. Finally, Golding says,

> Future generations are members of our moral community because, and insofar as, our social ideal is relevant to them, given what they are and their conditions of life.[2]

Up to a point, I find Golding's argument compelling. In essence, he is saying that if we are to establish a bond of claims, rights and obligations with future generations, it has first to be shown that, somehow, they are one with us—that, though remote in time, they are part of our own moral community. And he develops a way of showing how in principle this could be the case.

I would want to supplement Golding's argument in two ways. First, it seems critical that, when we talk of "our moral community," the phrase be understood to encompass the entire human community. Otherwise the ground is set for hazardous exclusions, of a kind which has ever plagued the human community: the judgment by one human group that another is not worthy of respect or protection. What was the institution of slavery other than the result of a judgment that African blacks were not part of "our moral community"— "our" in that case meaning the white Western community, which presumed the right to make such determinations? Golding's argument, it strikes me, is at least ambiguous on the point of whether the possession of a human nature is in itself sufficient to warrant inclusion in "our moral community." The introduction of other specifications, while perhaps necessary to specify greater or lesser obligations, would at least have to be handled delicately. To be sure, to state that we have moral obligations to "the community of all human beings" introduces its own problems. One of them turns on the practical impossibility of effectively discharging obligations to "all human beings." I grant the problems there and will assist the skeptics on that point by adding in their behalf that the difficulties mount immeasurably if future humans are added to the list of those toward whom we have obligations.

A second way I would supplement Golding's argument would be by laying a greater stress on the relationship between obligations to the past and to the future. The immediate problem here turns on the way in which, if at all, we are to establish an obligation—any obligation—toward other human beings, born or to-be-born. Allow me to evade that larger question, and take up a related one more directly pertinent to the question being considered in this article— our obligation to future generations. Golding quotes a passage from Burke's *Reflections on the Revolution in France* which characterizes "society" as "a partnership not only between those who are living, but between those who are living, those who are dead and those who are to be born."[3] But neither that passage nor the citation as a whole shows why anyone of us is obliged to become participants in the partnership, to take up the burdens and obligations which it entails. None of us, to put the matter baldly, was given any choice about whether we would be born or not, or be thrust into that partnership which is society. Why then ought we to feel any obligation to the partnership — we did not create it nor were we asked if we wanted to be part of it?

My own response, which can only be sketched here, is that it cannot be otherwise, either biologically or morally. That we exist at all puts us in debt to those who conceived us — our parents — and in debt to that society in which we were born, without which we might have been conceived but could not have survived (for our parents were not sufficient unto themselves). We could not be asking or discussing any of these questions if we did not exist; and we would not exist had not someone and some society taken some responsibility for our welfare. The condition for raising the question of whether we owe the past anything at all is that the past (concretized in the form of parents and society) took upon itself an obligation toward us — to bring us into existence and to sustain us. If we value our own life at all, then we must value and feel some obligation toward those who made that life possible; we did not arrive in this world on our own, nor did we come to maturity on our own. (One might, of course, curse the conditions under which he was raised, and those who raised him. But, if he is still alive at all and not psychotically bent on suicide, he cannot rationally curse the fact that, as an infant, someone listened to his cries of hunger and fed him. That may not be much to say in behalf of the wretched parents, but it is something; they could have done otherwise.)

From our obligation to the past stems our obligation to the future. On the one hand, we owe to those coming after us at least what we ourselves were given by those who came before us: the possibility of life and survival. On the other hand, we also owe to the future an amelioration of those conditions which, in our own life (and by our own lights), lessened our possibilities for living a full human life. Ruth Benedict, in discussing the Japanese concept of "on" (a concept akin to, but not identical with, the Western notion of obligation), wrote that

> . . . devoted care of one's children is a return on one's indebtedness to one's parents when one was oneself helpless. One makes past payment on *on* to one's parents by giving equally good or better rearing to one's children. The obligations one has to one's children are merely subsumed under *on* to one's parents.[4]

This notion can be extended. There is a necessary biological link between generations, each dependent upon the other: later generations exist because of burdens assumed by earlier generations. This is most evident in the case of close successor generations; the later requires the earlier. But it is no less present even when the generations are separated over time. To live at all is to be linked in an inextricable way to the past, and to be a determinant of future generations.

Where I would only want to supplement Golding's way of developing the basis of our obligation to future generations, I want to differ on the problem of how problematic our obligations to remote future generations are. Golding asks whether *our* conception of the good life for man is *relevant* to future generations. As long as we can show the pertinence of our social ideal to distant generations, and thus show that they are members of our moral community, all is well — obligations can be established. But, he says,

> it appears to me that the more *remote* the members of this community are, the more problematic our obligations to them become. That they are members of our moral community is highly doubtful, for we probably do not know what to desire for them.[5]

Golding is arguing that, on the one hand, it is possible to show the theoretical basis for obligations to future generations; but is saying, on the other, that conditions necessary to activate these obligations do not exist. Because remote future generations are so distant in time, we do not know what to desire for them; and this is true even with genetic constitutions. He concludes that section of his discussion by saying:

> One might go so far as to say that if we have an obligation to distant future generations it is an obligation not to plan for them. Not only do we not know their conditions of life, we also do not know whether they will maintain the same (or a similar) conception of the good life for man as we do. Can we even be fairly sure that the same general characterization is true for both them and us? . . . We would be both ethically and practically well-advised to set our sights on more immediate generations and, perhaps, solely upon our immediate posterity. After all, even if we do have obligations to future generations, our obligations to immediate posterity are undoubtedly much clearer.[6]

This conclusion leaves me uncomfortable, and for a couple of reasons. The first stems from the way Golding, at the outset of his paper, talks about our obligations to future generations.

> Obligations to future generations are essentially an obligation to produce — or attempt to produce — a desirable state of affairs *for* the community of the future, to promote conditions of good living for future generations.[7]

I am struck by the fact that he casts this obligation solely in terms of positive obligations, things we must do to *enhance* their life. I should think it no less obvious that we would also be obliged to refrain from doing things which might be harmful to future generations. Quite apart from trying to produce good we should also avoid causing harm.[8] And the two are not necessarily identical. While our ignorance of the desires of future generations may make it practically impossible to know what to work for positively in their behalf — and thus relieve us of some of our obligations — we cannot claim total ignorance when it comes to knowing what might be very harmful to them. We know enough about radiation hazards, for instance, to be sure that a widespread testing of nuclear devices would have harmful genetic consequences for future generations. Unless we suppose they might actually desire those consequences — which would be capricious on our part — we could hardly excuse our nuclear weapons testing on the grounds of our ignorance of what would be "relevant" to the life of those generations. Thus it would seem that, in some circumstances, our knowledge of harmful long-range consequences would be sufficient to restrain us from certain kinds of acts.

The pertinence of this consideration comes to the fore also when we consider ecological destruction and excessive population growth. While it may be impossible for us to know the desires of future generations, we know it is possible — though remote — that the present generation could destroy the environment in some irrevocable way. And it is at least conceivably possible that the present generation could so heavily populate the earth that it would be impossible for that earth to sustain the large numbers of people which could result from a continuation of high population growth rates. If we do nothing about these hazards, then we would have at least a moral certainty that our actions would be storing up evils for future generations — breakdown of culture, overcrowding, critical shortages — evils of a kind that they would not have brought upon themselves and that they would not be able to cope with. Once again, assuming we could surmise the existence of these hazards from our present behavior, we would have a situation which would seem to demand that we refrain from certain kinds of acts for the sake of future generations. (It is not crucial, for the sake of the moral logic, to prove these hazards; the logic says "if there are hazards, then . . ." — the hazards must of course be established.)

Golding is quite right to say that, because of our ignorance, we should not plan for distant generations. But this does not relieve us of our obligation to make certain (a) that there will be future generations — which is a way of reaffirming the value we attribute to our own life; and (b) that the possibility of those generations planning for themselves is not irrevocably destroyed by our failure now to refrain from those acts which could have evil consequences for them; we have no right to preempt their choices.

A second point that makes me uneasy is Golding's minimization of our obligation to future generations on the ground of our ignorance about whether they will maintain the same ideals we do. I feel the same discomfort when I hear some moral theologians argue that we cannot have fixed ethical norms because of purported changes in "man's nature." Perhaps I am deficient in my science fiction imagination, but I see no reason to suppose that future human beings will have desires and ideals dissimilar to our own. Is it unreasonable to suppose that they will have a will to life? If they do not, then they will cease existing and there will be nothing more for anyone to concern themselves with. And is it unreasonable to suppose that they will need food, clothing and shelter, and the use of natural resources, and that they will need to be able to think and to will? They may not need the same *kind* of food we do, or the same *kind* of clothing and shelter — one's imagination can run wild on those points — but they will need nourishment and they will have to protect themselves from the environment. Even if we assume they will have discovered ways of satisfying these needs in ways utterly different from our own, these ways will undoubtedly require the use of intelligence; thus they will need good minds. In addition, one must assume that they will have to devise ways of living with each other, regulating their individual relationships and ordering their societies. They will need a social structure, ethical codes and a political order. That we may not be able to imagine the contents of these structures, codes and orders is less important than the likelihood that the formal requirements of human life together will remain similar to our own.

From a moral point of view, the problem is not whether we can peer into the future and determine what future human beings will need and desire. It is possible to conceive — as distinguished from imagine — that future generations will be so different that our social ideal will no longer pertain. Golding may, in that sense, be right. I am only asserting that since we cannot *know* what their social ideal will be, we should act on the assumption that it will not be all that dissimilar from our own; we have no special reason to think otherwise. Hence, the course of responsible behavior in this generation would be to take what we do know, and can reasonably project, and act accordingly. Moreover, whatever the ideals and ways of life which may evolve in future generations, they will have to evolve from the legacy bequeathed them by our generation, at least in part. If we are not certain what a good legacy would be, we can make some reasonable guesses about what they might count as a bad legacy. At the very least, we owe to future generations an effort to preclude those bad legacies. In this sense, we must act on their behalf, and our obligation in this respect increases proportionately to our knowledge or sensible guesses about what, minimally, they will need to ensure their own survival and to have the opportunity to fashion their own life.

If I am correct in this line of reasoning, then I think, contrary to Golding, that we do have some important obligations even to far distant generations. Until it can be proved otherwise — and I do not see how it could — we must act as if they will be part of our moral community and will share to some degree our social ideal. I do not want to develop the point here, but I would also go so far as to suggest that we have the right to enhance the possibility that our own ideals will be perpetuated through time. Part of our present social ideal, for instance, is that human communities should be peaceful, fulfilling of the best human aspirations, permeated by love, justice and freedom. It could be said of course that distant future generations may not have similar ideals and may not desire to hold on to what we now value. I think I would reply to that, however, that I do not know what it could possibly mean to speak of a human community which did not want those goods, that I would want to know why, in that case, the word "human" any longer pertains. So far as I am concerned that would be a bad state of affairs, and I would accordingly feel obliged to do whatever I could to preclude it from arising.

2. *What is the relationship between our obligations to future generations and our obligations to the present generation?* If it can be agreed that we do have real obligations to distant generations, we are left with the problem of determining how we are to balance those obligations against our obligations to the present generation. In existing generations, moral dilemmas arise because of real or apparent conflicts among or between obligations. We do not know how to serve fully two or more goods at the same time, doing equal justice to all of them. It is conceivable that the same kind of dilemmas can arise across the generations, where the discharging of our obligations to the living could require acting in ways which would have harmful consequences for future generations. While I would aggressively not include myself among them, there are some, we should recall, who feel that if the price for maintaining our present Western way of life is a world-wide nuclear war, then that price should be paid, regardless of the environmental and genetic consequences for future generations. They really believe that it is better to be dead than red, and not only us, but, if necessary, all those who come after us. To choose death rather than slavery for oneself is one thing; to choose it for one's children quite another — the former is more easily justified than the latter. This seems to me a social ideal gone berserk, but for some it is the ideal. Arguments of this type seem, then, to presume that our main obligation is to the living or those who will immediately come after us.

At the other extreme are those who would apparently give our obligations to future generations a greater weight than those we owe to the living. Thus some biologists and ecologists speak as if our obligation to preserve the human species, or our obligation to preserve forests and wildlife, takes precedence over all other obligations. Garrett Hardin can discount the notion of individual conscience and the respect due it on the grounds that it is dysfunctional in ensuring control of population growth, without which all future generations, and the species itself, are radically endangered. Others have contended that, faced with a choice of cutting down the last redwoods to plant crops to feed the starving, our choice should clearly go to preserving the trees. For we have an obligation, they say, to preserve those trees for the enjoyment of future generations. If the price of this preservation is a few thousand lives, we can do no less for those who will come after us. Redwoods are in short supply; people are not.

I have presented some extreme positions, but it is possible to discover others which present what I think are genuine as distinguished from apocalyptic ethical dilemmas. Let us return to the contention that our present rate of consumption of natural resources combined with our present, and constantly expanding, rate of pollution of the environment may permanently despoil the earth. This will not happen at once, and for that matter our children and grandchildren may be able to survive; but sooner or later, a limit will be reached, a point of no return. We will not personally suffer, but others will, especially if what we are doing now will, if not stopped, make it impossible for future generations to survive, much less to live a decent life. One major argument against genetic engineering is that our present attempts at intervention may introduce irrevocable changes, which future generations will not be able to undo. Thus we would, in effect, have imposed ourselves upon them, leaving them no option but to accept our legacy.

These concerns are to be taken seriously. If it is the case—and that of course needs to be established—that our present behavior can prove harmful to future generations, then, according to my earlier argument, we have an obligation to refrain *as far as possible* from that behavior. The key phrase is "as far as possible." For it may well be the case that, in order to do justice to the present generation, some acts may be required which will jeopardize either the life or the quality of life of future generations. Let us imagine an improbable though ethically suggestive chain of events. Let us imagine that the nations of the world gave up the arms race and decided to turn all their efforts to the alleviation of hunger and disease, the development of the underdeveloped nations, and the establishment of a minimally decent standard of living for all. And let us assume they wanted to do this at once. However, if they wanted to do it at once—to save those now living—they would by and large have to do so with the tools of existing technologies. They would not have time to invent fertilizers which could guarantee a non-pollution of the earth, or time to invent factories which do not emit noxious fumes, or time to devise substitutes for nonrenewable resources, or time to find ways of raising crops which would not require the destruction of some wildlife and some primitive forest areas. All those steps could require years. At that point, of course, the ecologists would become violently alarmed, for they could easily foresee what the long-term price for the short-term salvation of individual lives could be. Well, to whom, then, do we owe what?

I think there is a partial way of resolving this dilemma. One thing that can be said for the present generation over against future generations is that they have *existing* rights: the right to life, liberty and the pursuit of happiness (to choose one familiar formulation). They are here and the future generations are not. The claim of future generations against us is a conditional claim, in the sense that it depends upon their existing to make the claim. That we know they will exist is enough to determine that their claim is not a fictitious one; but it is conditional in the sense that a number of conditions have to be fulfilled before the claim can be entered, the most important of which is that they exist in actuality and not just potentially. Over against that situation are presently living human beings, whose claims are actualized claims, whose rights are in no sense conditional. In this respect, it is difficult to see how one could set aside these claims in the name of claims as yet not made—even though we have a moral certainty they will be made. I am only saying that, so far as claims of rights are concerned, those who are living take priority over those who do not as yet exist. But more strongly, I do not see how one could *deny* the claim to a very basic human right made by a person now living in favor of the conditional claim which can be made by someone who will exist in the future.

Now if that were all there was to the matter, there would be no real dilemma. But I think that an assertion of the priority of the claims of the living over the claims of the yet-to-be-born cannot be turned into an absolute priority, of a kind which would not require us to give any thought to the claims which will be made by future generations. The limit of the claims of the present generations extends, I would argue, only to those rights which are fundamental to their own human existence. I mean by "fundamental" here not just gross survival, the right to life only, but also those rights which we judge are minimally necessary to live a life which can be said to have human dignity — the right to a safe and secure life, the right to those freedoms necessary for us to frame and live by our own values, the right to knowledge, the right to due process of law, and so on. (One can, to be sure, argue about just what rights are fundamental and indispensable to a life of human dignity, but that does not disturb my main point.)

If the present generation does have those rights, and their present claims give those rights a priority, it can still be asked how much of an exercise of those rights is really necessary for human dignity. Here, with an apology to Herbert Marcuse, I would like to coin the concept of a surplus-exercise of rights. By a surplus-exercise of rights I mean that exercise of rights which goes well beyond what is minimally or even moderately necessary for a decent human life. For instance, most of us would grant the right to decent housing. A surplus-exercise of that right might consist of insisting that we could, without compunction, consume all existing redwood trees in order to satisfy our desire to live in houses made of that kind of wood. Or, given our right to life, we might claim the right to produce those kinds of foods which most pleased our palate, at whatever the cost to the environment. Or, if we construe the right to pursue happiness as entailing the right to some entertainment, we might claim the right to ruin lakes by filling them with oil-spilling power boats, that being the kind of entertainment which pleases us.

To be sure, it might be possible to say that rights just do not extend that far. But that could be hard to sustain, especially if people are to have some choice about what they consider a valid and meaningful implementation of their fundamental rights. Hence, I prefer to speak of a surplus-exercise of rights — an exercise which might under some conditions be acceptable, but not under others. One of the circumstances under which they would not be acceptable would be when it came to be seen that such an exercise would jeopardize future generations. Indeed, one might say that a surplus-exercise comes into being at just that point when we discover that the *way* we exercise our rights jeopardizes the rights which future generations will claim, i.e., those fundamental rights we now claim.

3. *What ethical norms would be appropriate for that behavior of our present generation which has implications for the lives of future generations?* Let me try to suggest some summary rules concerning our obligations toward future generations:

a. Do nothing which could jeopardize the very existence of future generations.

b. Do nothing which could jeopardize the possibility of future generations exercising those fundamental rights necessary for a life of human dignity.

c. If it seems necessary, in the interests of the existing rights of the living, to behave in ways which could jeopardize the equivalent rights of those yet to be born, do so in that way which would as far as possible minimize the jeopardy.

d. When trying to determine whether present behavior will in fact jeopardize future life, calculate in as responsible and sensitive a manner as one would in trying to determine whether an act with uncertain consequences would be harmful to one's own children. If you would not conjure up the possibility of magical solutions occurring to save your own children at the last moment from the harmful consequences of your gambling with their future, do not do so even with future generations.

These are, of course, very general rules; and I would invite others who take up the topic of this paper to change, amend or further specify them. Of the four rules suggested, the last has a special importance. In trying to determine a model or a prototype of what it means to have an obligation toward future generations, we must begin with models or prototypes of what it means to have obligations toward those now living. The most pertinent present model is the obligation of parents toward their children. For what are future generations other than the children of children, each of whom in turn becomes a parent and thus extends through time the obligations which present parents bear toward their children? There is no way to break the chain of obligation which is passed from one generation to another; it is the very condition of there being successor generations. The essence of the parent-child relationship is the responsibility which the parent undertakes to give the child what he or she needs. The parent does not in all respects know exactly what that child, as a particular individual, needs. The parent can only act in terms of what it appears that the child needs, beginning with the minimal requirements of physical survival. Of necessity, the parent's interpretation of the child's needs will be conditioned by the parent's understanding of life, and this will be time- and culture-bound. While the parent may be aware of this, there is little he can do about it; he has no place to begin except where he is, hoping that the choices he must make in the child's behalf will not, should they prove wrong, be irredeemable.

If we extend the same model to let it serve as a prototype of our obligations toward future generations, then two conclusions appear inescapable: first, that we must use our own and present understanding of human life as the basis for any projections into the future—no other is available; and, second, that there are no grounds for introducing, in judging that behavior of ours with implications for future generations (close or distant), any norms sharply at variance with those we would employ in judging our obligations to those presently alive. This is only to say that, because we will be linked with future generations, we bear a responsibility toward them. While that is just the beginning of the ethical problem, it is an important beginning. We know that we cannot ignore them, that they are dependent upon us (for we are their parents, both literally and symbolically), that, in trying to discharge our obligations toward them, we are doing no more than our parents did for us. The burden is not necessarily a light one.

NOTES

1. Martin P. Golding, "Obligations to Future Generations," in the "Philosophy and Public Policy" issue of *The Monist* (January 1972), p. 86. I am indebted to Professor Golding for making his paper available to me prior to publication. [Callahan is referring here to the paper by Golding which immediately precedes this paper in this anthology. —ED.]

2. Golding, op. cit., p. 95. [p. 68, above].

3. E. Burke, *Reflections on the Revolution in France* (London: Dent, 1910), pp. 93–94: cited in Golding.

4. R. Benedict, *The Sword and the Chrysanthemum* (Rutland, Vt.: Charles E. Tuttle, 1946), p. 102.

5. Golding, op. cit., p. 97. [p. 69, above].

6. Golding, op. cit., pp. 97–98. [p. 70, above].

7. Ibid., p. 86. [p. 62, above].

8. I am not implying that the avoidance of doing harm constitutes the full range of ethical responsibilities. I am only saying that in the case of our obligations to future generations, where our duty to enhance their welfare is problematic, we can and should have recourse to the limited ethical goal of avoiding harm.

PART TWO

The Duty to Posterity
Some Perspectives

Part 2. The Duty to Posterity
Some Perspectives

Introduction

The papers in the previous section were selected for the purpose of posing moral questions concerning the duty to posterity. The papers of this section are intended to offer not so much specific answers to these questions as conceptual contexts and structures, or "points of view," from which morally appealing responses might best be evaluated. This distinction is blurred by the understandable and even desirable circumstance that the authors in the first section often attempt to answer the questions they pose, while writers in this second section state the questions and issues to which they propose to respond. Accordingly, many of these papers have been assigned to one group or the other on the rather arbitrary basis of emphasis. The reader is thus cautioned not to make too much of the section titles (". . . Issues," ". . . Perspectives"). Both sections are intended to introduce and illuminate the general topic of this anthology, the moral responsibility of the living to future generations.

In the first paper, philosopher Ronald Green, writing in *BioScience* for scientists, proposes and examines three "moral axioms of intergenerational responsibility." These axioms are, in order: (1) "We are bound by ties of justice to real future persons"; (2) "The lives of future persons ought ideally to be 'better' than our own and certainly no worse"; (3) "Sacrifices on behalf of the future must be distributed equitably in the present, with special regard for those presently least advantaged." Green adopts a "contractarian" approach to these questions that is similar to that of one of his teachers at Harvard, philosopher John Rawls.

"The rational aim of life," writes Charles Hartshorne, "is to contribute value to . . . the entire future." In this evocative, speculative, even religious essay, Hartshorne urges that concern and responsibility for the future is essential to a moral perspective and to the practice of a moral life. What future? Not the future of particular persons, but the future of the cosmic, universal *whole* that is the ground of values and the context of personal well-being.

Gregory Kavka asks: Are we obliged to afford future "strangers" the same moral consideration of beneficence and nonmalfeasance that we are obliged to show contemporary strangers? Kavka believes that we are. He arrives at this conclusion by examining, and discounting, three proposed reasons for *rejecting* such moral consideration for future "strangers": (*a*) that future persons have a different "temporal location," (*b*) that we are *ignorant* of them (that is, we do not know them as identifiable, individual persons), and (*c*) that their existence is contingent. Kavka then turns to the task of justifying the intuitive affirmation that the human race should continue far into the future. The essay closes with an examination of the question of the distribution of resources between present and future generations.

Holmes Rolston III invites the reader to adopt the perspective of human history, and even of life-history—a moral point of view "writ large." He adopts, at the outset, the metaphor of human life, both personal and specieswide, as a "river." To the moral spectator of all time and life—that is, of the "river of life"—basic and traditional philosophical polarities, such as "the actual and the potential," "the self and the other," "the human and the natural," "the present and the historical," and "the *is* and the *ought,*" are seen to flow together. From this perspective, writes Rolston, we see that "it would be a present, intrinsic wrong to deprive ourselves of a future, as it would also be wrong for us not to be instrumental for future good." (This perspective is urged elsewhere in this anthology by Hartshorne, Partridge, and Hartmann.)

Ronald M. Green

Intergenerational Distributive Justice and Environmental Responsibility

From the beginning of the nuclear age, through the Pugwash Conferences of the late 1950's, down to the environmental movement of our own decade, scientists have played a leading role in alerting us to the dangers posed by our present habits and technologies. Each problem in what Platt[1] has termed the "storm of crisis problems" facing mankind today—population growth, resource depletion, environmental degradation, and the control of nuclear energy—has typically first been identified and publicized by members of the scientific community.

Since a distinguishing feature of all these problems is that they threaten massive evil for generations yet unborn, scientists have also performed the important task of reminding us of our moral responsibility to future generations. More than many of us, scientists have been alert to the fact that our moral obligations extend beyond our contemporaries to the generations that will follow us. But although scientists have tended to assume the existence of a responsibility to the future, they have not commonly discussed the more abstract question of the nature of that responsibility, its basis, extent, or limits.

As an ethicist, I want to take the modest step here of remedying this lack of discussion by proposing three very basic guides to our thinking about obligations to the future. I call these "axioms" of intergenerational responsibility. They are so "commonsensical" that I suspect that most scientists concerned with the future already share them. Nevertheless, each does involve some serious conceptual difficulties, and it may be useful to look at these moral axioms with some of the same care that scientists bring to questions of fact.

Bonds With the Future

The first axiom is: *We are bound by ties of justice to real future persons.*

Reprinted with permission, from the April 1977 issue of *BioScience,* published by the American Institute of Biological Sciences.

Even though the belief that we have obligations to future generations is widely held, the very idea of obligations to persons in the future is quite odd. In a discussion of this issue, Stearns[2] pointed this out when he asked: "Why should there be obligations to future generations? We have made no commitments to them. We have entered no social compacts with them. . . . Under any moral theory, why should there be obligations to nonexistent persons?"

One response to these puzzling questions may be offered by utilitarian moral theory, which reduces all obligation to the single requirement that we act to produce "the greatest happiness for the greatest number of persons."[3] Since, from a utilitarian point of view, it is immaterial where or for whom happiness is produced, this requirement clearly extends to the future and helps explain our obligation to future persons.

Though this may be so, utilitarianism also entails some puzzling difficulties of its own. For example, if we are obligated to maximize happiness, might we not be obligated to multiply the number of persons who could experience happiness? Indeed, so long as the aggregate or overall gains to happiness produced this way proved greater than the corresponding loss to per capita well-being resulting from crowding, a utilitarian approach might even counsel indefinite growth in population. A utilitarian utopia might thus be characterized by burgeoning populations living at or near the subsistence level.

This possible utilitarian conclusion seems to illustrate the old saw that there is no position so foolish that some philosopher has not defended it. But utilitarianism is not just foolish. It represents a serious effort to answer the question of why we should be obligated to persons who are not yet even alive.

Nevertheless, we do not have to accept utilitarianism or its possible conclusions to understand our obligations to the future. In fact, the utilitarian error is a very basic one. Morality does not really involve any kind of lofty commitment to maximizing human happiness, nor even, as some have believed, to minimizing suffering.[4] Rather, morality has a far more mundane purpose: It is primarily an instrument for adjudicating possible conflicts between persons and for facilitating a noncoercive settlement of social disputes. It is an effort to replace the play of force and power in human affairs with principles to guide our conduct derived from reasoned, common agreement.[5]

Moral Reasoning

This understanding of morality is reflected in the recent return by some philosophers to a social contract method of moral reasoning. According to Rawls, for example, moral principles may be thought of as those basic rules agreed to by free, equal, self-interested and rational persons under conditions of strict impartiality.[6] Specifically, Rawls proposes that we view our moral principles as deriving from a hypothetical (not real) contract situation in which each of us seeks best to protect our possible interests. To prevent an unfair distortion of the outcome and to produce a result acceptable to all, however, he asks that we also think of ourselves as deprived of knowledge of our own particular strengths and weaknesses, advantages or disadvantages. The outcome of this hypothetical reasoning process would be a set of principles to which all could agree.

Rawls' view has many complexities, but the basic idea is as familiar as the everyday counsel to "put yourself in the other fellow's shoes." What Rawls is telling us is that if we are rationally to settle our social disputes and to construct a harmonious social order, we must adopt a moral point of view that involves choosing rationally but impartially before the array of competing interests and claims.

These considerations suggest just why we are obligated to future generations. It is not, as utilitarians mistakenly believe, because we have a duty to promote human happiness. Rather, it is because our wishes and behavior can conflict with those of future persons. We live, after all, in a finite world with limited space, resources, and opportunities, and not even the most optimistic prospects of technological change in the future are likely to remove all limits. By reducing these resources or opportunities, our conduct in the present can injure those who follow us, and they, in turn, in anger, resentment, or ignorance can inflict injury on their descendants.

For these reasons, moral obligations between generations are as important as any obligations we possess. In fact, they clearly form a part of the total requirements of distributive justice that bear upon us; as we must equitably distribute scarce goods and opportunities in the present, so must we do so over time. If we fail to do so, if we neglect our just responsibilities to the future, we risk reducing ongoing human relations to the Hobbesian "war of all with all" that morality aims to prevent.

Who Is the Future?

As elemental as this understanding is, it has some important implications. For one thing, it suggests that we need not morally concern ourselves with the welfare of merely "possible" future persons — with those human beings whose very coming into existence depends on our reproductive decisions. Persons who will never come into being cannot conceivably occasion social conflict, so merely "possible" persons need not enter into our moral thinking at all. Concretely, this means that there is no such thing as a "right to come into being" or a "right to be born."[7] It also means that in our collective population decisions we are primarily called upon to minimize injury to *real* future persons. Zero population growth, with its goal of improved life circumstances for smaller future numbers, is a valid conclusion from these basic premises.

Actually, the population issue is a bit more complex than this. Even with merely "possible" persons out of the picture, population policy can involve a conflict between generations. To some degree, it is in the interests of certain segments of present generations to have unrestrained procreative liberty, whereas it is generally in the ineterests of future generations to have earlier population growth limited. Apart from the emotional satisfactions produced by children, for example, there are often concrete reasons why parents in agrarian societies opt for numerous offspring. At the same time, larger family size can disadvantage the children themselves, a fact that has led some demographers to speak of the "parental exploitation of children" in the underdeveloped setting.[8]

This raises the question of how disputes of this sort are to be settled. The answer, I think, is furnished by the kind of contract method Rawls proposes. Specifically, each of us must ask: "If I were a member of a hypothetical contract situation seeking my possible advantage, but if I were denied knowledge of which generation I live in, what population policy would I propose?" Elsewhere I have tried to consider this question at length, but a general answer seems clear: In view of the many future generations aided by stationary population levels, and the relatively slight sacrifices imposed on the present, a nogrowth policy is a good choice under conditions of radical impartiality.[9] Zero population growth is right. Indeed, negative growth rates to enhance the circumstances of future generations are also justifiable, and it goes without saying that rampant population growth under conditions of poverty is absolutely unacceptable. Quite apart from the question of whether such growth threatens physical survival, the miserable survival it produces is a severe injustice to those born into progressively more impoverished generations.

More important than this almost undisputed conclusion, however, is the method of arriving at it. What I am trying to suggest under the heading of this first axiom is a way of thinking about our obligations to the future and, at the same time, a rational way of determining the extent of those obligations. This method, moreover, is as applicable to other problems of intergenerational justice, including environmental responsibility and resource planning, as it is to population policy. In each of these cases, I suggest, we are called upon to ask a simple question: "Which policy would I find most advantageous if I were deprived of the knowledge of the generation to which I belonged?" Obviously, this question alone will not solve our problems. Complex factual matters must also be faced on each issue, and the expertise of many disciplines must be drawn upon. But it may be of some help at the outset to see that the right question is being asked.

Future Should Be Better

The second axiom is: *The lives of future persons ought ideally to be "better" than our own and certainly no worse.*

Ordinarily, when we act out of respect for other persons, we can at least entertain the possibility that when their turn comes, they will act out of respect for us as well. But virtually no possibility of such reciprocity exists between generations. Except, perhaps, by respecting our memory, future generations cannot really compensate us for the sacrifices we make on their behalf. This consideration has led some philosophers to suggest that human history displays a kind of chronological unfairness; the earliest generations are called upon to make sacrifices whose benefits they can never enjoy.[10] A similar oddity has been noted by economists and others who have discussed the matter of capital savings for the future. A policy of savings, they observe, benefits every generation but the first, which experiences only sacrifice.[11]

It is tempting to conclude that policies which disadvantage one individual or group for the sake of others must be unjust. This need not be true. Where circumstances allow no alternative, policies of this sort can be just, and this seems to be the case where obligations to the future are concerned. Not only is restraint on behalf of the future required, but deliberate sacrifices on our part aimed at making life better for all our descendants also are justified.

To see this, we need only regard the choices impartially. We can refuse to sacrifice or save, and we can insist on a strict equality of expectations across generations. This probably is to our advantage if we happen to be in any initial generation when savings are proposed. But it is clearly to our disadvantage if we belong to any subsequent generation. Each of these receives something from its predecessors and benefits generally from the process of savings as the circumstances of life continue to improve. Deprived of knowledge of the generation to which we belong, therefore, it seems reasonable to opt for some kind of saving policy. Morally this expresses itself as the duty to strive, even at some expense to ourselves, for the betterment of the conditions of life of those who follow us.

My use of the terms *savings* and *betterment* interchangeably may suggest that I construe this duty to improve the welfare of our descendants primarily in economic terms—as some kind of unending growth in material productivity. Certainly, money income and consumer goods of one sort or another are candidates for consideration among the values we ought to increase for our descendants. But they cannot be the sole goods because we know that increase in these goods has characteristically been accompanied by the degradation of other important and choiceworthy values, including human emotional health, cultural richness, and environmental quality.

The fact that many evils associated with an expanding economy are external to any one generation has led some economists to view commodity production and consumption as an undisputed good, something that persons with divergent ends can all support. But any perspective which takes future generations into account must question this emphasis. Even responsible economists today agree that adequate income measurements must encompass the cross-generational costs of environmental deterioration and resource depletion.[12]

The Quality of Life

These considerations raise the complex question of "quality of life." If we agree that we ought to improve the real quality of life of our descendants, which criteria should we select for doing so? What constitutes a good or "better" life? So many moralists have tried to answer this question that it would be presumptuous of me to try to resolve it here. But a few modest suggestions may be in order. For one thing, the fact that it is far easier to identify what constitutes a deterioration in the quality of life than what constitutes an improvement makes it minimally incumbent upon us not to worsen the lot of our successors. This means that we must be careful not to squander or dissipate the legacy of natural and cultural values we have inherited from the past. In particular, we must respect the integrity of our physical environment, since all future progress presumes environmental stability.

In considering the direction actual progress in the future should take, we might keep in mind the fact that, here as elsewhere, moral choice requires a process of impartial but informed reasoning. This means that we must not allow our choices for the future to be guided by narrow preferences and special interest groups. Neither those who would make us into insatiable consumers nor those who would have us all become philosophers deserve our exclusive attention. A realistic assessment of the plurality of human ends must guide our thinking about the world we hand down to the future.

The fact that moral choice requires impartiality, however, does not mean that it presumes ignorance. On the contrary, full general information is essential to sound moral reasoning. Even the hypothetical contractors of Rawls' theory are assumed to know all the "general laws and theories" that bear on their choice.[13] This means that scientists have a particularly important role in helping us make our choices for the future. True, in choosing goods and weighing values, or even in judging scientific matters outside their areas of competence, scientists have no more expertise than educated laymen.[14]

But within their broad areas of specialization scientists have the vital task of alerting us to the dangers and opportunities in our actions and of identifying for us the natural conditions of human flourishing. In this respect, science is an irreplaceable "instrument of service" to the total moral community.[15]

It may well be that scientific inquiry will inform us that an overall improvement in our condition requires *less* of some of the goods or activities we presently cherish, or even, perhaps, a measure of deliberately programmed austerity and hardship in our lives.[16] Keeping this in mind, we should not forget that it is still our obligation to help improve the lives of those who follow us. Whatever the intent, appeals for an end to economic growth may have recently had the effect of casting the very idea of progress into disrepute.[17] Although this conclusion is understandable, it can encourage a defection from our obligation to the future. Our responsibility is not to abandon a striving for progress so much as to identify and develop those areas where significant human progress remains possible.

Whatever positive directions we select for the future, it remains true that we are minimally required not to worsen the future quality of life. Any historical process displaying a retrogression in human prospects would violate the deepest possibilities of the human enterprise. Unfortunately, an unprecedented capacity to inflict deliberate, mammoth, and irreversible injury on our descendants is a distinguishing feature of our era. Our exercise of this capacity is illustrated by our near exhaustion of petroleum resources and by the serious insults we inflict on delicate environmental systems. Among the most vivid illustrations of irresponsibility to the future, however, are the recent proposals for development of a plutonium recycle economy.[18] . . .

Distributing Sacrifices for the Future

The third axiom is: *Sacrifices on behalf of the future must be distributed equitably in the present, with special regard for those presently least advantaged.*

From the beginning of my remarks, I have tried to suggest that our obligations to the future are obligations of justice. They form part of the total moral question of how we are to distribute the limited material resources and opportunities our environment affords. There is nothing new in this understanding. It was emphasized almost two centuries ago by Thomas Robert Malthus, one of the pioneers in intergenerational thinking, when he argued against unrestrained procreation. The procreatively irresponsible, Malthus said, can be thought of as unjustly pushing their numerous offspring forward to the limited places at some future banquet table of life.[19] Recently, in a classic article, Hardin made the same point by comparing groups of nations with high fertility to abusers of the commons.[20] Even more than Malthus, Hardin's discussion indicates the element of injustice in abuse over time of a shared environment.

However, if we grant that it is unjust to force our excess progeny on others or that it is unjust to consume more than our generation's share of resources, what does this imply for our total moral responsibility and particularly for the question of how we ought to distribute needed sacrifices in the present? Very specifically, can we demand just treatment for the future while neglecting justice in the present? Can we require some persons to sacrifice on behalf of all our descendants while we refuse to treat those same persons by the strictest standards of justice? Can justice itself be compartmentalized in this way?

I believe the answer to these questions must be no. Just regard for the future is inseparable from just policies in the present. We cannot pick and choose our areas of moral exertion, encouraging or demanding regard for some persons but not for others. Unfortunately, this awareness has sometimes escaped participants in the population and resource debate. From Malthus to Hardin, many proponents of environmental responsibility have been quick to champion just policies protective of the future. But they have sometimes been equally slow to recognize the just claims of less advantaged groups or individuals in the present. In the case of Malthus, this partiality was a deliberate expression of his aristocratic and antidemocratic bias, and it deservedly earned him the enmity of radical defenders of the poor.[21]

Malthus' followers have not always shared his social preferences. Some have been convinced that restraints on consumption and population are very much to everybody's eventual advantage. Although this may be true, it obscures the fact that just demands on behalf of the future are first of all precisely that— demands. As such, they necessarily bring up the whole question of distributive justice.

What Distributive Justice Entails

This is all rather abstract, but it has some important concrete implications. Within our own nation it suggests that we must be especially careful to see that when we institute policies to protect the future, we do not disproportionately injure our less advantaged citizens in the present. I do not want to maintain that individuals or families earning less than, say, the median income are being unjustly treated. Justice need not require equality of income.[22] But certainly departures from equality require justification, and even when they are justified lesser shares of income can frequently generate resentment. To ask our less affluent fellow citizens to bear a special share of the burden of protecting the future, therefore, risks compounding injustice or exacerbating resentment.

We might also keep in mind the fact that the less affluent and the poor often have fewer reasons to identify with the future generations we seek to protect. Neither inner-city residents nor blue-collar workers, for example, typically enjoy optimum natural environments. One government report recently termed our urban poor as among our environmentally "most endangered" citizens.[23] Therefore, we should not be surprised if appeals for environmental responsibility go unheeded by members of these groups, or if they reject these appeals as an "elitist" preoccupation.

More serious than this is the fact that the less affluent can rarely afford the special sacrifices needed for the future, although these sacrifices very often tend to fall directly on them. Both in this country and abroad, for example, high fertility is usually associated with low income groups partly because members of these groups have the greatest need for the various kinds of basic security that large families can provide.[24] However necessary, and however much it may eventually benefit all families, therefore, population limitation can often severely disadvantage low income parents by requiring them to limit the size of their families before alternative social security programs are available and before adequate local health care can guarantee survival of all their children.

The same is true of the related environmental and resource issues. Recently, for example, measures aimed at protecting our environment have tended to strike lower-middle-class or poor workers the hardest. Not only can these workers barely afford to pay the extra costs or taxes for these measures, but they often depend for a livelihood on marginal firms whose viability is jeopardized by demands for pollution control or recycling equipment.

The energy issue offers a similar picture. As recent hearings on United States energy policy make clear, it is the poor and middle class that most sorely feel the bite of added energy costs.[25] Members of these groups tend to pay a large percentage of their income for fuel and gasoline, and they are tied to aging homes or automobiles, whose energy consumption is disproportionately high.

Implications

All those engaged in efforts to marshal support for programs protective of future generations should keep these facts in mind. It is not only that we potentially commit an injustice against the less privileged members of our community by causing them to bear a larger share of our intergenerational distributive responsibility. It is also that, in doing so, we endanger our very efforts to protect future generations. When those who are less well-off are treated in a way they regard as unjust, they may respond with resentment and resistance, which can paralyze efforts on behalf of future generations. Indeed, the recent erosion of public support for environmental programs during this recessionary period, and particularly the resistance of lower-middle-class workers fearful of losing their jobs, may serve as warning that these dangers are very real.

The third axiom of intergenerational justice has implications for a number of policy issues, ranging from the very specific matter of establishing fair rate schedules for promoting energy conservation to the broader matter of how we can best formulate strategies for eliciting environmental concern. It also has application to the international arena where it may counsel a change in the tone, if not the content, of demands for population restraint on the part of the poorer nations. These demands rightly proceed from a sense of the injustice of such unrestrained procreation (injustice to *all* our descendants).

But some of the most strident of these demands have been voiced by citizens of other nations or by indigenous elites whose own conduct, not only in matters of population or resource consumption but in a host of other social relations as well, has been morally questionable. Strict justice in the matter of population does not, as some have mistakenly believed and objected, require toleration of serious reproductive irresponsibility.[26] Those who fail to limit the number of their offspring are themselves guilty of violating strict standards of justice. The recognition that our objection to this behavior is based on considerations of justice, however, may caution us to be aware of our own inadequacies when we call on the procreatively irresponsible to respect our common future.

Conclusions

This is not the place to explore all the implications and applications of these axioms. My aim, instead, has been to present a way of thinking about intergenerational responsibility. Working out all the details of these axioms and the method that underlies them is an important but separate task. In moral reasoning, as in science, the method of thinking about problems may be more important than specific conclusions, "the act of judging more critical than the judgment."[27]

Although these three axioms may be taken singly, there is some value in regarding them all together. Like organic life, justice is a seamless webb.[28] If these axioms offer any lesson, it is that, although we are responsible to the future, our efforts to improve the future quality of life must not become an excuse for neglecting our responsibilities to our neighbors in the present.

The last point may have special importance for scientists. Perhaps because they work so closely with the delicate natural systems on which all of our lives depend, or perhaps just because they naturally have "the future in their bones," as C. P. Snow puts it, scientists, and particularly biologists, have been at the forefront of efforts at environmental preservation.[29] In the very urgent task of protecting the environment, however, scientists must be careful not to align themselves with those privileged individuals, groups, or nations whose calls for sacrifice are directed primarily at the poor.

Scientists must also be careful that their efforts to shock us into responsibility do not help generate the "me-first" attitude of survival more appropriate to a battlefield or lifeboat than an ongoing human community. If scientists allow their foresight to be used as an ideology by the privileged, if they fail to keep in mind the strict relationship between justice to the future and justice to the less fortunate in the present, both science and future generations will be the losers.

NOTES

1. John Platt, "What Must We Do?" *Science,* 166 (1969), 1115–1121.

2. J. B. Stearns, "Ecology and the Indefinite Unborn," *Monist,* 56 (1972), 612–625.

3. J. S. Mill, *Utilitarianism* (London: Longman, 1864). H. Sidgwick, *The Methods of Ethics,* 7th ed. (New York: Dover Publications, 1907).

4. J. Narveson, "Utilitarianism and New Generations," *Mind,* 76 (1967), 62–72.

5. D. Baier, *The Moral Point of View* (Ithaca, N.Y.: Cornell University Press, 1958). G. J. Warnock, *The Object of Morality* (London: Methuen, 1971).

6. J. Rawls, *A Theory of Justice* (Cambridge, Mass.: Harvard University Press, 1971).

7. J. Feinberg, "The Rights of Animals and Unborn Generations," in *Philosophy and Environmental Crisis,* ed. W. T. Blackstone (Athens, Ga.: University of Georgia Press, 1974).

8. T. P. Schultz, "An Economic Perspective on Population Growth," in National Academy of Sciences, *Rapid Population Growth* (Baltimore, Md.: Johns Hopkins Press, 1971).

9. R. Green, *Population Growth and Justice* (Missoula, Mont.: Scholars Press, 1976).

10. I. Kant, "Idea for a Universal History with a Cosmopolitan Purpose," in *Kant's Political Writings,* ed. H. Reiss (Cambridge, England: Cambridge University Press, 1970).

11. D. C. Mueller, "Intergenerational Justice and the Social Discount Rate," *Theory and Decision* (1974), 5:263–273. J. Rawls, *A Theory of Justice* (Cambridge, Mass.: Harvard University Press, 1971).

12. E. Dolan, *Tanstaffl: The Economic Strategy for Environmental Crisis* (New York: Holt, Rinehart & Winston, 1971). E. F. Schumacher, *Small Is Beautiful* (New York: Harper & Row, 1973). J. Spengler, "The Aesthetics of Population," *Population Bulletin,* 13 (1957), 61–75.

13. J. Rawls, *A Theory of Justice* (Cambridge, Mass.: Harvard University Press, 1971).

14. B. Glass, *Science and Ethical Values* (Chapel Hill, N.C.: University of North Carolina Press, 1965).

15. K. Thimann, "Science as an Instrument of Service," *Science,* 164 (1969), 1013.

16. R. DuBos, *Man Adapting* (New Haven, Conn.: Yale University Press, 1965). V. R. Potter, *Bioethics* (Englewood Cliffs, N.J.: Prentice-Hall, 1971).

17. K. E. Boulding, "The Economics of the Coming Spaceship Earth," in *Environmental Quality in a Growing Economy,* ed. H. Jarrett (Baltimore, Md.: Johns Hopkins Press, 1966). D. H. Meadows, D. L. Meadows, J. Randers and W. W. Behrens III, *The Limits to Growth* (New York: Universe Books, 1972). E. J. Mishan, *The Costs of Economic Growth* (New York: Praeger, 1967).

18. In its original form, Professor Green's paper proceeded at this point with a discussion of the moral implications of a decision to produce energy from a "plutonium recycle" technology. Because the same issue is discussed from the same point of view but at greater length later in this anthology (by Richard and Val Routley), Professor Green's presentation has been deleted. – ED.

19. T. R. Malthus, *Essay on the Principle of Population,* 2nd ed. (London: J. Johnson, 1802).

20. G. Hardin, "The Tragedy of the Commons," *Science,* 162 (1968), 1243-48.

21. R. Meek, *Marx and Engels on Malthus* (London: Lawrence & Wishart, 1953).

22. J. Rawls, *A Theory of Justice* (Cambridge, Mass.: Harvard University Press, 1971). N. Rescher, *Distributive Justice* (Indianapolis, Ind.: Bobbs-Merrill, 1967).

23. Environmental Protection Agency, "Report to the Administration of the Environmental Protection Agency by the Task Force on Environmental Problems of the Inner City" (Washington, D.C.: EPA, 1971).

24. L. S. El-Hamamsy, "Belief Systems and Family Planning in Peasant Societies," in *Are Our Descendants Doomed?* ed. H. Brown and E. Hutchings, Jr. (New York: Viking Press, 1972). J. B. Gordon and J. E. Wyon, *The Khanna Study* (Cambridge: Mass.: Harvard University Press, 1971).

25. Federal Energy Administration, "Project Independence" (Washington, D.C.: Government Printing Office, 1974).

26. G. Hardin, "Living on a Lifeboat," *BioScience,* 24 (1974), 561-568.

27. J. Bronowski, *Science and Human Values* (New York: Julian Messner, 1956).

28. R. Neuhaus, *In Defense of People* (New York: Macmillan, 1971).

29. C. P. Snow, *The Two Cultures and the Scientific Revolution* (London: Cambridge University Press, 1959).

Charles Hartshorne

The Ethics of Contributionism

Since it takes time for decisions to have their effect, all obligations in principle concern the future. Indeed, the entire rational significance of the present is in its contribution to future good. This does not mean that present happiness is of no value but that its being "valuable" means that its significance will not be simply canceled out by its becoming past. This preservation of value is effected partly by our enjoying (while we live) the memory of past happiness, partly by others enjoying that memory or somehow profiting by it, and finally (in my religious view) by all these values, immediate and subsequent, being inherited by the cosmic or divine reality that cherishes all creatures, and upon the inclusiveness, permanence, and universal relevance of whose valuations all rational or objective value depends. These are the assumptions of this brief essay.

The rational aim of life, according to this view, is to contribute value to the future, in principle the entire future, beyond any finite time limit. The question, "Whose future?" is secondary—apart from the cosmic or divine recipient, which or who is conceived to inherit all the values that are actualized anywhere, once they are actualized. Apart from this religious aspect, the answer to the question, "Value for whom?" depends on various considerations. Our own futures are always relevant, though as our conscious life nears its end the possible effects of our decisions on ourselves may become less and less important relative to the effects on others and should be so viewed by us. In my partly Buddhist, partly Peircean or Whiteheadian, and partly unique philosophy, there is no absolute difference between self and other persons. ("We are members one of another." Buddha knew this before Saint Paul.)

"Future persons" are only potentialities, but now existing persons, so far as one can affect them, are at least slightly future and in this regard not strictly actual at present. Nevertheless, there is a relative difference—important morally and legally—between future actualities forming states of persons now existing and already on the human level of awareness (as a fetus is not), and the mere possibility or probability of persons not in the normal sense "identical" with any now existing. So I think it is better to speak, as we commonly particular entities already in being though labeled future. Ultimate obligations are, in my religious view, to the cosmic Reality, not to this or that person or set of persons. Of course this transcends secular legal obligations. But there are only two ways we can fulfill the ultimate obligation: by achieving our own happiness and furthering future happiness in other persons or animals.

I agree with those who view critically any 'right to be born.' A fetus (by all the evidence we have) is not on the human level of awareness. Only as a potentiality has such a creature any value beyond that of adult animals on a considerably lower level than the human. As a potentiality it is one among countless value possibilities, and its realization may in some cases prevent the realization of other values whose probability and worth we are in a better position to estimate.

The more remote the future in question is, the greater the danger that we mistake future needs of life. Still, there are rational probabilities about these needs. It seems safe to assume that our descendants will need food and water, also electricity (and some form of energy for producing it), and that gas, if available, will be a convenient means of cooking. Energy waste (e.g., in extravagant forms of heating) or land uses that make the ground unproductive can hardly be in our children's children's interest. Substitutes will have to be found for nonrenewable resources, but it will require human labor to make them available; and the fossil fuels, while they last, will always be valuable and should be conserved.

It is said that our descendants will feel even less need to experience the beauties of wild nature than much of our population does now. This is arguable, but it is clear enough to some of us that if this happens it will mean a real loss. The beauty of wild nature is not merely a matter of opinion. Forests have, in each small area, a much richer diversity of plant and animal forms than parks, backyards, plantations, pastures, and other humanly transformed landscapes. Yet the natural diversity is harmonized by the laws of symbiosis, the mutual adaptations that evolution produces and maintains.

I submit that if our contribution to the future is not our justification we have none. I deduce from this that a grave defect of our American ethic has been its failure to even begin to do justice to the obligation to use resources economically. Setting thermostats needlessly high in winter and needlessly low in summer is not made innocent by the fact that our incomes enable us to pay for such practices. Future society as a whole will pay for it also. In many religions saintliness has meant making modest demands on the labor of others and on the supply of natural means for civilized living. The secular ideal in this country has tended to be the opposite, showing one's importance by "conspicuous waste." Thorstein Veblen's invention of this apt phrase has yet to be sufficiently appreciated.

Something worse than mere bad taste is involved. Democracy ideally means that resources are so divided that all can live with dignity and in health, and indulgence in great waste here is bound to interfere with reasonable sufficiency there. We now know that extravagant plenty for all is the least likely outcome in any future that is reasonably foreseeable.

It is important to realize that the realm of possible values is shot through with incompatibilities. We in this country probably could feed double our present population, but then could we also go on using land even more extensively for nonagricultural purposes, such as suburbs, highways, parking lots, strip-mining areas, and so on, and besides all this have large surpluses of food for exportation to help needy nations and help ourselves in our balance of payments problem, aggravated by huge importations of oil? We can (and we had better) construct solar power plants, but they will not come for nothing and will take resources from other operations that are also needed. Every possible good is partly competitive with other possible goods.

Pro-life monomaniacs (or, if you prefer, one-idea'd persons) tell us that one cannot set a price on "life." They forget—and this we know, if we know anything—that poverty more or less directly kills multitudes of people. And these are mostly people actually on the human level of awareness, not (by comparison) mindless fetuses. Economic questions are very human questions, in part questions of life and death. The mounting costs of medical care are only one of the countless evidences for this relationship.

The notion of individual rights is a tricky thing. I fail to see that potentialities for individuation are already actual individuals with the rights of individuals. A fetus is an individual animal but not an individual person. It has not the developed brain and consciousness of a person. It is significant that we do not recall ourselves as fetuses. There was no self, on a human level psychologically, to recall in that animal stage of "our" existence. And the individuals of the future are not individuated already. Our ultimate obligations are to the future in an impersonal or superpersonal sense, to humanity, nature, and God.

Jefferson, Washington, Lincoln, and countless others tried to leave a good heritage to future generations of people in this country, but it would never occur to me and could not have occurred to them that they were discharging obligations to you or me. There was then no such you or me for them to be obligated to. But there was a virtual certainty that there would be people in this country who for generations or centuries would enjoy or suffer the consequences of what Jefferson and the others were doing. Also, they nearly all had some belief in God, with whose beneficent purposes for his creation it was our duty to conform. This was their understanding of their obligations to future generations.

It is of course now conceivable that the combination of (only too natural) human errors and weaknesses in our own and other nations may produce nuclear warfare on such a scale that no posterity worth thinking about will be left. But we can hardly make this conceivability an excuse for dismissing the claims of future humanity. Rather we should try to study the ways of improving our diplomacy and of mitigating our appallingly heavy reliance on nuclear threats (already superabundantly prepared for by stocks of terrible explosives) so that the conceivable will not happen. Any direct dangers from civil uses of atomic power are small compared to the danger of the military use. This applies to the waste disposal problem, which we would have with or without the nonmilitary installations. The primary nuclear problem is military. (However, the civilian use can be a stepping stone to military and terrorist applications. Probably, for this and other reasons, the nuclear power option must be written off as a sad mistake.) No obligation to posterity can exceed this one of trying to diminish the nuclear threat. We must learn how to subdue our arrogant nationalism sufficiently to take more seriously than our ancestors were able to do our obligations to humanity. President Truman used atomic bombs; according to Daniel Ellsberg, presidents Kennedy, Eisenhower, and Nixon threatened to do so. We need to reflect on how such behavior looks to other nations.

The impersonal or superpersonal aspect of obligation is clear in the case of patriotic duties. In the early history of humanity, families and small tribes represented the beginning of this aspect of ethics. But the nation cannot be the last word in this development. The nuclear threat makes this even more obvious than it already was, for example, to Immanuel Kant. But is even humanity the last word?

The whole idea that our final obligation is to groups of animals, whether human alone or (as I would say) human and subhuman, is to my mind utterly inadequate. Here all religions largely agree. If the cosmos has no value, neither, by any rational standard, do animals or persons. The parts are for the whole, the ephemeral for the abiding. And the only aspects of the whole that we can influence or benefit are future aspects. I call this doctrine *contributionism*. It is essentially Whitehead's view, and I regard it as implicit in all the religions.

Our secular culture is in difficulties about values. Neither the state nor science can, it seems, choose among the religions. And in my opinion every religious tradition is shot through with human—all *too* human—error. Yet no nonreligious scheme of thought really makes sense of life. The dilemma is in essence as simple as that.

The inclusive obligation, I have been arguing, is to optimize our gifts to the future, including our gift of present happiness. Gifts to what future? Any future able to inherit and use the gifts. As merely ours, our joys are, from a long-run point of view—the rational point of view—"passing whiffs of insignificance" (Whitehead). Only as possessions of the Encompassing, as Jaspers calls it, have they objective and permanent importance. Humanity as a whole, or sentient life on this planet as a whole, is relatively encompassing, but it, too, merely by itself is a fragment of reality. It symbolizes rather than constitutes the Encompassing. By contributing to the human and animal future we indefinitely magnify our gifts to life, but we do not thereby render it objective and permanent, put it where "neither moth nor rust doth corrupt nor thieves break through and steal."

Science could give us a genuine substitute for traditional religions only if it could arrive at a consensus supporting the proposition that our careers have worth for the inclusive and everlasting Reality. And this science could hardly do. Only religion and philosophy can give human life a human meaning.

The other animals live largely by feeling; we have to live far more by thought. Merely practical or scientific thinking only makes us extremely clever animals. Religious or philosophical thought alone can lift our feelings to the full human level on which we dare to face not simply this bit or that bit of the future but the future as such, so far as our decisions are relevant to it. The scope of the relevance of our decisions for the future is an enigma for science and also for practical common sense. But science does help us see that, however much the relevance may transcend the effects we can have on the future of our species and of life on our planet, it must certainly include those effects, which (thanks to science) are more drastic by far than our forefathers knew. We do indeed have obligations to posterity. As Denis Hayes remarks, "after me the deluge" is no better coming from a whole generation than from a French king.

Gregory Kavka

The Futurity Problem

Whether we should allow population and industry to grow essentially un-
checked, as we have in the past, is currently the subject of an active debate
within the scientific and intellectual community. Pessimists, such as the
authors of the Club of Rome Report, *The Limits to Growth,*[1] warn that this
would lead — perhaps within a few generations — to extreme shortages of food,
clean air, fossil fuels, and other resources needed to sustain human life and
civilization. The result would be a cataclysmic decline in population and industrial output, and human death and suffering on an unprecedented scale. On
the other hand, optimists, such as Herman Kahn of the Hudson Institute,
argue that the modernization of presently underdeveloped countries will produce a natural plateau in world population at a level that the earth's environment and resources can easily support, given probable technological advances.[2]
I shall not enter this debate, but shall simply *assume* that the dire warnings of
the pessimists, who seem to be in the majority, are credible. If this is so, a serious moral question confronts our generation (i.e. those presently living). Are
we morally obligated, in order to prevent impending catastrophe for mankind,
to impose strict limits on population growth, pollution, and resource use, at
the cost — to many of us — of a significant decrease in our material standard of
living and our freedom to have large families?

Answering this question adequately would require solving two difficult
problems in moral theory. The first concerns whether (relatively) rich individuals and groups are morally obligated to offer aid to strangers in desperate
need, if so doing would impose substantial costs on those rich individuals and
groups or on their friends and loved ones. (It is generally acknowledged that
rendering aid under such circumstances is praiseworthy and good, but it is by
no means obvious whether it is morally required.) Because it concerns the

Reprinted from *Obligations to Future Generations,* R. I. Sikora and Brian Barry, eds. (Philadelphia: Temple University Press, 1978), pp. 186–203, with permission of the publisher and
author.

extent to which morality permits one to favor the interests of one's friends (including oneself) over the interests of strangers, I call this the Friends and Strangers Problem. Our second problem concerns whether future people are different, in morally relevant ways, from present people. The following formulation of the problem makes clear its independence from the first problem; putting aside considerations based on special relationships such as love, friendship, or contractual obligation, ought one, in his moral decision making, assign equal weight to the interests of present and future persons? In other words, if we think of "strangers" as those to whom one stands in no such special relationships, are the interests of *future* strangers worthy of equal consideration with those of presently existing strangers? Let us call this the Futurity Problem.

The relationship between these two problems and the question of our obligations to future generations may be explained as follows. Suppose that we are obligated to aid desperately needy strangers who are now alive, even at substantial cost to ourselves and our friends. If the needs and interests of future people are as important, morally speaking, as those of present people, it would apparently follow that we are obligated to make substantial sacrifices, if necessary, to prevent *future* strangers from being desperately needy.[3]

Of our two problems, the Friends and Strangers Problem has received much more attention in the philosophical literature.[4] However, the Futurity Problem is equally interesting and important, and I shall leave the other aside to focus on it. Thus, instead of trying to prove that we are obligated to sacrifice for future generations, I seek only to establish the more modest conditional conclusion that *if* we are obligated to make sacrifices for needy present strangers, then we are also obligated to sacrifice for future ones. We may arrive at this conclusion by considering, and rebutting, three sorts of reasons that might be offered for *not* giving the interests of future people equal consideration with those of present people: the temporal location of future people, our ignorance of them, and the contingency of their existence.

I. The Temporal Location of Future People

The most obvious difference between present and future people is that the latter do not yet exist. Does this difference in temporal location in itself constitute a reason for favoring the interests of present over future persons? It does not seem so. Location in space is not a morally relevant feature of a person, determining his worthiness for consideration or aid. Why should location in time be any different? Further, it is part of our general conception of the rational person that he assign the same importance to the satisfaction of a desire whether he has it now, or knows he will have it in the future.[5] Since rational prudence (which concerns the satisfaction of desires) sees no intrinsic importance in the temporal location of a desire, it would seem that rational morality (which concerns the well-being of people) should attach no intrinsic importance to the temporal location of people.

Now, of course, temporal location does make a difference to morality — when that location is in the *past*. For surely, it would be absurd to give equal weight to the desires of living and dead persons. This, however, may be admitted without affecting the claim of equal status for *future* people. There are two main reasons for favoring the desires of the living over those of the dead. First, nearly all of the desires of the dead concerned matters in their own lifetimes that are now past and cannot be changed. Second, consider those desires of persons now dead that were directed toward future states of affairs that living people might still bring about. Since the persons having had those desires will not be present to experience satisfaction in their fulfillment or disappointment in their non-fulfillment, it is reasonable to downgrade the importance of these desires (and perhaps ignore them altogether) in our moral decision making. Now, it is clear that neither of these two reasons applies to the desires of future people. We *are* in a position to act to make it more likely that many of the desires of future people will be satisfied, and future people *will* be around to experience the fulfillment or non-fulfillment of their desires. Again, the analogy to rational prudence is instructive. We regard it as rational for a person to give equal weight to his present and (known) future desires, even though we would regard it as silly for him to give equal weight to past desires. It may be concluded that while there are sound reasons, when deciding *whose* desires to satisfy, to favor present over *past* people, the difference in their temporal location does not constitute a reason for favoring present over *future* people.

II. Our Ignorance of Future People

While the temporal location of future people is, in itself, not a reason for discounting their interests, other factors resulting from their temporal location might be. In particular, it could be argued that our *ignorance* of future people renders us less able to promote their interests than those of present people. For future people are not around to tell us what their desires are (or will be). Also, our ability to shape future events generally decreases as they become temporally more distant, so it may be thought that we would be less able to satisfy the desires of future than of present people, even if we knew in detail what those desires will be.

Does this relative ignorance of what future people will want, and how to get it for them, justify us in paying less attention to their interests in decision making? I am doubtful that it does to any substantial degree. For we do know with a high degree of certainty the basic biological and economic needs of future generations — enough food to eat, air to breathe, space to move in, and fuel to run machines. The satisfaction of these needs will surely be a prerequisite of the satisfaction of most of the other desires and interests of future people, whatever they may be. Further, if the pessimist's warnings are correct, certain burdensome things our generation could do now would substantially promote the satisfaction of these needs and interests. First, our generation could limit population growth, pollution, and the use of non-renewable resources. Second, we could make very heavy investments in research in what may be called the *survival sciences*—agriculture, population control, energy production, war prevention, etc. Third, we could develop and design institutions and organizations to represent the interests of future generations. Their purpose would be to propose social programs to benefit posterity, advise policy makers, pressure legislators to take the interests of posterity into account, and encourage the public to evaluate policies in terms of their effects on future, as well as present, generations.

What I am suggesting is that we view our ignorance of the interests of future people as being analogous to a young adult's ignorance of the desires and interests he will have in old age, say, after retirement. It is unlikely that a young adult will know in detail the goals and desires he will have in forty years: whether, for example, he will wish to spend his time traveling, doing volunteer work, or drinking beer. However, he can believe with a high degree of confidence that his important needs and interests will include good health, adequate food and shelter, and security for his loved ones. And there are definite things he can do now that will make it more likely that these needs will be met: saving or investing a portion of his income, eating properly, exercising regularly, etc. Rational prudence will advise him to do these things, despite his ignorance of the details of the desires he will have when old. Similarly, morality advises us to take steps to insure an adequate supply of resources for future generations, despite our ignorance of the details of the desires that future people will have.

An interesting variant of the argument from ignorance is presented by Martin Golding, in an article titled "Obligations to Future Generations."[6] Golding contends that we should regard future people as members of our moral community, whose interests we should look after, only if we know what to desire for them. But, he claims, we know what to desire for them only to the extent that we can expect them to share our conception of the good life for man. Since this expectation becomes less credible as we consider more distant generations, Golding concludes that we essentially ought to confine our attention to helping "immediate posterity" achieve our shared conception of the good life.

I do not find this argument convincing. For, depending upon how one understands the notion of "a conception of the good life," it seems that the argument either goes against the grain of our deep-seated beliefs about human equality or fails to establish the conclusion that Professor Golding reaches. To see this, let us briefly examine the claim—fundamental to our moral tradition— that all men are equal and are worthy of equal consideration.

When we say that all men are equal, we are asserting that they are alike in certain important respects. Clearly, people are *not* alike, but are widely diverse in their cultural practices, political ideologies, religious beliefs, life-styles, and values. If most or all people *are* alike in significant ways, it is, as I pointed out in an earlier paper,[7] in virtue of their possession of certain very general features: their vulnerability to physical and mental suffering and to death, their capacity for enjoyment (including the enjoyment of complex activities and interactions with others), their self-consciousness, their capacity for long-range purposive planning and action, and their capacity for cooperation and identification with others. These general features are, among other things, what make human beings capable of entering into and benefiting from moral relations with others; they are, as I see it, the valid basis of the claim that all men are equal.

Two aspects of this elucidation of the traditional conception of human equality are worth noting. First, there are not degrees of membership in the human moral community. One is a full and equal member of that community if one possesses a sufficient number of the above features in sufficient degree. (The cut-off point of membership may, of course, be vague and ill-defined.) Second, membership in the human moral community is not dependent upon possessing any particular *substantive* conception of the good life; though those possessing the credentials for membership will doubtless share our *formal* conception of the good life as one in which the individual engages in a variety of complex and cooperative activities with others, in which the desires he regards as important are usually satisfied, and in which the projects he cares most about are generally carried forth to successful completion.

The implications of these observations are these. The features in virtue of which we regard *present* persons of other cultures, nations, political persuasions, and life-styles, as equal with ourselves, are quite general features that will certainly be shared by future people for very many generations. The moral status of such persons and our reasons for promoting their interests are not dependent upon their sharing our substantive conception of the good life. (Admittedly, complications would arise if we had good reason to suppose that their conception of the good life would be the same as our conception of a morally evil or inhuman life; but it is doubtful we have such reasons.) Hence, our ignorance of the degree to which, in fact, future generations will share our substantive conception of the good life does not seem to be a valid reason for favoring present over future strangers, much less a reason for ignoring, in our planning and practices, the well-being of all generations save the next few.

III. The Contingency of Future People

Having rejected the temporal location of future people and our ignorance of them as substantial reasons for downgrading the importance of their interests, we must now deal with the most perplexing and least tractable feature of future people—their contingency. The trouble with future people, we might say, is not that they do not exist *yet,* it is that they might not exist *at all.* Further, what and how many future people will exist depends upon the decisions and actions of present people. To see how this existential dependence of future persons on the decisions of present ones affects the moral relationship between the two, let us consider two analogies.

First, suppose that a moral person realizes that he cannot fulfill both of two promises he has made, though he can fulfill either one. If he cannot obtain release from either promise, he will decide what to do by considering such factors as how much each promisee would be harmed by his failure to keep the promise in question, and how adequately he would be able to compensate each promisee for non-fulfillment. Now imagine that he has this same realization about two promises — one that he has already made and a second that he has been planning to make in the future. It would be wildly wrong-headed for him to proceed, as in the previous case, by weighing such considerations as his ability to compensate each promisee for non-fulfillment. For he has not yet made the second promise and thus has available to him the option, which he clearly ought to adopt, of keeping the first promise and simply not making the second. The fact that this second, "potential" promise is contingent upon his own decision gives him strong reason not to treat that promise on a par with promises he has already made.

A second and somewhat closer analogy to the situation of the present generation with respect to future generations involves a poor couple that has some children and is planning to have more. Should they treat the interests of their prospective children on a par with those of their existing children, by husbanding resources that could be used by the latter? Not if this would cause the existing children to suffer serious deprivation. For in that case, they should simply not have any more children.

These two examples suggest that, under conditions of scarcity, resource distributors have reason to show preference for existing resource consumers (e.g. people or promises) over future resource consumers whose very existence is dependent upon the distributor's decisions and actions. It is important, however, not to misunderstand the nature of these reasons or the kind of preferences they support. Under scarcity, there seems to be reason to meet the needs of existing consumers rather than bringing into existence too many new consumers who will make demands on scarce resources. This does not mean, however, that consumers that one assumes or knows *will exist* are less important or less worthy of receiving resources than those presently existing. To see this, suppose that the parents in our example *know* they will not change their mind about having more children, even if they save no resources to care for them. Under these circumstances, they ought to give their prospective children equal consideration with their present ones.[8]

The implications of these examples with respect to our relationship to future generations are as follows. Suppose, following the pessimists, that we (i.e. those presently living) cannot (i) consume as much as we want and could, and (ii) have as many children as we want and could, and (iii) still leave sufficient resources to take care of the needs of future people. Then, we must either consume less or produce fewer children, if we are to leave enough for future generations. Now, our examples do not indicate that the contingency of future people in any way warrants our abandoning the goal of conserving resources adequate to the needs of future people. What they do suggest is that producing *fewer* future people (than we could), so as to allow us both to provide for the needs of those future people who are produced and still to consume what we want, would be a morally viable option.

A different face of the contingency issue appears when we consider situations *not* involving great scarcity. Suppose that a happy childless couple is deciding whether to have a child. Imagine that they know that each would be somewhat less happy in the long run if they had the child, but that the child would be a happy one, and that its happiness would greatly exceed the loss of happiness they would suffer as a result of having it. If we proceed to evaluate each of their alternatives — having and not having a child — in terms of the happiness of the people that would be affected by it, an odd result emerges. Whichever act they choose turns out to be the better one! For suppose that they have the child. This is better because the child's happiness more than makes up for the small loss in happiness they each suffer. But if they do not have the child, this also turns out to be better. For they have benefited (i.e. done better for themselves than if they had produced the child), and *no one* has been adversely affected.[9]

The oddity, that of each of two alternatives seeming better than the other, arises out of the contingency of the child's existence on the decision in question. Because of this contingency, the act of not having the child is evaluated in terms of its effects on the parents alone, while the act of having the child must be evaluated in terms of its effects on a different set of people — the parents *and* the child. This produces the odd result of each act being better than the other, when evaluated by what seems to be the same criterion: the happiness of those affected. This oddity can be avoided only by making the controversial move of treating non-existence as a harm or opportunity-cost suffered by the non-existent child.[10]

This puzzling aspect of the contingency issue relates to an important theoretical question about our moral relationship to posterity. It was suggested above that limiting the size of the next generation to allow more consumption in this generation would not be an objectionable policy. But suppose this policy were carried to its farthest extreme. Suppose, that is, that everyone now living voluntarily agreed to forego the pleasures of childbearing and agreed to undergo sterilization, so that they could live out their lives consuming and polluting to their heart's content without worrying about the effects on future generations. (This would be in some ways analogous to the parents in our last example foregoing having a child, so they could be as happy as possible.) Would there be anything morally wrong about our generation (or some later generation) doing this? Or, to put the matter somewhat differently, does a moral person have any reason to care that the human race survive?

Note that this question has interest aside from its implications concerning the purely imaginary possibility that people will unanimously decide not to reproduce. For some pessimists fear that, if we do not control the growth of population and pollution, the very existence of human species, as well as the existence of modern civilization, will be endangered. Hence, whether we, as moral persons, have reason to care that mankind survive, is a question that bears on our attitudes toward uncontrolled growth. It is this question that I wish to consider next.

IV. The Survival of the Human Species

Setting aside their particular desires to have and raise children, why shouldn't present people simply refrain from producing future people, so that they can live out their lives consuming and polluting at will? No doubt the cessation of reproduction would force serious readjustments in the economy. And if carried through to the bitter end, such a program would lead to the last people alive suffering from severe loneliness and a shortage of services. But, such considerations aside, would it be morally wrong for present people to act collectively in this way if they freely chose to do so? One might be tempted to object to such action on the grounds that it would be unfair to future generations.[11] But this objection flounders in the face of the fact that, if the action were successfully carried out, there would *be* no future generations to have been treated unfairly by it. Leaving fairness aside, the central question becomes whether we, as moral persons, have any reason to care about the survival of our species. Some philosophers, e.g. Jan Narveson,[12] suggest we do not. I should like to set out my reasons for thinking that we do.

It is generally acknowledged that human life has value, and hence the lives of existing people are, with rare exceptions, worth preserving. If we dare to venture the question of *why* human life is valuable and worth preserving, the answers we receive — religious answers aside — are likely to fall into three categories. First, there are answers that explain the value of life in terms of the pleasures contained therein. Second, it may be held that certain human experiences or relationships (e.g. loving another person) are valuable in themselves, beyond the pleasures they contain, and it is the having of such experiences (or the possibility of having them) that makes human life valuable. Third, it may be thought that the value of human life is to be found in the human capacity for accomplishment, the fact that human beings set and achieve goals, and exercise and develop various complex capacities. What is of interest here is that, whichever of these views of the value of human life (or combination of such views) one adopts, it turns out that the lives of future people would almost certainly possess the properties that make the lives of present people valuable, and hence would be valuable themselves. This seems to be a reason for creating such lives; that is, for bringing future people into existence.

Now this last claim is presumably what my opponents would deny. They would contend that the fact that one state of affairs contains more equally valuable elements than another does not constitute *any* reason to bring the former rather than the latter about. This contention is sometimes expressed using the following example. Imagine God deciding between creating a universe with one planet occupied by n happy people, and a universe with two planets, *each* occupied by n people just as happy as those in the first universe. Does the fact that there are twice as many happy people in the latter universe constitute a reason for God preferring to create it? My opponents would say, No. Notice that our problem concerning future generations is quite analogous to this one, the difference being that the extra equally happy people are located in later generations rather than on another planet. Now I confess to being one of those who strongly feels it would be better for God to create the greater number of equally happy planets (or generations). [13] I doubt, however, that this point can be argued. The preference for *more* happy people seems to rest on a basic intuition, comparable perhaps with Mill's intuition that some pleasures are more choiceworthy than others of equal intensity. I hope and expect that others share this intuition, but I cannot prove it to be a valid one.

There is, however, an argument for preserving our species that does not depend upon this basic intuition, though it depends on others perhaps equally controversial. This concerns certain collective enterprises of man, the shared accomplishment of our species. There are few of us who have not at some time or other been awed and inspired by mankind's intellectual, artistic, scientific, or technological accomplishments. Implicit in this attitude of awe is the view that these accomplishments are marvelous, valuable, and worthy of admiration for reasons that transcend their usefulness to us. If this attitude is not misguided, the accomplishments of mankind in the intellectual, artistic, and scientific spheres, and the likelihood of continued progress in these fields, give us a substantial reason to wish the race to survive. For if the life of our species ends, so will these collective enterprises; while if it continues, spectacular accomplishments in such fields of endeavor are highly probable. One suspects that at least some of those who are indifferent to whether happy people will exist in the future will not be indifferent to the continuation and progress of these admirable human enterprises, and will regard their development as a reason for wanting mankind to go on.

The notion that our species should be preserved gains additional support from an analogy that can be constructed between the life of the species and the life of an individual. Imagine an individual choosing between two strategies for living. First, living to the fullest for a few years, consuming and creating at a rapid rate but dying soon as a result. Second, consuming and creating at a moderate pace in the near future and living a long life of progressively greater accomplishments, with total accomplishments far surpassing those that could be attained in a short life. Choosing the short life in such circumstances would be analogous to our generation's cutting out reproduction in favor of unlimited present consumption. Choosing the long life would be analogous to our generation's limiting consumption and growth so that the species can survive and progress for a very long time. In the individual case, we are strongly inclined to approve the choice of the longer life, to have greater respect for the individual making that choice than for the individual who chooses the short but sweet life. This suggests, by analogy, that we should prefer a longer life of increasing accomplishment for mankind, to having human history cut short to facilitate present consumption.

This analogy between individual and species life also helps us see what is wrong with an objection that has been raised against caring about the survival of the species. [14] The objection is based on the prediction that the expanding sun will swallow up the earth within twelve billion years or so. It is, in effect, claimed that, since our species will ultimately be extinguished anyway, we have no reason to act to prolong its existence. To see that this claim is fallacious, it is sufficient to note that each of us knows that he, individually, is mortal. It hardly follows that one has no reason to prolong his own life, especially if, as in the case of the species, one has reason to suppose that one's accomplishments will grow in magnitude with age.

A final implication of the analogy between individual and species life is that our desire for the survival of the species should not be *unconditional*. If a person recognizes that his continued existence would uncontrollably result in his moral, intellectual, and physical degeneration, he has good reason to wish for an early death, even to commit suicide. Similarly, if we knew that future generations would inevitably descend into bestiality or a Hobbesian war of all against all, it might be reasonable for us to put an end to the species deliberately. Fortunately, we do not know this. Such a future for our species could come about as a result of extreme scarcity brought on by uncontrolled population growth and pollution, or as a result of large-scale nuclear war. But if we had the will and means to end reproduction deliberately, we would, *ipso facto,* be in a position to alleviate the former danger. And the threat of nuclear war, while hardly negligible, is not so imminent and certain as to make voluntary suicide of the species a preferable alternative to living under that threat.

To summarize, there seem to be two main sorts of reasons that moral persons will appreciate for wanting the human species to survive. First, human life has value and is generally a good thing to those possessing it. Second, the continuation of our species will very likely mean the continuation of its collective artistic, intellectual, and scientific accomplishments. Further, certain features of the analogy between the life of an individual and the life of the species suggest the reasonableness of the preference for continuation over termination of the species. Taken together, these considerations suggest that a moral person should not be indifferent to mankind's survival.

V. Aid Between Nations and Generations

In this concluding section, I should like to consider briefly the implications of our discussion of the Futurity Problem with respect to two issues: the form in which rich countries give aid to very poor ones, and the distribution of resources between generations. To take the aid question first, let us suppose that a rich nation has decided to give a fixed quantity of aid to a very poor and overpopulated nation with many starving people in it. (The question of how large this quantity of aid ought to be falls under the Friends and Strangers Problem and will not be taken up here.) Should the aid be given (i) in the form of food or (ii) in the form of birth control devices, machinery, help in governmental and educational planning, etc?

It seems at first that the aid ought to be in the form of food to save people from starvation. But then, it would be pointed out, some forms of aid (e.g. food aid) tend to accelerate population growth while other forms (e.g. birth control and education) tend to inhibit population growth. Thus, giving aid in the form of food could be expected to result in more starving people in the country in the long run than if the aid were given in other forms.[15] Now the arguments offered in sections I–III above indicate that the needs of future people deserve equal consideration with those of present people. Hence, it is as important to prevent those who will be born later from starving as it is to prevent people who exist now from starving. Does this imply that, in view of the danger of producing starvation on a larger scale in the future, it must be wrong to give aid in the form of food? Not necessarily, for there is always the possibility that technological discoveries in birth control or food production will obviate scarcity problems in time to keep later generations of the country's citizens from starving. If we had a reliable estimate of the likelihood of such technological developments, we could use it to calculate which form of aid would, on average, lead to fewer starvation deaths in the long run. But it is more realistic to suppose that any such estimate is, at best, an educated guess, and should not be heavily relied upon in making our choice. Under these circumstances, it would not be unreasonable to give aid in the form of food, on the grounds that this may enable us to prevent starvation in both the present and future, while the alternative policy would assure the starvation deaths of many of the country's present citizens.[16]

Let us turn from the issue of aid between countries to the more general one of aid between generations. The question to be considered is: How much of the earth's resources may any given generation use up and how much should it preserve for use by later generations? Of course, we cannot determine the *obligations* of our generation to save resources for later generations without solving the Friends and Strangers Problem. For most of our friends (i.e. those to whom we stand in special relationships, including ourselves) are in our own generation; hence, morality may allow us to show, in our actions, a bias in favor of our own generation. We can, however, explicitly set aside considerations based on special relationships; we can ask what ideal standard of generational resource use follows from the view, defended above, that the interests of future persons are worthy of equal consideration with those of present persons.

John Locke supposes that men in the state of nature are moral equals and that God has given to them, in common, the use of the earth and its resources. He claims that, under these conditions, an individual may fairly appropriate land for his own use — without belying the equal status of his fellows — provided that he (i) uses rather than wastes what he appropriates and (ii) leaves "enough and as good for others."[17] Locke justifies the latter condition on the ground that one who appropriates a resource but leaves enough and as good for others, leaves others as well off as they were prior to the appropriation. Hence, they are not injured by his act and have no complaint against him.[18] Given that present and future persons are moral equals with equal claim to the earth and its resources, Locke's analysis can be extended to apply to the problem of generational resource use. Accordingly, we say that a generation may use the earth's resources provided that it (i) does not waste them (i.e. uses them to satisfy human interests) and (ii) leaves "enough and as good" for future generations. In the spirit of the justification Locke offers for his second condition, I interpret this to mean that, in this context, the generation in question leaves the next generation at least as well off, with respect to usable resources, as it was left by its ancestors. (In which case, later generations cannot be said to have been injured by this generation's use of resources.) Since it is individuals, and not generations *per se,* that are regarded as equal, I understand the relevant measure of usable resources to be relativized to population. This means that if a given generation insists on having more than one descendant per capita, it is to aim at leaving proportionally more total resources.

It might at first appear impossible that any generation live up to the Lockean standard. For questions of waste aside, how could a generation use *any* resources at all and leave even an equal number of descendants with as many resources as they themselves inherited? The question is readily answered by noting that some physical resources are renewable or reusable, and that knowledge—especially scientific and technological knowledge—is a usable resource that grows without being depleted and enables us to increase the output of the earth's physical resources. Thus, what the Lockean standard recommends is that each generation use the earth's physical resources only to the extent that technology allows for the recycling or depletion of such resources without net loss in their output capacity. Aside from its equity, perhaps the most attractive feature of this standard is the following. If all succeeding generations abided by it, mankind could go on living on earth indefinitely, with living standards improving substantially from generation to generation, once world population were stabilized. Or, to put the point somewhat differently, the Lockean standard prescribes a world in which the fixed natural capital supplied by our planet is essentially preserved, and men live off the ever increasing interest generated by expanding technology.

Is the Lockean standard unfair to our generation? It appears so when we consider that vast investments to speed development in poor countries may have to be made soon, if those countries are to be eased through the demographic transition in time to stabilize world population at supportable levels. Won't our generation then have to use more than our share of resources to deal with the threat to later generations of disastrous overpopulation? Perhaps so. But this special use of resources can be accommodated to the general framework of the Lockean standard in either of two ways. First, by treating the case of our generation as special, so that our task is one of creating initial conditions in which future generations may attain compliance with the Lockean standard without excessive sacrifice. Second, by treating the pronatal practices, institutions, and attitudes that we have inherited from our ancestors as a special kind of *negative* resource, so that our extra use of other resources would be balanced out if we eradicated this negative resource; we would be leaving our descendants as well off as we were left, all things considered.

I close with a brief summary of my conclusions. The temporal location of future people and our comparative ignorance of their interests do not justify failing to treat their interests on a par with those of present people. While the *contingency* of future people *does* justify granting priority to the needs of existing people, it does so only in the sense of warranting population limitation as a means of limiting the total needs of future generations. However, population limitation carried to the utmost extreme, i.e. the end of the species by collective decision not to reproduce, would not be morally justified. Granting the equality of present and future people, it follows that it is not morally wrong for rich nations to consider the population-related effects of various forms of aid in determining how to help poor overpopulated nations. Finally, the equal moral status of present and future persons suggests that our generation should, ideally, aim collectively at leaving our descendants a planet as rich in usable per capita resources as that we have inherited from our ancestors.[19]

NOTES

1. Donella and Dennis Meadows, Jorgen Randers, and William Behrens III, *The Limits to Growth* (New York: Universe Books, 1972).

2. Herman Kahn, William Brown, and Leon Martel, *The Next 200 Years* (New York: William Morrow, 1976).

3. This would be so even if the amount of aid needed by present strangers alone were more than the maximum we (relatively rich people) are obligated to give. For, in that case, we should use a portion of our aid for the benefit of future strangers, even though this would mean failing to meet the needs of some present strangers we could otherwise have helped. See the opening paragraphs of Section V, below.

4. See, e.g., the essays in William Aiken and Hugh La Follette, eds., *World Hunger and Moral Obligation* (Englewood Cliffs, N.J.: Prentice-Hall, 1977).

5. I assume the rationality of discounting one's *expected* future desires to take account of the possibilities that one's expectations are wrong or that one will die in the interim. Similarly, we should discount the interests of any expected future generation by the probability that the human race will die out prior to that generation. The implications of our uncertainty about what future generations will want are discussed in Section II, below.

6. Martin Golding, "Obligations to Future Generations," *Monist,* 56 (1972): 97–98. [In this anthology, pp. 61–72.]

7. "Equality in Education," in John M. McDermott, ed., *Indeterminacy in Education* (Berkeley: McCutchan, 1976).

8. They should, of course, take account of the possibility that they will be unable to produce more children, and discount the interests of their prospective children accordingly.

9. It should be emphasized that the problem discussed here is *not* the same as the average versus total utility problem. This can readily be seen if we let x be the total happiness of the two parents if they do not have the child, $x - y$ be their total happiness if they do have it, and z be the child's happiness (if it exists). If $z > y + \frac{1}{2}x$, both total and average happiness would be maximized by the production of the child. Yet, if they do not have the child, the parents have still maximized utility for those affected by their act.

10. I make this move, in a special context and for a limited purpose, in my "Rawls on Average and Total Utility," *Philosophical Studies* 27 (1975), 241.

11. Mistakenly, I did not resist a similar temptation in "Rawls on Average and Total Utility," 250.

12. Jan Narveson, "Utilitarianism and New Generations," *Mind* 76 (1967), 62–72.

13. I do not endorse the stronger claim that God would be obligated to create the greatest possible number of happy people (generations). For it is likely there is no limit on the number of happy people (generations) an omnipotent being could create. Cf. Robert M. Adams, "Must God Create the Best," *Philosophical Review* 81 (1972), 317.

14. This objection is cited, but not endorsed, by Robert Heilbroner in "What Has Posterity Ever Done for Me?," a postscript to his *An Inquiry Into the Human Prospect* (New York: W. W. Norton, 1975). [In this anthology, pp. 191–94.]

15. An argument of this form is pressed by Garrett Hardin, in "Living in a Lifeboat," *BioScience,* 24:10 (October, 1974). [See also the selections by Hardin and by Michael Bayles in this anthology. — ED]

16. I rely here on the following principle of rational choice under conditions of uncertainty, which I call the Disaster Avoidance Principle: Among alternatives, any of which might lead to disaster, choose the act that maximizes the chances of avoiding all disastrous outcomes. This principle is elaborated, discussed, and applied to a practical problem of a different sort, in my paper "Deterrence, Utility, and Rational Choice," *Theory and Decision,* forthcoming.

17. John Locke, *Two Treatises of Government,* ed. by Peter Laslett (New York: New American Library, 1965), Second Treatise, secs. 4, 26–27, pp. 309, 328–329.

18. Locke, Sec. 33, p. 333.

19. This is a slightly revised version of a paper read on December 2, 1977, at the conference on Obligations to Future Generations at the University of Delaware. I am indebted to Virginia Warren and Joseph Runzo for helpful comments.

Holmes Rolston III

The River of Life: Past, Present, and Future

To speak of a river of life is more poetry than philosophy, but images have an evocative power that may launch critical reflection. Life is organic, and much too complex to be illuminated by many of the features of a simple, inorganic river. Our purpose here is only to abstract out the notion of a current, a naturally impelled flow that is energetically maintained over time. Life is often said to be a countercurrent to entropy, its negatively entropic flow in that respect the reverse of a merely physical current; still the notion of a current is generic enough to provide considerable insight into the life process. It provides the thought of continuity and ceaseless flow in a life-stream that transcends the individual, and here we gain a model fertile in its capacity to channel together ideas that under other gestalts become differentiated into troublesome opposites. In this processive on-rolling we can find a confluence of the actual and the potential, the self and the other, the human and the natural, the present and the historical, and the *is* and the *ought*.

Most of us attach life to the immediate present, to encapsulated individuals, and we locate the ethical life in the interrelations of subjective human selves. We often find life to be a notion that belongs incongruously to biology and to ethics, to nature and to culture. We do not here mean to deny that the individual human life is a substantive matter, of moral concern, when we notice that it is also an adjectival property of a collective, still more substantive flow, which also is of moral concern. This concept of a current in which the individual is buoyed up and on is at once biologically viable, culturally informed, and satisfying to many of our deepest ethical intuitions. Its corporate nature perhaps does not give due place to that individual integrity that is so well served by the more atomistic paradigms, but our experiment here is to discover an ethical vision of more scope, one with a more open run than any single life can provide. The thesis here is that an individualistic ethic is shortsighted and needs to be corrected by a collective vision, as a result of which we have clearer insight in five areas especially problematic under traditional ethical analysis.

1. *The actual and the potential.* Our notions of justice have been finely honed around the concept of individual rights as these can be defended against the interests of others, and the casuistry that has here developed has some cross-generational usefulness. Still, when we move beyond our grandchildren, we falter; for future persons are indeterminate and remote, and one wonders how present persons have duties to such faceless nonentities. Our ethical skills deploy ahead uncertainly, owing to the lack of concrete, identifiable rights-carriers. We who are actually present do not know how to adjudicate our interests against such a potential "they," claimants all too nebulous and "iffy." These anomalies dissipate in part when life is observed as a corporate current, for then there is a present carrier of this possibility. This future belongs not to some abstract, hypothetical others; it is our future, which we who exist now do bear and transmit. It does not appear *ex nihilo,* but flows through us, it is the future of our generation, the future we generate, the downstream of our life. We are dealing with a potentiality of and in the actual.

The river has a geographical extension, which, though we typically view the stream at one point, we easily keep in mind. As an analogy it helps us to realize that, though we now see life locally, it has chronologically extended reality. We may then say that this present life, which we now compose, ought to have this tensed potential. Humans have, so to speak, a class right to the future; this race ought to run on, collectively, statistically, although we cannot individuate our posterity or prejudge entirely now "their" needs, "our" needs then. The mature self is able to envision itself in any present moment as enjoying but one slice in a temporally extended life. To be a self is to endure over time, in the processive stages from birth to death. But those endpoints of articulation, so vital in an egoistic ethic, are submerged in this life-pulse, which overflows those very individuals that it flows through. We pass away, but we pass life on. We share a common life with posterity, not in that they now are available for reciprocal obligations, but in that a common life is transported from here to there. This corporate passage also treats as concurrent what are usually separated out as deontological and teleological concerns. It would be a present, intrinsic wrong to deprive ourselves of a future, as it would also be wrong for us not to be instrumental to future good.

For a living thing to be actual is to be generative. If we think electrically, no current actually flows except as maintained by a potential. Life is another sort of current, more autonomously propelled, in which being actual and having potential are much the same thing; being is always becoming. Biologically, life must be procreative; the life-stream is one of parenting and growing, sowing and reaping, a dynamism that turns acorns into oaks into acorns into oaks. Further, this natural, seminal adventure has its human, educational extensions. We are so built as to be both reproductively and culturally *projective.* That is the notion of *con/sequences,* that there are "sequences" that follow "together with" past and present acts, and these consequences overleap the death of the individual. When there appear any living things, any life ways, whose consequences are not sufficiently projective, those forms may enjoy local successes and values, but they soon vanish. That is so, and, we shall later add, it ought to be so.

The river flows under the force of gravity, and the life-stream moves under an inner conative urge. The philosopher may have trouble supplying rational arguments why this life, now instantiated in me, should want to flow on, but he is unlikely to eradicate this natural passion. If any do fall into an entire disconcern to project themselves, careless about the future, they will soon be eliminated as unfit, the stream of life by-passing them. Such failure of nerve will be swept aside by other currents in which more fight remains. Most of us are going to find that the will to life which we have inherited from past generations floods through us, and thence to the future. Thus, fortunately, to a certain point, our class right, and our duty, and our compelling natural urge are discharged in the production of a surviving, future generation.

Unfortunately, this is not entirely so, else we should not have the problem of the *ought* and the *is,* to which we will come. More unfortunately still, we appear to have reached troubled waters, where these productive urges to reproduce and build will, without ethical control, become pathogenic and misfit us for survival. Our actual lifestyle might now be reducing our potential, which would be lamentable both biologically and ethically.

2. *The self and the other.* A person's ethical capacity can be roughly measured by the span of his "we." Egoism marks off an isolated "I," and beyond this boundary discovers only "he" and "she," finding ethical contests in the clashes of these irreducible cores, the one against the many, each unit pursuing its own enlightened interest. Altruism finds "others" and is also pluralistic, but there now appear sympathetic capacities. Beyond both egoism and altruism, the "I" is sometimes so moved to identify with a "you" that the capacity to say "we" emerges. My self is stretched over to the other, and ethical concern does not stop with my skin but overflows to my kin. Ethical maturity comes with a widening of that sense of kinship, and, with broad enough recognition of this togetherness, the self is immersed in a communal life.

Most of us can dissociate our identity beyond our own memory traces and reassociate it with parents and children, even with our ethnic and national kind. We could not be biologically or culturally successful without the capacity to do this, for we could not, as we have said, be sufficiently projective. There is a certain biological and psychological soundness to egoism's focus on the individual organism, but we also have to recognize the provision for regeneration. Thus we have a natural beginning for the development of the moral sense in the defense not merely of the self but of the in-group. The two senses of *kind,* "considerate" and "related," have a single etymological origin. The evolution of conscience proceeds with a widening out of both senses of *kind* so that they become less familial, less tribal, more ecumenical, reaching in the end a universal moral intent, and this extended sweep is not only a global but a chronological one.

We may notice here that far-off descendants and distant races do not have much "biological hold" on us. Across the era of human evolution, little in our behavior affected those remote from us in time or in space, and natural selection shaped only our conduct toward those closer. Now that our actions have such lengthened impact, we may indeed need ethics to survive, since this is required to enlarge the scope of concern for which we are biologically programmed. If our ethical concern can evolve to equal our awesome modern capacities to help and to hurt, around the globe and across generations to come, in such moral development, we would no doubt find new truth in the old moral paradox that a concern for others benefits one's own character.

In this life-current, distinctions that earlier were so clear begin to dissolve. Even the egoist knows that a person can have a duty to his future self, and hence he sacrifices for his retirement. All his stages are eventually present, and "now" has no favored status. But what of parents who bequeath possessions to their children and grandchildren, what of the farmer who for them conserves his soil, what of donors who endow the communities and institutions they have cherished? If we narrowly define the self, we shall say that prudence has become charity. But if we recognize the larger, more enduring group from which the self takes its identity, we will redescribe as a sort of corporate egoism what first seemed private charity; for the enlarging self extends into and continues in the course of the things that it loves. What then happens as this sense of kinship widens further under influences less ethological, less ethnological, more ethical? We may wonder whether egoism has vanished and altruism remains, or vice versa, as we wonder whether the drop of water remains or dissolves in the river. There are those who insist that every corporation is a fiction and that any goods and interests it may have are analyzable into those of individuals, and they will have here somehow to assign fractions to egoism and to altruism. But this is a type of ethical nominalism, not well served by recent biological and sociological theory where the goods and interests of the individual are constituted interdependently with the larger genetic and social movements out of which that person is composed.

When one pauses to consider the life that one "has," only an ignorant person would think of oneself as really "self-made" or "self-sufficient"; it is rather the lonesome self that is closer to fiction. The natural and cultural truth is in this otherness of the self, that we are participants in a shared flow, of which the self is an integral but momentary instantiation, rightly to be cherished in what autonomy it is given but responsibly and responsively to be emplaced in its supporting matrix. The old Jewish fathers put this aphoristically: "If I am not for myself who will be for me? And if I am only for myself, what am I?" (Hillel) The train of thought and of life we are following here lets us apply this to a generation; and if there are those who find this application difficult, we recommend that they go and stand at their great-grandparents' graves.

Love cares what happens after we are gone. The biological roots of this lie in parenting, but this concern matures and bears fruit in culture and in ethics. All authentic love is causally transitive, propagative, projecting that level of life that one most enjoys, but in this it goes out to invest itself in the other. Where this is not so, where one is careless about what happens after the demise of the local self, then there is only pretended, inauthentic love, stagnant self-love, unworthy of survival. Where this is so, we gain a much richer notion of the "commons" than has lately been current, for we no longer have self-aggrandizing egos, each wresting out its share of the commons, kept in check from stupidly overloading it only by finding some keener, more calculating self-interest to which we can appeal.[1] The self can live in love in and on this commons which we commend, but on the fought-over one it can live only in careful fear. Those who join this collective current find new meaning in the earth's carrying capacity.

3. *The human and the natural.* It is no coincidence that environmental ethics and intergenerational ethics are often a single issue, for our survival requires a habitat. It is typically, though not invariably, the case that what is good now for the environment is good for the human future, and we next find that the flow of this living river erodes and rounds off the sharp edges of the human/natural distinction. Soil, air, water, forests, grasslands, seas, the fauna, the flora are confluent with what, seen too narrowly, too artificially, some call the course of human events. Ecology has taught us vastly to expand our notions of circulation; human life moves afloat on a photosynthetic, nutritional biocurrent, with organic life in turn dependent on hydrologic, meteorologic, and geologic cycles. Life does not stop at the skin here either; it is an affair of natural resources. All that we are and have was grown or collected. If that word *resources* by its prefix "re" introduces the thought of a source that has been "turned into" human channels, away from its spontaneous course, it recalls more prominently the substantive earthen "source" out of which all springs.

No life form, the human included, can be projective enough to survive if it is not also, at a minimum, environmentally homeostatic. "Homeostasis" is not so much a static word as it is a hydraulic word, portraying in its biological use the steady state of a life-current maintaining itself over time in exchange with supporting movements in the physical environment. Consumption is always at odds with conservation; life endures in a delicate tension of the two. In prehuman life this balance is nondeliberate; with human life the challenge emerges to make this deliberate — and ethical. Homeostasis need not preclude evolution or historical development, but it does specify that any future human course shall include the carrying on of these natural processes with which collectively we move. We can "regenerate" only if our sources are "renewable." In both these words the prefix "re" no longer has to do with the making over of something natural into something human but, rather, with a human continuance by fitting into an uninterrupted flow of earthen sources. It was those concerned with natural conservation who early became concerned about future generations.

Life is a current in organismic as well as in environmental biology. Being water-based, life nowhere proceeds without its fluids, whether it be the sap in the trees or the blood in our veins. These support the protoplasmic process, and when we consider its future we speak still further of a genetic flow. Though individuals are the necessary carriers of genes, this notion again is not so individualistic as it is populational. No one of us carries all the human genetic load, each one draws an integral humanity from a pool that enormously transcends what any one person owns. It is to the regeneration of that communal reservoir that I contribute. Biologically, I am perhaps urged to preserve my germ line in that pool, as this may be edited by natural selection for the most viable genetic reservoir; ethically, the self can also enlarge its concern to care more broadly for the entire genealogical stream. If this seems to reduce our human life too much to the microscopic, genetic level, then we can readily return to the macroscopic, personal life, where the phenotype expresses a genotype, but always remembering how the subjective self manifests this genetic current.

It is fruitful to view the evolution of life as a kind of information flow. Against a basic physical flow, the disordering tendency to increase entropy, a biocurrent emerges with the capacity to build up and reproduce ordered, organic structures, passing this constructive information along genetically. In this nondeliberate sense all life is intelligent, logical, communicative, and the linguistic models employed in genetics give evidence of this. This flow diversifies, becomes more sophisticated and creative, more sentient and intelligent, until at length there emerges the capacity in humans for culture; and then a radically new sort of information flow appears, surpassed in significance only by the initial appearance of the negatively entropic life process itself. Acquired information can be transmitted, linguistically stored, and evaluated, and intelligence becomes deliberate. But the cultural process is still a part of, if the apex of, a natural life process. Life is always a cybernetic question, one of information transfer, as life is steered along over time, with both biological and civilized currents. The projecting of ourselves biologically and culturally, different though these may be, are inseparably integrated facets in the survival process.

Life is one of nature's projects, but it has flowed on so as to become one of our projects. We are the tip of an iceberg. We do dramatically emerge out of nature, but beneath the surface life remains nine-tenths natural. What is often wrong with the model of a "contract," in terms of which ethics is argued out, is that it is anti-natural, finding individualistic humans reluctantly banded together against threatening nature. There, rights-talk understandably appreciates individuals and depreciates nature. This countercurrent of the human before the natural is not wrong, as the notion of a countercurrent of the organic before the inorganic is not wrong, but both become fragmentary truths when placed in a still larger picture that sees an interflowing of the human and the natural, the biological with the physical. Nature gives us *objective* life, of which the *subjective* life of the individual is but a partial, inner face. Upon this given ecosystem we are what biologists call obligate parasites, and at this point we become interestingly confused — are we morally obligated to conserve and value merely the human or also the natural, since these have fused? Those who are ethically conservative will prefer to insist that ethics applies only to the human race, with all other processes auxiliary to this; those who are ethically liberal may find that their moral concern ranges over this catholic river of life and even includes the landscapes over which it flows.

4. *The present and the historical.* The river is a billion years long and persons have traveled a million years on it, recording their passage for several thousand years. If the river were to stretch round the globe, the human journey would be halfway across a county and we would have kept a journal for only a few hundred feet. The individual's reach would be a couple of steps. Such a linear scale admits the natural length of the river, yet it does not record an increasing turbulence in the human epoch, owing to the augmented information-flow. What is upstream flows down so as progressively, logarithmically to become tributary to more depth and stir. This past distance traveled is only partially forgotten and gone; it is rather largely here. It survives in us; for the present is what endures out of the past.

We are, as it were, the "*is*-ness of the was," not only in an evolutionary sense but also in an educational sense. Socrates and Moses, Jesus and Buddha, Newton and Copernicus, are not merely prior to us; their effects have been carried here by thousands now nameless who cherished and taught them, so transmitting them across time that something of them is recomposed in our composition. We sometimes think of the past as a kind of corpse; the dead are nothing but memories and phantoms. But if life is an on-rushing current, this is not so; for it is the past that germinates us. Our present life is just that past life in a cumulative, contemporary incarnation. In a legal phrase, we are both the executors and beneficiaries of the "wills" of our forebears, which outlast them. We do well to "will" that this providence lasts on, to ensure the "*will-be-ness of the is.*" In a natural idiom, we have roots, and we ought to have fruits.

Life is a splendid sort of "project," the ultimate drama. Some of its meanings are, and ought to be, transient. But the deepest meaning is found not merely in the present but, as in all narrative, when leading features of the past survive, deepen, and cohere to govern across repeated chapters in a whole plot. Incidentals may be delighted in for the present, but they pass away, peculiar to an era. Discontinuities and emergents surprise us; still each generation's noblest adventures are tributary to a meaning flow that is intergenerational. In the flow of a symphony, the present melody is enjoyed in itself, but not only so; it often recapitulates and leads. Else there is less beauty and no real movement. That we cannot entirely foresee the outcome is a positively dramatic feature, and so we do not and cannot know the future course of this life tide, whether of success or of catastrophe. But that does not diminish in present actors a duty to thrust forward what they most cherish. Nor does this duty diminish their own immediate integrity; it rather establishes it.

Every scientist, every humanist, every educator, and every parent knows how the single life needs these dimensions of retrospect and prospect. We are set in motion with what was delivered to us; we carry it on a bit, but not to its conclusion; we pass from the scene, and our students, disciples, and children carry on. This age has seen the remarkable revelations of Watson and Crick, but only as they follow those of Darwin, Mendel, and Linnaeus; and others will continue the succession. Democracy has been a long time building, and most of us would die to pass it on. The musician, the artist, the novelist, the philosopher — all flourish in the heritage of their predecessors, and they themselves create works to be appreciated now but also to pass into the objective public domain. Particular lives and labors are most often forgotten, but that does not mean that they were not part of the cybernetic circuits over which a culture was transmitted.

No one should deny important asymmetries between past, present, and future; they are well recognized in what McTaggart called the temporal A-series, where a knife-edged present moves inexorably across time to convert the future into the past. But it is likewise possible, more scientific, and just as moral, to view time as what he called a B-series, having only an earlier-than/later-than in a serial whole.[2] If we couple these series, past, present, and future are not three things, with only one convincingly real. But there is one life-stream that bears the predicates of the past into the future by conveying them through the present. Past, present, and future are not strung together like beads on a string, each a detachable existent *simpliciter*. They flow together like the upstream and downstream of a river, only more organically. The myopic, arrogant "now" generation thinks of the past as dead, the future as nonbeing, with only the present alive. The far-sighted see that to be alive in the present is to carry the past on to the future; and, if so, it is rather the ephemeral "now" generation that is as good as dead, for they do not know what survival means. We are constituted in memory and hope, and it is indeed a prophetic truth that where there is no vision, the people perish.

5. *The* is *and the* ought. Life flows on. Life ought to flow on. Few can specify how we make that descriptive-prescriptive jump, but here, where biology and history draw so close to ethics, it is made easier than anywhere else. Fact and fact-to-be-desired join in "the *ought*-ness in the *is*," which is not to endorse all, nor to deny that some life-forms are passing, but to cheer for this fabulous life project. Not only in our genes but also in our consciences we are constructed for a sort of keeping faith with those upstream and down. Here are joined the twin meanings of "conduct" that constrain the present; we ought each and all to *conduct* ourselves (to behave responsibly) so as to *conduct* ourselves (to lead the race safely on) from past to future. Life protects life; such survival is "becoming," again in biological and ethical senses. Should we fail, that would abuse our resources and abort our destiny.

This judgment is not entirely shared by those who find life's currents to be all in tragedy. The older, Indian Buddhists called the world a maelstrom of dependent origination, one misery causing another, but they hoped to find a deliverance by putting out these urges in a quiescent *nirvana*. We may agree with them that an unrelieved, individualistic plurality is bad, an illusory gestalt, that intensifies suffering, but we disagree in our wish to conserve and corporately to integrate the world of birth and death, preserving just that blessed life-stream that survives these agonies. The recent nihilists screamed that life was absurd and, in despair, said they cared nothing about its going on. Both rightly perceived life's suffering, but underwent it so intensely that they misperceived its meaning. This suffering, however, can become a sacrament of life; it takes on significance as, and only as, in these tears, we insist on the projection in this world of this life-stream. And, whatever their theories, in practice both still found life heroic—the compassionate Buddhists in their reverence for life, and the adamant nihilists in their protest that we manufacture meaning despite our nothingness.

These extremes aside, most of us find our earthen life to be more a gift than a meaningless given, a gift that obligates us as trustees to the task of carrying it on. Against all the arguments, sometimes forceful ones, about nature's heartlessness and culture's mindlessness, here we are, alive and even well, products at once of nature and of culture, glad of it, and rather persuaded that the real tragedy, the ultimate in absurdity, lies not in our being here but in the possibility of our failing to pass life forward.

We do not suppose that there is no discontinuity when the *ought* emerges where hitherto there was only an *is*. In the wild, each fends for itself competitively. The cooperative flow is an unintended consequence of this self-interest, which is edited by natural selection to shape the survival of the most vigorous species. Life is advanced by a kind of libido, and, while we must be careful not to judge this to be bad, neither is it moral. Looking out after oneself has its necessary place in this ensuring of life, although this is not sufficient for its continuance; it must be kept in check by the interests of others, by ecosystemic balances and evolutionary pressures. What *is* the case in the prehuman world, and often even in the premoral human world, can and henceforth *ought* at deliberative levels to be accomplished morally.

One's self-interest, which is still required, can now be kept in its desirable place, sufficiently checked by capacities for sympathy, by judgments finding rightness in the corporate currents of life, to which one belongs. What before was externally and genetically controlled can by this advance be internalized and freely acted upon. The moral sense then becomes a new form of cybernetic control. But the effect of that switch can be, and ought to be, to ensure the continuity of a life process that has long been under way. Indeed, such are our recently maturing powers for the exercise of self-interest that, unless these ethical capacities also unfold, the earlier natural checks may no longer be effective and we may plunge into that terminal tragedy which we most fear.

In front of Eiheiji, Dogen's mountain temple in Japan, there stands the Half-Dipper Bridge, so named because the Zen sage was accustomed to drink there; but he would take only half a dipperful and pour the rest back into the river, rejoicing in its onward flow. We may puzzle about whether this denies or fulfills that earlier, Indian Buddhist estimate of the *samsara* world, to which we just referred, but we must surely admire so simple a gesture with such a rich ethical concern. There is much scientific analysis now of the "energy throughput" in the biosystem and in the economy. A moral concern for a "life throughput" would help even more. A fair criticism of what we have proposed is that it is impressionistic and difficult to make "operational," so accordingly we do also need the ethical logic that unfolds under other models of life and responsibility. Their arguments may help us, in the conflict of life against life, to protect individual integrity, to compute maximums in quantity and quality, and to balance each against the other. But we operate as impressed by our metaphors too, as well as by our calculations, whether those images are of the survival of the fittest, or the social contract, or lifeboat ethics, or the way of the cross. If seen as a symbol, this river of life is no longer merely a metaphor, it is a truth that bears moral insight, because it helps us see more deeply how the life process is and how it ought to be.

NOTES

1. Garrett Hardin, "The Tragedy of the Commons," *Science,* 162 (Dec. 13, 1968), 1243–1248.

2. J. M. E. McTaggart, *The Nature of Existence,* vol. 2 (Cambridge: University Press, 1921), chap. 33.

PART THREE

Can Future Generations Be Said to Have Rights?

Part 3. Can Future Generations Be Said to Have Rights?

Introduction

Each of the writers that we have encountered thus far acknowledges that the living have moral duties to members of future generations. Likewise, we will find that each of the five authors in this next section also affirms such duties. The dispute in this section centers around the additional question of whether future generations can be said to have *rights*. Three writers (Feinberg, Pletcher, and Baier) argue that they can. The others (De George and Macklin) deny that posterity can properly be said to have rights now.[1] The issue may be one of enormous moral and practical significance, for a duty to respect another's rights generally carries greater weight and thus overrules a competing "uncorrelated" duty, such as a duty to be charitable. Thus, for example, we assume that we can write a check to the March of Dimes *only* if we have cash on balance *after* paying our bills and installment debts. Our creditors have a *right* to our money, but the charitable agencies do not. Need is irrelevant: the situation is unaltered by the fact that our creditor might be Exxon, and that the potential beneficiaries of our charity include the wretched of the earth. In short, *rights* have a stringency and urgency that benefactions do not.

But there is more. Beings with rights deserve respect. As Joel Feinberg states in a paper not included here, *rights* command our attention and demand our response:

> Their characteristic use and that for which they are distinctively well-suited, is to be claimed, demanded, affirmed, insisted upon. They are especially sturdy objects to "stand upon," a most useful sort of moral furniture. . . . Having rights enables us to "stand up like men," to look others in the eye, and to feel in some fundamental way the equal of anyone. To think of oneself as the holder of rights is not to be unduly but properly proud, to have the minimal self-respect that is necessary to be worthy of the love and esteem of others. Indeed, respect for persons (this is the intriguing idea) may simply be respect for their rights, so that there cannot be the one without the other; and what is called "human dignity" may simply be the recognizable capacity to assert claims. To respect a person then, or to think of him as possessed of human dignity, simply *is* to think of him as a potential maker of claims.[2]

Thus, if future generations have rights-claims against us, they will have no cause to be "grateful" to us for preserving a viable ecosystem; for they will have received their due. On the other hand, if we violate this duty, their appropriate response will be not simply *regret* but moral *indignation*. Moral duties born of *rights* weigh more heavily upon the duty-bearers. Thus, to the degree that our policy-makers and legislators respond to valid moral arguments, the interests of future generations will be far better served if we can succeed in defending the notion that succeeding generations have rights-claims against the living who, in turn, have the moral duty to respect and respond to these rights. In other words, this stronger claim transforms the moral case – a point of no small significance for those whose job it is to propose and defend environmental policies.[3]

It is customary for anthologists to separate and group contestants in a philosophical debate according to the "sides" they take in the dispute. The following five papers will not follow that format. Instead, the section will begin with Joel Feinberg's *defense* of the claim that future generations have rights. Feinberg's paper has been so chosen for its excellent explication of the concept of *rights* – an explication that will serve the reader well as he continues through the section. Feinberg's view that "rights" are grounded in the "interests" of sentient beings enjoys widespread, though less than unanimous, support among moral philosophers. His case in support of the rights of future persons is skillfully developed through an examination of the purported "rights" of "borderline cases" such as animals and fetuses, and so on. Richard De George and Ruth Macklin dissent from Feinberg's view that posterity has rights now. Because the papers by Galen Pletcher and Annette Baier are responsive to arguments presented by De George and Macklin, these are appropriately placed at the close of the section.

The issue of the alleged "rights of future persons" is discussed in several of the works in this anthology. Each of the papers (especially the Routleys' paper) in the final section, "Applications," deal with the issue of posterity's "rights" and, as the reader may recall, the preceding papers by Passmore, Golding, and Callahan also give explicit attention to the question.[4]

All the papers in this section, except Feinberg's, are derived from a specific occasion, namely, a symposium at the 1973 annual meeting of the Eastern Division of the American Philosophical Association in Atlanta, Georgia. (The topic of the symposium, in full, was: "Can Future Generations Properly Be Said to Have Rights – e.g., the Right to Breathe Clean Air?") Professor De George's remarks were later refined, expanded, and then published. The paper included here is from a published source. The essays by Macklin, Pletcher, and Baier were revised at the request of this editor.

NOTES

1. Once again, I would urgently and emphatically remind the reader that both Macklin and De George *affirm* that there are moral constraints upon what the living

may do that will foreseeably affect the future. What they deny is that these constraints can properly be categorized as *rights* of future persons.

2. Joel Feinberg, "The Nature and Value of Rights," *The Journal of Value Inquiry,* 4 (Winter 1970), p. 252.

3. It should be noted, however, that not all moral philosophers agree that the attribution of "rights" makes all that much difference with regard to duties to future persons. For example, see Annette Baier, below [p. 171], and Edwin Delattre (1972).

4. For a categorical denial of *both* duties to and rights of future persons, see Thomas Thompson's "Are We Obligated to Future Others" [this anthology, p. 195] and Thomas Schwartz's "Obligations to Posterity" (in Barry and Sikora, 1978).

Joel Feinberg

The Rights of Animals and Unborn Generations

Every philosophical paper must begin with an unproved assumption. Mine is the assumption that there will still be a world five hundred years from now, and that it will contain human beings who are very much like us. We have it within our power now, clearly, to affect the lives of these creatures for better or worse by contributing to the conservation or corruption of the environment in which they must live. I shall assume furthermore that it is psychologically possible for us to care about our remote descendants, that many of us in fact do care, and indeed that we ought to care. My main concern then will be to show that it makes sense to speak of the rights of unborn generations against us, and that given the moral judgment that we ought to conserve our environmental inheritance for them, and its grounds, we might well say that future generations *do* have rights correlative to our present duties toward them. Protecting our environment now is also a matter of elementary prudence, and insofar as we do it for the next generation already here in the persons of our children, it is a matter of love. But from the perspective of our remote descendants it is basically a matter of justice, of respect for their rights. My main concern here will be to examine the concept of a right to better understand how that can be.

The Problem

To have a right is to have a claim[1] *to* something and *against* someone, the recognition of which is called for by legal rules or, in the case of moral rights, by the principles of an enlightened conscience. In the familiar cases of rights, the claimant is a competent adult human being, and the claimee is an office-holder in an institution or else a private individual, in either case, another

Reprinted from *Philosophy and Environmental Crisis,* ed. William Blackstone, by permission of the University of Georgia Press and the author. Copyright 1974 by The University of Georgia Press.

competent adult human being. Normal adult human beings, then, are obviously the sort of beings of whom rights can meaningfully be predicated. Everyone would agree to that, even extreme misanthropes who deny that anyone in fact has rights. On the other hand, it is absurd to say that rocks can have rights, not because rocks are morally inferior things unworthy of rights (that statement makes no sense either), but because rocks belong to a category of entities of whom rights cannot be meaningfully predicated. That is not to say that there are no circumstances in which we ought to treat rocks carefully, but only that the rocks themselves cannot validly claim good treatment from us. In between the clear cases of rocks and normal human beings, however, is a spectrum of less obvious cases, including some bewildering borderline ones. Is it meaningful or conceptually possible to ascribe rights to our dead ancestors? to individual animals? to whole species of animals? to plants? to idiots and madmen? to fetuses? to generations yet unborn? Until we know how to settle these puzzling cases, we cannot claim fully to grasp the concept of a right, or to know the shape of its logical boundaries.

One way to approach these riddles is to turn one's attention first to the most familiar and unproblematic instances of rights, note their most salient characteristics, and then compare the borderline cases with them, measuring as closely as possible the points of similarity and difference. In the end, the way we classify the borderline cases may depend on whether we are more impressed with the similarities or the differences between them and the cases in which we have the most confidence.

It will be useful to consider the problem of individual animals first because their case is the one that has already been debated with the most thoroughness by philosophers so that the dialectic of claim and rejoinder has now unfolded to the point where disputants can get to the end game quickly and isolate the crucial point at issue. When we understand precisely what *is* at issue in the debate over animal rights, I think we will have the key to the solution of all the other riddles about rights.

Individual Animals

Almost all modern writers agree that we ought to be kind to animals, but that is quite another thing from holding that animals can claim kind treatment from us as their due. Statutes making cruelty to animals a crime are now very common, and these, of course, impose legal duties on people not to mistreat animals; but that still leaves open the question whether the animals, as beneficiaries of those duties, possess rights correlative to them. We may very well have duties *regarding* animals that are not at the same time duties *to* animals, just as we may have duties regarding rocks, or buildings, or lawns, that are not duties *to* the rocks, buildings, or lawns. Some legal writers have taken the still more extreme position that animals themselves are not even the directly intended beneficiaries of statutes prohibiting cruelty to animals. During the nineteenth century, for example, it was commonly said that such statutes were designed to protect human beings by preventing the growth of cruel habits that could later threaten human beings with harm too. Prof. Louis B. Schwartz finds the rationale of the cruelty-to-animals prohibition in its protection of animal lovers from affronts to their sensibilities. "It is not the mistreated dog who is the ultimate object of concern," he writes. "Our concern is for the feelings of other human beings, a large proportion of whom, although accustomed to the slaughter of animals for food, readily identify themselves with a tortured dog or horse and respond with great sensitivity to its sufferings."[2] This seems to me to be factitious. How much more natural it is to say with John Chipman Gray that the true purpose of cruelty-to-animals statutes is "to preserve the dumb brutes from suffering."[3] The very people whose sensibilities are invoked in the alternative explanation, a group that no doubt now includes most of us, are precisely those who would insist that the protection belongs primarily to the animals themselves, not merely to their own tender feelings. Indeed, it would be difficult even to account for the existence of such feelings in the absence of a belief that the animals deserve the protection in their own right and for their own sakes.

Even if we allow, as I think we must, that animals are the intended direct beneficiaries of legislation forbidding cruelty to animals, it does not follow directly that animals have legal rights, and Gray himself, for one,[4] refused to draw this further inference. Animals cannot have rights, he thought, for the same reason they cannot have duties, namely, that they are not genuine "moral agents." Now, it is relatively easy to see why animals cannot have duties, and this matter is largely beyond controversy. Animals cannot be "reasoned with" or instructed in their responsibilities; they are inflexible and unadaptable to future contingencies; they are subject to fits of instinctive passion which they are incapable of repressing or controlling, postponing or sublimating. Hence, they cannot enter into contractual agreements, or make promises; they cannot be trusted; and they cannot (except within very narrow limits and for purposes of conditioning) be blamed for what would be called "moral failures" in a human being. They are therefore incapable of being moral subjects, of acting rightly or wrongly in the moral sense, of having, discharging, or breeching duties and obligations.

But what is there about the intellectual incompetence of animals (which admittedly disqualifies them for duties) that makes them logically unsuitable for rights? The most common reply to this question is that animals are incapable of *claiming* rights on their own. They cannot make motion, on their own, to courts to have their claims recognized or enforced; they cannot initiate, on their own, any kind of legal proceedings; nor are they capable of even understanding when their rights are being violated, of distinguishing harm from wrongful injury, and responding with indignation and an outraged sense of justice instead of mere anger or fear.

No one can deny any of these allegations, but to the claim that they are the grounds for disqualification of rights of animals, philosophers on the other side of this controversy have made convincing rejoinders. It is simply not true, says W. D. Lamont,[5] that the ability to understand what a right is and the ability to set legal machinery in motion by one's own initiative are necessary for the possession of rights. If that were the case, then neither human idiots nor wee babies would have any legal rights at all. Yet it is manifest that both of these classes of intellectual incompetents have legal rights recognized and easily enforced by the courts. Children and idiots start legal proceedings, not on their own direct initiative, but rather through the actions of proxies or attorneys who are empowered to speak in their names. If there is no conceptual absurdity in this situation, why should there be in the case where a proxy makes a claim on behalf of an animal? People commonly enough make wills leaving money to trustees for the care of animals. Is it not natural to speak of the animal's right to his inheritance in cases of this kind? If a trustee embezzles money from the animal's account,[6] and a proxy speaking in the dumb brute's behalf presses the animal's claim, can he not be described as asserting the animal's *rights?* More exactly, the animal itself claims its rights through the vicarious actions of a human proxy speaking in its name and in its behalf. There appears to be no reason why we should require the animal to understand what is going on (so the argument concludes) as a condition for regarding it as a possessor of rights.

. . . H. J. McCloskey,[7] I believe, accepts the argument up to this point, but he presents a new and different reason for denying that animals can have legal rights. The ability to make claims, whether directly or through a representative, he implies, is essential to the possession of rights. Animals obviously cannot press their claims on their own, and so if they have rights, these rights must be assertable by agents. Animals, however, cannot be represented, McCloskey contends, and not for any of the reasons already discussed, but rather because representation, in the requisite sense, is always of interests, and animals (he says) are incapable of having interests.

Now, there is a very important insight expressed in the requirement that a being have interests if he is to be a logically proper subject of rights. This can be appreciated if we consider just why it is that mere things cannot have rights. Consider a very precious "mere thing"—a beautiful natural wilderness, or a complex and ornamental artifact, like the Taj Mahal. Such things ought to be cared for, because they would sink into decay if neglected, depriving some human beings, or perhaps even all human beings, of something of great value. Certain persons may even have as their own special job the care and protection of these valuable objects. But we are not tempted in these cases to speak of "thing-rights" correlative to custodial duties, because, try as we might, we cannot think of mere things as possessing interests of their own. Some people may have a duty to preserve, maintain, or improve the Taj Mahal, but they can hardly have a duty to help or hurt it, benefit or aid it, succor or relieve it. Custodians may protect it for the sake of a nation's pride and art lovers' fancy; but they don't keep it in good repair for "its own sake," or for "its own true welfare," or "well-being." A mere thing, however valuable to others, has no good of its own. The explanation of that fact, I suspect, consists in the fact that mere things have no conative life: no conscious wishes, desires, and hopes; or urges and impulses; or unconscious drives, aims, and goals; or latent tendencies, direction of growth, and natural fulfillments. Interests must be compounded somehow out of conations; hence mere things have no interests. *A fortiori,* they have no interests to be protected by legal or moral rules. Without interests a creature can have no "good" of its own, the achievement of which can be its due. Mere things are not loci of value in their own right, but rather their value consists entirely in their being objects of other beings' interests.

So far McCloskey is on solid ground, but one can quarrel with his denial that any animals but humans have interests. I should think that the trustee of funds willed to a dog or a cat is more than a mere custodian of the animal he protects. Rather his job is to look out for the interests of the animal and make sure no one denies it its due. The animal itself is the beneficiary of his dutiful services. Many of the higher animals at least have appetites, conative urges, and rudimentary purposes, the integrated satisfaction of which constitutes their welfare or good. We can, of course, with consistency treat animals as mere pests and deny that they have any rights; for most animals, especially those of the lower orders, we have no choice but to do so. But it seems to me, nevertheless, that in general, animals *are* among the sort of beings of whom rights can meaningfully be predicated and denied.

Now, if a person agrees with the conclusion of the argument thus far, that animals are the sort of beings that *can* have rights, and, further, if he accepts the moral judgment that we ought to be kind to animals, only one further premise is needed to yield the conclusion that some animals do in fact have rights. We must now ask ourselves for whose sake ought we to treat (some) animals with consideration and humaneness? If we conceive our duty to be one of obedience to authority, or to one's own conscience merely, or one of consideration for tender human sensibilities only, then we might still deny that animals have rights, even though we admit that they are the kinds of beings that *can* have rights. But if we hold not only that we ought to treat animals humanely but also that we should do so for the animals' own sake, that such treatment is something we owe animals as their due, something that can be claimed for them, something the withholding of which would be an injustice and a wrong, and not merely a harm, then it follows that we do ascribe rights to animals. I suspect that the moral judgments most of us make about animals do pass these phenomenological tests, so that most of us do believe that animals have rights, but are reluctant to say so because of the conceptual confusions about the notion of a right that I have attempted to dispel above.

Now we can extract from our discussion of animal rights a crucial principle for tentative use in the resolution of the other riddles about the applicability of the concept of a right, namely, that the sort of beings who *can* have rights are precisely those who have (or can have) interests. I have come to this tentative conclusion for two reasons: (1) because a right holder must be capable of being represented and it is impossible to represent a being that has no interests, and (2) because a right holder must be capable of being a beneficiary in his own person, and a being without interests is a being that is incapable of being harmed or benefitted, having no good or "sake" of its own. Thus, a being without interests has no "behalf" to act in, and no "sake" to act for. My strategy now will be to apply the "interest principle," as we can call it, to the other puzzles about rights, while being prepared to modify it where necesary (but as little as possible), in the hope of separating in a consistent and intuitively satisfactory fashion the beings who can have rights from those which cannot.

Vegetables

. . . Plants are not the kinds of being that can have rights. Plants are never plausibly understood to be the direct intended beneficiaries of rules designed to "protect" them. We wish to keep redwood groves in existence for the sake of human beings who can enjoy their serene beauty, and for the sake of generations of human beings yet unborn. Trees are not the sorts of beings who have their "own sakes," despite the fact that they have biological propensities. Having no conscious wants or goals of their own, trees cannot know satisfaction or frustration, pleasure or pain. Hence, there is no possibility of kind or cruel treatment of trees. In these morally crucial respects, trees differ from the higher species of animals.

Yet trees are not mere things like rocks. They grow and develop according to the laws of their own nature. Aristotle and Aquinas both took trees to have their own "natural ends." Why then do I deny them the status of beings with interests of their own? The reason is that an interest, however the concept is finally to be analyzed, presupposes at least rudimentary cognitive equipment. Interests are compounded out of *desires* and *aims,* both of which presuppose something like *belief,* or cognitive awareness. . . .[8]

Human Vegetables

Mentally deficient and deranged human beings are hardly ever so handicapped intellectually that they do not compare favorably with even the highest of the lower animals, though they are commonly so incompetent that they cannot be assigned duties or be held responsible for what they do. Since animals can have rights, then, it follows that human idiots and madmen can too. It would make good sense, for example, to ascribe to them a right to be cured whenever effective therapy is available at reasonable cost, and even those incurables who have been consigned to a sanatorium for permanent "warehousing" can claim (through a proxy) their right to decent treatment.

Human beings suffering extreme cases of mental illness, however, may be so utterly disoriented or insensitive as to compare quite unfavorably with the brightest cats and dogs. Those suffering from catatonic schizophrenia may be barely distinguishable in respect to those traits presupposed by the possession of interests from the lowliest vegetables. So long as we regard these patients as potentially curable, we may think of them as human beings with interests in their own restoration and treat them as possessors of rights. We may think of the patient as a genuine human person inside the vegetable casing struggling to get out, just as in the old fairy tales a pumpkin could be thought of as a beautiful maiden under a magic spell waiting only the proper words to be restored to her true self. Perhaps it is reasonable never to lose hope that a patient can be cured, and therefore to regard him always as a person "under a spell" with a permanent interest in his own recovery that is entitled to recognition and protection.

What if, nevertheless, we think of the catatonic schizophrenic and the vegetating patient with irreversible brain damage as absolutely incurable? Can we think of them at the same time as possessed of interests and rights too, or is this combination of traits a conceptual impossibility? Shocking as it may at first seem, I am driven unavoidably to the latter view. If redwood trees and rosebushes cannot have rights, neither can incorrigible human vegetables.[9] The trustees who are designated to administer funds for the care of these unfortunates are better understood as mere custodians than as representatives of their interests since these patients no longer have interests. It does not follow that they should not be kept alive as long as possible: that is an open moral question not foreclosed by conceptual analysis. Even if we have duties to keep human vegetables alive, however, they cannot be duties *to* them. We may be obliged to keep them alive to protect the sensibilities of others, or to foster humanitarian tendencies in ourselves, but we cannot keep them alive for their own good, for they are no longer capable of having a "good" of their own. Without awareness, expectation, belief, desire, aim, and purpose, a being can have no interests; without interests, he cannot be benefited; without the capacity to be a beneficiary, he can have no rights. But there may nevertheless be a dozen other reasons to treat him as if he did.

Fetuses

If the interest principle is to permit us to ascribe rights to infants, fetuses, and generations yet unborn, it can only be on the grounds that interests can exert a claim upon us even before their possessors actually come into being, just the reverse of the situation respecting dead men where interests are respected even after their possessors have ceased to be. Newly born infants are surely noisier than mere vegetables, but they are just barely brighter. They come into existence, as Aristotle said, with the capacity to acquire concepts and dispositions, but in the beginning we suppose that their consciousness of the world is a "blooming, buzzing confusion." They do have a capacity, no doubt from the very beginning, to feel pain, and this alone may be sufficient ground for ascribing both an interest and a right to them. Apart from that, however, during the first few hours of their lives, at least, they may well lack even the rudimentary intellectual equipment necessary to the possession of interests. Of course, this induces no moral reservations whatever in adults. Children grow and mature almost visibly in the first few months so that those future interests that are so rapidly emerging from the unformed chaos of their earliest days seem unquestionably to be the basis of their present rights. Thus, we say of a newborn infant that he has a right now to live and grow into his adulthood, even though he lacks the conceptual equipment at this very moment to have this or any other desire. A new infant, in short, lacks the traits necessary for the possession of interests, but he has the capacity to acquire those traits, and his inherited potentialities are moving quickly toward actualization even as we watch him. Those proxies who make claims in behalf of infants, then, are more than mere custodians: they are (or can be) genuine representatives of the child's emerging interests, which may need protection even now if they are to be allowed to come into existence at all.

The same principle may be extended to "unborn persons." After all, the situation of fetuses one day before birth is not strikingly different from that a few hours after birth. The rights our law confers on the unborn child, both proprietary and personal, are for the most part, placeholders or reservations for the rights he shall inherit when he becomes a full-fledged interested being. The law protects a potential interest in these cases before it has even grown into actuality, as a garden fence protects newly seeded flower beds long before blooming flowers have emerged from them. The unborn child's present right to property, for example, is a legal protection offered now to his future interest, contingent upon his birth, and instantly voidable if he dies before birth. As Coke put it: "The law in many cases hath consideration of him in respect of the apparent expectation of his birth";[10] but this is quite another thing than recognizing a right actually to be born. Assuming that the child will be born, the law seems to say, various interests that he will come to have after birth must be protected from damage that they can incur even before birth. Thus prenatal injuries of a negligently inflicted kind can give the newly born child a right to sue for damages which he can exercise through a proxy-attorney and in his own name any time *after* he is born.

There are numerous other places, however, where our law seems to imply an unconditional right to be born, and surprisingly no one seems ever to have found that idea conceptually absurd. One interesting example comes from an article given the following headline by the *New York Times:* "Unborn Child's Right Upheld Over Religion."[11] A hospital patient in her eighth month of pregnancy refused to take a blood transfusion even though warned by her physician that "she might die at any minute and take the life of her child as well." The ground of her refusal was that blood transfusions are repugnant to the principles of her religion (Jehovah's Witnesses). The Supreme Court of New Jersey expressed uncertainty over the constitutional question of whether a nonpregnant adult might refuse on religious grounds a blood transfusion pronounced necessary to her own survival, but the court nevertheless ordered the patient in the present case to receive the transfusion on the grounds that "the unborn child is entitled to the law's protection."

It is important to reemphasize here that the questions of whether fetuses do or ought to have rights are substantive questions of law and morals open to argument and decision. The prior question of whether fetuses are the kind of beings that can have rights, however, is a conceptual, not a moral, question, amenable only to what is called "logical analysis," and irrelevant to moral judgment. The correct answer to the conceptual question, I believe, is that unborn children are among the sort of beings of whom possession of rights can meaningfully be predicated, even though they are (temporarily) incapable of having interests, because their future interests can be protected now, and it does make sense to protect a potential interest even before it has grown into actuality. The interest principle, however, makes perplexing, at best, talk of a noncontingent fetal right to be born; for fetuses, lacking actual wants and beliefs, have no actual interest in being born, and it is difficult to think of any other reason for ascribing any rights to them other than on the assumption that they will in fact be born.[12]

Future Generations

We have it in our power now to make the world a much less pleasant place for our descendants than the world we inherited from our ancestors. We can continue to proliferate in ever greater numbers, using up fertile soil at an even greater rate, dumping our wastes into rivers, lakes, and oceans, cutting down our forests, and polluting the atmosphere with noxious gases. All thoughtful people agree that we ought not do to these things. Most would say that we have a duty not to do these things, meaning not merely that conservation is morally required (as opposed to merely desirable) but also that it is something due our descendants, something to be done for their sakes. Surely we owe it to future generations to pass on a world that is not a used up garbage heap. Our remote descendants are not yet present to claim a livable world as their right, but there are plenty of proxies to speak now in their behalf. These spokesmen, far from being mere custodians, are genuine representatives of future interests.

Why then deny that the human beings of the future have rights which can be claimed against us now in their behalf? Some are inclined to deny them present rights out of a fear of falling into obscure metaphysics, by granting rights to remote and unidentifiable beings who are not yet even in existence. Our unborn great-great-grandchildren are in some sense "potential" persons, but they are far more remotely potential, it may seem, than fetuses. This, however, is not the real difficulty. Unborn generations are more remotely potential than fetuses in one sense, but not in another. A much greater period of time with a far greater number of causally necessary and important events must pass before their potentiality can be actualized, it is true; but our collective posterity is just as certain to come into existence "in the normal course of events" as is any given fetus now in its mother's womb. In that sense the existence of the distant human future is no more remotely potential than that of a particular child already on its way.

The real difficulty is not that we doubt whether our descendants will ever be actual, but rather that we don't know who they will be. It is not their temporal remoteness that troubles us so much as their indeterminacy—their present facelessness and namelessness. Five centuries from now men and women will be living where we live now. Any given one of them will have an interest in living space, fertile soil, fresh air, and the like, but that arbitrarily selected one has no other qualities we can presently envision very clearly. We don't even know who his parents, grandparents, or great-grandparents are, or even whether he is related to us. Still, whoever these human beings may turn out to be, and whatever they might reasonably be expected to be like, they will have interests that we can affect, for better or worse, right now. That much we can and do know about them. The identity of the owners of these interests is now necessarily obscure, but the fact of their interest-ownership is crystal clear, and that is all that is necessary to certify the coherence of present talk about their rights. We can tell, sometimes, that shadowy forms in the spatial distance belong to human beings, though we know not who or how many they are; and this imposes a duty on us not to throw bombs, for example, in their direction. In like manner, the vagueness of the human future does not weaken its claim on us in light of the nearly certain knowledge that it will, after all, be human.

Doubts about the existence of a right to be born transfer neatly to the question of a similar right to come into existence ascribed to future generations. The rights that future generations certainly have against us are contingent rights: the interests they are sure to have when they come into being (assuming of course that they will come into being) cry out for protection from invasions that can take place now. Yet there are no actual interests, presently existent, that future generations, presently nonexistent, have now. Hence, there is no actual interest that they have in simply coming into being, and I am at a loss to think of any other reason for claiming that they have a right to come into existence (though there may well be such a reason). Suppose then that all human beings at a given time voluntarily form a compact never again to produce children, thus leading within a few decades to the end of our species. This of course is a wildly improbable hypothetical example but a rather crucial one for the position I have been tentatively considering. And we can imagine, say, that the whole world is converted to a strange ascetic religion which absolutely requires sexual abstinence for everyone. Would this arrangement violate the rights of anyone? No one can complain on behalf of presently nonexistent future generations that their future interests which give them a contingent right of protection have been violated since they will never come into existence to be wronged. My inclination then is to conclude that the suicide of our species would be deplorable, lamentable, and a deeply moving tragedy, but that it would violate no one's rights. Indeed if, contrary to fact, all human beings could ever agree to such a thing, that very agreement would be a symptom of our species' biological unsuitability for survival anyway.

Conclusion

For several centuries now human beings have run roughshod over the lands of our planet, just as if the animals who do live there and the generations of humans who will live there had no claims on them whatever. Philosophers have not helped matters by arguing that animals and future generations are not the kinds of beings who can have rights now, that they don't presently qualify for membership, even "auxiliary membership," in our moral community. I have tried in this essay to dispel the conceptual confusions that make such conclusions possible. To acknowledge their rights is the very least we can do for members of endangered species (including our own). But that is something.

NOTES

1. I shall leave the concept of a claim unanalyzed here, but for a detailed discussion, see my "The Nature and Value of Rights," *Journal of Value Inquiry,* 4 (1971), 263-277.

2. Louis B. Schwartz, "Morals, Offenses and the Model Penal Code," *Columbia Law Review,* 63 (1963), 673.

3. John Chipman Gray, *The Nature and Sources of the Law,* 2nd ed. (Boston: Beacon Press, 1963), p. 43.

4. And W. D. Ross for another. See *The Right and the Good* (Oxford: Clarendon Press, 1930), App. 1, pp. 48-56.

5. W. D. Lamont, *Principles of Moral Judgment* (Oxford: Clarendon Press, 1946), pp. 83-85.

6. Cf. H. J. McCloskey, "Rights," *Philosophical Quarterly,* 15 (1965), 121, 124.

7. Ibid.

8. Professor Feinberg's intriguing discussion of the putative "rights" of dead persons has been omitted. Though this is a fascinating and difficult issue in its own right, the exclusion of this section of Feinberg's paper does not materially affect his case for the "rights" of future generations. For a further discussion of this issue, see Feinberg's "Harm and Self Interest," *Law, Morality and Society: Essays in Honor of H. L. A. Hart,* ed. P. M. S. Hocker and J. Raz (Oxford: Clarendon Press, 1977), pp. 284-308. See also my "Posthumous Interests and Posthumous Respect," forthcoming in *Ethics.* —ED.

9. Unless, of course, the person in question, before he became a "vegetable," left testamentary directions about what was to be done with his body just in case he should ever become an incurable vegetable. He may have directed either that he be preserved alive as long as possible or else that he be destroyed, whichever he preferred. There may, of course, be sound reasons of public policy why we should not honor such directions; but if we did promise to give legal effect to such wishes, we would have an example of a man's earlier interest in what is to happen to his body surviving his very competence as a person, in quite the same manner as that in which the express interest of a man now dead may continue to exert a claim on us.

10. As quoted by Salmond, *Jurisprudence,* p. 303. Simply as a matter of policy the potentiality of some future interests may be so remote as to make them seem unworthy of present support. A testator may leave property to his unborn child, for example, but not to his unborn grandchildren. To say of the potential person currently in his mother's womb that he owns property now is to say that certain property must be held for him until he is "real" or "mature" enough to possess it. "Yet the law is careful lest property should be too long withdrawn in this way from the uses of living men in favor of generations

yet to come; and various restrictive rules have been established to this end. No testator could now direct his fortune to be accumulated for a hundred years and then distributed among his descendants"—Salmond, ibid.

11. *New York Times,* (June 17, 1966), p. 1.

12. In an essay entitled "Is There a Right to Be Born?" in *Understanding Moral Philosophy,* ed. James Rachels (Belmont, Calif.: Wadsworth, 1976), I defend a negative answer to the question posed, but I allow that under very special conditions, there can be a "right *not* to be born." See also *The Problem of Abortion* (Belmont, Calif.: Wadsworth, 1973), pp. 7–8, and 161–179.

Ruth Macklin

Can Future Generations Correctly Be Said to Have Rights?

Questions about the rights of future generations arise in a variety of contemporary settings. They have been invoked by legislators, philosophers, health policy makers, proponents of environmental protection, and generally concerned citizens. The things to which future generations are often said to have rights include: clean air and water; the beauty, integrity, and the very existence of the natural landscape; a fair share of the earth's diminishing energy resources; freedom from the unabated spread of genetically transmitted diseases. The present discussion is sufficiently general to cover this rather wide range of goods. My arguments do not rest on the details or circumstances of particular cases, but are directed, instead, to some basic features of the concept of rights.

A great deal of emphasis has recently been placed on the topic of rights in social, political, medical, and other contexts. Rights claims of individual persons or groups of persons are easily generated with too little attention paid to their origin or justification. In thinking about the rights of future generations, we should bear in mind that not all of our obligations, or the things we ought to do, can be derived from the rights of some person or group of persons.

The question of whether future generations can correctly be said to have rights must, I think, be answered in the negative. Nevertheless, it does not follow from this that the present generation ought not to take steps or engage in actions with an eye to, or for the sake of, future generations. The chief argument in support of the position that future generations cannot correctly be said to have rights rests on the premise that the ascription of rights is properly to be made to actual persons—not possible persons.[1] Since future generations can only be viewed as consisting of possible people, from any vantage point at which the description "future generations" is applicable, it would follow from

A revision of a symposium paper read at the Eastern Division meeting of the American Philosophical Association, December 28, 1973. This paper has not been previously published.

151

the aforementioned premise that rights cannot properly be ascribed to future generations. I shall attempt to offer some reasons in support of the premise, and then go on to argue that the present generation (consisting of actual people) ought to act in the present with an eye to the future, in the belief that there will, in the future, *be* actual people.

What reasons might be given for holding that rights are properly to be ascribed only to actual persons? First, let me make clear that the account presented here in no way supposes that there may not be any future generations. That is, I do not rest the argument on the possibility that the human race might be eliminated in the present generation (however one individuates generations) by thermonuclear war or accident, universally fatal plague, the "greenhouse effect," or other such catastrophe. Rather, the argument contends that while it is appropriate to ascribe rights to a class of persons, in general, such ascription is inappropriate when the class in question has no identifiable members. Now the class describable as "future generations" does not have any identifiable members — no existing person or persons on whose behalf the specific right can be claimed to exist. Even if we believe that there will be such actual persons in the future, their rights cannot be said to exist until they (the persons) exist. The possible persons comprising the class of future generations are not identifiable in the present by any of the means ordinarily used to identify actual persons.

It is evident that rights are often ascribed to classes of persons, as shown by the legal practice of class action suits — legal proceedings undertaken on behalf of a class of persons who are believed to be wronged in some manner by an individual, a corporation, or the government. But the class of persons involved in such a suit is comprised of identifiable individuals. These are actual persons to whom we can ascribe duties as well as rights. For those who claim that future generations can correctly be said to have rights, it would be well to reflect on whether we can correctly ascribe *duties* to the possible people comprising future generations. For, it would seem, where it is inappropriate to assign duties, it is similarly inappropriate to ascribe rights. If the defender of the rights of future generations were to reply that when these possible persons become actual persons they will have all the duties ordinarily assigned to persons, then his answer is precisely that of ours: When these possible persons become actual persons, they will have all the *rights* ordinarily assigned to persons. It does not make sense to claim that persons who do not now exist have duties *in the present*. I propose that, if this is the case for duties, so should it be for rights. In spite of our inclinations to the contrary, we should not consider that it makes sense to speak of the present rights of persons who do not now exist. The question under discussion is not whether future generations will have rights, for example, the right to clean air and water. Of course they will, just as we do in the present. And future generations of polluters will have duties, too, for example, the duty to refrain from polluting the air and water.

A natural reply to these grounds for denying that future generations have rights is that the concept of duties and the concept of rights are not similar in relevant respects. That is, while it does not appear to make sense to speak of the present duties of future persons, it does make sense to speak of rights that can be assigned (in the present) to possible (future) persons. There is one chief argument in support of this view about the asymmetry between rights and duties. I shall discuss this argument next and try to show that it does not succeed in demonstrating the correctness of ascribing rights to future generations.

This line of argument claims that there are other sorts of cases in which it is appropriate to ascribe rights but inappropriate to assign duties to the same individuals. These sorts of cases include all those individuals who are functionally incapacitated or undeveloped in some way and, hence, to whom it is unreasonable to assign duties: infants, the severely retarded, the insane, the aged, to mention a few. It is clearly not the case that infants can be viewed as having any duties, as W. D. Ross argues,[2] because they are not moral agents (although Ross adds that this case is complicated by the fact that infants are potential moral agents). A good deal of attention has been paid recently to the rights of special groups of persons—the retarded, the mentally ill, dying patients—where there is general agreement that it is wholly inappropriate to assign the usual or even any sorts of duties to such individuals. I think the chief reason these individuals are properly viewed as having rights is that they are all sentient creatures. While sentience seems to be a sufficient condition for ascribing to persons such rights as freedom from harm or injury by other persons, it is not sufficient for assigning duties. So there is an asymmetry between rights and duties: the conditions under which it is appropriate to assign the latter are more extensive (i.e., the possession of a range of human capacities including some appropriate degree of rationality) than the condition for ascribing the former.

How does this asymmetry bear on the question at issue, namely, the correctness of ascribing rights to future generations? The answer is, I think, that it has no bearing at all. Sentience is not only a sufficient condition for ascribing rights to persons; it is also a necessary condition. This condition is not met in the case of possible persons. Individuals who are not actual persons are obviously not sentient creatures and do not, therefore (until they become sentient creatures), possess rights. This constitutes the grounds for holding that rights are properly to be ascribed only to actual persons. The necessary condition of sentience also explains why it is senseless to speak of trees, plants, and insects as having rights.

There is an interesting borderline case that has claimed much recent attention: the rights of the (human) fetus. I propose not to get entangled in the abortion argument here, but it is worth noting that some clarity may be introduced into the current controversy over whether or not the fetus can be said to have rights by focusing on the notion of actual or possible persons. Those who hold that a fetus is a person (whether from the moment of conception or later) are most likely to proclaim the rights of the fetus, that is, freedom from abortion. Those who hold that the fetus is not (yet) a person, are more likely to deny that the human embryo can properly be said to have rights. I think this latter view rests on the premise on which I am basing the argument about future generations — namely, that rights are properly to be ascribed to actual persons, not possible persons. The reason, of course, that the case of the fetus is a borderline case is that a fetus seems to be "closer" to being an actual person than do the possible persons constituting future generations. Proponents of the rights of the fetus might plausibly argue that the fetus acquires rights at the time it becomes sentient. Resolution of this issue will surely not settle the abortion controversy; and this is because, even if it is agreed that a fetus at any stage cannot properly be said to have rights, it does not automatically follow that abortion is morally permissible.

Similarly, even if it is agreed that future generations cannot correctly be said to have rights, it does not follow that there are no moral restrictions whatever on acts in the present that will have foreseeable effects upon the future. Indeed, as I shall argue in the conclusion below, our moral decisions should be made in the light of future consequences, to the best that these can be ascertained, and we ought morally to consider the probable effects on future generations of actions performed in the present.

The fundamental justification for the view that the present generation ought to take steps or engage in actions with an eye to, or for the sake of, future generations is a utilitarian one. If, among a range of alternative actions open to us in the present, some of these are likely to have more undesirable consequences than others, then we ought to engage in those actions that will have the best consequences on the whole. Leaving aside the obvious effects on currently existing persons, it seems clear that allowing increasing amounts of pollutants to be thrown into the air and water is likely to have undesirable consequences for future generations in the form of health hazards, further limitation of available natural resources, increased costs of using those resources, and so on. Thus, even if there were no undesirable consequences *in the present* resulting from allowing pollution to continue unabated, still, when one considers the likelihood that such actions will have consequences for persons who *will* exist, then these consequences must be taken into account in our moral decision making. The justification for claiming that it is morally wrong to engage in actions that are likely to affect future generations adversely must, I think, be utilitarian in nature. The justification need make no mention of rights, but remains, nonetheless, a moral justification for a particular line of action.

If the arguments presented above are sound, they suggest that a deontological conception of morality may be too narrow to encompass all the actions properly subject to moral review. This is not, of course, to argue that considerations of rights and duties are generally inappropriate or that they do not have a central place in the moral arena. It is, rather, to suggest that where considerations of rights and duties are inappropriate — as in their ascription to possible or future persons — it does not follow that the area under consideration is inappropriately viewed as an area of ethical concern and moral decision making. I do not claim that we need to abandon deontological considerations in our moral decision making, or even that utilitarianism is a superior moral theory because it has been shown to be broader in the respects argued here. But if future generations cannot be said to have rights, it does not follow that it is morally permissible to ignore consequences of our actions that are likely to affect future generations for better or for worse. We ought (morally) to take steps or engage in actions with an eye to, or for the sake of, future generations as long as we believe that actual persons will exist in the future.

NOTES

1. The discussion of future generations as "possible persons" owes much to the work of Professor Derek Parfit of Oxford University. I am not following Parfit's arguments here but simply his mode of conceptualizing future generations.

2. Ross's discussion appears in his *The Right and the Good* (London: Oxford University Press, 1930), pp. 48 ff.

Richard T. De George

The Environment, Rights, and Future Generations

The rapid growth of technology has outstripped our moral intuitions, which are consequently unclear and contradictory on many environmental issues. As we try to handle new moral problems we stretch and strain traditional moral concepts and theories. We do not always do so successfully. The difficulties, I believe, become apparent as we attempt to deal with the moral dimension of the depletion of nonrenewable resources.

Consider the use of oil, presently our chief source of energy. The supply of oil is limited. Prudence demands that we not waste it. But who has a right to the oil or to its use? From one point of view the owners of the oil have a right to it. And we each have a right to the amount we are able to buy and use. From another point of view everyone has a right to oil, since it is a natural resource which should be used for the good of all. Americans, as we know, use a great deal more oil than most other people in the world. Is it moral of us to do so? Will our use preclude people in other parts of the world from having it available to them when they will need it for uses we presently take for granted? Will some unborn generations not have the oil they will probably need to live as we presently do?

These questions trouble many people. They have a vague sense of moral uneasiness, but their intuitions concerning the proper answers are not clear. They feel that they should not waste oil or fuel or energy. They feel that they should not keep their houses as cool in summer and as warm in winter as they used to. They feel that they should impose these conditions on their children. Yet they are not, simply on moral grounds, ready to give up too much in the way of comfort. Once forced to do so by economics, they will. But they are somewhat uneasy about their own attitude. Is it morally proper that affluent individuals or nations are able to live in greater comfort and will have to make

Reprinted from *Ethics and Problems of the 21st Century*, edited by Kenneth E. Goodpaster and Kenneth M. Sayre (Notre Dame, Ind.: University of Notre Dame Press, 1979), with permission.

fewer sacrifices than the less well-to-do, simply because they have more money?

My intuitions on the issue of energy and oil are in no way privileged. I do not know how much oil or energy I have a right to; nor can I say with any certainty how much those in underdeveloped countries presently have a right to, or how much should be saved for them, or how much should be saved for generations yet to come. Nor do I know clearly how to weigh the claims to oil of the people in underdeveloped countries vis-à-vis the future claims to oil of generations yet unborn. If all presently existing members of the human race used energy at the rate that the average American does, there would obviously be much less left for future generations. Does this mean that others in the world should not use as much oil as Americans; or that Americans should use less, so that those in other countries will be able to use more; or that people in less developed countries should not use more in order that future generations of Americans will be able to use as much as present-day Americans?

Though our intuitions are not very clear on these issues, there is some consensus that present people have moral obligations vis-à-vis future generations. Yet stating the grounds for even these obligations is not an easy task and it is one that I do not think has been adequately accomplished. The attempt to state them in terms of rights has not been fruitful. And the utilitarian or consequentialist approach has fared no better. Lack of clarity about collective responsibility further magnifies the complexity of the problem.

In this paper I shall not be able to solve the question either of the proper use of oil or of the basis of our obligations to future generations. I shall attempt only to test the ability of some moral theories and language to express them adequately. I shall negatively show why some approaches are not fruitful lines to pursue. And positively I shall argue for some considerations which I think are applicable, though by themselves they are not adequate to solve the moral problems at issue.

Talk about rights has proliferated in recent years.[1] Moral feelings and concerns have been put in terms of rights in a great many areas. It does not fit in some of them. Thus for instance some people concerned with the environment have come to speak of the rights of nature, or the rights of trees, or the rights of a landscape.[2] The intent of people who use such language is easy enough to grasp. They are concerned about man's abuse of the environment, his wanton cutting of trees, or his despoiling the countryside. But those who wish to attribute rights to nature or trees or landscapes must come up with some way of interpreting the meaning of rights which makes their assertions plausible. The usual ways of unpacking rights in terms of justifiable moral claims, or in terms of interests, or in terms of freedom do not apply to nature or trees.[3] Yet failure to provide an interpretation which both grounds the purported rights of trees and relates them to the rights of humans, while accounting for the obvious differences between them, leads to confusion and precludes arriving at a satisfactory solution to the moral problems posed.

These attempts are nonetheless instructive. For rights can be ascribed and rights-talk can be used with respect to almost anything,[4] even if the claims involved cannot always be adequately defended. When we restrict our use of rights-talk to human beings, therefore, it should be clear that the question of whether people have rights is not a factual one comparable to the question of whether they have brains, or whether they usually have two arms or two legs. The question of whether future generations have rights is similarly not one simply of fact; and the answer is compounded because there is no consensus and little precedent. Thus simply looking at ordinary language, or simply unpacking the concepts of person or rights, will not yield a definitive answer. Since the question is not a factual one, it is to be solved in part by making a decision. It is possible to say that future generations have rights. But I shall argue that we avoid more problems if we maintain that, properly speaking, future generations do not presently have rights, than if we say they do.

Future generations by definition do not now exist. They cannot now, therefore, be the present bearer or subject of anything, including rights. Hence they cannot be said to have rights in the same sense that presently existing entities can be said to have them. This follows from the briefest analysis of the present tense form of the verb 'to have'. To claim that what does not now exist cannot now have rights in any strong sense does not deny that persons who previously existed had rights when they existed, or that persons who will exist can properly be said to have rights when they do exist, or that classes with at least one presently existing member can correctly be said to have rights now. Nor does it deny that presently existing persons can and sometimes do make rights claims for past or future persons. It emphasizes, however, that in ascribing rights to persons who do not exist it is the existing person who is expressing his interests or concerns.

Those who claim that present existence is not necessary for the proper ascription of present rights sometimes cite the legal treatment of wills as a counterexample. In this instance, they argue, the courts act as if the deceased continued to have rights, despite the fact that he no longer exists. But this is not the only way of construing wills or the actions of courts. If we consider those countries in which inheritance laws were suddenly changed so that all the property of a deceased went to the state rather than to the heirs named in a will, it would be more plausible to argue that the rights of a particular heir were violated rather than the rights of the deceased. Equally plausible construals can, I believe, be made for each of the other standard supposed counterexamples.[5]

Consider next the supposed present rights of some future individual. Before conception potential parents can and should take into account the obligations they will have in connection with caring for the children they might produce. They can and should consider the rights their children will have if they come into being. But since the children do not yet exist, we should properly say they do not now have rights. Among the rights they do not have (since they have none) is the right to come into existence. By not bringing them into existence we do not violate *that* right, and we can obviously prevent their having any other rights. Now if we attempt to speak otherwise, I suggest, we invite confusion. What sense would it make to say that some entity which was not conceived had a right to be conceived? We cannot sensibly or intelligibly answer the question of whose right was infringed when there is no bearer of the right.

A similar difficulty, and therefore a similar reason for not using rights-talk, arises in speaking of the rights of future generations, providing we mean by that term some generation no members of which have presently been conceived and so in no sense presently exist. Such future generations could at least in theory be prevented from coming into existence. If they were never produced it would be odd to say that their rights had been violated. For since they do not now exist they can have no right to exist or to be produced. Now, they have no present rights at all.

Nonetheless possible future entities can be said to have possible future rights. And future generations when they exist have rights at that time. But the temptation to consider all rights as temporally on a par should be resisted. Moreover, the weight which should now be given to the rights claims which future individuals or future generations will have should be proportional to the likelihood that such individuals will exist, and by analogy with the case of parents the obligations should be borne by those individuals (and collectively by those groups) most responsible for bringing the individuals into existence.

Future persons do not, individually or as a class, presently have the right to existing resources. They differ from presently existing persons who in general have the right to the judicious use of the goods necessary for them to continue in existence. And if some of these goods, because of present rational demands, are used up, then it is a mistake to say that future persons or future generations have or will have a right to *those* goods and that we violate their rights by using them up. Future generations or future individuals or groups should correctly be said to have a right only to what is available when they come into existence, and hence when their possible future rights become actual and present.

Many people feel that this is incorrect and that future persons and generations have as much right as presently existing persons to what presently exists, for example, in the way of resources. A few considerations, however, should suffice to show that such a view is mistaken. The first consideration is conceptual. Only once a being exists does *it* have needs or wants or interests. It has a right only to the kind of treatment or to the goods available to it at the time of its conception. It cannot have a reasonable claim to what is not available. Consider this on an individual level. Suppose a couple are so constituted that if they have a child, the child will have some disease, for example, sickle-cell anemia. Suppose the woman conceives. Does the fetus or baby have a right not to have sickle-cell anemia? Before it was conceived there was no entity to have any rights. Once it is conceived, its genetic make-up is such as it is. It makes no sense to speak of *its* having the right not to have the genetic make-up it has, since the alternative is its not being. This does not mean that it does not have the right to treatment, that if genetic engineering is able to remedy its defect it does not have the right to such remedy, and so on. But it does mean that there is no *it* to have rights before conception, and that once conceived it is the way it is. There is therefore no sense in speaking of the antecedent right for it not to be the way it is, though it may have a subsequent right to treatment. Similarly, prehistoric cave men had no right to electric lights or artificial lungs since they were not available in their times, and we have no right to enjoy the sight of extinct animals. To claim a right to what is not available and cannot be made available is to speak vacuously. Some future people, therefore, will have no right to the use of gas, or oil, or coal, if, when they come into existence, such goods no longer exist. If the goods in question are not available, *they* could not be produced with a right to them.

Second, suppose we attempt to speak otherwise. Suppose we assume that all future generations have the same right to oil as we do; and suppose that since it is a nonrenewable resource, it is used up — as it is likely to be — by some future generation. What of the next generation that follows it? Should we say that since that generation cannot be produced without violating its right to oil it has a right not to be produced? Surely not. Or should we say that if it is produced one of its rights is necessarily infringed, and that the right of all succeeding generations will similarly necessarily be infringed? It is possible to speak that way; but to do so is at least confusing and at worst undermines the whole concept of rights by making rights claims vacuous.

The third reason for not speaking of the rights of future generations as if their rights were present rights is that it leads to impossible demands on us. Suppose we consider oil once again. It is a nonrenewable resource and is limited in quantity. How many generations in the future are we to allow to have present claim to it? Obviously if we push the generation into the unlimited future and divide the oil deposits by the number of people, we each end up with the right to a gallon or a quart or a teaspoon or a thimble full. So we must reconstrue the claim to refer to the practical use of oil. But this means that we inevitably preclude some future generation from having oil. And if all future generations have equal claim, then we necessarily violate the rights of some future generations. It is clear, then, that we do not wish to let unending future claims have equal weight with present claims. The alternative, if we do not consistently treat future rights differently from the rights of presently existing persons, is arbitrarily to treat some rights, those of sufficiently distant generations, as less deserving of consideration than the same claims of generations closer to us. What I have been arguing is that our approach turns out to be less arbitrary and more consistent if we refuse to take even the first step in considering future rights as anything other than future, and if we do not confuse them or equate them with the rights of presently existing people.

To ascribe present rights to future generations is to fall into the trap of being improperly motivated to sacrifice the present to the future, on the grounds that there will possibly (or probably) be so innumerably many future generations, each of which has a presently equal right to what is now available, as to dwarf the rights of present people to existing goods. The trap can be avoided by maintaining that present existence is a necessary condition for the possession of a present right. To the extent that rights-talk tends to be nontemporal and future generations are considered to have present rights, such talk tends to confuse rather than clarify our obligations for the future, and the ground for such obligations. For this and similar reasons future generations should not be said to have present rights.

If the argument so far is correct, however, we have not solved a problem, but merely seen how not to approach it if we want a solution. That future generations do not have present rights does not mean that present people, individually and collectively, have no obligations to try to provide certain kinds of environment and to leave open as many possibilities as feasible for those who will probably come after them, consistent with satisfying their own rational needs and wants. How are we to describe this felt moral imperative?

If the language of rights will not do, a theory such as utilitarianism does not fare much better. Consider once again the problem of how much oil we can legitimately use and how much we are morally obliged to save for future generations. Let every person count for one and let us decide on the basis of what produces the greatest good for the greatest number of people. The task is difficult enough in dealing with micro-moral problems, though we have the history of human experience to help us solve with at least a certain amount of assurance many ordinary moral questions. We can be fairly sure that lying in general is wrong, as is murder, and theft, and perjury, and so on.

When we try to carry out the analysis with respect to nonrenewable resources, the question of how many future generations we are to count is one problem. We have already seen the difficulties it leads to. Second, we cannot know how long people will actually need oil. We cannot know when a substitute will be found. We therefore do not know how many generations to count and how many to discount. Third, generations of people lived long before oil was discovered and put to its present uses. As oil becomes less available, if no substitute is found people may have to go back to doing things the way they did before the discovery of oil. Will such a world be morally poorer than ours? On a utilitarian calculation the answer may well be negative. But we can plausibly argue that good is not maximized if we waste our resources, and that more good will probably be done for more people if we stretch out our resources while providing for our own rational needs. The difficulty, of course, consists in specifying our rational and justifiable needs. Utilitarianism does not help us do this, nor does it help us decide between the somewhat greater good (however defined) of presently existing people versus the lesser good of more people in the future when the totals are equal. Therefore this approach, too, does not provide the key for determining the proper use of our nonrenewable resources. . . .

. . . There is no moral imperative that requires each generation to sacrifice so that the next generation may be better off than it is. Parents do not owe their children better lives than they had. They may wish their children to have better lives; but they do not owe it to them. If there is to be a peak followed by a decline in the standard of living, and if such a peak is tied to the use of natural resources, then providing there is no profligate waste, there is no reason why the present rather than a future generation should not enjoy that peak. For no greater good is served by any future group enjoying the peak, since when its turn comes, if enjoying the peak is improper for us, it will be improper for them also.

We do not owe future generations a better life than we enjoy nor do we owe them resources we need for ourselves. When dealing with renewable resources, other things being equal, they should not be used up faster than they can be replaced. When they are needed at a greater rate than they can be replaced, they raise the same problem raised by nonrenewable resources. We should use what we *need,* but we should keep our needs rational, avoid waste, and preserve the environment as best we can. How this is to be translated into the specific allocation of goods and resources is not to be determined a priori or by the fiat of government but by as many members of the society at large who are interested and aware and informed enough to help in the decision-making process. Part of that process must involve clarifying the moral dimensions of the use of resources and developing the moral theory to help us state consistently and evaluate our moral intuitions.

Up until relatively recent times it may have seemed that each generation was better off than the previous one, and that just as each successive generation had received a better lot than its predecessor, it had an obligation to continue the process. But we are now at the stage where our own efforts are frequently counterproductive. Our progress in transportation has led to pollution; our progress in pest control has led to new strains of insects resistant to our chemicals or has resulted in pollution of our food; our expansion of industry has taken its toll in our rivers and in the ocean; and so on. We are now faced with shortages of the type we used to experience only during war times. So we can argue that in some ways we are already over the peak and will all be forced to cut down on certain kinds of consumption. That our children have to bear our fate is no reason for reproach. What would be reprehensible on the individual level is if we live in luxury and allowed our children to exist at a subsistence level. It is appropriate that we help them to live as well as we, where that is possible. But we have no responsibility for helping them live better at great expense to ourselves. Nor does it make much sense to speak in those terms where overlapping generations are concerned.

What I have been maintaining is that we should be careful not to assume the burden of the future on some mistaken notion of the need to sacrifice the present to the future. The past appeal of the call to sacrifice the present to the future depended on the foreseeable future being increasingly better, and each generation both being better off than the previous one and worse off than the following in an unending chain. The realization that the goods of the earth are limited should mitigate somewhat that appeal. The earth will not in the foreseeable future be able to support limitless numbers of human beings at a high standard of living.

There is one last caveat that I should like to add, however. I have been arguing that we do not owe the future more than we have in the way of goods of the earth or in terms of standard of living. This does not mean that we do not owe them the benefit of what we have learned, that we should not preserve and pass on culture, knowledge, moral values — all increased to the extent possible. For standard of living is not the only good in life and quality of life should not be confused with quantity of goods. In fact, if we do soon suffer a decline in our standard of living either voluntarily by freely sacrificing for others or simply because we use up our resources before we find adequate substitutes, then what we should pass on to our children are the qualities of mind and spirit which will help them to cope with what they have, to live as fully as possible with what is available, and to value the quality of life rather than the quantity of goods they have.

My three claims are not a solution to the problems of limited resources or a full analysis of what we owe to future generations. They are a start which needs a fuller theory to ground it and a set of institutions to work within. But they do not constitute a call to selfishness. Enlightened self-interest may well benefit mankind as a whole more than unenlightened self-sacrifice, even if the latter could be sold to large segments of the world's population. For we have come to a point where, if we limit our use and abuse of the environment, it is in our self-interest to do so. The needs of the present and of already existing generations should take precedence over consideration of the needs of those who may exist at some far distant time. Perhaps all we can expect is that each generation look that far ahead.

The moral issues raised by environmental questions are in some ways truly new and test both our moral intuitions and concepts. Not all our moral values and intuitions are inapplicable. But we have much analytic work to do before we can fully and clearly state — much less solve — some of the problems which face us.

NOTES

1. See Rex Martin and James W. Nickel, "A Bibliography on the Nature and Foundations of Rights 1947–1977," *Political Theory* (forthcoming).

2. See, for example, Aldo Leopold, *A Sand Country Almanac and Sketches Here and There* (New York: Oxford University Press, 1949); Christopher Stone, *Should Trees Have Standing?: Toward Legal Rights for Natural Objects* (Los Altos, Calif.: Kaufmann, 1974).

3. H. L. A. Hart, "Are There Any Natural Rights?" *Philosophical Review,* 64 (1955), 175–91, argues that the natural right of men to be free is basic; Joel Feinberg, "Duties, Rights and Claims," *American Philosophical Quarterly,* 3 (1966), 137–44; David Lyons, "The Correlativity of Rights and Duties," *Nous,* 4 (1970), 45–57.

4. H. J. McCloskey, "Rights," *Philosophical Quarterly,* 15 (1965), 115–27, raises the question of whether art objects can have rights. A number of philosophers have recently argued for the rights of animals: Andrew Linzey, *Animal Rights* (London: S.C.M. Press, 1976); Peter Singer, *Animal Liberation* (London: Jonathan Cape, 1976); on the other hand, see Joseph Margolis, "Animals Have No Rights and Are Not Equal to

Humans," *Philosophic Exchange,* 1 (1974), 119–23. See also M. and N. Golding, "Value Issues in Landmark Preservation," in *Ethics and Problems of the 21st Century,* edited by Kenneth E. Goodpaster and Kenneth M. Sayre (Notre Dame, Ind.: University of Notre Dame Press, 1979).

　5. Joel Feinberg, "The Rights of Animals and Unborn Generations," *Philosophy and Environmental Crisis,* ed. William T. Blackstone (Athens: University of Georgia Press, 1974), pp. 43–68, defends the opposite view. [Reprinted in this anthology, pp. 139–50.]

　6. See Peter A. French, ed., *Individual and Collective Responsibility: Massacre at My Lai* (Cambridge, Mass.: Schenkman, 1972); Joel Feinberg, "Collective Responsibility," *Journal of Philosophy,* 45 (1968), 674–87; W. H. Walsh, "Pride, Shame and Responsibility," *The Philosophical Quarterly,* 20 (1970), 1–13; D. E. Cooper, "Collective Responsibility," *Philosophy,* 43 (1968), 258–68.

Galen K. Pletcher

The Rights of Future Generations

In what follows, I shall argue that future generations do have rights and that these can be seen as special cases of rights that every person has. It is undeniable that sometimes the rights of existing people are very little infringed by actions that seem to be very injurious to future generations. For example, it is alleged that the most crucial dangers to be found in the continually proliferating use of the internal combustion engine are dangers to future life, consisting in the depletion of fossil fuels and petro-chemicals and the irrevocable alteration of world climate. It is in cases of this sort that it is especially important to decide if we should, in considering the moral ramifications of our actions, consider also the welfare of those who have not yet been born.

The importance of these cases to moral theory, of course, is that, if future generations have rights to certain things, then it would seem that living people may well have obligations to provide those things. In arguing this way, I am following Richard Brandt, who says that " 'X has a prima facie right to enjoy, have, or be secured in y' means the same as 'it is someone's objective prima facie obligation to secure X in, or in the possession of, or in the enjoyment of y, if X wishes it.' "[1] I will assume that in talking about the rights of future generations we may, by implication, be talking of the obligations of living persons to secure those things to which these future generations are entitled. (Of course, rights of future generations can also entail obligations to persons of generations other than our own, including members of those very future generations.) At the end of this paper, I shall say something about the difficulty of specifying exactly who it is on which such obligations rightly fall. (Note also that I am ignoring any attempts to specify duties to future generations in terms of duties to God to respect His creation.)

One of the sources of uneasiness about the position that future generations have rights is expressed by the following question: How can we, or anyone, be

This paper is a revision of a symposium paper read at the Eastern Division meeting of the American Philosophical Association, December 28, 1973, and has not previously been published.

said to have obligations to people who do not exist? (That is, how can people who do not exist be said to have rights?) I think we can make sense of such talk, because this question suggests a kind of mystery that the case does not have. For example, if I have been camping at a site for several days, it is common to say that I have an obligation to clean up the site — to leave it at least as clean as I found it — for the next person who camps there. We assume, of course, that the person who will use it next does exist somewhere; but it is not necessary to assume this, just as it is not necessary to know who he or she is or when he or she will use the site. We have an obligation that might be called an "obligation-function,"[2] because it is to some as yet unspecified person or persons. There is a preliminary "right-function" in this case, which can be stated: "For any x, if x is a person who wants to camp at this site, then x has a right to a clean campsite." I am strongly inclined to think that our obligation in this case derives from this right; but since I am assuming that rights and obligations are correlative, it is not crucial to decide that question. Consider as another example the obligation I have to brake my car properly when it is parked on an incline. When, on a certain day at a certain time, I do properly brake my car, I doubtless have no particular persons in mind who have the right correspondent to my obligation to brake it. Nevertheless, if I fail to brake my car and it rolls over Smith, then I have done Smith a moral wrong; I have failed to fulfill an obligation I had to him (and to anyone else who came by). (We commonly say, "We have a right to assume that someone will properly brake his car." But that is too weak, because it is a proposition of epistemology. Smith had a right to a state of affairs, not [merely] a right to entertain a certain belief.)

I think that there is a broad area of normative ethical theory that can best be expressed in terms of what I have called "right-functions" or "obligation-functions." Difficulties with the concept of the rights of future generations derive from focusing on such moral obligations as promises, borrowings, and spoken contracts, instead of more general obligations that must be stated with no particular person in mind. If I am correct in thinking this, namely, that there *are* rights of the form "for any x, if x has Q, then x has R" (where Q is a set of circumstances and R is a right), then these right-functions must range over all people at all times, even to those who are not yet born. If, happily, I have discovered a campsite so removed from the beaten track that the next person to discover it is someone who wasn't even alive when I last camped there, it still is true of that lucky person that he has a right to a clean campsite, and I had an obligation to secure to him that state of affairs. My conclusion can thus be stated: If any moral obligations or rights can properly be stated in terms of "obligation-functions" or "right-functions," then these apply also to future generations.

Treating rights of future generations as special cases of right-functions provides a good way of answering questions about exactly what rights belong to future generations. For example, do they have a right to a higher standard of living than we enjoy? It is said that Thomas Edison was able to continue through the many disappointments and setbacks in his attempt to develop a workable light bulb because of his firm belief that it would make the lives of future generations better. Yet surely we did not have a *right* to the light bulb; Mr. Edison's achievements, evaluated from the moral point of view, were supererogatory. Experimentation with attempts to provide the corresponding right-function will show this. In general, and perhaps this should come as no surprise, the rights that belong to future generations will be forms of freedom of action, commonly stated as life, liberty, and the pursuit of happiness. Basically, they are rights that state that everyone is entitled to a world that shall not have been so changed by the actions of others that it offers many impediments to choices and actions that rational people can be expected to want to carry out. Seen in this way, not only do future generations have a right to clean air, they may even have a right to a world without war.

Attention to this question about how people who do not exist can have rights might lead one to propose as parallel to this a situation that is not really parallel: the situation where we say that a person has obligations to his or her unborn children. We might say, for example, that someone planning to be a parent has an obligation not to be knowingly so financially irresponsible that the children, when they arrive, cannot possibly be cared for properly. This case is more nearly what I would call a "moral inconsistency" than it is the violating of a prima facie obligation-function to these children. The difference is that one can rid oneself of a moral inconsistency by giving up one half of the offending pair. If someone decides not to become a parent, then many financial undertakings that would be irresponsible in the face of imminent parenthood will not be any longer irresponsible at all. But if there are obligations to future generations, then we cannot get rid of them in this way. Their being construed as special cases of obligation-functions shows that nothing we can do will discharge these obligations, consistent with morality, other than the fulfilling of them. (It would in this context be either bad faith or a bad joke to suggest that the world is in such a shape that there is no reason to expect that there will *be* future generations.) What I want to say is that the moral inconsistency case is not a case of genuine obligation. A genuine obligation cannot be waived by the person on whom the obligation falls (although it can be waived by the person who has the corresponding right). But in the moral inconsistency case, the person on whom the obligation falls can get out of it by performing some nonmoral action. So the question that I have answered affirmatively is: Can there correctly be said to be *genuine* obligations toward future generations? A discussion of this question is not illuminated by concentrating on the case of parenthood.

There remains the difficulty of deciding on whom such obligation-functions shall fall. This is faced, of course, by any theory that claims that general obligations, whether to future generations or not, are valid. For example, it is faced by any theory that claims that everyone has a right to a basic education.

Suppose that we are inclined to endorse the following as a right-function: Anyone has a right to clean air. We should say, I think, that the people on whom the obligations correspondent to this shall fall are all those people who are in a position at some time to deprive some person or set of persons of clean air. In theory, this is clear, but two problems will loom large (for *any* theory, be it noted, that espouses general obligations). First is the problem of how much weight the rights of future generations are to receive. Are we all obliged to stop driving cars entirely? After all, presently existing people have rights, too, such as the right to leisure activities and the prima facie right to unfettered travel. This difficulty will best be solved, I think, by attending to the second of the major problems with such theories: that of *assessing* the detrimental effect that our actions will have in depriving others (present and future) of their rights. For example, is my continuing to burn leaves really a threat to the children of A.D. 2010? These will be ticklish, but they are, after all, factual questions, and we do seem to have the technical expertise to decide some such questions fairly certainly, and others with at least some degree of probability. As our understanding of the long-range effects (spatial and temporal) of our actions increases, ignorance of the deleterious effects of one's actions will no longer be an acceptable excuse for the morally irresponsible infringing of such "right-functions" as there may be.[3]

NOTES

1. *Ethical Theory* (Englewood Cliffs, N.J.: Prentice-Hall, 1959), p. 439.
2. In speaking of "obligation-functions" and "right-functions," I do not mean to imply that these are somehow less compelling, or less substantial, than obligations and rights *simpliciter*. I mean to emphasize that obligations and rights can be spoken of, in these cases, independently of knowledge of what persons have these obligations or enjoy these rights. That they are otherwise perfectly compelling obligations, and perfectly valid rights, is explicitly assumed.
3. This paper has profited from extensive comments and criticisms by Lawrence C. Becker, Ernest Partridge, F. R. Adams, Jr., Ronald J. Glossop, John A. Barker, and Charles A. Corr. They are not to be blamed for errors that have withstood their efforts.

Annette Baier

The Rights of Past and Future Persons

No one doubts that future generations, once they are present and actual, will have rights, if any of us have rights.[1] What difference is made if we say, not that they *will* have, but that they *do* have rights — *now?* I see two main points of difference — first, that those rights will then give rise to obligations on our part, as well as on their contemporaries' part; and, second, that what they have a right *to* will be different. In addition to whatever political and civil rights they have or will have, they will also each have a right to a fair share of what is then left of the earth's scarce resources. If they *now* have rights, they have rights to a share of what is *now* left of those scarce resources. To believe that they have rights is to believe that *we* must safeguard those rights and that, where the right is to a share, that we must share with them, and that the size of our share is affected by their right to share.

Should we believe that future persons not merely *will* have rights, but that they presently *do* have rights? To decide this I shall first consider whether any conceptual incoherence would result. Having eliminated that threat, I shall turn to the question of what rational or moral grounds there might be for the belief. I shall argue that some of the reasons for recognizing obligations to future persons are closely connected with reasons for recognizing the rights of past persons and that these reasons are good ones. In addition there are the obligations that arise from our responsibility for the very existence of those future persons, through our support of social policies that affect the size and nature of the human population in the future. I shall argue that we have good reason to recognize these obligations to future persons, whether or not we see them as arising out of their rights.

I turn first to the question of what we are committed to in asserting that a person has a certain right. I take it that this is to assert:

This is a revision of a paper originally read in a symposium at the Eastern Meeting of the American Philosophical Association, December 28, 1973. It has not been previously published.

(*a*). That at least one other person has an obligation to the right-holder. This obligation may be to refrain from interfering with some activity of the right-holder or to take some positive steps to secure for the right-holder what he or she has a right to. These steps may be ones that benefit the right-holder or some third party, as would be the case if I have promised a friend to feed his cat. He thereby has a right to my services that are intended to benefit the cat. Following Feinberg's[2] terminology, I shall say that the obligation is *to* the right-holder and *toward* whomever is the intended beneficiary.

(*b*). There is, or there should and could in practice be, socially recognized means for the right-holder, or his or her proxy, to take appropriate action should the obligations referred to in (*a*) be neglected. This action will range from securing belated discharge of the obligation, to securing compensation for its neglect, to the initiation of punitive measures against the delinquent obligated person.

I think that this account covers both legally recognized rights and also moral rights that are more than mere "manifesto" rights,[3] since clause (*b*) requires that effective recognition could be given to such rights. Such effective recognition can of course be given only to a set of nonconflicting rights, and so I assume that to claim anything as a right is to claim that its effective recognition is compatible with the effective recognition of the other rights one claims to exist.[4] To claim a moral right to something not effectively recognized as a right is to claim that it could without contradiction to other justifiably recognized rights *be* given recognition, that only inertia, ignorance, greed or ill-will prevents its recognition.

This account of what it is to have a right differs in another sense from the account that is more commonly given. The point of difference lies in the extension of power to claim the right from the right-holder to his spokesman, vicar, or proxy. This extension is required to make sense of the concept of rights of past or future generations. I think we already accept such an extension in empowering executors to claim the rights of the deceased whose wills they execute. The role of executor is distinct from that of trustee for the heirs. We recognize obligations both *to* and *toward* the legal heirs, and *to* the person who made the will. Where the legal heirs are specified only as the "issue" of certain persons known to the will-maker, we already accept the concept of an obligation, owed by the trustees, to look after the interests of such not-yet-determinate persons.

Can those who protect the rights of future persons be properly regarded as their spokesmen, claimants of their rights in the present, when they, unlike executors of wills, cannot be appointed by the original right-holder? The rights of past persons, claimed by their recognized spokesmen, are person-specific rights to have their legally valid powers exercised, while the rights in the present claimed for future persons will be general human rights. No one needs to be privy to the individual wills of future persons to claim their right to clean air. Already recognized spokesmen for known past persons, claiming their particular rights, need knowledge of them, their deeds, and their wishes, and so are sensibly required to have a special tie to the original right-holder, initiated by him. Spokesmen for future persons, claiming general rights, need no such tie.

If future generations have rights, then we, or some of us in some capacity, have obligations to and presumably also toward them, and their spokesman should be empowered to take action to see to it that we discharge those obligations. I see no conceptual incorrectness in attributing such rights. Admittedly we do not now recognize any person as the proper spokesman, guardian, and rights-claimant for future generations. But we could, and perhaps we should.

The fact that future generations are not *now* living persons is irrelevant to the issue, if, as I have argued, we are willing to speak of the rights of those who are no longer living persons. The fact that we do not and cannot have knowledge of the special characteristics and wishes of future generations is, I have claimed, also irrelevant to the recognition of their rights to basic nonspecial human requirements, such as uncontaminated air. Our dependence on fossil fuels may be, compared with the needs of past generations, quite special, and there may be good reason not to extrapolate that need into the distant future. But there is no reason to think that the need for air will be lessened by technological progress or regress in the future. Our ignorance of precisely *who* future generations will be, and uncertainty of how numerous they will be, may be relevant to the priority of our obligations to them, compared with obligations to the living, should conflicts arise; but it is not relevant to the reality of obligations to future persons, nor to the moral priority of such obligations over our tastes for conspicuous consumption or our demands for luxury and for the freedom to waste or destroy resources.

As lawful heirs of specific past persons, some of us may have a right to what those persons intended us to possess, should there be sufficient moral reason to recognize the disputed right to pass on private property and to inherit it. By contrast, we all inherit a social order, a cultural tradition, air and water, not as private heirs of private will-makers but as members of a continuous community. We benefit from the wise planning, or perhaps the thoughtless but fortunate conservation, of past generations. In so far as such inherited public goods as constitutions, civil liberties, universities, parks, and uncontaminated water come to us by the deliberate intention of past generations, we inherit them not as sole beneficiaries but as persons able to share and pass on such goods to an indefinite run of future generations. It was, presumably, not for this generation in particular that public spirited persons in past generations saved or sacrificed.

Rights and obligations are possessed by persons not in virtue of their unique individuality but in virtue of roles they fill, roles that relate to others. For example, children, *qua* children, have obligations to and rights against parents *qua* parents. My obligations as a teacher are owed to my students, whoever they may be. When I discharge obligations to them, such as ordering textbooks, I do not and need not know who those students will be. As long as I believe that determinate actual persons will fill the role of students, will occupy a position involving a moral tie to me, my obligations are real and not lessened by my ignorance of irrelevant details concerning those role-fillers. As long as we believe there will be persons related to us as we are related to past generations, then any obligations and rights this relation engenders will be real. Whether there will be such persons is something about which we can have well-based beliefs, especially as it is to some degree up to us whether to allow such roles to be filled.

The ontological precariousness of future generations that some see as a reason for not recognizing any rights of theirs is not significantly greater than that of the future states of present persons. In neither case does ignorance of details about the future, or the possible nonexistence in that future of those who would benefit from discharge of obligations in the present, affect the reality of our obligations. To make sacrifices *now* so that others may benefit in the future is always to risk wasting that sacrifice. The moral enterprise is intrinsically a matter of risky investment,[5] if we measure the return solely in terms of benefits reaped by those toward whom obligations are owed. Only if virtue is its own reward is morality ever a safe investment. The only special feature in a moral tie between us and future generations lies in the inferiority of our knowledge about them, not in the inferiority of their ontological status. They are not merely possible persons, they are whichever possible persons will in the future be actual.

So far I have found no conceptual reason for disallowing talk of the rights of future persons. Neither their nonpresence, nor our ignorance of *who* exactly they are, nor our uncertainty concerning how many of them there are, rules out the appropriateness of recognizing rights on their part. The fact that they cannot now claim their rights from us puts them in a position no different from that of past persons with rights in the present — namely, a position of dependency on some representative in this generation, someone empowered to speak for them. Rights typically are *claimed* by their possessors, so if we are to recognize rights of future persons we must empower some persons to make claims for them.

Another thing that can be done with a right is to waive it. Past persons who leave no will waive the right that they had to determine the heirs of their private property. Since nothing could count as a sign that future generations waive their rights against us, then this dimension of the concept of a right will get no purchase with future generations, unless we empower present persons not merely to claim but also to waive rights of future persons. Waiving rights and alienating them by gift or exchange are both voluntary renunciations of what a right puts in the right-holder's secure possession. However, waiving rights, unlike alienating them, does not involve a transfer of the right. Since the rights that are transferred are always special rights, and the rights of future persons that we are considering are general ones, there can be no question of transferring such rights. But might a proxy waive them? Guardians of present persons (children, incompetents) do have the power to waive some rights on behalf of their wards, but the justification for this practice, and any exercise of it, depends upon the availability of special knowledge of what will and will not benefit the right-holder. It is barely conceivable that we or any official we appointed could have such knowledge of the special needs of some future generations. If we were facing the prospect of a nuclear war and foresaw that any immediate successor generations would live in the ruins of civilization as we have known it, we might judge that there was no point in trying to preserve, say, the Bill of Rights for one's successors, although they had a *prima facie* right to inherit it. One might on their behalf waive that right, in extreme conditions, and bury the Constitution, rather than prolong our agony to fight for it. But such scenarios are bizarre, since it is barely conceivable that those who would bequeath to future generations the effects of a nuclear war would care about the rest of their bequest, about the fragments that might be shored against our ruin. The benefits that might be gained for future generations by empowering any of their ancestors to waive some of their rights seem minimal. Still, this is a question not of the conceptual absurdity of waiving a recognized right of future generations but of the practical wisdom of giving another this power.

I conclude that no conceptual error is involved in speaking of the rights of future generations. The concept of a right includes that of the justified power of the right-holder or his spokesman to press for discharge of obligations affecting his particular interests, or to renounce this power. The concept has already shown itself capable of extension to cover the rights of past persons and could as easily accommodate the rights of future generations if we saw good reason thus to extend it.

What might give us such a reason? I have already spoken of our position in relation to past generations whose actions have benefited us, either by planning or by good luck. The conservative way to decide the *moral* question is to ask whether we ourselves claim anything as a matter of right against past generations. Do we feel we had a *right* to be left the relatively uncontaminated water we found available to us, as a generation? Do we feel that the Romans, whose cutting down of forests left barren, eroded hillsides, violated a right of later generations? I think that we do not usually attribute to past generations the obligation to save for us, we do not accept their savings as only our just due, we do not usually condemn past generations where their actions have had bad effects in the present. But the reason for this may be that we are reluctant to attribute obligations where we are uncertain of the ability to meet them. Past generations, unlike ours, were rarely in a position to foresee the long-term effects of their actions, so are rightly not blamed by us for any harm they caused. Where what they did had good consequences for us, we accept these not as our due but as our good fortune. Where past generations deliberately saved or conserved for us, we accept their savings not as something they owed us, even when they may have believed they did owe it, but as something they chose to give us, where the "us" in question includes future generations.

It is possible that we stand to future generations in a relation in which no previous generation has stood to us; so that, although we have no rights against past generations, future generations do have rights against us. This is a possible position one might defend. Our knowledge and our power are significantly different even from that of our grandparents' generation, and might be thought to give rise to new moral relationships and new obligations. Before turning to consider how we might determine what those new obligations are, and how to find for them a common ground with old obligations, I want to look more closely at our relations to past generations and to ask if there is anything they might have done that would have given us a reason to blame them for failing in their obligations to us.

I take as an example of a benefit made possible by the actions of earlier generations my own education at the University of Otago in New Zealand. This university was founded extraordinarily early in the establishment of the colony because of the high priority the Scottish colonists gave to education and to its free availability. The existence of a distinguished university, and of the institutions supporting and financing it, was due to the efforts of people in my great grandparents' generation. Had they not made that effort, or had they or later generations established a university that only the wealthy could attend, I would have had no ground for complaint against them. They did not owe me a university education. But had an intervening generation allowed the university and its supporting institutions to founder, and done so from unwillingness to spend on its upkeep the resources that could be used for personal profit, I and my generation *would* blame those who failed to pass on the public benefits they themselves inherited. One obligation that every generation has toward subsequent generations is to leave "as much and as good" of the public goods previous generations have bequeathed them. This obligation arises as much from a right of past persons to have their good intentions respected as it does from any right of future persons, but I think there *is* a right to have passed on to one those public goods that, but for ill will or irresponsibility, would have been passed on. If I had been deprived of an education because a previous generation had destroyed an already founded university for the sake of its own greater luxury, I would feel that *my* rights, as well as those of the university's founders, had been overridden. It is interesting to note that the rights of past benefactors and their future beneficiaries give rise to one and the same obligation. Indeed, if we consider the motivation of the university's founders, who were heirs to a Scottish tradition of investment in public education, we find that they saw themselves as much as *preservers* as creators, as passing on, in new and difficult conditions, a heritage they had themselves received. As one of their hymns put it:

> They reap not where they laboured,
> We reap where they have sown.
> Our harvest will be garnered
> By ages yet unknown.

The metaphor of seed and harvest is the appropriate one where what is passed on, sown, is the same good as was received or harvested from the earlier sowing by others. The obligation that each generation has, which is owed equally to past and future generations, is the obligation to preserve the seed crop, the obligation to regenerate what they did not themselves generate.

That this obligation can be seen as due, indifferently, to past or future persons shows something of considerable importance about obligations in general and about the moral community. Earlier I said that rights are possessed not in virtue of any unique individuality but in virtue of roles we fill. The crucial role we fill, as moral beings, is as members of a cross-generational community, a community of beings who look before and after, who interpret the past in the light of the present, who see the future as growing out of the past, who see themselves as members of enduring families, nations, cultures, traditions. Perhaps we could even use Kant's language and say that it is because persons are *noumenal* beings that obligations to past persons and to future persons reinforce one another, that every obligation is owed by, to, and toward persons as participants in a continuing process of the generation and regeneration of shared values.

To stress the temporal continuity of the moral community is not to deny that accumulating knowledge and increasing power make a difference to the obligations one has. Earlier I said that the reason we do not morally condemn earlier generations for those actions of theirs whose consequences are bad for us is the reasonable doubt we feel about the extent to which they knew what they were doing. If the overgrazing that turned grasslands into deserts were thought by us to have been a *calculated* policy to increase a past generation's nonrenewed wealth, at our expense, we would condemn them for it. Any obligations we have to generations future to us that find no exact analogue in obligations past persons owed us arise, I believe, both from special features of our known control over the existence and the conditions of life of future generations and from our awareness of what we owe to past generations. We are especially self-conscious members of the cross-generational community, aware both of how much, and how much more than previous generations, we benefit from the investment of earlier generations and of the extent to which we may determine the fate of future generations. Such self-consciousness has its costs in added obligations.

Another sort of obligation we may have to future generations arises out of our failure to discharge other obligations to them. We, unlike earlier generations, are in a position to control population growth and to attempt to gear it to the expected supply of essential resources. Where we are failing to use this ability responsibly, we incur obligations to compensate our victims in a future overcrowded world for the harm we have thereby done them. Special efforts to increase, not merely to conserve, needed food and water resources are the appropriate accompaniment to our neglect of the obligation not to overbreed.

Our special position, relative to previous generations, in the procession of human possessors of knowledge and power, gives us the ability to end the sequence of human generations as well as to be self-conscious and deliberate in our procreative or regenerative activities. It is a consequence of my version of the cross-generational moral community that this power to end the human community's existence could justifiably be exercised only in conditions so extreme that one could sincerely believe that past generations would concur in the judgment that it all should end. I do not think that anyone, past, present, or future, has a right to exist, and certainly no merely possible person has such a right. But we do not need the rights of possible persons to restrain us from bringing about the end of human life, the rights of past persons and the very nature of membership in a moral community rule that out in all except the very direst circumstances. Just as we have no *right* to use up all scarce resources in our generation for our own luxury or whim but, rather, an obligation to renew what we use, to pass on what we received, so we have no right to decree the ending of an enterprise in which we are latecomers. To end it all would not be the communal equivalent of suicide, since it would end not only our endeavors but those invested endeavors of all our predecessors. Only if they could be seen as concurring in the decision not to renew human life, or not to allow it to be renewed, could such a decision be likened to suicide.

I have said almost nothing about the theoretical basis for the obligations and rights I have claimed exist. Indeed, I am not sure that theories are the right sort of thing on which to ground assertions about obligations. In any case I shall not here go into the question of which moral theory would best systematize the sorts of reasons there are for recognizing the rights and obligations I have invoked. Kant's moral theory, if it could be stripped of its overintellectualism, Burke's account of a cross-generational community, if it could be stripped of its contractarian overtones, Hume's account of the virtues recognized by us humans who see ourselves as "plac'd in a kind of middle station betwixt the past and the future" who "imagine our ancestors to be, in a manner, mounted above us, and our posterity to lie below us,"[6] Rawls's idea of social union, of a continuing community in which "the powers of human individuals living at any one time takes the cooperation of many generations (or even societies) over a long period of time,"[7] if this could be used, as he does not use it, to give an account of the right as well as the good, all these give us assistance in articulating the reasons that we should recognize obligations of piety to past persons and responsibility to future ones. I do not think that either utilitarian theories or contractarian theories, or any version of any moral theory I am familiar with, captures the right reasons for the right attitudes to past and future persons. Perhaps we need a new theory, but the "intuitions" it will ground are, I believe, very old ones. I have relied, rather dogmatically, on those intuitions that I think are fairly widely shared, but before attempting to summarize in broad outline the factors relevant to our obligations to future generations I need to make clear a few points about the community in which such obligations arise.

First, it is not a community to which one *chooses* to belong, but one in which one finds oneself. By the time any moral reflections arise, one is already heir to a language and a way of life, and one has already received benefits from those particular older persons who cared for one in one's initial extreme dependency and who initiated one into a way of life. This way of life typically includes conventions to enable one voluntarily to take on obligations as well as to renounce and transfer some rights; but not all obligations are self-imposed, and those that are are arise from institutions, like that of promising, which depend for their preservation on other obligations that are not self-imposed. As Hume said: "We are surely not bound to keep our word because we have given our word to keep it."[8] We may, and usually do, "agree," as Hume put it, or go along with the customs we find in force, including the custom of promising and demanding that promises be kept, since we see the benefits of having such a practice; but any obligations there may be to support existent practices depend not on the prior consent of the obligated but on the value of the practice to all concerned and on their reliance on it.

Reliance creates dependency, and the second point I wish to make is that the relations that form a moral community, and which, once recognized, give rise to obligations, all concern dependency and interdependency. Some of these dependency relations are self-initiated, but the most fundamental ones are not. The dependency of child on parent, for example, is a natural and inevitable one, and the particular form it takes is socially determined but certainly not chosen by the child. Socially contrived dependencies shape, supplement, and balance natural and unavoidable dependencies. Rights and duties attach to roles in a network of interdependent roles, which if it is wisely designed will conserve and increase the common store of goods, and if it is fairly designed will distribute them equitably. Some morally significant and interrelated roles are ones we all occupy in sequence—the dependent child becomes the adult with children in his care, those who care for the dependent elderly themselves become old and in need of care. Similar to these roles in their reference to earlier and later persons, but unlike them in that we do not occupy them in temporal succession, are the roles of inheritor from past generations, executor and determiner of the inheritance of future generations. In filling these roles one both receives and transfers goods, but the transfer involved is of necessity nonreciprocal, only a *virtual* exchange, and the taking begins to occur too early to be by choice.

The third point is that the cross-temporal moral community in which one finds oneself is not restricted to those who share one's own way of life, but extends to all those with whom one stands, directly or indirectly, in dependency or interdependency relations. Although a seventeenth-century Scotsman may have had no ties, social or economic, with Maoris in New Zealand, or even any knowledge of them, he has indirect ties if his descendants have economic and social and political relations with them. Interdependency is transitive, and so relates me to all those with whom either earlier or later participants in my particular way of life have stood in interdependent relationships.[9] Thus the tie linking "those who are living, those who are dead, and those who are yet to be born"[10] is a cross-cultural one and brings it about that (at least) no one human is alien to me.

What facts about our own dependency relations to past and future generations are relevant to deciding what rights and duties those relations should entail? As far as our own duties to past and future generations go, the relevant facts are these: first our relatively privileged material position, compared with that of most members of most previous generations; second, our dependency for this on past generations as well as our own generation's efforts; third, our power to affect the lot of future generations; fourth, our comparatively extensive knowledge of the long-term effects of our policies; and fifth, the fact that when past generations conserved or saved deliberately for the sake of future generations (in creating parks, writing and fighting for constitutions) there is no reason to think that it was for us in particular, but rather that it was done on the assumption that we would pass on the inheritance. To sum up, the chief facts are our indebtedness to the past and our dangerously great ability to affect the future. We, like most of our forebears, are the unconsulted beneficiaries of the sacrifice of past generations, sometimes seen by them as obligatory, often in fact nonobligatory. If we owe something in return, what is it, and what can we do for those who benefited us? The most obvious response is to continue the cooperative scheme they thought worth contributing to, adapting our contributions to our distinctive circumstances. What is distinctive is our increased ability to plan and foresee the future (and to recognize the dangers of overplanning). If we say that all generations have owed it to the moral community as a whole, and to past generations in particular, to try to leave things no worse than they found them, then we too have that obligation. In addition, in as far as past generations, by supererogatory effort, left things *better* than they found them, we owe it to them to pass on such inherited benefits. We must not poison the wells, even such wells as we have deepened.

We, unlike our ancestors, are better able to judge and control what will benefit and harm our descendants, so our obligations are correspondingly more determinate. Does our special position warrant speaking of the rights of future generations and not just of our obligations toward them? I have argued that past generations have rights against us, that we not wantonly waste or destroy what they made possible for us to have, not intending it for us only. It would therefore be appropriate to recognize spokesmen for their rights. Should spokesmen for future generations, as well as for past generations, be empowered to ensure that we discharge our obligations, take our "trusteeship" seriously, and should we see our obligations as arising out of the rights of future generations?

When we speak of obligations as arising out of rights, we do several morally pertinent things. First, we put a certain emphasis on determinate interests that these rights protect and individuate our obligations by reference to these individual interests of persons. Second, we give a certain guarantee of moral priority to the protection of these definite central interests over negotiable goods. Third, we give the person whose interest a right protects a certain power of individual initiative to claim or demand or waive the right.[11] In all three aspects the concept of a right goes along with that of a certain individualist version of respect for persons and involves seeing obligations as arising out of this respect.

I have argued for a convergence of important interests of past and future persons, so that obligations to future persons do not stem from consideration of their interests alone. But their interests are of undeniable importance and merit a high priority, so that the first two dimensions of rights apply here. The third ingredient, respect for the rightholder's initiative in claiming a right, could only be fictionally present in the case of future generations, if we recognized a spokesman for them. I see no reason in principle why we should not speak of rights of future generations as well as of our obligations to them, but on the other hand I see nothing very important to be gained by doing so. As long as we recognize our obligations to consider the good of the continuing human community, it matters little whether we speak of the rights of future persons. Whether an official agency to execute our collective obligations were seen as a guardian of the interests of future persons or as a spokesman for their rights would make little difference to the responsibility of such an agency. To speak of their rights would be to commit ourselves to the priority of whatever rights we recognized over our own lesser interests. Until we are clear exactly what priority we are willing to give to the interests of future persons, and to which of their interests we will give this priority, it would be less misleading not to use the language of rights. We should first recognize that we have obligations, then devote ourselves to clarifying the precise content of these. If when that is done we find that we do believe we should give priority to certain definite individuated rights of future persons, we can then recognize and itemize such rights.

I have not detailed the content of our obligations to future persons, but have addressed myself only to the general question of whether there are any. I shall end by repeating the features of our own relationship with future persons that I have claimed to be relevant to these obligations. Future persons stand to us in several morally pertinent roles that give rise to obligations on our part:

1. As those who, like us, depend upon naturally self-renewing resources like air, soil, and water, which none of us produced, they are owed the use of these resources in an unpoisoned state.
2. As intended heirs, with us, of the public goods past generations created, often at great cost and sacrifice, they are owed their share in these goods.
3. As those whose existence we could have prevented, but which we owe it to past generations not to prevent wantonly or for our own increased luxury, they have a right to a tolerable and so to a not-too-crowded existence. Our duty to the past is to ensure that, short of catastrophe, there be future persons. Our duty to those persons is to ensure that there not be too many of them.
4. As victims of our probable failure to meet the last mentioned obligation, they are owed some compensation from us. This means, for example, that we as a society should be working on methods to increase food supplies beyond those that would be needed should our justifiable population policies succeed.

I have claimed that there is no conceptual counter-reason, and that there is good moral reason, to recognize obligations to future generations, to recognize that either they, or past generations, or both, have a moral right to our discharge of such obligations. I agree with Golding that "if obligation to the past is a superstition, so is obligation to the future,"[12] and I have tried to suggest that, if both these are superstitions, then all obligation is superstition.

NOTES

1. I do not take it for granted that any of us do in any morally significant sense have rights. We do of course have legal rights, but to see them as backed by moral rights is to commit oneself to a particular version of the moral enterprise that may not be the best version. As Hegel and Marx pointed out, the language of rights commits us to questionable assumptions concerning the relation of the individual to the community, and, as Utilitarians have also pointed out, it also commits us more than may be realistic or wise to fixing the details of our moral priorities in advance of relevant knowledge that only history can provide.

2. J. Feinberg, "Duties, Rights and Claims," *American Philosophical Quarterly,* vol. 5, no. 2 (April 1966).

3. J. Feinberg, *Social Philosophy* (Englewood Cliffs, N.J.: Prentice-Hall, 1973), p. 67. The term 'manifesto rights' is from Joel Feinberg, who writes, "[I am] willing to speak of a special 'manifesto sense' of 'right,' in which a right need not be correlated with another's duty. Natural needs are real claims, if only upon hypothetical future beings not yet in existence. I accept the moral principle that to have an unfulfilled need is to have a kind of claim against the world, even if against no one in particular. . . . Such claims, based on need alone, are 'permanent possibilities of rights,' the natural seed from which rights grow." (p. 67)

4. I assume that while it makes sense to speak of *prima facie* and possibly conflicting obligations, statements about rights gave final moral decisions, so there are no *prima facie* or conflicting rights.

5. I have discussed this in "Secular Faith," *Canadian Journal of Philosophy* (March 1979).

6. David Hume, *Treatise of Human Nature,* ed., Selby Bigge (Oxford University Press, 1968) p. 437.

7. John Rawls, *A Theory of Justice,* p. 525. Rawls uses this idea of a cross-temporal social union to explicate the concept of the good, but in his account of justice he restricts the relevant moral community, those who make an agreement with one another, to contemporaries who do not know their common temporal position.

8. David Hume, *Enquiry Concerning the Principles of Morals,* ed., Selby Bigge (Oxford: Clarendon Press, 1935), p. 306.

9. This transitivity of dependency and interdependency does not imply any strong cultural continuity; but I do assume that, where the dependency is recognized and so is obligation-engendering, there is sufficient common culture for some sort of understanding of intentions to be possible. Even if, as those like Michael Foucault believe, there is radical discontinuity in human culture, so that we are deluded if we think we can understand what Plato or Hume meant, it is nevertheless a significant fact that we try to understand them and that we get insight from those attempts. Indeed, part of the

intention of any writer, artist, or producer of other meaningful human works, may be to provide something that can be reinterpreted. We do not need to see the heritage of the past to be fixed in form in order to value it, nor see future persons as strict constructionists, finding only our intentions in our works, in order to work for them.

10. Edmund Burke, *Reflections on the Revolution in France* (London: Macmillan, 1910), pp. 93–94.

11. H. L. A. Hart stresses this element in the concept of a right in "Are There Any Natural Rights?", *Philosophical Review,* vol. 64 (1955), and in "Bentham on Legal Powers" in *Oxford Essays in Jurisprudence.* Second Series, ed., A. W. B. Simpson (Oxford: Clarendon Press, 1973).

12. M. P. Golding, "Obligations to Future Generations," *Monist* (January 1972), p. 91. [Reprinted in this anthology, pp. 61–72.]

PART FOUR

Can We, and Should We, *Care* About Future Generations?

Part 4. Can We, and Should We, *Care* About Future Generations?

Introduction

The papers in the foregoing sections of this anthology have explored the nature and the moral stringency of the duty to posterity. Next we shift our attention to moral psychology as we ask: "Are human beings *capable* of caring about the effects of their acts and policies upon the welfare of future generations?" This question may be even more basic than the moral issues raised earlier; for, if members of the current generation are psychologically incapable of caring and acting in behalf of remote posterity, they may have no moral responsibility to do so. This conclusion follows from the fundamental rule of metaethics, "*Ought* implies *can*." It must be noted, however, that the rule does *not* state that *ought* implies *must*." In other words, for an act to be morally significant it is necessary (though not sufficient) that the agent be capable of the act or else have an operative commitment to the rule that commands the act. The *capacity* to act must not, however, be a result of coercion or be otherwise inevitable, since the element of free choice is essential to the moral significance of the act.

Are human beings psychologically equipped to care for the future, and to care enough to make deliberate sacrifices in behalf of future persons? In his sensitive exploration of this question, Robert Heilbroner points out that "care" has several dimensions. Following David Hume and Adam Smith, Heilbroner points out that on the level of casual, unreflective, even "primitive" mood and impulse, we care more about personal itches and pangs than we do about the welfare of all humanity. But this is not the level at which moral reflection and decision-making takes place. At this "higher level" of abstraction, reflection, and ideal commitment, we might find adequate moral enthusiasm and motivation for significant effort and sacrifice in behalf of future persons. We *might,* but *will* we? In a brief space, Heilbroner has clearly and eloquently posed the question and left it open. That is quite enough for his purpose and ours.

In his essay, Heilbroner writes: "No argument based on reason will lead me to care for posterity or to lift a finger on its behalf." The point is reiterated throughout his paper and repeated in Garrett Hardin's piece in this section.

The reader might ask: Upon what conception of "rationality" is this assertion based? Is it based upon the calculation of that strange abstraction "economic man"? Is this a conception of "rationality" that many contemporary philosophers and psychologists would adopt? In this anthology, Passmore, Hartshorne, Rolston, and Partridge express and defend differing conceptions of moral "rationality." (See also the moral writings of Michael Scriven, Kurt Baier, and John Rawls.)

The next two papers in this section propose sharply contrasting answers to the question, suggested by Heilbroner, of whether human beings, by and large, have the capacity, and thus the duty, to care for the future. Thomas Thompson is convinced that mankind is not capable of such concern and is thus absolved of the responsibility of caring for and acting in behalf of "future others." Ernest Partridge takes the opposite view, arguing that human beings are not only capable of such "self-transcending concern," but that such concern is a fundamental component of a healthy personality. In fact, he further argues, a life without self-transcending concern is impoverished and pitiable.

In the final essay of this section, Garrett Hardin examines the question of care and provision for the future in terms of economic and political considerations. "Purely economic" cost-benefit calculations, he points out, indicate that the future should be "discounted," that is, that future benefits should "count less" than present benefits. (The policy of "discounting the future," which seems virtually axiomatic to most economists, is widely disputed by moral philosophers—particularly by Bayles and the Routleys in the final section of this anthology.[1]) Hardin then suggests that operative and effective concern for the future is directly proportional to the availability of surplus wealth and material comfort. It follows, then, that poor "developing" countries are not likely to manifest responsibility toward the future unless these countries are governed by secure and affluent elites with the political power to enforce provision for the future. In the second section of Hardin's paper, the obligation to care for the needs of those presently impoverished is balanced with the obligation to forestall even worse emergencies in the future. In the face of such compelling moral dilemmas, Hardin pleads for an ecological approach. This means, first, that when an aid policy is proposed, the well-intentioned government or agency should ask "and *then* what?" Second, the policy-maker must take a "situationist" or "contextualist" approach; that is to say, he must remember that "the morality of an act is a function of the state of the system at the time the act is performed." Finally, an aid policy must, above all, protect the "carrying capacity" of the land, which must sustain present and future generations. This latter part of Hardin's contribution, which briefly summarizes some of his recent and controversial pronouncements concerning "lifeboat ethics," serves as a "bridge" to the final section of the anthology, the first essay of which (by Michael Bayles) is directly responsive to Hardin's proposals.

NOTE

1. The forthcoming anthology by Peter Brown and Douglas MacLean, *Energy Policy and Future Generations* (for the Center for Philosophy and Public Policy, University of Maryland), to be published by Rowan and Littlefield (Tottowa, N.J.), examines this issue of "discounting the future" with care and thoroughness. The advanced drafts and working papers from this study group that I have seen (by Rolf Sartorius, Derek Parfit, and Douglas MacLean) contain superb discussions of the concept of "discounting."

Robert L. Heilbroner

What Has Posterity Ever Done for Me?

Will mankind survive? Who knows? The question I want to put is more searching: Who cares? It is clear that most of us today do not care—or at least do not care enough. How many of us would be willing to give up some minor convenience—say, the use of aerosols—in the hope that this might extend the life of man on earth by a hundred years? Suppose we also knew with a high degree of certainty that humankind could not survive a thousand years unless we gave up our wasteful diet of meat, abandoned all pleasure driving, cut back on every use of energy that was not essential to the maintenance of a bare minimum. Would we care enough for posterity to pay the price of its survival?

I doubt it. A thousand years is unimaginably distant. Even a century far exceeds our powers of empathetic imagination. By the year 2075, I shall probably have been dead for three quarters of a century. My children will also likely be dead, and my grandchildren, if I have any, will be in their dotage. What does it matter to me, then, what life will be like in 2075, much less 3075? Why should I lift a finger to affect events that will have no more meaning for me seventy-five years after my death than those that happened seventy-five years before I was born?

There is no rational answer to that terrible question. No argument based on reason will lead me to care for posterity or to lift a finger in its behalf. Indeed, by every rational consideration, precisely the opposite answer is thrust upon us with irresistible force. As a Distinguished Professor of political economy at the University of London has written in the current winter issue of *Business and Society Review:*

> Suppose that, as a result of using up all the world's resources, human life did come to an end. So what? What is so desirable about an indefinite continuation of the human species, religious convictions apart? It may well be that nearly everybody

Reprinted from the *New York Times Magazine,* January 19, 1975. Copyright 1975 by the New York Times Company. Reprinted with permission.

191

who is already here on earth would be reluctant to die, and that everybody has an instinctive fear of death. But one must not confuse this with the notion that, in any meaningful sense, generations who are yet unborn can be said to be better off if they are born than if they are not.

Thus speaks the voice of rationality. It is echoed in the book *The Economic Growth Controversy* by a Distinguished Younger Economist from the Massachusetts Institute of Technology:

> . . . Geological time [has been] made comprehensible to our finite human minds by the statement that the 4.5 billion years of the earth's history [are] equivalent to once around the world in an SST. . . . Man got on eight miles before the end, and industrial man got on six feet before the end. . . . Today we are having a debate about the extent to which man ought to maximize the length of time that he is on the airplane.
>
> According to what the scientists now think, the sun is gradually expanding and 12 billion years from now the earth will be swallowed up by the sun. This means that our airplane has time to go round three more times. Do we want man to be on it for all three times around the world? Are we interested in man being on for another eight miles? Are we interested in man being on for another six feet? Or are we only interested in man for a fraction of a millimeter—our lifetimes?
>
> That led me to think: Do I care what happens a thousand years from now? . . . Do I care when man gets off the airplane? I think I basically [have come] to the conclusion that I don't care whether man is on the airplane for another eight feet, or if man is on the airplane another three times around the world.

Is it an outrageous position? I must confess it outrages me. But this is not because the economists' arguments are "wrong"—indeed, within their rational framework they are indisputably right. It is because their position reveals the limitations—worse, the suicidal dangers—of what we call "rational argument" when we confront questions that can only be decided by an appeal to an entirely different faculty from that of cool reason. More than that, I suspect that if there is cause to fear for man's survival it is because the calculus of logic and reason will be applied to problems where they have as little validity, even as little bearing, as the calculus of feeling or sentiment applied to the solution of a problem in Euclidean geometry.

If reason cannot give us a compelling argument to care for posterity—and to care desperately and totally—what can? For an answer, I turn to another distinguished economist whose fame originated in his profound examination of moral conduct. In 1759, Adam Smith published "The Theory of Moral Sentiments," in which he posed a question very much like ours, but to which he gave an answer very different from that of his latter-day descendants.

Suppose, asked Smith, that "a man of humanity" in Europe were to learn of a fearful earthquake in China—an earthquake that swallowed up its millions of inhabitants. How would that man react? He would, Smith mused, "make many melancholy reflections upon the precariousness of human life, and the vanity of all the labors of man, which could thus be annihilated in a moment. He would, too, perhaps, if he was a man of speculation, enter into many reasonings concerning the effects which this disaster might produce upon the commerce of Europe, and the trade and business of the world in general." Yet, when this fine philosophizing was over, would our "man of humanity" care much about the catastrophe in distant China? He would not. As Smith tells us, he would "pursue his business or his pleasure, take his repose or his diversion, with the same ease and tranquillity as if nothing had happened."

But now suppose, Smith says, that our man were told he was to lose his little finger on the morrow. A very different reaction would attend the contemplation of this "frivolous disaster." Our man of humanity would be reduced to a tormented state, tossing all night with fear and dread—whereas "provided he never saw them, he will snore with the most profound security over the ruin of a hundred millions of his brethren."

Next, Smith puts the critical question: Since the hurt to his finger bulks so large and the catastrophe in China so small, does this mean that a man of humanity, given the choice, would prefer the extinction of a hundred million Chinese in order to save his little finger? Smith is unequivocal in his answer. "Human nature startles at the thought," he cries, "and the world in its greatest depravity and corruption never produced such a villain as would be capable of entertaining it."

But what stays our hand? Since we are all such creatures of self-interest (and is not Smith the very patron saint of the motive of self-interest?), what moves us to give precedence to the rights of humanity over those of our own immediate well-being? The answer, says Smith, is the presence within us all of a "man within the beast," an inner creature of conscience whose insistent voice brooks no disobedience: "It is the love of what is honorable and noble, of the grandeur and dignity, and superiority of our own characters."

It does not matter whether Smith's eighteenth-century view of human nature in general or morality in particular appeals to the modern temper. What matters is that he has put the question that tests us to the quick. For it is one thing to appraise matters of life and death by the principles of rational self-interest and quite another *to take responsibility for our choice.* I cannot imagine the Distinguished Professor from the University of London personally consigning humanity to oblivion with the same equanimity with which he writes off its demise. I am certain that if the Distinguished Younger Economist from M.I.T. were made responsible for determining the precise length of stay of humanity on the SST, he would agonize over the problem and end up by exacting every last possible inch for mankind's journey.

Of course, there are moral dilemmas to be faced even if one takes one's stand on the "survivalist" principle. Mankind cannot expect to continue on earth indefinitely if we do not curb population growth, thereby consigning billions or tens of billions to the oblivion of nonbirth. Yet, in this case, we sacrifice some portion of life-to-come in order that life itself may be preserved. This essential commitment to life's continuance gives us the moral authority to take measures, perhaps very harsh measures, whose justification cannot be found in the precepts of rationality, but must be sought in the unbearable anguish we feel if we imagine ourselves as the executioners of mankind.

This anguish may well be those "religious convictions," to use the phrase our London economist so casually tosses away. Perhaps to our secular cast of mind, the anguish can be more easily accepted as the furious power of the bio-genetic force we see expressed in every living organism. Whatever its source, when we ask if mankind "should" survive, it is only here that we can find a rationale that gives us the affirmation we seek.

This is not to say we will discover a religious affirmation naturally welling up within us as we career toward Armageddon. We know very little about how to convince men by recourse to reason and nothing about how to convert them to religion. A hundred faiths contend for believers today, a few perhaps capable of generating that sense of caring for human salvation on earth. But, in truth, we do not know if "religion" will win out. An appreciation of the magnitude of the sacrifices required to perpetuate life may well tempt us to opt for "rationality"—to enjoy life while it is still to be enjoyed on relatively easy terms, to write mankind a shorter ticket on the SST so that some of us may enjoy the next millimeter of the trip in first-class seats.

Yet I am hopeful that in the end a survivalist ethic will come to the fore—not from the reading of a few books or the passing twinge of a pious lecture, but from an experience that will bring home to us, as Adam Smith brought home to his "man of humanity," the personal responsibility that defies all the homicidal promptings of reasonable calculation. Moreover, I believe that the coming generations, in their encounters with famine, war, and the threatened life-carrying capacity of the globe, may be given just such an experience. It is a glimpse into the void of a universe without man. I must rest my ultimate faith on the discovery by these future generations, as the ax of the executioner passes into their hands, of the transcendent importance of posterity for them.

Thomas H. Thompson

Are We Obligated to Future Others?

Only a short time has elapsed since the appearance of *The Limits to Growth* and Robert Heilbroner's *An Inquiry Into the Human Prospect.* But the time has been sufficient for the message of disaster to percolate through to almost everyone. Many experts are thoroughly convinced that present trends extrapolated into the future will produce deterioration and ultimately threaten us with cataclysm. Eventually we and our descendants will have brought on the demise of civilization.

You've heard the details before. The population of the world is roughly four billion and doubling about every thirty-five years. In the first decade of the next century there will be eight billions. An already shaky food supply will be by then chaotically short. Famine will be endemic. Nuclear accident or nuclear gangsterism will have happened or become more probable. Resource exhaustion will restrict our indulgent way of life even as we sicken more readily from industrial effluents.

The cumulative effect of these familiar factors is what produces the scenarios of doom. Each factor is subject to argument and revision. But I shall not — here and now — argue any one of them. Nor will I attack the general accuracy of the projection.

Instead, I begin by *postulating* the general accuracy of the doom-model as a plausible image of the relatively near future of global mankind. I will simply assume that the world as it is now — extrapolated into the fairly near future — will yield an environment no longer supportive of the style of life in our region of the world. Human civilization lives under a sentence of death.

Students of the future invariably have two related messages to communicate. The sky is falling is the loudest part of their prophecy — so loud that the second message tends to be obliterated. But every futurist jeremiad is also

Reprinted from *Alternative Futures,* 1:1 (Spring 1978), with permission of the publisher and author.

tinctured with hope. The hope is slender and difficult to argue because the statistical projections of disaster lend themselves to easier exposition and have an aura of hard fact about them.

Yet all the futurists I know are more like preachers than pure scientists. They resemble biblical prophets in that they tell us their scary tales of the future in order to bring us back to virtue and sense. Or they are like evangelical ministers in that they paint a picture of future fire and brimstone only in order to hold forth a gospel of salvation. To share an analogy with fiction, the futurists are Dickensian. They invoke the Ghost of Christmas Future — the cloaked figure who escorted old Scrooge through the graveyard right up to his own tombstone — in order to frighten us into a change of heart. The prophet of doom is also very close to Dante. When Dante sat down to chart the progress of the human soul through Hell, he did not have in mind that journey only. It was his conviction that in order to understand the puzzling justice of a loving God, one had to begin with Hell in order to be spiritually prepared for the journey of hope. Similarly, the futurists' goal is only incidentally a horror story. Their second emphasis is on what must be done to realize the hope of salvation on this earth.

The end-product of these new prophecies should be a new man — a man of changed understanding, a man who, when he understands, will change his heart as well. When that happens, the scary future will be tamed and an alternative future will have a chance for realization.

It is not difficult to describe the new man in whom the hope of the future resides:

He has a longer and broader horizon of time and space than we.

He has a range of sympathetic fellow-feeling that soars beyond himself, his kinfolk, friends, and fellow-nationals, and embraces both present and future humanity.

Having acquired the knowledge needed, he has also found the will to assign the survival of civilization a higher priority than his own and his friends' temporary well-being.

He is more patient than we, preferring long-range rational solutions to global problems while suspending irrational demands for short-range local fixes.

He is all these things, finally, because he loves the world and its people for themselves alone — for him the world and its humanity is not merely the first act of a drama whose climax lies outside the human context.

I have not copied my new man directly from any particular futurist. But I claim that from Meadows to Heilbroner, from Ehrlich to Boulding, from Falk to Lester Brown, this image of a new man is what gives their work its moral center.

The futurist moralist has an uphill fight on his hands. Those who hear the message tend to hear only its first part. They assume that the futurist is *predicting* the collapse of civilization. They are deaf to the message of hope that is its implicit peroration. Of course the deafness is understandable.

I myself listen and try to understand, but then — I forget it. The demands of the present and the nearest future are so insistent that my time and energy-budgeting simply cannot accommodate continual awareness of horror stories.

I am immensely impressed with the tendency to forgetfulness in myself. I am even more impressed with its apparent effect on the behavior of others. Speaking of death, Camus remarked: "Everyone acts as if nobody knew." That is my point precisely. Even futurist prophets present a very questionable role model for the kind of behavior they hope will rapidly emerge in others. Their life-styles, with few exceptions, are indistinguishable from those they condemn as the architects of the coming doom. It is understandable, even if not forgivable then, that the gap is huge between intellectual understanding of future troubles and the will to change oneself to avert those troubles.

The fact is that the future has a heavy discount-rate applied to it. It follows an informal inverse-square law. Next week may be about 75% real. Next year slumps to 20% reality. The year 2000 is lucky if its discount-rate is not 100%. My guess is that the reason for the discount-rate on the future lies in our genetic programming. Evolution has installed in each of us an apprehension of just that degree of future time awareness that serves the blind purpose of animals unconsciously attempting to leave more offspring behind than others. Our time sense is adjusted to the past of the whole phylum of vertebrates, plus some mammalian quirks. Far future awareness is not a trait selected with very great frequency, hence our abiding concentration on the present. A few years of rational exhortation understandably has had little effect on the average time-future sense of the human population, even allowing for a few mutants — the futurists themselves. The schizoid separation of near future considerations from serious long-run implications is a short-run benefit to competing species. It is, just as surely, a long-range threat to the survival of the human species.

Let me cite one specific example among many. We know very well that the forests are vulnerable resources that may not be replaceable. That knowledge has not stopped clear-cutting of timber — yet. I would argue that clear-cutting is directly analogous to overgrazing of pastures by ruminants. Can you argue that men are more foresighted than sheep?

Serious futurists are also plagued by another form of deafness to their message of hope. Certain students of the history of British foreign policy have identified what I have in mind as "muddle-through." What does this optimism amount to? It says: We need not radically change ourselves in order to change the future enough to get by.

The most virulent form of this false optimism is the secular faith in the "technological fix." This faith is easier to illustrate than to define. Sobersided utilities board members admit that natural gas will be gone in a few years. So nuclear power plants will more than make up the deficit. But, wait — those nuclear plants may be more dangerous than at first anticipated. No matter. Breeder reactors will supply a "fix" for the unanticipated side effects of the previous "fix." If population expansion threatens to leave only standing room for new arrivals on earth, we will create colonies in space to absorb the over-plus. With what unanticipated consequences? And so on.

It cannot be demonstrated that technological fixes will not keep us going for a long time. But the probabilities (given the overdetermination inherent in the long list of factors that can kill us) suggest that future technological fixes will have as many toxic side effects as those now in evidence. We will succeed in worsening our long-run chances of survival even as we pursue temporary remedies for our previous thoughtlessness.

I see two basic reasons for the ultimate failure of technological fixes:

1. *The human spirit, as it relentlessly pursues manipulative remedies, will one day find its inventiveness stopped by the finite limits of the world. What the Greeks called pride will find its sorrow even if Zeus and Apollo have departed.*

2. *The technological environment—which has almost wholly replaced the natural environment—grows increasingly more complicated, more inter-dependent, and more fragile. We cannot do without it and we must ex-pand it. As we do so, we come ever closer to the chaotic dispersal of the whole teetering system. A few well-aimed blows can wreck the techno-logical house of cards.*

Permit me a gross illustration. The Pentagon cannot give me any assurance whatever that the tax monies devoted to military expenditures can any longer buy increased security of person. This is true no matter how many techno-logical marvels are brought on line by the Army, Navy, and Air Force. Public assurances to the contrary I regard as outright lies—lies known to be lies by the respected public figures who purvey them. The world has run out of "security" based on hardware.

As we continue to manipulate the limited group of variables addressed by practical technology, the area of total ignorance of unanticipated negative-feedbacks will probably be enough, by itself, to destroy civilization. "Muddle through" is nonetheless the basis for a great deal of the deafness of the general population to warnings about the truly long-range future. Allied with forget-fulness, it is a formidable enemy to the futurists' message of hope in a new man.

The roadblocks in the way of realization of the new man as preached by salvationist futurism are as nothing in the face of one more problem I now wish to discuss. The problem is absolutely crucial to the enterprise of change. I think it is insoluble. If it is, we will probably be extinguished as a species. At the very least, the ideals of individualism and wide-ranging personal freedom they entail will be destined to disappear for good.

My two theses are these:

1. *The ideological underpinnings of liberal democracy are done for; con-viction in their truth has eroded to almost nothing. The present world*

contains only remnants and residues of these underpinnings. Yet there will not be a real future unless a faith is found that carries us beyond self to the worth of the global person, including the total humanity of the future.

2. *The superstructure of traditional religious beliefs is also done for; conviction in its truth has eroded to almost nothing.*

Democratic liberalism arose from the dream of John Locke and became the dominant ideology of the eighteenth century Enlightenment which in its turn became the political faith of American society. Locke's dream of the future said this: There is a natural moral law that sets forth human rights and human obligations simultaneously. While this law is not written, every individual has access to it through reason. The law dwells inwardly in every individual man in the form of rational conscience. Thus we all know our rights and obligations to others with fair certainty. True, in a state of natural anarchy, emotion may sometimes becloud reason — particularly when personal interests are at stake. But on the whole, everyone knows how to govern himself while allowing others the same prerogative. Government, therefore, is merely a device to receive the deputized powers of individuals; its judgments are given in their stead. If not, the people will know when the time has come to dissolve the fiduciary arrangement.

My observation on this creed is a simple one — maybe banal. I say that nobody believes in a natural law of morality or in a rational conscience founded upon it. If not, then individualism is without a political rudder.

I admit that people participate in the political process, make speeches, and even testify privately to their abiding faith in the principles of our founding fathers. What I deny is that the average behavior of those who claim a Lockean heritage would lead an unprejudiced observer to conclude that such words record the actual motives of their daily lives.

Locke's natural law setting forth the rights of individuals was addressed to *all* men — everywhere — past, present and future. I recall no restrictive covenant that validated the rights of territorial nationalism or the right of present individuals to prevail over the ultimate rights of all other rational beings.

When I say that "nobody" believes these things, I mean that *almost* no one believes them in the sense that he is ready to practice them in his daily choices — the choices that, when accumulated, make a life. Furthermore, no one believes them in the sense that he is ready to make conscientious sacrifices of self in order to serve the future interests of those beings of the future whose rights — rationally — are the same as our own. The Preamble to the Constitution mentions approvingly "the blessings of liberty to ourselves *and our posterity.*" My judgment is that the behavioral intention of the present generation of Jefferson's descendants is to enjoy as many blessings of liberty as they can, while leaving to posterity what one author has called "a used up garbage dump."

Traditional religious belief was the victim of Enlightenment rationalism. What remained after that criticism was rendered irrelevant by the substitution of technological progress for the promise of spiritual progress. Locke's optimistic assessment of the rationality of human nature in contact with a law of nature was an attempt to substitute a basis of moral certainty without dependence on revelation. Adam Smith's "invisible hand" was just as clearly a substitute for the fading Providence of God, although he attributed it to the workings of the natural laws of economics. But, if I am correct, the substitutes themselves have eroded to almost nothing. Few would be willing to argue that the daily choices of Western man are influenced to any great extent either by the original faith or by the substitutes.

Why, then, should I be moral? If a twentieth century futurist preacher calls upon me to sacrifice my short-term good to forfend the suffering of others who may live in some far-off future, why should I change my ways? Why should I become a "new man"?

Why indeed? If God is not there to instruct me, to reward me, or to punish me, why should I regard those faceless, potential beings as my "neighbors"? There must be some way to interpret the parable of the Samaritan to make it appropriate for Palestinians of old but inappropriate for the worldlings of today. All I need is a little hermeneutical ingenuity. If that should fail, I may simply join in the average behavior which has ignored the parabolic teaching without bothering to refute it.

But if they cannot command the righteous wrath of a just God, what have the futurist preachers to offer in its place? What avenging Furies will pursue me or mine if I continue to follow my present policy of short-term personal prudence? Surely their offerings are stones instead of bread. They hold up population charts, computer print-outs, and horror stories featuring far-off neighbors as the victims. Jesus could at least offer the lawyer the prospect of eternal life if he changed his ways and became a new man. If I were to change mine, the futurist preacher cannot promise me that my future "neighbors" will survive eternally. Much less can he promise me that *I* will. So—why should I be moral?

I want to introduce my conclusion by analyzing a portion of what strikes me as the most influential of futurist broadsides—Robert Heilbroner's *An Inquiry into the Human Prospect*. The first part of his book is a review of neo-Malthusian futurist prophecy. The second part is devoted to the problem of this essay. Heilbroner can best be described as a defeated liberal. He too believes that religion and the liberal ideology are no longer viable universal faiths. He believes, in fact, that we are so far gone toward perdition that no freely chosen social medicine will cure the sickness of civilization. That sickness, untreated, is a sickness unto death.

Only an authoritarian government enforcing a monastic community will stem the tide. For he argues (in a Hobbesian vein) that we are all so shortsighted and so selfish that we must trade off freedom for survival. Not our own survival but the survival of our kind in the future. Some of Heilbroner's bargaining with the future coincides with my own assertions: neither traditional religion, capitalism, nor socialism can save us. My agreement stops short at his next principle. He claims that a mythology of stoic endurance can do the job. As he says, "If, within us, the spirit of Atlas falters, there perishes the determination *to preserve humanity at all cost and any cost, forever*" (italics mine). I hope I was able to make the italics as written sound as portentous and as important as they are to Heilbroner's conclusion: we are obliged to preserve humanity — *at all cost and any cost, forever*. The supreme intrinsic moral value is now to be the survival of humanity — forever. But this version of the new morality simply leads me to again ask: why should I be moral?

For Heilbroner, morality is necessary only because there should be one single tie between me and the otherwise awful tragedy of the future. That tie is a full-bodied, almost fanatical identification of myself with the humans of the future. The identification must be so profound, the sympathy so immense, that I will allow myself to be coerced to sacrifice my good for their sheer survival. Their freedom, note well, has already been bargained away. They are, I shall have to believe, my "neighbors" and my "brothers." My own survival is less important than theirs. All my values shall be transvalued to reflect the *summum bonum* of their survival as people bound to a tyrant.

Well, I'm not going to stand still for it. The demands of existent beings have a claim on me — wife, children, and a few others. There are some dim claims from all my global neighbors. But the hordes of future "neighbors" will have to put up with my indifference. Future beings, being nonbeings, can have no demands to make upon me. Even if they did, they have no reality, save potential reality, sufficient to establish an emotive bond of identification with me. How I form identifications with others is a hazy matter, but it is clear enough so that I can say with certainty that beings of the future can never be conscientiously internalized as primary moral ends. They are too diffuse, too abstract, too impersonal. Moreover, the Kantian principle that *ought* implies *can* applies here. If I cannot in fact melt my own destiny into the destinies of those unreal others, it is fatuous to command me to do so.

I am told that of all the species extant in the history of the world, about ninety-five percent are now extinct. The terrifying denouement that Heilbroner fears for Homo sapiens has already overtaken them. The very urge to reproduce one's kind — so strong in the male mantis that it transcends his very existence — is not so much an intrinsic value as it is a physiological compulsion. As such it may have a chemical description but it completely lacks an evaluative justification. If the neo-Malthusian scenario comes true one day and mankind becomes extinct, the event would not be unprecedented. It would be quite a normal event, an expected event in a typical evolutionary history of a species.

Why then, should I be moral? Can it be that the supreme value is merely the endless replication of the human species for the sake of that same endless replication? I can't believe it. I have no particular stake in it. On the contrary, if I consider myself and my kind a *part* of nature rather than standing transcendently outside nature, a sensible ethic might counsel me to let humanity perish. Such apparent "defeats" are, after all, the staging grounds for new phases of evolutionary development. The dominant reptiles had to fade out to make way for the incoming mammals. So why should I not give my loyalty to the evolutionary process itself, rather than to a temporary phase of it, the dominance of Homo sapiens? Why not, indeed?

I am led to believe that the unconscious motivation underlying Heilbroner's peroration, culminating in his exhortation to preserve humanity forever at all and any cost, stems from unexamined Judeo-Christian residues bubbling up from his former liberalism. If man is just the latest dominant animal species in a scheme of evolutionary development, there is no good factual or moral reason to regard his demise as an occasion either for sorrow or joy. It just happens—if it happens. Only if man is somehow still the apple of God's eye, only if the earth was created to be the setting for man's struggles and trials before he enters a New Kingdom, only if God's Providence is watching over him until Grace finally brings him into a right relation with God and his own Better Nature, only then is the extinction of man an unbearable tragedy.

Otherwise, to take our cue from Atlas is silly.

From the evolutionary point of view extended far into the future, the ideal of ensuring the eternal survival of humanity is, while not flatly impossible, very highly improbable. The law of entropy, unless somehow repealed, will ensure just the opposite of eternal human survival, no matter what we do. We will all disappear from the face of the earth once our ecological niche becomes uninhabitable. Unless by that time we have beat a strategic retreat to a better universe next door, that will be the end of us. In time even that redoubt will crumble. No sacrifice of mine or ours has the potency to stay the sentence of execution. The immortality of the species might make some kind of sense, given its Christian undertow. Without it, the sheer continuation of the human species for a certain time beyond my own death strikes me as a boring, value-less repetition.

In conclusion, I have to confess that I go on my selfish and polluting way with a certain amount of bad conscience—as I imagine you do. But your guilty self-indulgences may bother you a little less if you try to believe—as I do— that we are not obligated to future others.

Ernest Partridge

Why Care About the Future?

In this section, Professors Heilbroner, Thompson, and Hardin variously pose a question that is central to any discussion of the issue of the duty to posterity. The question is this: Are human beings, for the most part, *capable* of caring for the remote future? Thompson's answer to this question is starkly and uncompromisingly negative, and thus his challenge is the most likely to arouse intuitive discomfort and opposition. But his answer has the merit of reaching to the heart of the problem of whether human beings are the sort of creatures that are capable of caring for their remote posterity.

Professor Thompson's challenge (as well as those of Heilbroner and Hardin) draw their significance from a fundamental criterion of moral responsibility: *stability*. This criterion (examined and defended with considerable care by John Rawls in his monumental work, *A Theory of Justice*), states that no moral principle can claim our allegiance unless human beings are generally capable of obeying the principle, unless, as Rawls puts it, the principle can withstand "the strains of commitment."[1] The criterion, in turn, follows from the metaethical rule that "*ought* implies *can*." Thompson argues, in effect, that human beings are generally incapable of caring for the remote future and thus are absolved of a moral obligation to do so.

In this paper I will accept Rawls's criterion of stability and will argue, against Thompson, not only that it is *possible* to care about the remote future, but, even more, that failure to do so exacts a considerable cost in well-being to those individuals and those societies that disavow any care for the future.[2]

There is, I believe, a persuasive empirical case against the claim that human beings are disinclined to care for the future, much less to act upon such cares. We need only consider the present existence of national parks and forests, trust funds, donated public buildings, educational and charitable foundations, and numerous other specific examples of care and provision for "future others."[3]

A briefer version of this paper appeared in *Alternative Futures*, November 1980.

But, while the empirical evidence is abundant, it is not my task to cite such evidence. Instead, through a series of speculations in moral psychology, I wish to suggest not only that humans commonly display a concern for future others but also that it is both morally correct to do so and, even more, that such interest is grounded in identifiable and rational features of human social, personal, and moral life—features that reflect and manifest fundamental aspects of human nature and development. Accordingly, if one feels no concern for the quality of life of his successors, he is not only lacking a moral sense but is also seriously impoverishing his life. He is, that is to say, not only to be *blamed*; he is also to be *pitied*.

The alleged need of a well-functioning person to care for the future beyond his own lifetime rests upon a more basic need that I will call "self transcendence." In short, then, the purpose of this paper is to demonstrate that we have sound personal and social, as well as moral, reasons to care about our impact upon the living conditions of both our contemporaries and successor generations.

The Concept of Self Transcendence. By claiming that there is a basic human need for "self transcendence," I am proposing that, as a result of the psychodevelopmental sources of the self and the fundamental dynamics of social experience, well-functioning human beings identify with, and seek to further, the well-being, preservation, and endurance of communities, locations, causes, artifacts, institutions, ideals, and so on, that are outside themselves and that they hope will flourish beyond their own lifetimes. If this is so, then John Donne spoke for all mankind when he wrote: "No man is an island, entire of itself." Thus we cannot regard our decisions and the values that we hold to be restricted to and isolated within our lifetimes.

This claim has a reverse side to it, namely, that individuals who lack a sense of self transcendence are acutely impoverished in that they lack significant, fundamental, and widespread capacities and features of human moral and social experience. Such individuals are said to be *alienated,* both from themselves and from their communities. If such individuals lack concern for self-transcending projects and ideals because of a total absorption with themselves, they are said to be *narcissistic* personalities.

"Self-transcendence" describes a class of feelings that give rise to a variety of activities. It is no small ingredient in the production of great works of art and literature, in the choice of careers in public service, education, scientific research, and so forth. In all this variety, however, there is a central, generic motive, namely, for the self to be part of, to favorably effect, and to value for itself the well-being and endurance of something that is *not* oneself.

An awareness of this need for self transcendence might be evoked (among those who have and acknowledge this need) by a simple thought-experiment. Suppose that astronomers were to determine, to the degree of virtual certainty, that in two hundred years the sun would become a nova and extinguish all life and traces of human culture from the face of the earth. In the words of the poet Robinson Jeffers:

> . . . These tall
> Green trees would become a moment's torches and vanish, the
>   oceans would explode into steam,
> The ships and the great whales fall through them like flaming
>   meteors into the emptied abysm, the six mile
> Hollows of the Pacific sea bed might smoke for a moment
>   the earth would be like a pale proud moon,
> Nothing but vitrified sand and rock would be left on the earth.[4]

Suppose, then, that this were known to be, in two hundred years, the fate of our planet. Would not this knowledge and this awareness profoundly affect the temperament and moral activity of those persons now living who need not fear, for themselves or for anyone they might love or come to love, personal destruction in this eventual final obliteration? How, in fact, is the reader affected by the mere contemplation of this (literal) catastrophe?

For most, I believe, it would be dreadful to contemplate the total annihilation of human life and culture even two hundred years hence. But if, in fact, most persons would be saddened by this thought, we might ask *why* this obliteration is so dreadful to contemplate. We *need* not care personally, and yet we *do* care. We are not indifferent to the fate of future persons unknown and unknowable to us, or to the future career of institutions, species, places, and objects that precede and survive our brief acquaintance thereof. Furthermore, we seem to feel that, if without exorbitant cost we can preserve and enhance natural areas or human artifacts and institutions for the use and enjoyment of future generations, we have a *prima facie* reason to do so.

Apparently, our pride of community, of culture, and of self is enhanced by the assurance that, having accepted the gift of civilization, we have, through our involvement with self-transcending projects, increased its value to our successors. We wish, that is, to perceive ourselves in the stream of history not only as recipients of a culture and tradition but also as builders of the future, as determiners of the conditions of future lives. "To the extent that men are purposive," writes Delattre:

> The destruction of the future is suicidal by virtue of its radical alteration of the significance and possibilities of the present. The meaning of the present depends upon the vision of the future as well as the remembrance of the past. This is so in part because all projects require the future, and to foreclose projects is effectively to reduce the present to emptiness.[5]

Thus it is likely that we would feel a most profound malaise were we to be confronted with the certain knowledge that, beyond our lifetimes but early in the future of our civilization, an exploding sun would cause an abrupt, final, and complete end to the career of humanity and to all traces thereof. Fortunately, the available scientific evidence indicates that the sun will burn safely and constantly for several more billions of years. But whatever the solar contingencies, the physics of the sun is quite beyond our present or projected control.

On the other hand, current social policies and technological developments *are* within our control, and many now being contemplated and enacted may bear portentous implications for the conditions of life for generations yet unborn. Among these developments are nuclear power and genetic engineering (examined by Hardy Jones and the Routleys later in this anthology). In addition, our generation might significantly affect the future through the continuing use of fluorocarbons (e.g., aerosol propellants), which could deplete the stratospheric ozone, or through the use of chlorinated hydrocarbons (e.g., DDT), which could permanently damage the integrity of the world ecosystem. Each of these practices, and many others both current and projected, pose enduring threats to the earth's biosphere and thus to the security and abundance of life for future generations. Surely we of this generation wield an unprecedented power to enhance or to diminish the life prospects of our posterity. With this power comes dreadful responsibility; we may choose to ignore it, but we cannot evade it. To paraphrase Lincoln, we of this generation will be held accountable in spite of ourselves. Who cares? Most of us, I dare say, *do* care. We care about the remote effects of our voluntary and informed choices and policies — even effects so remote in time that they will take place beyond the span of our own lives and the lives of our children and grandchildren. Furthermore, those who feel and manifest this concern display psychological health and well-being, while those who lack such concern are personally impoverished and genuinely deserving of *pity*.

The Self and Society. It is time, now, to attempt to justify these bold claims. First, is "self transcendence," as I contend, essential to the very nature of a well-functioning human personality? A strong case for this position is to be found in the writings of George Herbert Mead and John Dewey.[6] (I will focus most of my attention on Mead, mindful that Dewey's position is, in most significant respects, quite similar.) Mead suggests, in effect, that the notion of a totally isolated self is a virtual contradiction. The *self,* he argues, has its origin, nurture, and sustenance in social acts. Furthermore, says Mead, the mind emerges through the acquisition, in social acts, of communication skills and the consequent absorption of the medium of "significant symbols" known as *language.* Accordingly, the self is defined and identified (i.e., "self-conscious") only in terms of social experience and the consequent perception of a "generalized other" (or, roughly speaking, internalized norms or "conscience"). Moreover, even in moments of solitary reflection, the mind employs, in silent soliloquy, the fund of meanings (i.e., the language) of the community.

The upshot of the position of Mead and Dewey would seem to be that the self, *by its very origin and nature,* transcends the physical locus (of body, of sense impressions, and of behavior) that identifies the individual. "Self transcendence" becomes, then, not a moral desideratum but a basic fact of the human condition. To be sure, some persons may withdraw from human society and claim to be unconcerned with their effects upon others and with the future fate of mankind. However, Mead and Dewey would argue, those who claim total psychic and moral autonomy are deceived. For, despite this manifest autonomy, their personality and selfhood have their origin in social acts and contexts, and their denial of this nature is a symptom of personality disorder. In brief, to be a healthy, well-functioning person is to have "significant others" in one's life and to wish to be significant *to* others and to affect consequences *for* others. Furthermore, this desire to extend one's self to others (either directly or through institutions and works) does not require that the significant persons, things, and events be physically proximate or contemporary with one's lifetime. The self, then, from its earliest origins in infancy, is *essentially* "transcendent." To be human is to "relate out," to identify with others, and to show concern for the well-being and endurance of (at least some) communal values, artifacts, and institutions.

If this admittedly impressionistic account is roughly accurate (both of Mead's and Dewey's position, and of human motivation), its significance is clear: "self transcendence" is *not* a more-or-less occasional and accidental characteristic of individuals and cultures. It is a consequence of universal conditions and circumstances of individual human development. A sense and expression of self-transcendence is thus as necessary for mental health as is exercise for physical health.

The Law of Import Transference. A second approach to self transcendence is suggested by George Santayana's account of "beauty" as "pleasure objectified."[7] By this Santayana means that, when an object is perceived as beautiful, the pleasure of the aesthetic experience is projected into the object and interpreted as a quality thereof. While I do not wish either to defend or criticize this controversial theory, I find it quite illustrative of a psychological phenomenon that is widespread, familiar, and most significant to our account and defense of the motive of self transcendence. This psychological phenomenon may be summarized by what I will call "the law of import transference." The law states that if a person P feels that X (e.g., an institution, place, organization, principle, etc.) matters *to him,* P will also feel that X matters *objectively and intrinsically.* In other words, the significance and importance of an object *to* the agent is interpreted *by* the agent as a quality *of* the object itself. Thus the well-being and endurance of the significant object apart from, and beyond the lifetime of, the agent may become a concern *of* and a value *to* the agent — a part of his inventory of personal *interests or goods.* John Passmore expresses the point quite eloquently:

> When men act for the sake of a future they will not live to see, it is for the most part out of love for persons, places, and forms of activity, a cherishing of them, nothing more grandiose. It is indeed self-contradictory to say: "I love him or her or that place or that institution or that activity, but I don't care what happens to it after my death." To love is, amongst other things, to care about the future of what we love. . . . This is most obvious when we love our wife, our children, our grand-

children. But it is also true in the case of our more impersonal loves: our love for places, institutions and forms of activity.

The application of this point to posterity, then, is quite clear:

> There is . . . no novelty in a concern for posterity, when posterity is thought of not abstractly — as "the future of mankind" — but as a world inhabited by individuals we love or feel a special interest in, a world containing institutions, social movements, forms of life to which we are devoted — or even, a world made up of persons some of whom might admire us.[8]

The "law of import transference," I suggest, describes a universal phenomenon familiar to all of us. It is manifested in acts and observances of patriotism, and in the donation of time, talent, and substance to various causes, places, and institutions. It is also seen in posthumous trusts and bequests. Most dramatically, import transference is found in the willingness of a hero or a saint to die for the sake of other persons, his country, his religious beliefs, or his ideals.

"Unfortunately," the critic may reply, "there are still *other* cases of import transference that may *not* manifest a motive for 'self transcendence,' or at least not the kind of 'transcendence' that would encourage just provision for future persons." For example, the miser "transfers import" to money to the degree that this normally instrumentally good medium of exchange becomes, to him, an *intrinsic* good. He desires to own and to hoard money (something other than himself) for the sake of ownership alone and not for whatever might be purchased therewith. More generally, the selfish and acquisitive person (e.g., the landowner who "locks up" his holdings, or the art collector who keeps his collection in a vault, not for investment but for mere possession itself) does not fail to value things for themselves. Surely he does value them, but, in addition, he desires to *own* them.

The difference, I suggest, is that in the case of the selfish individual, the "transfer of import" is partial, while, for the artist, scholar, or philanthropist enjoying self transcendence in his work or in his benefactions, the transference is more complete. How is this so? Because the selfish person desires the well-being of other-than-self (e.g., his money, his land, or his art objects) for *his* sake. The "transcending" individual desires the well-being of the other-than-self (e.g., institution, artifact, place, ideal, etc.) for *its* sake, or perhaps for the sake of other persons who might benefit thereby. Thus we may suppose that the miser cares or thinks little of the fate of his hoard after his death (except, perchance, to wish that he could "take it with him"), while to the artist the anticipated fate of his creations after his death is of great interest and concern. In short, we may say that one is "fully self transcendent" when (*a*) he regards something other than himself as good in itself, *and* (*b*) when he desires the well-being and endurance of this "something else" for its own sake, apart from its future contingent effects upon him. Though the selfish person may fulfill the first condition, he fails the second.

We are left with an unsettled problem of no small significance. Even if we assume the truth of the law of import transference, we find that this law gives rise either to selfish behavior or to "fully self-transcendent" concern and involvement. (The possibility of still other results has not been excluded.) It follows, then, that of itself this "law" can supply no proof of a basic "need" for self transcendence. In other words, "import transference" is apparently *not* a sufficient cause of a motive for self transcendence. It may, however, be a necessary condition, in which case self transcendence may be said to be "grounded in," or supported by, this alleged behavioral law. We thus find ourselves at the threshold of a difficult ethical challenge; we must show that rational, informed persons would prefer a mode of life with self-transcendent concerns (in the "full" sense) to a life that is wholly selfish. Later in this paper, I will attempt to show that it is, paradoxically, in our own best present interest to anticipate, care about, and prepare for a remote future that we will never see or enjoy.

Significance and Mortality. Another, somewhat existential account of the motive of self transcendence is based upon the universal human awareness of physical mortality—a price that each man must pay for his rationality and self-consciousness. Despite an abundance of religious and metaphysical doctrines of spiritual immortality and of physical resurrection, the time of personal presence and efficacy in the affairs of familiar and significant persons, places, and institutions is universally acknowledged to be coterminous with one's physical life-span.

Surely I need not argue that the finitude of human life is a source of much preoccupation and regret. A myriad of religious doctrines and philosophical systems have been devised to offer hope, consolation, or at least perspective in the face of this common fate. All this is obvious and commonplace and thus can be set aside. However, there is one response to the awareness of mortality that is of considerable importance to our analysis, namely, the investment and devotion of time, talent, concern, loyalty, and financial substance in behalf of enduring and permanent causes, ideals, and institutions.

While there are, of course, many possible motives for these kinds of activities, I would like to focus upon one motive in particular, namely, the desire to extend the term of one's influence and significance well beyond the term of one's lifetime—a desire evident in arrangements for posthumous publications, in bequests and wills, in perpetual trusts (such as the Nobel Prize), and so forth. In such acts and provisions, we find clear manifestations of a will to transcend the limits of personal mortality by extending one's self and influence into things, associations, and ideals that endure. Nicolai Hartmann offers an eloquent expression of this need to transcend the limits of one's immediate life and circumstances:

> In such a [self-transcending] life is fulfilled something of man's destiny, which is to become a participant in the creation of the world. . . . But what will that signify,

if [a person's] life-work dies with him, or soon after? It is just such work that requires permanence, continuation, a living energy of its own. It inheres in the nature of all effort that looks to an objective value, to go on beyond the life and enterprise of the individual, into a future which he can no longer enjoy. It is not only the fate but is also the pride of a creative mind and is inseparable from his task, that his work survives him, and therefore passes from him to others, in whose life he has no part.

. . . The content of a fruitful ideal necessarily lies beyond the momentary actual. And because it reaches beyond the limits of an individual life, it naturally reduces the individual to a link in the chain of life, which connects the past with the future. Man sees himself caught up into a larger providence, which looks beyond him and yet is his own.[9]

With the awareness of mortality comes existential anguish and dread—the heavy price we pay for self-awareness, time-perception, and abstract knowledge of the external world and our place in it. But a consciousness of mortality also evokes some of our finer moral qualities. For instance, mindful of our finitude, we make provision for a future beyond our own lifetimes, and, conversely, we feel morally obligated to honor the wills and reputations of the deceased. But both the preparing and the honoring of wills would make no sense if we egoistically confined all import and values to our own experiences and satisfactions. Yet provision for a posthumous future and respect for the previously recorded wishes of those now dead is commonplace and universally sanctioned. Such behavior is possible only in a community of individuals who share and exercise capacities for self-consciousness, hypothetical reflection, self-transcending interests, and abstract moral reasoning. Given these capacities, and through them an operative and effective provision for the posthumous future, the personal, moral, social, and material well-being of the community is significantly enhanced from generation to generation. For, just as our lives are enriched by the knowledge that we might make provision for our children and grandchildren (not to mention unrelated members of future generations), so too has each of us benefited from the private and public bequests that have followed from our predecessors' desires to benefit those who would live after them.[10]

Alienation: The Self Alone. I have, to this point, attempted to indicate that self transcendence is a basic and virtually universal human need. In defense of this assertion, I have cited what seem to be necessary and general conditions of human development, evaluation, and awareness. I would like now to examine the issue of self transcendence from a different perspective. Specifically, I would like to examine the results of even a partial deprivation of the alleged "need" for self transcendence. If, as I have suggested, this need is basic to human nature, a denial thereof should produce clear and dramatic results.

In much contemporary sociological and psychological literature, this denial of self transcendence has been described as "alienation." In the introduction to their anthology *Man Alone,* Eric and Mary Josephson present a vivid account of the broad range of sources and manifestations of alienation in contemporary life:

> Confused as to his place in the scheme of a world growing each day closer yet more impersonal, more densely populated yet in face-to-face relations more dehumanized; a world appealing ever more widely for his concern and sympathy with unknown masses of men, yet fundamentally alienating him even from his next neighbor, today Western man has become mechanized, routinized, made comfortable as an object; but in the profound sense displaced and thrown off balance as the subjective creator and power. This theme of the alienation of modern man runs through the literature and drama of two continents; it can be traced in the content as well as the form of modern art; it preoccupies theologians and philosophers, and to many psychologists and sociologists, it is the central problem of our time. In various ways they tell us that ties have snapped that formerly bound Western man to himself and to the world about him. In diverse language they say that man in modern industrial societies is rapidly becoming detached from nature, from his old gods, from the technology that has transformed his environment and now threatens to destroy it; from his work and its products, and from his leisure; from the complex social institutions that presumably serve but are more likely to manipulate him; from the community in which he lives; and above all from himself — from his body and his sex, from his feelings of love and tenderness, and from his art — his creative and productive potential.[11]

Clearly the Josephsons have described here a sizable array of social and personal disorders. I should not, and will not, attempt to respond to more than a few of them. Most of the symptoms that I will discuss fall under the category of *personal or psychological alienation.*

Erich Fromm eloquently describes personal alienation as "a mode of experience in which the person experiences himself as an alien. He has become, one might say, estranged from himself. He does not experience himself as the center of his world, as the creator of his own acts — but his acts and their consequences have become his masters, whom he obeys, or whom he may even worship." In other words, says Fromm, an alienated person "does not experience himself as the active bearer of his own powers and richness, but as an impoverished 'thing,' dependent on powers outside of himself, unto whom he has projected his living substance."[12]

It is all too easy to find examples of alienation in contemporary life. For example, the worker finds that he, or she, is a replaceable part in the assembly line or shop. His job activity is governed by machines (most ubiquitously, the clock). The product of his labor shows no evidence of his distinct personality or skills. Even if he wears a white collar and brings an inventory of acquired professional skills to his work, he may perform as a faceless functionary, with little personal style evident or required in his task. The management of his household, his shopping habits, travel arrangements, even his leisure activities, are mechanized and impersonal. The utilities and services that sustain his life and creature comforts are themselves maintained by an unfathomable network of electronic, mechanical, and cybernetic devices that at any moment could collapse from the weight of their own complexity. Economic and political forces that may radically disrupt his life are unresponsive to his needs and beyond his control; indeed, they may even be beyond the conscious and deliberate control of *any* persons, either in public or in private offices.

In brief, the alienated person shrinks into himself. He loses control over the social, economic, and political forces that determine his destiny. With loss of control comes indifference and apathy. Because, in his social contacts, he is responded to ever more in terms of his *functions,* and ever less in terms of his personality and autonomy, he becomes estranged from the wellsprings of his own unique personal being. He becomes, that is, alienated from *himself.* He is left aimless, vulnerable, insignificant, solitary, and *finite.* In such a condition not only does he lose his self-respect; even worse, he is hard-pressed to recognize and define the *identity* of his own self.

In alienation we find the very antithesis of self transcendence. There is no feeling, within a state of alienation, of a personal contribution to grand projects, no sense of involvement in significant events, no investment and expansion of one's self and substance into enduring causes and institutions. Surrounded by institutions, machines, individuals, social trends, for which he has no significance and to which he can thus "transfer" no "import," one truly lives in an alien world. Surely alienation is a dreadful condition, made no less so by its widespread and growing manifestations in contemporary society. It is a condition that no rational person would happily wish upon himself.

And what is the alternative, even more the *remedy,* for this dismal condition? Clearly, it would appear to be a life committed to self-transcending concerns and interests. Such a life, writes Kenneth Keniston, displays "human wholeness," by which he means "a capacity for commitment, dedication, passionate concern, and care—a capacity for wholeheartedness, and single-mindedness, for abandon without fear of self-annihilation and loss of identity."[13] For Erich Fromm, the commonplace word "love" describes the transcending reach from self to another self, or to an ideal.

> There is only one passion which satisfies man's need to unite himself with the world, and to acquire at the same time a sense of integrity and individuality, and this is *love. Love is union* with somebody, or something, outside oneself, *under the condition of retaining the separateness and integrity of one's own self.* It is an experience of sharing, of communion, which permits the full unfolding of one's own inner activity. The experience of love does away with the necessity of illusions . . . [T]he reality of active sharing and loving permits me to transcend my individualized existence, and at the same time to experience myself as the bearer of the active powers which constitute the act of loving.[14]

Furthermore, writes Fromm, the self-transcending lover, as the "bearer of active powers," is a creator, for "in the act of creation man transcends himself beyond the passivity and accidentalness of his existence into the realm of purposefulness and freedom. In man's need for transcendence lies one of the roots for love, as well as for art, religion, and material production."[15]

Narcissism: The Self Contained. A lack of self-transcending concern is also a feature of *narcissism,* a personality disorder that is currently attracting widespread attention and interest in the social and behavioral sciences.[16] In his popular and provocative book *The Culture of Narcissism,* Christopher Lasch describes the narcissist as one who experiences

> intense feelings of emptiness and inauthenticity. Although the narcissist can func-
> tion in the everyday world and often charms other people . . . , his devaluation of
> others, together with his lack of curiosity about them, impoverishes his personal
> life and reinforces the "subjective experience of emptiness." Lacking any real intel-
> lectual engagement with the world—notwithstanding a frequently inflated esti-
> mate of his own intellectual abilities—he has little capacity for sublimation. He
> therefore depends on others for constant infusions of approval and admiration.
> He "must attach [himself] to someone, living an almost parasitic" existence. At the
> same time, his fear of emotional dependence, together with his manipulative,
> exploitative approach to personal relations, makes these relations bland, super-
> ficial, and deeply unsatisfying.[17]

The essence of narcissism, writes Fromm, is "a failure of relatedness." In fact, "one understands fully man's need to be related only if one considers the outcome of the failure of any kind of relatedness, if one appreciates the meaning of *narcissism.* Narcissism is the essence of all severe psychic pathology. For the narcissistically involved person, there is only one reality, that of his own thought processes, feelings and needs. The world outside is not experienced or perceived *objectively,* i.e., as existing in its own terms. . . . Narcissism is the opposite pole to objectivity, reason and love . . . The fact that utter failure to relate oneself to the world is insanity, points to the other fact: that some form of relatedness is the condition for any kind of sane living."[18]

Of particular interest to our analysis is the effect of the narcissistic orientation in our culture upon "the sense of historical time." We live these days for ourselves, writes Lasch, and "not for [our] predecessors or posterity." We are, he claims, "fast losing the sense of historical continuity, the sense of belonging to a succession of generations originating in the past and stretching into the future."[19] This loss of historical consciousness, coupled with a general lack of self-transcending concern, exacts a heavy penalty as one approaches the second half of his life. For at mid-life, writes Lasch, "the usual defenses against the ravages of age—identification with ethical or artistic values beyond one's immediate interests [!], intellectual curiosity, the consoling emotional warmth derived from happy relationships in the past—can do nothing for the narcissist." And he is "unable to derive whatever comfort comes from identification with historical continuity."[20] Lasch quotes Kernberg, who observes that "to be able to enjoy life in a process involving a growing identification with other people's happiness and achievements is tragically beyond the capacity of narcissistic personalities."[21] And so, "the fear of death takes on a new intensity in a society that has deprived itself of religion and shows little interest in posterity."[22]

In contrast, the "traditional consolations of old age" are available to those with an authentic and active sense of self-transcending concern. Of these consolations, "the most important . . . is the belief that future generations will in some sense carry on [one's] life work. Love and work unite in a concern for posterity, and specifically in an attempt to equip the younger generation to carry on the tasks of the older. The thought that we live on vicariously in our children (more broadly, in the future generations) reconciles us to our own supercession."[23]

Is self-transcendent concern an appropriate "prescription" for the narcissist? Perhaps. But that simple answer, and even worse that simple question, may be wholly inadequate and inappropriate in the face of the complexity of the issue of narcissism.[24] Some narcissists may be beyond relief. At best, narcissism appears to be one of the more difficult personality disorders to treat (due, in part, to the narcissist's virtuoso skills at manipulation, evasion, and self-deceit).[25] But these considerations are of psychiatric interest. Our question is more fundamental: Is "self-transcendent concern" essential to a healthy and fulfilling human life? And, conversely, is a life without such concern a basically impoverished life—a life that a rational disinterested person would not choose for himself? This brief sketch of the psychopathology of narcissism suggests that an examination of this personality disorder gives us further reason to suppose that to be a healthy, happy, fulfilled person, one *needs* self-transcending interests and concerns. Beyond that, humane sympathy and concern should lead us to support efforts to *prevent* narcissistic disorders (e.g., through social reform, moral education, etc.), and to support efforts to treat those who, nonetheless, suffer from this disorder. But, while these are worthy objectives, a discussion thereof would lead us away from the topic of this paper.

Two Contrary Cases: The Recluse and the Playboy. Earlier it was suggested that alienation is "the very antithesis of self transcendence. But isn't this an overstatement? Might we not find cases of individuals who appear to be both "self transcendent" and alienated, and still other cases of individuals (e.g., *narcissists*) who appear to be *neither* self-transcendent nor alienated?[26]

In the first case, consider such solitary persons as Henry David Thoreau and John Muir. Though these individuals voluntarily withdrew from their communities, surely their lives cannot be said to have been unproductive and without purpose. Indeed, in their own views and that of others, Thoreau and Muir pursued lives of transcending significance. However, they were *not alienated.* To be sure, while Thoreau was alienated from the commonplace, commercial, and civic routines of Cóncord, he nevertheless perceived himself as a member of a community of ideas and, of course, a community of nature. He shunned the way of life of his neighbors not because he felt his life had no significance but because he sought a variant and, he believed, a *deeper* significance. He chose, that is, to "march to the sound of a *different* drummer." He did not refuse to "march" at all. His writing is directed to causes, issues, and times that extend far beyond his immediate circumstances. Thoreau's life supplies eloquent evidence that *solitude* need not imply alienation.

But can a life display *neither* self transcendence nor alienation? Consider the "playboy," the self-indulgent, narcissistic hedonist who "takes no care for the morrow," much less posterity. If such a person is healthy, wealthy, personable, and attractive, can he be said to be "alienated"? It would seem, quite to the contrary, that he is living not in an "alien" world but in a world quite friendly to his tastes and whims. And if the playboy is not alienated, then isn't he, necessarily, the opposite, that is, self-transcendent? But how could this be so? Or might he not, in fact, be neither alienated nor self-transcendent, and yet, for all that, lead an enviable life?

These questions lead us to an important point, namely, that a life not filled during every waking moment with self-transcendent causes and projects is not necessarily an alienated life. Neither is a person who is *occasionally* self-absorbed a narcissist. While there are appropriate times in any life for simple, trivial, egoistic, self-sufficient activities and pleasures, a life *totally* devoid of any awareness of, concern for, involvement with, or valuing of things, persons, institutions, and ideals, *for the sake thereof,* would in fact be an alienated life, and a person *totally* absorbed in his self-interested concerns would be properly described as a narcissist. Consider, then, that paradigmatic hedonist, Hugh Hefner, the publisher of *Playboy* magazine. Is he "alienated?" Apparently not, for despite all his mansions, jets, hi-fi's, and bunnies, Hefner has also established "The Playboy Foundation" (which is involved in such public issues as civil liberties), he has published a "playboy philosophy" (a philosophical position, of sorts), and he has contributed generously to various social and political causes. All of these enterprises and benefactions would seem to manifest a desire for self transcendence.

If not even Hugh Hefner presents a refuting case, let us then concoct an extreme paradigm. Imagine a person with health, wealth, sophistication, social grace, and so on, who cares for nothing in life but his own personal satisfaction, and values nothing except as it immediately contributes to this satisfaction—in other words, a textbook example of a narcissist. Assume, further, that, with his generous endowments, his selfish interests are routinely satisfied. Would such a person, having no concern for the well-being of anything else (for *its* own sake), lead an enviable life—the sort of life that a rationally self-interested individual would desire for himself?

Despite all his good fortune and opportunity, such a person might, I suspect, be inclined to feel that his life was confined and confining. By hypothesis, nothing would matter to him, unless it had impact upon the course of his personal life plan. He would have no interest in persons he would never meet, places he would never see, and events and circumstances outside the span of his lifetime. In other words, those persons, places, and events with which he was not directly involved would be "alien" to him. With all significant events confined to the span of his lifetime, the consciousness of his own mortality would be especially burdensome.[27] While this is a life-style that we might be tempted to try for a while (given the chance), I wonder if we could bear it for a lifetime. ("A great place to visit, but I wouldn't want to live there.") If, as I suspect, such a life does not "wear well," this might explain why it seems that those new to wealth are more inclined to indulge themselves with gadgetry, diversions, and opulence, while those born to wealth generally involve themselves with such self-transcendent concerns as philanthropy, the arts, social work, and political issues.

I have said that I "suspect" that an opulent, self-centered, narcissistic life would be confining and, concerning all things outside the small egocentric confinement, *alienating*. Unfortunately, we shall have to close with nothing more substantial than this "suspicion." Surely much literary and psychological evidence might be brought to bear upon the question of the relationship between self-indulgence and alienation. Furthermore, one might conceive of some sort of direct empirical study of the issue, albeit the execution of such a study might be a trifle awkward (e.g., "Tell me, Howard Hughes, are you *really* happy?"). All this, however, is beyond the scope of this inquiry. What remains is the tentative conclusion that, while an enlightened egoist might prefer the life of the alienated, narcissistic millionaire to that of some other possible choices, given the additional happy option he would, I believe, much prefer to utilize the millionaire's resources and circumstances in a life containing self-transcending projects and concerns.

The Paradox of Morality. Throughout these explorations of the proposed "need for self transcendence," we have found manifestation of evidence of what is often called "the paradox of morality." Briefly, the paradox is found in the common circumstance that one appears to live best for oneself when one lives for the sake of others. While the rule may seem pious and banal, it points to a profound and recurring theme in religion and moral philosophy, a theme that is especially prominent in the writings of contract theorists from Thomas Hobbes to John Rawls.[28] Statements of the moral paradox are abundant in the writings of contemporary philosophers. For instance, Kai Nielsen writes: "There are good Hobbesian reasons for rational and self-interested people to accept the moral point of view. A rational egoist will naturally desire the most extensive liberty compatible with his own self-interest, but he will also see that this is the most fully achievable in a context of community life where the moral point of view prevails."[29] Consider also Michael Scriven's position:

> Each citizen's chances of a satisfying life for himself are increased by a process of conditioning all citizens *not* to treat their own satisfaction as the most important goal. Specifically, a system which inculcates genuine concern for the welfare of others is, it will be argued, the most effective system for increasing the welfare of each individual. Put paradoxically, there are circumstances in which one can give a selfish justification for unselfishness.[30]

"The paradox of morality," then, supplies still another argument for self transcendence. But it is an argument with a difference. In our earlier discussion of the motive of self transcendence, we adopted a psychological approach; that is, we considered the need for self transcendence from the perspective of its origin and sustenance in human experience and behavior. Thus a life "transcended" is perceived to be a healthy life, while an alienated or narcissistic life is perceived to be impoverished. In contrast, the argument from the moral paradox directly *recommends* self transcendence (in the form of "the moral point of view") as a more prudent policy for achieving self-enrichment and personal satisfaction.

At the outset of this discussion of "the paradox of morality," I admitted that, on first encounter, this principle seemed "pious and banal." I hope I have, in the intervening paragraphs, added some substance to the notion. Perhaps the paradox seems less "pious and banal," and is given a more severe testing, when it is applied to the question of the duty to posterity. In such a case, those who defend such a duty and urge thoughtful and responsible provision for the future might wish to affirm that life is immediately enriched by the collective agreement of the living to provide for the well-being of the unborn. This is the position of economist Kenneth Boulding:

> Why should we not maximize the welfare of this generation at the cost of posterity? *Après nous le déluge* has been the motto of not insignificant numbers of human societies. The only answer to this, as far as I can see, is to point out that the welfare of the individual depends on the extent to which he can identify himself with others, and that the most satisfactory individual identity is that which identifies not only with a community in space but also with a community extending over time from the past into the future. . . . This whole problem is linked up with the much larger one of the determinants of the morale, legitimacy, and "nerve" of a society, and there is a great deal of historical evidence to suggest that a society which loses its identity with posterity and which loses its positive image of the future loses also its capacity to deal with the present problems and soon falls apart.[31]

If I interpret Boulding correctly, he is saying, in essence, that we need the future, *now.*

"Self Transcendence": A Summary. In this paper I have tried to defend the position that healthy, well-functioning human beings have a basic and pervasive need to transcend themselves; that is, to identify themselves as a part of larger, ongoing, and enduring processes, projects, institutions, and ideals. Furthermore, I have contended that, if persons are deceived into believing that they can live in and for themselves alone, they will suffer for it both individually and communally. If my presentation of the concept of "self transcendence" has been even moderately successful, we may be prepared to answer the cynic's taunt: "Why should we care about posterity; what has posterity ever done for us?" Our duty to make just provision for the future, I contend, is *not* of the form of an *obligation*—not, that is, a contractual agreement to exchange favors or services. To be sure, posterity does not actually exist *now.* Even so, in a strangely abstract and metaphorical sense, posterity may extend profound favors for the living. For posterity exists as an *idea,* a potentiality, and a valid object of transpersonal devotion, concern, purpose, and commitment. Without

this idea and potentiality, our lives would be confined, empty, bleak, pointless, and morally impoverished. In acting for posterity's good we act for our own as well. Paradoxically, we owe it to *ourselves* to be duty-bound to posterity, in a manner that genuinely focuses upon future needs rather than our own. By fulfilling our just duties to posterity, we may now earn and enjoy, in our self-fulfillment, the favors of posterity.[32]

NOTES

1. John Rawls, *A Theory of Justice* (Cambridge, Mass.: Harvard University Press, 1971), pp. 145, 176.

2. It is, I think, a bit unsporting for an editor to invite a paper, only to prop it up as a target for his own polemic. It is especially so when the author of the target has no opportunity for rebuttal. And so, rather than abuse my advantage, I shall simply point out my differences with Professor Thompson in these opening paragraphs and then make no further mention of his paper during the remainder of this piece.

3. Apparently this is not a rare or trivial sentiment, for, as Peter Laslett points out, "no little portion of political life rests upon" the premise that we have moral duties toward the yet-unborn. He continues:

> The speeches of ministers, the propaganda of parties, the actions of planners, the demands of administrators, unhesitatingly assume that men ordinarily recognize the right of generations yet to come. The additional and significant paradox here is that this assumption is well founded in behavior. We do in fact respond quite spontaneously to an appeal on behalf of the future. [Peter Laslett, "The Conversation Between the Generations," in *The Proper Study,* Royal Institute of Philosophy Lectures, vol. 4 (New York: Macmillan, 1971), p. 78.]

4. Robinson Jeffers, "Nova," *The Selected Poetry of Robinson Jeffers* (New York: Random House, 1927), p. 597.

5. Edwin Delattre, "Responsibilities and Future Persons," *Ethics,* 82 (April 1972), p. 256.

6. John Dewey, *Experience and Nature* (LaSalle, Ill.: Open Court, 1958), chapter 6. George Herbert Mead, *Mind, Self and Society* (Chicago: Phoenix, 1956). The social-psychological theories of Mead and Dewey are exceedingly complex (a circumstance aggravated by the obscurity of their writing styles), and I haven't the space even to attempt an adequate summary thereof.

7. George Santayana, *The Sense of Beauty* (New York: Random House Modern Library, 1955).

8. John Passmore, *Man's Responsibility for Nature* (New York: Scribner, 1974), pp. 88-9.

9. Nicolai Hartmann, *Ethics,* vol. 2: *Moral Values* (New York: Macmillan, 1932), pp. 313, 324 [in this anthology, pp. 305-08].

10. The critical reader will justifiably object that I have presented in this paragraph a statement of position without much of a supporting argument. I should therefore point out that support for these conclusions, as well as an elaboration of this position, may be found in Parts 4-6 of my paper, "Posthumous Interests and Posthumous Respect," *Ethics,* 91 (January 1981).

11. Eric and Mary Josephson, Introduction to *Man Alone: Alienation in Modern Society* (New York: Dell, 1962), pp. 10–11.

12. Erich Fromm, *The Sane Society* (New York: Fawcett, 1955), pp. 111, 114.

13. Kenneth Kenniston, *The Uncommitted* (New York: Harcourt, Brace and World, 1960), p. 441.

14. Fromm, pp. 36–37, 41–42.

15. *Ibid.*

16. How is *narcissism* related to *alienation?* Is narcissism a *type* of alienation? A *cause* of alienation? Are they otherwise related? These are complicated and interesting questions whose resolutions rest upon differing definitions of these terms, different theories of their etiology, and different accounts of their symptomatology. We cannot, and fortunately need not, devote much space to these questions. It suffices for our purposes to note that both alienation and narcissism are unenviable conditions and are characterized by a lack of self-transcending concern.

17. Christopher Lasch, *The Culture of Narcissism* (New York: Norton, 1978), pp. 39–40. The quotations within are from Otto Kernberg. Kernberg's primary work on this topic is *Borderline Conditions and Pathological Narcissism* (New York: Jason Aronson, 1975).

18. Erich Fromm, pp. 39–41. It should be noted that Lasch is quite impatient with Fromm's habit of expanding the scope of the concept of "narcissism," thus "drain[ing] the idea of its clinical meaning" (Lasch, p. 31). Even so, I believe that the passage from Fromm, quoted above, serves my purpose well without seriously compromising Lasch's sense of the term "narcissism."

19. Lasch, p. 5.

20. Lasch, p. 41.

21. Otto Kernberg, quoted in Lasch, p. 41.

22. Lasch, p. 208.

23. Lasch, p. 210.

24. Even so, "transcendence" seems to be a favored treatment strategy of some psychotherapists. For instance, Lasch cites Heinz Kohut in this regard: "Useful, creative work, which confronts the individual with 'unsolved intellectual and aesthetic problems' and thereby mobilizes narcissism on behalf of activities outside the self provides the narcissist with the best hope of transcending his predicament" (Lasch, p. 17n). The source from Kohut is *The Analysis of the Self . . .* (New York: International Universities Press, 1971), p. 315.

25. Lasch, pp. 40–1.

26. Even if we conclude that alienation and self transcendence are "antitheses," there is no contradiction in stating that a person is transcendent with regard to some X, while at the same time alienated from a distinct Y. The life of Thoreau seems to be a case in point.

27. As we have seen, this seems to be precisely the fate of the narcissistic personality.

28. Thus Jesus said: "Whosoever will save his life shall lose it, and whosoever will lose his life for my sake shall find it" (Matthew 16:25). In a contemporary paraphrase of this scripture, William Frankena writes:

> If we believe psychologists like Erich Fromm and others, . . . for one's life to be the best possible, even in the non-moral sense of best, the activities and experiences which form one side of life must (1) be largely concerned with objects or causes other than one's own welfare and (2) must be such as to give one a sense of achievement and excellence. Otherwise its goodness will remain truncated and incomplete. He

that loses his life in sense (1) shall find it in sense (2). [*Ethics,* 1st ed. (Englewood Cliffs, N.J.: Prentice-Hall, 1963), pp. 76-7.]

For a suggestive and influential application of "the moral paradox" to ecological issues, see Garrett Hardin's justly celebrated essay, "The Tragedy of the Commons," *Science,* 162 (1968), 1243-8.

29. Kai Nielsen, "Problems of Ethics," *The Encyclopedia of Philosophy,* vol. 2 (New York: Macmillan & Free Press, 1967), p. 132.

30. Michael Scriven, *Primary Philosophy* (New York: McGraw-Hill, 1966), p. 240.

31. Kenneth Boulding, "The Economics of the Coming Spaceship Earth," in *The Environmental Handbook,* ed. Garrett de Bell (New York: Ballantine, 1970), pp. 99-100.

32. Over half of this paper appeared originally in Section 42 of my doctoral dissertation, *Rawls and the Duty to Posterity* (University of Utah, 1976). This version was prepared especially for this anthology. I am grateful to Dr. R. Jan Stout for advising me of the appropriateness of my use of psychiatric terms and concepts in this version. Much of the final work on this paper was accomplished during the term of a Fellowship in Environmental Affairs from the Rockefeller Foundation. I am grateful to the Foundation for this support.

Garrett Hardin

Who Cares for Posterity?

I

Two centuries ago the American poet John Trumbull (1750–1831) posed a question that has ever since disturbed those who want to put a wholly rational foundation under conservation policy. Why, Trumbull asked, should people act

> . . . as though there were a tie
> And obligation to posterity.
> We get them, bear them, breed, and nurse:
> What has posterity done for us?[1]

The question is surely an ethical one. One would think that philosophers who have been dealing with ethics for more than two thousand years would by this time have developed a rather impressive intellectual apparatus for dealing with the needs of posterity; but they nave not. In a thought-provoking essay on "Technology and Responsibility," Hans Jonas points out that ethical literature is almost wholly individualistic: it is addressed to private conduct rather than to public policy.[2] Martin Buber epitomized this spirit well when he oriented his ethics around the *I-Thou* dyad.[3] That sounds fine until a close reading reveals that the author means no more than *I-Thou, Here and Now.* The standard ethical dialogue is between people who stand face to face with each other, seeking a reasonable basis for reciprocal altruism. Posterity has no chance to show its face in the here and now.

Except for Jonas's valuable comments, contemporary philosophy still evades the hard problem of caring for posterity's interests. Probably no recent

Part I is reprinted from *The Limits of Altruism* (Indiana University Press, 1977), pp. 70–84, and part II from "Carrying Capacity as an Ethical Concept," *Soundings,* 59 (Spring 1976), 131–134, with permission of the publishers and the author.

work is as well known or spoken of with such awe as John Rawls's *A Theory of Justice,* so we should see what this book has to say about "the problem of justice between generations," as Rawls puts the problem.[4] In §44 the author candidly admits that in his hopefully comprehensive system of analysis the problem "seems to admit of no definite answer." One might suppose that he would then drop the matter but he somehow manages to talk about it for another fourteen pages without adding anything more positive than statements such as "men have a natural duty to uphold and to further just institutions." This pronouncement is less than revolutionary; it is hardly operational. Perhaps we have expected too much from philosophers.[5] Can economists throw any more light on the problem of posterity?

Time is of the essence. In cost–benefit analysis we attempt to list and evaluate all the costs (negative benefits); similarly with all the (positive) benefits; then we strike a balance for the whole, on which action can be based. If the balance is plus, we go ahead; if minus, we stop. The decision is simple if costs and benefits are encountered at practically the same moment. But what if they are separated by a considerable gap in time? What if the benefits come now and the costs do not turn up for a generation? Contrariwise, what if costs have to be paid now for benefits that come later? How do we balance costs against benefits when time is interposed between the two?

To begin with let us take up the benefits-first problem, which throws an interesting light on human nature. When the High Aswan Dam was proposed for the Nile only its expected benefits were publicized: the additional electricity it would generate and the additional land that could be irrigated with the impounded water. The huge financial cost of the dam was acknowledged, but the world was told that it would be well worth it. It would bring the blessings of "development" to the poor people of Egypt.

People were not told certain other costs that were well known to some agricultural experts. Agriculture in the Nile below Aswan had always depended on a yearly flooding of the flat fields. This flooding accomplished two things: it leached out the salts accumulated from the preceding year's evaporation of irrigation water, and it left behind one millimeter of silt, which served as fertilizer for the next year's crops. This system of agriculture had been successful for six thousand years—a unique record of long-term success. Now technologists proposed to put an end to it.

Had there been any national or international debate on the subject the debaters should have wrestled with this question: Do today's short-term benefits of more electricity and more agricultural land in the upper reaches of the river outweigh tomorrow's losses in the lower valley resulting from salination and loss of fertility? The gains are necessarily short term: all dam-lakes eventually silt up and become useless as generators of electricity and sources of abundant water. The process usually takes only a century or two, and often much less. No economically feasible method has ever been found for reclaiming a silted-up dam-lake. The loss from salination of irrigated land is also virtually permanent; treatment requires periodic flooding, but that is what the

High Aswan Dam was designed to prevent. The Tigris–Euphrates valley, in which irrigation was practiced for centuries, was ruined by salination two thousand years ago—and it is still ruined.

How a cost–benefit balance would have been struck had these facts been known to the decision makers we do not know. Probably their reaction would have been that of Mr. Micawber in *David Copperfield*: "Something will turn up." Such is the faith of the technological optimists. "Eat, drink, and be merry—for tomorrow will find a solution to today's problems. We will learn how to dredge out dam-ponds—economically. We will learn how to desalinate farmland—economically. Don't wait until we've solved these problems. Plunge ahead! Science will find an answer in time."

Curiously, economists have more confidence in science and technology than scientists do. Could it be that too much knowledge is a bad thing? Should conservatism in ecological matters be labeled a vice rather than a virtue? So say the technological optimists.

Well, the High Aswan Dam has been built now, and the returns are coming in. They are worse than expected. There has not been time for appreciable salination or significant loss of soil fertility—which no one expected this soon anyway—but other disadvantages we had not foreseen have turned up. Water behind the dam is rising more slowly than had been hoped, because of unexpected leakage into surrounding rock strata and greater than expected evaporation from the surface of the lake. The present steady flow of water in irrigation channels (instead of the former intermittent flow) favors snails that carry parasitic worms. As a result, the painful and debilitating disease of schistosomiasis is more widespread among Egyptians now. There are medical measures that can be taken against the disease and sanitary measures to combat the snails, but both cost money, which is what the Egyptians are short of. In addition, the reduction of the flow of the Nile has opened the delta to erosion by the currents of the Mediterranean; as a result, precious delta farmland is now being swept into the sea. And the stoppage of the annual fertilization of the eastern Mediterranean by flood-borne silt has destroyed 95 percent of the local sardine fisheries.[6] The dam is proving a disaster, and sooner than anyone had thought.

Mr. Micawber, where are you now?

We come now to the opposite problem, that of weighing present costs against future benefits. For this question there is a rational economic theory. Let us see if it is adequate.

Suppose I offer to sell you something that will be worth $100 ten years from now: how much should you be willing to pay for it? If you are the standard "economic man," equipped with a hand calculator, you will say something like this: "Well, let me see: assuming the interest rate for money stays at 6 percent, I cannot afford to pay you more than $55.84 for this opportunity. So if you want to close the deal you'll have to accept $55.84 or a bit less to get me to opt for $100 ten years from now."

The reasoning is as follows. A person with some money to spare can either put it in the bank at 6 percent interest or invest it in this enterprise. Put in the bank, $55.84 (at compound interest) will amount to $100 ten years later: the proposed investment should be able to do that well. If the investor thinks the proposal is speculative he will make a lower bid (i.e., expect a higher rate of interest). If he is worried about inflation (and thinks he knows another investment that is inflation-proof) he will demand a still lower price.

In economic terms, we "discount" the future value at a discount rate (rate of interest), calling the discounted value the "present value." The present value of $100 ten years from now at a discount rate of 6 percent is $55.84; if the discount rate is 10 percent the present value is only $38.55 The formula for these calculations is:

$$\text{Present value} = \text{Future value} \div e^{bt}$$
$$\text{where: } e = \text{base of natural logarithms (ln)}$$
$$b = \ln{(1 + \text{interest rate})}$$
$$\text{and} \quad t = \text{time}$$

The economic theory of discounting is a completely rational theory. For short periods of time it gives answers that seem intuitively right. For longer periods, we are not so sure.

A number of years ago I decided to plant a redwood tree in my backyard.[7] As I did so I mused, "What would my economist friends say to this? Would they approve? Or would they say I was an economic fool?"

The seedling cost me $1.00. When mature the tree would (at the then current prices) have $14,000 worth of lumber in it — but it would take two thousand years to reach that value. Calculation showed that the investment of so large a sum of money as $1.00 to secure so distant a gain would be justified only if the going rate of interest was no more than 0.479 percent per year. So low a rate of interest has never been known. Plainly I was being a rather stupid "economic man" in planting that tree. *But I planted it.*

The theory of discounting scratches only the surface of the problem. What about the quid pro quo? The quid ($1.00) is mine to pay; but who gets the quo, two thousand years from now? Not I, certainly. And it is most unlikely that any of my direct descendants will get it either, history being what it is. The most I can hope for is that an anonymous posterity will benefit by my act. Almost the only benefit I get is the thought that posterity will benefit — a curious sort of quo indeed. Why bother?

I am beginning to suspect that rationality — as we now conceive it — may be insufficient to secure the end we desire, namely, taking care of the interests of posterity.[8] (At least, some of us desire that.) I can illustrate my point with a true story, which I shall embellish with a plausible historical explanation.

During the Second World War certain fragments of information, and fragments of wood, coming out of China led the California botanist Ralph Chaney to believe that the dawn redwood, which had been thought to be extinct for hundreds of thousands of years, was still in existence. Fortunately Chaney was a person of initiative and independent means, and he promptly set out for China to look for the tree. Getting to the interior of this war-torn country was no small accomplishment, but he did it. He found the tree. It was in an area that had suffered severe deforestation for several thousand years, and there were fewer than a thousand dawn redwoods left. They were still being cut down for fuel and cabinetmaking. Most of the living specimens were in temple courtyards — and thereby hangs our tale.

What is so special about being in a temple courtyard? Just this: it makes the object sacred. The word *sacred* is not easy to define, but whatever we mean by it we mean something that stands outside the bounds of rationality, as ordinarily understood. Let me illustrate this by a fictional conversation between a priest and a peasant in a Chinese temple a thousand years ago. Knowing almost nothing of Chinese social history I cannot make the conversation idiomatically correct, but I think the sense of it will be right.

A peasant from the deforested countryside, desperate for fuel to cook his rice, has slipped into a temple courtyard and is breaking twigs off the dawn redwood when he is apprehended by the priest.

"Here, here! You can't do that!"

"But, honorable sir, I have to. See, I have a little rice in this bowl, but it is uncooked. I can't eat it that way. I'm starving. If you'll only let me have a few twigs I can cook my rice and live another day."

"I'm sorry," says the priest, "but it is forbidden. This tree is sacred. No one is allowed to harm it."

"But if I don't get this fuel I will die."

"That's too bad: the tree is sacred. If everybody did what you are trying to do there soon wouldn't be any tree left."

The peasant thinks a few moments and then gets very angry: "Do you mean to tell me that the life of a mere tree is more valuable than the life of a human being?"

Now this is a very Westernized, twentieth-century question; I doubt that an ancient Chinese would have asked it. But if he had, how would the priest have replied? He might have repeated his assertion that the tree was sacred; or he might have tried to frighten the peasant by saying that touching it would bring bad luck to him in the future. That which is sacred or taboo is generally protected by legends that tend to make the taboo operational: bad luck, the evil eye, the displeasure of the gods. Are such stories consciously concocted because the idea of posterity is too remote to be effective? Or is it just a coincidence that objects so protected do survive for posterity's enjoyment? Whatever the case, being treated as sacred can protect an object against destruction by impoverished people who might otherwise discount the future in a simplistically rational way.

Once the peasant realized that the tree was sacred (or that its destruction would bring him bad luck) he would probably have slunk out of the courtyard. But suppose we continue to endow him with twentieth-century sentiments and see what happens.

"Sir," says the peasant, "your position is a self-serving one if I ever heard such. It's all well and good for you to be so thoughtful of posterity, for you get your three square meals a day no matter what. But what about me? Why do I have to serve posterity while you stuff your belly? Where's your sense of justice?"

"You're right," admits the priest. "I *am* the beneficiary of special privilege. There's only one thing to do," he says, as he takes off his clothes, "and that is to trade positions. Take your clothes off and trade with me! From now on you are the priest and I am a peasant."

That is a noble gesture — but surely the point is obvious? The gesture solves nothing. The next day, when the priest-turned-peasant comes begging for wood, the peasant-turned-priest must refuse him. If he doesn't the tree will soon be destroyed.

But the dawn redwood did survive. The conversation was fictional but the event — saving the trees by labeling some of them sacred — is true. The ginkgo tree was also saved in this way: it was known only in temple courtyards when Western men first found it in China. Special privilege preserved the trees in the face of vital demands made by an impoverished people.

Are we in the West capable of such severity? I know of only two stories of this sort, both from the USSR. The first dates from 1921, a time of famine there.[9] An American journalist visited a refugee camp on the Volga where almost half the people had already died of starvation. Noticing sacks of grain stacked in great mounds in an adjacent field, he asked the patriarch of the refugee community why the people did not simply overpower the lone soldier guarding the grain and help themselves. The patriarch explained that the sacks contained seed for planting the next season. "We do not steal from the future," he said.

Much the same thing happened again in the Second World War.[10] The siege of Leningrad by the Germans lasted 900 days, killing about a quarter of the population of three million. The cold and starving inhabitants had to eat dogs, cats, rats, and dried glue from furniture joints and wallpaper. All this time truckloads of edible seeds in containers were in storage in the All-Union Institute of Plant Industry. The seeds were a precious repository of genetic variety for Russian agriculture in the future. These seeds were never touched, though hundreds of thousands of people died.

Do these stories show that starving people are just naturally noble and take the long view? No. The behavior of people in prison camps shows that the opposite is the case. Altruism evaporates as egoism takes over.[11] It is egoism of the crudest sort: people will sacrifice every promise of tomorrow for the merest scrap of food today. It is as though the interest rate for discounting the future approached infinity.

Under severe survival conditions morality disappears, as became evident in an experiment carried out by American physiologists during the Second World War.[12] Foreseeing the need to treat starving victims of European concentration camps after the Germans were driven back, and recognizing that there was too little sound physiological knowledge, American scientists called for volunteers to take part in starvation experiments. Some conscientious objectors, members of the Church of the Brethren, volunteered. They were extremely idealistic young men, but as their ribs started to show, their ideals evaporated. They stole food from any place they could get it, including from one another. Many people do not like to face this sort of reality about human nature, but thoughtful religious men have known it for centuries. Thomas Aquinas summarized the situation very well when he said, "Necessity knows no law."[13]

It is futile to ask starving people to act against their own self-interest as they see it, which is an exclusively short-term self-interest. In a desperate community long-term interests can be protected only by institutional means: soldiers and policemen. These agents will be reliable only if they are fed up to some minimum level, higher than the average of the starving population. In discounting the future a man's personal discount rate is directly related to the emptiness of his stomach. Those who are the guardians of future stores must be put in a favored position to keep their personal discount rates low — that is, to make it possible for them to believe in, and protect, the future.

In a prosperous society the interests of posterity may often be served by the actions of a multitude of people. These actions are (or at least seem to be) altruistic. That cannot happen in a desperately needy society. When necessity is in the saddle we dare not expect altruism from "the people." Only institutions can then take actions that would be called altruistic were individuals to perform them. "An institution," as George Berg has pointed out, "can be considered as an anticipating device designed to pay off its members now for behavior which will benefit and stabilize society later."[14] An army, a police force, and a priesthood are institutions that *can* serve the needs of posterity — which they may or may not do.

Moralists try to achieve desired ends by exhorting people to be moral. They seldom succeed; and the poorer the society (other things being equal) the less their success. Institutionalists try to achieve desired ends by the proper design of institutions, allowing for the inescapable moral imperfection of the people on whose services institutions must depend. The Cardinal Rule is not violated: institution-designers count on people acting egoistically.

If there is complete equality of position and power in a needy society the interests of posterity are unlikely to be taken care of. Seeds for the future will be used for food today by a hungry people acting egoistically. To serve the future a few individuals must be put in the special position of being egoistically rewarded for protecting the seeds against the mass of people not enjoying special privilege. Well-fed soldiers acting egoistically (to preserve their institutional right to be well fed) can protect posterity's interests against the egoistic demands of today's hungry people. It is not superior morality that is most likely to serve posterity but an institutional design that makes wise use of special privilege.

I am not pleading for more special privilege in our own country. So far as posterity's interests are concerned the richer the country the less need it has for special privilege. We are rich. But I do plead for tolerance and understanding of special privilege in other countries, in poor countries. Political arrangements can never be wholly independent of the circumstances of life. We have long given lip service to this principle, recognizing that illiteracy, poverty, and certain traditions make democracy difficult. If we wish to protect posterity's interests in poor countries we must understand that distributional justice is a luxury that cannot be afforded by a country in which population overwhelms the resource base.

In a poor country, if all people are equally poor—if there is no special privilege—the future will be universally discounted at so high a rate that it will practically vanish. Posterity will be cheated; and being cheated it will, in its turn, be still poorer and will discount the future at an even higher rate. Thus a vicious cycle is established. Only special privilege can break this cycle in a poor country. We need not positively approve of special privilege; but we can only do harm if, like the missionaries of old, we seek to prevent it.

Special privilege does not insure that the interests of posterity will be taken care of in a poor country; it merely makes it possible. Those enjoying special privilege may find it in their hearts to safeguard the interests of posterity against the necessarily—and forgivably—short-sighted egoism of the desperately poor who are under the natural necessity of discounting the future at a ruinous rate. We will serve posterity's interests better if we give up the goal of diminishing special privilege in poor countries. We should seek instead to persuade the privileged to create altruistic institutions that can make things better for posterity, thus diminishing the need for special privilege in the future.

Special privilege may be *pro tempore,* as it is for drafted or enlisted soldiers (in the stories told of the USSR); or it may extend over generations by virtue of hereditary privilege. The privileged always seek to make privilege hereditary. There is much to be said against hereditary privilege, from both biological and political points of view; but it has a peculiar psychological merit from the point of view of posterity, a merit pointed out by Edmund Burke (1729-1797) when he said: "People will not look forward to posterity who never look backward to their ancestors."[15] The image evoked by this old-fashioned voice of conservatism is one of landed gentry or nobility, reared in baronial halls lined with the pictures of ancestors, looking out over comfortable estates, which they are determined to keep intact against the demands of the less fortunate, so that their children may enjoy what they enjoy. In some psychological sense posterity and ancestors fuse together in the service of an abstraction called "family."

If Burke's psychology is right (and I think it is), he points to several ways in which posterity may be served despite the strictures of hardheaded economics. A society in which prosperity is less than universal may institutionalize special privilege. (The desired result is not guaranteed: when ill used, special privilege can have the opposite effect, of course.) Where wealth is sufficiently great and more equitably distributed, a society that held Burke's assertion to be true would be expected to modify its institutions in a number of ways. Obviously it would see to it that the teaching of history played a large role in education.

Less obviously, a society interested in posterity might decide that the policy of encouraging a high degree of mobility in the labor force should be reversed. There is considerable anecdotal evidence to show that a person's identification with the past is significantly strengthened by exposure during childhood to the sight of enduring artifacts: family portraits, a stable dwelling place, even unique trees.[16] It is harder for a mobile family to achieve this unconscious identification with the past. It is the conventional wisdom of economics that labor mobility improves the productivity of a nation. In the short run that may be true; but if the Burkean argument presented here is sound it means that short-term economic efficiency is purchased at the expense of long-term failure to conserve resources.

One further and rather curious point needs to be made about this argument. If I believe it to be true that locational stability encourages the identification of the past with the future, that belief may have little direct effect on my own actions because my childhood is now beyond reach. Such a "belief" would be a conscious one, and it seems that only unconscious beliefs have much power to cause actions that run contrary to the dictates of simple rationality. I cannot willfully create within myself the psychological identification whose praises I sing. The most I can do (if I am powerful and clever enough) is modify the environment of other people—of children now growing up—so that they will unconsciously come to give preference to the interests of posterity.

Here is a curious question: if, because of my own childhood I myself lack a strong feeling for place and ancestry (and hence for posterity), what would lead me to try to inculcate it in others by working to modify their childhood experiences? Isn't this process a sort of lifting one's self by one's bootstraps, a sort of second-order altruism? The problem of posterity is rich in puzzles!

Whatever the answer may be to questions like these, this much should be clear: once a society loses a keen concern for posterity, regaining such a sense will be the work not of a few years but of a generation or more. If civilization should collapse worldwide, the second tragedy would be the loss of the will to rebuild it. Under the inescapable condition of dire poverty, augmented no doubt by a rejection of the past that had caused the collapse, effective concern for posterity would virtually disappear—not forever, perhaps, but until historical developments we cannot possibly foresee rekindled a concern for social continuity.

In the light of this conclusion questions of another sort should be raised. Do we yet have the knowledge needed to insure the indefinite survival of any political unit? Do we yet know how to prevent the collapse that overtook all previous civilizations? If we do, then it is safe to create One World (if we can); but if we do not, it is not advisable even to try. If collapse is still an inescapable part of the life cycle of political units then posterity would be poorly served by a fusing of all present states into one. We should instead preserve enough of the economic and social barriers between groupings of humanity so that the cancer of collapse can be localized.[17]

If knowledge of local wretchedness in distant states should lead us altruistically to create a resource commons we would thereby become a party to the ultimate metastasis of collapse. If our understanding of the physiology and pathology of political organizations is less than total, an overriding concern for the needs of the present generation can lead to a total sacrifice of the interests of posterity. I submit that our knowledge of the laws of political behavior is less than total.

II

. . . Students of charity have long recognized that an important motive of the giver is to help himself, the giver.[18] Hindus give to secure a better life in the next incarnation; Moslems, to achieve a richer paradise at the end of this life; and Christians in a simpler day no doubt hoped to shorten their stay in purgatory by their generosity. Is there anyone who would say that contemporary charity is completely free of the self-serving element?

To deserve the name, charity surely must justify itself primarily, perhaps even solely, by the good it does the recipient, not only in the moment of giving but in the long run. That every act has multiple consequences was recognized by William L. Davison, who grouped the consequences of an act of charity into two value-classes, positive and negative.[19] True charity, he said,

> confers benefits, and it refrains from injuring. . . . Hence, charity may sometimes assume an austere and even apparently unsympathetic aspect toward its object. When this object's real good cannot be achieved without inflicting pain and suffering, charity does not shrink from the infliction. . . . Moreover, a sharp distinction must be drawn between charity and amiability or good nature—the latter of which is a weakness and may be detrimental to true charity, although it may also be turned to account in its service.

To the ecologically minded student of ethics, most traditional ethics looks like mere amiability, focusing as it does on the manifest misery of the present generation to the neglect of the more subtle but equally real needs of a much larger posterity. It is amiability that feeds the Nepalese in one generation and drowns Bangladeshi in another.[20] It is amiability that, contemplating the wretched multitudes of Indians asks, "How can we let them starve?" implying that we, and only we, have the power to end their suffering. Such an assumption surely springs from hubris.

Fifty years ago India and China were equally miserable, and their future prospects equally bleak. During the past generation we have given India "help" on a massive scale; China, because of political differences between her and us, has received no "help" from us and precious little from anybody else. Yet who is better off today? And whose future prospects look brighter? Even after generously discounting the reports of the first starry-eyed Americans to enter China in recent years, it is apparent that China's 900 million are physically better off than India's 600 million.

All that has come about without an iota of "help" from us.

Could it be that a country that is treated as a responsible agent does better in the long run than one that is treated as an irresponsible parasite which we must "save" repeatedly? Is it not possible that robust responsibility is a virtue among nations as it is among individuals? Can we tolerate a charity that destroys responsibility?

Admittedly, China did not reach her present position of relative prosperity without great suffering, great loss of life. Did millions die? Tens of millions? We don't know. If we had enjoyed cordial relations with the new China during the birth process no doubt we would, out of a rich store of amiability, have seen to it that China remained as irresponsible and miserable as India. Our day-to-day decisions, with their delayed devastation, would have been completely justified by our traditional, posterity-blind ethics which seems incapable of asking the crucial question, *"And then what?"*

Underlying most ethical thought at present is the assumption that human life is the *summum bonum.* Perhaps it is; but we need to inquire carefully into what we mean by "human life." Do we mean the life of each and every human being now living, all 4,000,000,000 of them? Is each presently existing human being to be kept alive (and breeding) regardless of the consequences for future human beings? So, apparently, say amiable, individualistic, present-oriented, future-blind Western ethicists.

An ecologically oriented ethicist asks, "And then what?" and insists that the needs of posterity be given a weighting commensurate with those of the present generation. The economic prejudice that leads to a heavy discounting of the future must be balanced by a recognition that the population of posterity vastly exceeds the population of the living.[21] We know from experience that the environment can be irreversibly damaged and the carrying capacity of a land permanently lowered. Even a little lowering multiplied by an almost limitless posterity should weigh heavily in the scales against the needs of those living, once our charity expands beyond the limits of simple amiability.

We can, of course, increase carrying capacity somewhat. But only hubris leads us to think that our ability to do so is without limit. Despite all our technological accomplishments — and they are many — there is a potent germ of truth in the saying of Horace (65–8 B.C.): *Naturam expelles furca, tamen usque recurret.* "Drive nature off with a pitchfork, nevertheless she will return with a rush." This is the message of Rachel Carson,[22] which has been corroborated by many others.[23]

The morality of an act is a function of the state of the system at the time the act is performed—this is the foundation stone of situationist, ecological ethics.[24] A time-blind absolute ethical principle like that implied by the shibboleth, "the sanctity of life," leads to greater suffering than its situationist, ecological alternative — and ultimately and paradoxically, even to a lesser quantity of life over a sufficiently long period of time. The interests of posterity can be brought into the reckoning of ethics if we abandon the idea of the sanctity of (present) life as an absolute ethical ideal, replacing it with the idea of the sanctity of the carrying capacity.

Those who would like to make the theory of ethics wholly rational must look with suspicion on any statement that includes the word "sanctity." There is a whole class of terms whose principal (and perhaps sole) purpose seems to be to set a stop to inquiry: "self-evident" and "sanctity" are members of this class. I must, therefore, show that "sanctity" is used as something more than a discussion-stopper when it occurs in the phrase "the sanctity of the carrying capacity."

Some there are who so love the world of Nature (that is, Nature *sine* Man) that they regard the preservation of a world without humankind as a legitimate objective of human beings. It is difficult to argue this ideal dispassionately and productively. Let me only say that I am not one of this class of nature-lovers; my view is definitely anthropocentric. Even so I argue that we would do well to accept "Thou shalt not exceed the carrying capacity of any environment" as a legitimate member of a new Decalogue. When for the sake of momentary gain by human beings the carrying capacity is transgressed, the long-term interests of the same human beings — "same" meaning themselves and their successors in time — are damaged. I should not say that the carrying capacity is something that is *intrinsically* sacred (whatever *that* may mean) but that the rhetorical device "carrying capacity" is a shorthand way of dealing time and posterity into the game. A mathematician would, I imagine, view "carrying capacity" as an algorithm, a substitute conceptual element with a different grammar from the elements it replaces. Algorithmic substitutions are made to facilitate analysis; when they are well chosen, they introduce no appreciable errors. I think "carrying capacity" meets significant analytical demands of a posterity-oriented ethics.

In an uncrowded world there may be no ethical need for the ecological concept of the carrying capacity. But ours is a crowded world. We need this concept if we are to minimize human suffering in the long run (and not such a very long run at that). How Western man has pretty well succeeded in locking himself into a suicidal course of action by developing and clinging to a concept of the absolute sanctity of life is a topic that calls for deep inquiry. . . .

NOTES

1. John Trumbull (1782), "McFingal," canto II, lines 121ff. Reprinted in Edwin T. Bowden, ed. (1962), *The Satiric Poems of John Trumbull* (Austin: University of Texas Press), p. 129.

2. Hans Jonas (1974), *Philosophical Essays* (Englewood Cliffs, N.J.: Prentice-Hall). [Also in this Anthology, pp. 23–36.]

3. Martin Buber (1970), *I and Thou* (New York: Scribner's).

4. John Rawls (1971), *A Theory of Justice* (Cambridge: Harvard University Press). See especially pp. 284–93.

5. Rawls has become the darling of the liberal-to-radical branch of the political spectrum of our time; his theory of "justice as fairness" fits in perfectly with their political aims. Many professional philosophers, however, have not been taken in by Rawls. See

Brian Barry (1973), *The Liberal Theory of Justice* (Oxford: Clarendon Press). See also vol. 3, no. 1 of *Social Theory and Practice* (1974), a special issue devoted to Rawls. One is struck by the frequency with which a critical reviewer begins by identifying *A Theory of Justice* as "a work of major importance," or speaks of "my great respect for the author," before proceeding to dismember Rawls's argument, enthymeme by enthymeme. Charles Frankel is more forthright. In his essay "Justice, Utilitarianism, and Rights" (1974), *Social Theory and Practice* 3(1):27–46, Frankel says that Rawls's work is "not so much argument as atmospherics," and remarks that his prose "gives off that special aroma of diffident perplexity which has become, these days, the seal of good housekeeping in philosophy." Still more strongly Frankel states that "the confusion between fact and faith is not merely incidental in Rawls's argument, but indispensable to it." In the light of all the justifiable criticism that has been leveled against it the puzzle is why the popular-intellectual press—magazines like the *New York Review of Books*—treat Rawls with such awe. This is a problem in the sociology of the knowledge industry.

6. M. Taghi Farvar and John P. Milton, eds. (1972), *The Careless Technology* (Garden City, N.Y.: Natural History Press). See particularly the article by Carl J. George.

7. Garrett Hardin, "Why Plant a Redwood Tree?" in G. Tyler Miller (1975), *Living in the Environment* (Belmont, Cal.: Wadsworth).

8. Garrett Hardin (1974), "The Rational Foundations of Conservation," *North American Review* 259(4), 14–17.

9. Raymond Swing (1964), *Good Evening* (New York: Hardcourt, Brace & World), p. 137.

10. Jack R. Harlan (1975), "Our Vanishing Genetic Resources," *Science* 188:618–21.

11. Ancel Keys et al. (1950), *The Biology of Human Starvation* (Minneapolis: University of Minnesota Press).

12. H. S. Guetzkow and P. H. Bowman (1946), *Men and Hunger* (Elgin, Ill.: Brethren Publishing House).

13. St. Thomas Aquinas, *Summa Theologica,* translated by the Fathers of the English Dominican Province (New York: Benziger Bros., 1947), vol. 1, p. 1022.

14. George Berg (1968), "Environmental Pollution in the Inner City," *Scientist and Citizen* 10(5), 123–25.

15. Edmund Burke (1790), *Reflections on the Revolution in France* (Garden City, N.Y.: Doubleday, 1961), p. 45.

16. Melford E. Spiro (1956), *Kibbutz: Venture in Utopia* (Cambridge: Harvard University Press). The author tells how children brought up in a spartan, communal kibbutz, in which there is very little that can acquire the emotional aura of "home," develop emotional attachments to such fixed natural objects as trees.

17. Kenneth E. Boulding, "Commons and Community: The Idea of a Public," in Garrett Hardin and John Baden (1977), *Managing the Commons* (San Francisco: Freeman). Boulding makes this point forcefully, giving the mathematical theory on which it is based.

18. A. S. Geden (1928), "Hindu Charity (almsgiving)," *Encyclopedia of Religion and Ethics,* vol. 3 (New York: Scribner), pp. 387–89.

19. William L. Davidson (1928), "Charity," *Encyclopedia of Religion and Ethics,* vol. 3, op. cit., p. 373.

20. Earlier in this paper, in a portion not included here ("Carrying Capacity," p. 128), Hardin points out that "twenty-five years ago western countries brought food and medicine to Nepal." This led to a marked population rise in Nepal, which, in turn,

created an increasing demand for firewood, which then resulted in deforestation. With the forests gone, disastrous floods came to Bangladesh, downstream from the Nepalese watershed. — Ed.

21. Garrett Hardin (1974), "The Rational Foundation of Conservation," op. cit.
22. Rachel Carson (1962), *Silent Spring* (Boston: Houghton Mifflin).
23. M. Taghi Farvar and John P. Milton, eds., *The Careless Technology,* op. cit.
24. Garrett Hardin (1972), *Exploring New Ethics for Survival* (New York: Viking).

PART FIVE

Applications

Part 5. Applications

Introduction

What, then, is to be done? In view of the unprecedented emergencies and opportunities of our time, and of the concepts, principles, and imperatives that issue from an examination of the moral question of the duty to posterity, what are the morally acceptable limits and the morally required policies regarding our deliberate and informed dealings with the future? The moral concepts and principles examined above have endless applications, and many thoughtful and provocative papers have explained these applications. The four papers in this section have been chosen, first, to illustrate the wide range of applicability of the posterity question and, second, to recapitulate, *in application,* the principles and concepts explained earlier in this anthology.

The first paper, by Michael Bayles, is directly responsive to the question posed by Garrett Hardin in the preceding paper of how we are to balance the needs of the present generation with those of future generations.

Not only are we in a position to affect the food supply of future persons (i.e., through agricultural research and population policy), we are also able to determine the genetic make-up of future persons. We can do so now through deliberate policies of negative and positive eugenics (i.e., by preventing or promoting the transmission of certain recognized genes through sterilization or artificial insemination). The "genetic engineering" and even the cloning of human beings may soon be technologically possible, and with these innovations some profound and unprecedented moral problems will arise. Hardy Jones explains, analyzes, and projects some of these present and prospective issues.

Does the duty to future generations include a duty to produce future (or "potential") persons? This question is examined by Mary Anne Warren. All the papers heretofore have dealt primarily with the moral issue of "the duty to posterity" in exclusion of the related issue of "population policy." As noted in the general introduction, the former problem is concerned with duties to persons who may be assumed to exist in the future, while the latter deals with deliberate decisions to procreate or not to procreate. While the two issues can

be conceptually separated with little difficulty, in the arena of moral controversy and debate they are closely interrelated. Warren's essay has been chosen
to display this connection and to serve a "bridge" between the two issues. Warren defends a widely held, yet warmly contested, view that, while the living
have moral obligations not willfully to harm those who *will* exist, they have no
obligation to bring potential persons into existence. The truth or falsity of this
second claim has important implications for the duty to posterity. (For references to additional works dealing with the topic of "population policy," see
Note 10 of Warren's article, p. 273 below, and part 2 of the bibliography at the
end of this anthology.)

The final paper (excepting the "Afterword") in this anthology is also the
longest. In a careful, eloquent, and thoroughly researched argument against
nuclear power, Richard and Val Routley recapitulate many of the concepts,
principles, and issues developed and detailed earlier in this anthology. Several
of the papers included in this collection are cited and criticized by the Routleys. They contend that *no* "features of the future, such as uncertainty or
indeterminacy," are sufficient to excuse or allow the considerable burdens that
nuclear energy technology will inflict upon future generations.

Michael D. Bayles

Famine or Food: Sacrificing for Future or Present Generations

In two recent papers, Garrett Hardin has asserted: "Every life saved this year in a poor country diminishes the quality of life for subsequent generations," and "To be generous with one's own possessions is one thing; to be generous with posterity's is quite another."[1] An ecologically oriented ethics, he also claims, "insists that the needs of posterity be given a weighting commensurate with those of the present generation. The economic prejudice that leads to a heavy discounting of the future must be balanced by a recognition that the population of posterity vastly exceeds the population of the living."[2] On the other side, Callahan claims, "While we surely have obligations to future generations, our more immediate obligation is toward those now alive. There is no moral justification for making them the fodder for a higher quality of life of those yet to be born, or even for the maintenance of the present quality of life."[3]

In effect, then, food aid raises the dual issues of sacrifice within a generation and between generations. By "sacrifice" is meant people not having some goods or benefits they would have were a different policy adopted. As just explained, not giving aid in order to secure the quality of life of future people involves sacrifice between generations, because people currently alive will die sooner than they would were aid given. The giving of aid involves the sacrifice of those in the future for the sake of those presently alive. It also involves sacrifice within a generation, because the better-off give up some goods they might have for the sake of the worse-off. Thus, there are two sacrifices involved in the provision of aid. An argument in favor of it will have to take both into account.

The crux of Hardin's argument is that if food aid is given now, more people will starve later, and that consequences in future generations must be weighed equally with famine deaths which would occur now were food aid withheld.

From *Ethics, Free Enterprise, and Public Policy: Original Essays on Moral Issues in Business,* by Richard T. De George and Joseph A. Pichler (eds.). Copyright 1978 by Oxford University Press, Inc. Reprinted with permission.

However, on current ethical theories, it is not obvious that future famines would be a great evil. In support of Hardin's thesis, Joseph Fletcher and Tristram Engelhardt have both made the seemingly plausible claim that future famines would injure those alive then. Fletcher contends that those who subsequently starve will be injured.[4] However, one must compare what happens on the two alternatives of aid and no aid. If aid is given, they will live for a while and then starve. If aid is not given, many of them will never live at all. For the first option to be worse for them than the second, their brief lives would have to be so miserable that it would be better for them not to live at all; that is, their lives would have to be not worth living. While Fletcher holds that a rather high quality of life is essential for life to be worth living, there is little if any reason to believe that these people would not attain that level.[5]

Engelhardt presents a more subtle analysis. He does not claim that those who starve but would not have been born had no aid been given are injured. Instead, he claims the injury is only to those who would have been born anyway, their quality of life being lower than it would otherwise have been.[6] That is, he claims that if aid is not given, there will be a future generation of i people. If aid is given, then there will be a future generation of $i + j$ people. Fletcher claims the injury is to members of the i or j classes who starve. Engelhardt claims it is only to members of the i class who are worse off, whether by starvation or otherwise, due to the existence of the members of j.

Englehardt's analysis will not do. First, it assumes that the i class will be composed of the same individuals on either alternative, so that one may speak of the same persons being better off on one than the other. But the i class will not consist of the identical individuals on the two alternatives. The difference in policies would change the timing of births and different people would be born, at least as different as siblings.[7] Second, even if they were the same individuals, they would not be injured in the sense of having had goods taken from them. Instead, they would merely fail to receive benefits they might otherwise have had. The failure to provide benefits is not morally equivalent to injuring people. It is morally one thing not to give an employee a Christmas bonus and quite another to reduce his salary.[8]

Instead, the issue should be formulated as follows: Assuming justice within each generation, how much quality of life ought one generation to sacrifice for another? "Quality of life" does not refer simply to material goods, but to the total natural and social environment providing conditions and opportunities for a meaningful and rewarding life. A sacrifice may be by present generations for future ones, or by future generations for present ones. These sacrifices will usually be of forgone benefits rather than incurred losses. For example, one argument for Stalinist repression in the Soviet Union during the 1930's was that drastic measures were needed then to bring about rapid industrialization and improve the quality of life for future generations. Thus, the generation of the 1930's was sacrificing for the generation of the 1960's. On the opposite side, some people believe that the high quality of life in the United States during the 1950's and 1960's consumed material resources and created such pollution that subsequent generations—perhaps those of the 1970's and 1980's—will have a lower quality of life, at least as measured by pollution, resource consumption, and prices, than they would otherwise have had. Such sacrifices by future generations are always an involuntary forgoing of benefits.

It is a well-accepted principle of moral philosophy that time is irrelevant.[9] Whether an event or state of affairs occurs at one time or another is irrelevant to the evaluation of it or the choice that produces it. Of course, events in the far future may be less certain to occur than those in the near future and, therefore, less heavily weighted in evaluating the consequences of choices, but the lesser weighting is due to the uncertainty, not the time per se. Consequently, if one seeks to obtain the highest average or total quality of life over time, one may prefer a lower than possible quality of life now because it will be outweighed by a much higher one later, or vice versa. A high rate of savings and investment now would provide a lower quality of life at present than a low rate, but it might pay off in a much higher quality of life in the future. It follows on these principles that "generational sacrifice," the sacrifice of the well-being of one generation for another, is justifiable provided less suffering or greater well-being results when the well-being of all those existing at any time is considered.

The problem is, what precisely is the obligation of the present generation to future ones? One may perhaps approach it by roughly ranking the degrees of concern or benevolence one might have for future generations. A minimum concern might be that future generations survive long enough to reproduce themselves and continue the species. This degree of concern is roughly comparable to one that currently existing children survive to adulthood. A greater degree of concern would be to ensure that future generations have a minimum level of well-being or quality of life—higher than that for mere survival but not as high as it might be. Such a concern is analogous to a concern to provide a floor of welfare for currently existing people. A concern for a minimum well-being does not involve a concern for others equal to that for oneself, for presumably one desires more than minimum well-being for oneself. Consequently, a third level of concern would be that future generations be as well-off as the present. One would want others to have as much as one does oneself. Finally, one could be altruistic in the sense of wanting others to be better off than oneself. Thus, in order to make life even better for future generations, one would be willing to take less than what would leave them equally well-off.

Principles of moral obligation to future generations embody one of these levels of concern. The issue is what principle may be justified. As a first step in determining what principle is justified, one may explore the implications of there being any obligation to future generations.

Any degree of concern for future generations will impose some moral constraints upon what the present generation may do. Suppose the present generation has a quality of life of level p. Further, suppose it is accepted that future generations ought to be able to have a minimum quality of life of level q, which is less than p. This obligation may be called the minimum principle.

Then the present generation is not justified in acting in ways which would prevent future generations from attaining level q. However, this restriction leaves open the size of future generations, although freedom to have the children one desires is a factor in determining present quality of life. The quality of life of the present generation may not prevent the next generation from attaining level q, but it may necessitate its being smaller than it would otherwise have had to be. The present generation thus will not be able to have as many children as it might otherwise, but one may assume other benefits more than make up for losses in not having children. Consequently, provided each subsequent generation is smaller than it otherwise need to have been, it is possible for each generation to live at a higher quality of life (involving a more rapid consumption of resources, etc.). In short, the size of future generations may be sacrificed for present quality of life.

However, there is a limit to such sacrifices. If future generations become too small, they will not be able to sustain a quality of life of level q. Moreover, since moral principles are indifferent to time, it makes no difference whether it is a generation in the near or distant future which would become too small to sustain a population with a quality of life at level q. Consequently, the present generation is constrained to act so that a population with a quality of life of level q is indefinitely sustainable. The population which may be sustainable at that level might be considerably smaller than the present one. Moreover, the present generation may enjoy a much higher quality of life than q, and future generations may be able to live only at level q. Whether that is possible largely depends on how high level q is. In any case, this argument establishes a basic element of an obligation to future generations. Any obligation to future generations, even for mere survival to adulthood, requires the present generation to act so that future generations can be indefinitely sustained at that quality of life.

Suppose generations live in ways which are not indefinitely sustainable—for example, by producing pollution, consuming resources, or simply having large numbers of children. Then, sooner or later, there will be a generation which cannot live above level q and enable the following generations to attain a quality of life of level q. Consequently, in the long run, whatever level q is, if previous generations do not provide for more than that level, the population will be unable to live above it and indefinitely sustain a population at level q. Thus, the ultimate principle must be that a generation is not justified in acting in ways which will not permit the continuance of a population at the current quality of life. In short, the only principle of obligation to future generations which can be adopted in the long run is that the present generation act so that a population is indefinitely sustainable at the present quality of life.

While this is the only principle which may be justified in the long run, it does not follow that it must be adopted now. The conduct of the present generation may not allow for future ones to have an equally high quality of life but only a minimum level. However, one cannot let the standard of a minimum level to be sustained vary over time. If the present generation is at level $q + 2$, It might claim that the minimum level owed to future generations is q and so provide for the next generation. But the next generation may claim that the minimum level owed is $q - 1$ and so live at level $q + 1$. Repeated resetting of the minimum level owed would result in a constantly diminishing quality of life. Hence, the standard of the level owed future generations must be constant.

If one thinks q is the minimum owed others, one should act to assure its attainment. Only if people in future generations will agree to the principle can one be assured that it will be adhered to and no resetting occur. Thus, one should adopt a principle to which future generations may also be expected to agree and adhere. The principle states what generations are obligated to provide future ones, what it would be wrong not to provide. It thus sets limits to their self-seeking. Consequently, one may assume each generation will seek as high a quality of life for itself as is morally permissible. Each generation will hope previous ones set q as high as possible. The result, then, is that all generations will agree only if q is as high a quality of life as may be indefinitely sustainable. Consequently, the only principle which may realistically be expected to be adopted and adhered to is that each generation is obligated to provide future ones as high a sustainable quality of life as it achieves. This may be called the maximum principle.

Societies may violate this principle either with respect to population characteristics or to quality of life. For example, if the population is too large or small to sustain the present quality of life, then it should be decreased or increased. Similarly, the quality of life may be too high to be sustainable no matter what the size of the population, in which case it ought to be lowered. Also, the quality of life may be lower than is sustainable. That would not violate an obligation to future generations but it would probably violate obligations to members of the present one. However, one need not worry about this case, because most people desire and seek at least as good a life for themselves as is morally permissible. Since population characteristics such as size and age structure are not inherently valuable, one evaluates them by their impact upon the quality of life. That is, one first determines the maximum sustainable quality of life and population characteristics are adjusted to provide for it, keeping in mind that the opportunity to have children is one factor in the quality of life.

An objection to such obligations to far distant generations is that one cannot know what they will desire or need.[10] One cannot provide for their quality of life because one does not know what to provide. This objection has more force with respect to providing for a particular type of goods and services than it does with respect to providing for a quality of life. Quality of life is a broad concept covering natural and social conditions for life's worthwhileness. One can be pretty sure future generations will need a source of food; education; social institutions preventing violent conflicts; physical mobility; and the abilities to see, hear, and communicate.[11] Moreover, since the present generation is obligated to provide as high a quality of life as it enjoys, in the face of ignorance about future needs and desires, it should leave open as much freedom and opportunity as possible to allow an equally high quality of life in the future. If one does not know whether one will need to do A, B, or C next week, one reasonably tries to leave open all options. Thus, if the present generation does not know whether future ones will need arable lands, forests, etc., it should leave as much as possible for them.

The two principles of generational sacrifice may be applied to the issue of food aid. They require that the present generation make sacrifices if they are necessary to ensure future generations a minimum or equivalent sustainable quality of life. The difficulty in applying them is in determining what quality of life future generations would have. On Hardin's scenario, if food aid is given, there will be many more deaths by starvation in the future. What this result implies about the quality of life of that generation as a whole depends on the criteria used to determine the quality of life of a society. It is not possible here to develop an index for the quality of life of a society. Nonetheless, one may make a commonsense judgment that widespread famine, with concomitant social turmoil and human misery, would constitute a low quality of life. However, the alternative is current starvation and a lower present quality of life. On the maximum principle, the present generation ought to suffer current starvation to the extent that failure to do so would result in a lower quality of life in the future. In short, it should suffer a current famine if that will avoid a worse one, but it need not suffer any more starvation than that. On a minimum principle, one's obligation depends on what the minimum is and whether or not a future famine would reduce the quality of life below it. It would certainly not require permitting as much present starvation as the maximum principle, and it provides a weak basis for an argument against food aid.

A further difficulty is that it is not certain that the Hardin scenario of food aid would in fact materialize. First, it is not clear that food aid does contribute to larger future populations.[12] Second, if stringent programs of population control are implemented, then aid may eliminate an imminent famine and population control a later one. Whether population control can or will be effective in time is a matter about which experts disagree. One's willingness to provide aid depends upon one's attitude toward risk taking. If one is a gambler, then one will be willing to provide aid now in the hope that the future catastrophe will be avoided by policies taken in the meantime. If one is cautious, one will not take such chances and will not give aid now in order to be certain to avoid a later catastrophe.

NOTES

I wish to thank Tom Shannon, Jim Smith, and Onora O'Neill for helpful comments on previous versions of this essay.

1. "Living on a Lifeboat," *BioScience,* Vol. 24 (October, 1974), pp. 565 (italics omitted), 567.

2. Garrett Hardin, "Carrying Capacity as an Ethical Concept," *Soundings,* Vol. 59 (Spring 1976), p. 133. [See part 2 of preceding paper by Hardin in this anthology.]

3. Daniel Callahan, "Doing Well by Doing Good: Garrett Hardin's Lifeboat Ethic," *Hastings Center Report,* Vol. 4 (December, 1974), p. 4.

4. Joseph Fletcher, "Feeding the Hungry: An Ethical Appraisal," *Soundings,* Vol. 59 (Spring, 1976), p. 58.

5. See Joseph Fletcher, "Indications of Humanhood: A Tentative Profile of Man," *Hastings Center Report,* Vol. 2 (November, 1972), pp. 1-4; *idem,* "Four Indicators of Humanhood—The Enquiry Matures," *Hastings Center Report,* Vol. 4 (December, 1974), pp. 4-7.

6. H. Tristram Engelhardt, Jr., "Individuals and Communities, Present and Future: Towards a Morality in a Time of Famine," *Soundings,* Vol. 59 (Spring, 1976), p. 79.

7. Derek Parfit, "On Doing the Best for Our Children," in *Ethics and Population,* ed. by Michael D. Bayles (Cambridge, Mass.: Schenkman Publishing Co., 1976), pp. 101-102.

8. I elaborate the basic argument of this paragraph in "Harm to the Unconceived," *Philosophy and Public Affairs,* Vol. 5 (Spring, 1976), pp. 292-304.

9. John Rawls, *A Theory of Justice* (Cambridge, Mass.: Harvard University Press, Belknap Press, 1971), pp. 293-98; Henry Sidgwick, *The Methods of Ethics,* 7th ed. (London: Macmillan & Co., 1907), p. 381.

10. Martin P. Golding, "Obligations to Future Generations," *The Monist,* Vol. 56 (January, 1972), pp. 85-99; Robert L. Cunningham, "Ethics, Ecology, and the Rights of Future Generations," *Modern Age* (Summer, 1975), pp. 260-71. [Golding's paper is reprinted in this anthology.]

11. See also Daniel Callahan, "What Obligations Do We Have to Future Generations?" *American Ecclesiastical Review,* Vol. 164 (April, 1971), pp. 273-75. See also B.M. Barry, "Justice Between Generations," in *Law, Morality and Society: Essays in Honour of H. L. A. Hart,* ed. by P. M. S. Hacker and J. Raz (Oxford: Clarendon Press, 1977), pp. 274-75. [Callahan's paper is reprinted in this anthology.]

12. Lester R. Brown, for example, has claimed that "good nutrition is the best contraceptive"; *In the Human Interest: A Strategy to Stabilize World Population* (New York: Norton & Co., 1974), p. 119.

Hardy Jones

Genetic Endowment and Obligations to Future Generations

Are there any moral obligations to unborn and unconceived members of future generations? There appears to be an emerging philosophical controversy concerning the existence, analysis, and justification of such obligations.[1] In this paper I discuss one kind of obligation with regard to future persons — the responsibility of providing a good genetic constitution. There is a continuing social and biological controversy over the ethical implications of genetic control. Distinguished geneticists, such as H. J. Muller, have insisted for years that increasing numbers of undesirable mutations are harming the genetic endowments of human beings.[2] Genetic manipulation is, of course, not new: persons have practiced it with domestic animals and with human beings for a very long time. Modern developments, though, have contributed to the alleged need for it and to refined techniques for accomplishing it. Medical advances have rendered many genetically defective individuals able to reproduce. Because of this and several other factors it is claimed that, genetically, the human race is getting worse and worse all the time. Though some biologists are gloomier than others, there is general agreement that failure to adopt negative and positive eugenics measures will result in our descendants having to bear extremely serious genetic burdens. There is strong pressure to institute both mandatory and voluntary schemes to prevent some of these defects entirely and to reduce the incidence of those not totally eliminable.

Many intelligent and sensitive persons find such proposals quite alarming. There has been much discussion of the dangers of using biological knowledge and technique for genetic screening, mandatory sterilization and abortion, cloning, and selective reproduction. The benefits of such practices are thought to be outweighed by their potential for repression and injustice. In this controversy the moral principles on all sides are often unarticulated, confused, or unsupported.[3] In discussing the moral basis for determining genetic

---

Reprinted from and copyrighted by *Social Theory and Practice* (Florida State University), 4:1 (Fall 1976), with permission of the publisher and author.

endowments, I shall connect the special problems of genetic control with more general claims about obligations to, and rights of, members of future generations. The main question is this: what is the rationale for an obligation to provide good genetic endowments for future persons?

I

Advocates of far-reaching eugenics programs have sometimes claimed that every person has a right to a reasonably good genetic endowment. Dwight Engle, in *Who Should Have Children?*, says that "every child should have the right to a sound biological endowment and good environment. . . ."[4] It is then argued that this right places severe limits on the freedom of those who desire to have children. The noted geneticist Bentley Glass has asserted:

> In the new, far more regulated society of man which will inevitably be forced upon us by our exponential rates of increase, the present genetic types of man may not all permit happy adjustment. . . . The once sacred rights of man must alter in many ways. Thus, in an overpopulated world it can no longer be affirmed that the right of the man and woman to reproduce as they see fit is inviolate . . . the right that must become paramount is not the right to procreate, but the right of every child to be born with a sound physical and mental constitution, based on a sound genotype.[5]

The implicit argument is roughly as follows. Every person has a right to a good genetic endowment. The children of certain couples will have very poor genetic constitutions. The rights of these children will be violated if they are conceived and born. So these couples have obligations not to have children.

It may appear that such claims are very plausible, albeit in need of clarification and support. I believe, however, that assertions of a right to a good genetic endowment are quite seriously confused. How could someone have such a right? Suppose A is a person with genetically defective characteristics. If a person did not have the genetic endowment that A has, then A would not exist. If A's parents had produced a child with a different and better endowment, that child would not have been, could not have been, A. An individual's genetic endowment defines or determines who he is in a way that his other characteristics do not. (In this discussion "genetic endowment" is used to mean that genetic constitution possessed at the stage of conception. For reasons considered later, I wish to ignore cases of alteration of already established genetic makeups.)

Compare the claim of a right to a good genetic endowment with the following: Every person has a right to be born into a world with a clean and healthy environment. This claim, whether or not it is true, is a quite sensible one. We can think, alternatively, of an individual as living in a healthy environment or as living in an unhealthy environment. The clean environment is independent of the person's existence: he can exist with it or he can exist without it. His surroundings are things contingently attached, or not attached, to his life. But a genetic endowment cannot be thought about in this way: it is not theoretically "detachable." We cannot coherently think of *the same person* either as having the genetic endowment he possesses or as not having it. Gene alteration aside, one cannot sensibly imagine A's existing without the genetic inheritance with which he is endowed. For if someone did not have *that inheritance,* that someone could not be A.

The point may be brought out in a different way. We think of rights as entitlements that can — in principle, and at some time in the life of a normally developing person — be claimed and exercised. A future person who is born into a despoiled environment can coherently say, "My parents, and theirs before them, should have left a better environment for me to live in. They violated my rights by polluting and destroying the present environment." But the future person cannot sensibly assert: "My parents, and theirs before them, wronged me in giving me this bad genetic endowment. They violated my rights in not giving me a better one." This does not make sense, for if his parents had taken successful steps toward enhancing the genetic endowments of their offspring, their child could not have been the child they actually had. Having a child with defective genes cannot be a *violation* of that child's right because it is not possible to respect the alleged right by (a) not having him or (b) giving him a different genetic constitution.[6] The second alternative is clearly impossible. And (a) is not possible either; for without his parents having him, there is no one whose rights can be violated.[7]

The point should not be confused with the following strange claim: "After all, the genetically defective individual does exist, and he should be grateful for that even if he suffers from a bad genetic disease. A person in his place without the disease would not be he. So he should be thankful that he exists, genetic defects and all." The point is not a moral consideration about proper attitudes toward one's parents. And I am most certainly not claiming that genetically defective persons are undeserving of respect for their human rights. The issue is a conceptual and metaphysical one. Since the genetically diseased child could not exist without the disease — the disease is not detachable — he cannot have a right to be without it. The life of a genetically defective person is directly linked to the union of a specific egg and a specific sperm. If *that* egg and *that* sperm do not unite, he cannot come to exist. But if they do unite, then he has the genetic defect. So *he* cannot be without this defect, though someone similar to him could have been. And one cannot have a right not to have, and never to have had, something which is essential to one's existence. No right to a good genetic endowment can serve as the basis for an obligation to provide sound genetic constitutions. There is a persistent temptation to think of genetically defective persons as though something bad has been done *to* them. But it is only a confusion to regard them as being treated badly or harmed by receiving defective genes from parents and other ancestors.[8] Genetically defective persons are not analogous to existing individuals who subsequently acquire biologically bad qualities.

Some important qualifications are in order. The points made thus far presuppose a context of certain kinds of genetic controls. They apply to actions done at the present time to affect the genetic endowments of beings to be conceived in the future. They do not apply to biological techniques for gene transfer, gene therapy, or gene surgery — procedures for altering the genetic makeup of persons after they are conceived and born. The genetic controls relevant to my claim are eugenics schemes such as mandatory sterilization and screening, selective breeding, and artificial insemination with sperm banks. Genetic control at this level involves efforts to get good sperm and good eggs together and to prevent bad eggs and bad sperm from uniting. Genetic engineering at the other level has quite different ethical implications. The intriguing future possibilities of beneficial genetic surgery and induction of desirable mutations may make it very reasonable for persons to claim a right to a good genetic constitution. Suppose that in the distant future baby A is born with a serious genetic defect. Suppose further that genetic surgery can correct the problem without affecting the good features of his genetic makeup. If his parents choose not to have the surgery, then A can later claim quite coherently that they violated his right and failed to fulfill their obligation. In this kind of case there is no fundamental difference between genetic defects and nongenetic birth defects. The conceptual difficulties do not arise here, and no new theoretical problems arise for obligations to future generations. . . .

II

I shall take preliminary steps toward a defense of the view that we do have moral obligations with regard to the genetic endowment of future generations. The obligation to be defended potentially imposes serious limitations on the freedom to have children and on activities that worsen the gene pool and increase the incidence of genetic disease. I shall not attempt a general argument in favor of the existence of obligations to future generations. I do believe that there are many types of such obligations. John Rawls, in *A Theory of Justice,* has argued persuasively that there are duties of justice to members of future generations, and it seems wrong to waste natural resources so as to leave our descendants with little chance of living decent lives.[9] There are difficulties in specifying just who the individuals are to whom such obligations are owed. But such problems do not seem to be devastating, even if these future persons are not definitely specifiable. In cases of this sort we may think of future individuals *as existing.* We can do this because we know, or at least have excellent reasons to believe, that some members of future generations will exist on an expanse of land and water identical to that on which we now live. We regard them as existing and then imagine them as having clean air or polluted air, adequate energy or insufficient energy, and similarly with respect to other goods of life. These detachable goods do not present conceptual barriers to rights of and obligations to future persons.

On a less global level it appears that those contemplating parenthood have clear obligations to make provisions for their as yet unconceived children. They can make plans for security, education, health, and comfort. Again, such goods are detachable: future children can be born with these things or without these things. Prospective parents can also make provisions for nondetachable goods. They may be able to manage conception so that defective eggs and defective sperm fail to join any sperm and eggs. And it seems obligatory for them to do this—though, of course, not because their future children have rights to good genetic inheritances.

What, then, is the basis for an obligation to provide good genetic constitutions for members of future generations? Some biologists have based their appeals for eugenics schemes on utilitarian grounds. They have argued that much harm is being done by not having such programs, that much good would result from instituting them, and that more good than bad will be the net effect. Such points are fervently made, though it is left unclear just why one ought to maximize good and just why this justifies severe restrictions on freedom.[10] The position to be defended here is quite different. Its force rests on the intuitive appeal of a familiar, though not very philosophically refined, conception of morality. A morality is a structure of interconnected rights and duties. Among the most fundamental and most important rights are the right to life, the right to a certain measure of freedom, the right to be treated fairly, the right to be free of unnecessary suffering, and the right to be treated with respect. I do not, unfortunately, have an account of the ultimate rational foundation for this set of rights. But I believe that its widespread intuitive appeal is so great that very powerful (and as yet unknown) arguments would be required in order justifiably to deny that human beings have these rights. The intuitive appeal of any argument against them would have to be extremely strong to overturn our conviction that these are basic human rights that it would normally be grossly immoral to violate. These rights are so fundamental that any fully adequate moral theory must be consistent with them, must articulate and explain them, and must show why it is wrong to violate them.

This rudimentary idea is very useful for the defense of the claim that there is a strong moral obligation to provide members of future generations with good genetic endowments. It is first necessary, however, to assume that much genetic control is possible. Let us then suppose a few things not now in accord with the world as we know it. Suppose that we can devise feasible and effective methods for controlling and determining the genetic inheritances of those as yet unconceived. We can use our techniques for good or for evil. We can reduce the incidence of genetically transmitted disease, or we can increase it. We can, if we wish or if we do not care, make more and more people have worse and worse diseases. Or we can decrease the numbers of those who have genetic diseases and insure that genetic diseases become less and less severe. Suppose further that we can either improve human intelligence or use our powers to make our descendants even less intelligent than we are. We can produce persons who are more or less aggressive, more or less adaptable, more or less attractive than those living now. And so on and so on. In general, let us suppose, we have the technology and knowledge to determine whether future persons will have genetically desirable characteristics or genetically defective traits. At this point I do not wish to delve too far into vexing questions concerning (a) *how* one should determine what genetic traits are defective and (b) *who* should decide which traits are good and which are bad. Subsequent examples are confined to reasonably clear cases of bad traits and good traits. As I shall reemphasize later, determining which genetic traits are desirable or defective is no more difficult, from a moral or evaluative point of view, than determining which nongenetic human qualities are good or bad (though, from an epistemic standpoint, it may be more difficult to predict the consequences of having certain genetic traits and not having others).

Why exercise such control? We should make use of genetic control technology in order *to protect human rights.* We have very good reason to believe that there will be people living 50, 100, and 200 years from now. These persons will have the rights (to life, liberty, fairness, and respect) that I have mentioned. But it is likely that their rights will be less often respected and protected if they live amidst genetically defective persons. I want to introduce a special class of undesirable genetic qualities and call its members "morally defective genetic traits (MDGT)." One type of MDGT is that which causes the individual possessing it to perform bad and wrong actions involving violations of the rights of others. Among possible candidates are excessive aggressiveness, low intelligence, and lack of sensitivity. Some MDGT's will also cause their possessors to be good and to act rightly in some respects and for some purposes. Low intelligence might prevent an individual from being able successfully to perform acts which harm others' life and liberty. And high intelligence may provide the ability for rights violation to someone inclined to treat people unjustly. Many genetic traits are "mixed blessings" in that they can enable individuals to be morally bad or morally good at different times. I believe that this is primarily a problem of determining which groups of genetic qualities will be good or bad with regard to rights violations. It does not affect, from a theoretical standpoint, the moral basis for engaging in genetic control. The main point is that, to the extent that controls are feasible and reliable in producing and avoiding certain results, one should exercise them so as to produce individuals who will respect others' rights and to avoid the production of persons who will violate rights.

One problem immediately arises. How can a trait be morally defective if it is genetic and, if therefore not under the control of its possessor, renders him not responsible for the actions it generates? A complete answer to this would involve some attention to the issues of freedom and determinism. A similar question about responsibility can also be raised about nongenetic qualities of character over which an individual has no control. But nothing that I say implies that the genetically defective individual is responsible for acts generated by his genetic traits. The rights of others may be violated by those acts even if he is not responsible for them. An important point here is that those who control or determine someone's genetic inheritance are themselves (at least partially) morally responsible for, and blameworthy because of, genetically generated actions violating persons' rights. This assumes, of course, a large measure of actual genetic control. It also assumes that the "controllers" could have foreseen that a genetically defective person would be produced, that they could have prevented his production, and that there are no countervailing moral considerations requiring or justifying his production.

Another type of MDGT is one which causes its possessor to be an intolerable strain and drain on the lives of his contemporaries. Suppose that a person possesses a severely debilitating genetic disease and that his care requires much time, money, and equipment. The genetic trait responsible for the disease is a morally defective one if it causes his life to draw an excessive, unfair share of the resources of the society. I do not suggest that *he* is being unfair to his fellows or that he is being unjust in staying alive. But, on the assumptions that his not being produced was a viable alternative and that his condition was foreseeable, his controllers were wrong to have caused the resultant unfairness in that society. Now I am not, absolutely not, endorsing the view that his contemporaries are justified in killing him or withdrawing care for him as ways of rectifying injustice. Genetically defective though he may be, he has rights also. If they are to justify eliminating him or neglecting him, they must at least show that their own rights are more serious or more important than his. Their justification cannot be made to stand on the genetic source of unfairness in the form of the disease. The diseased person is not responsible for his fellows' extra burden; his producers are responsible. The rights of his contemporaries are violated because of his genetic disease, but he does not violate their rights by trying to live with it.

This case is interesting because it illustrates further the point made in the first section. The diseased person suffers because of his disease and he has a right not to endure suffering; but it does not follow that he has a right not to suffer from the disease. Those sufferings which result from the disease and which cannot now be eliminated are not violations of a right. Nor is his right to life violated if he dies of the disease despite the best efforts of those charged with his care. The disease is genetic, and he cannot sensibly complain about a genetic endowment without which he could not exist. He does not have a right not to suffer from a condition that is nondetachable (when that suffering cannot be alleviated by his contemporaries). His fellows also suffer from his having the disease. Their right not to endure suffering is violated, and it is sensible for them to complain because their suffering could have been prevented. Their suffering from his disease is detachable even though his is not. *Vis-à-vis them,* there is no fundamental moral difference between this case and one in which their time and money must be used to care for someone with a severe infectious disease produced deliberately by a malicious contemporary. Their rights are violated by that malicious person. *Vis-à-vis the person inflicted with disease,* however, there is a fundamental difference. The infectiously diseased person has a right which is violated by the person who caused the disease. His suffering is detachable, and he could have lived very well without it. But the genetically diseased person's rights are not violated by his possession of that disease and by his endurance of the unpreventable suffering that accompanies it. He can rightly complain if his contemporaries fail to try to alleviate his suffering; but he cannot complain that his producers violated his rights by producing a person who suffers.

Those operating the genetic controls ought to provide to members of future generations morally nondefective genetic constitutions. By doing so they can bring it about that many of the rights of many of those future persons will not be violated. They can prevent assault on human rights, and they can enhance respect for them. They can afford some measure of protection both to the genetically defective and to the genetically nondefective. They can prevent violations of rights of the nondefective that would be violated by the defective, but also rights of the defective that would be violated by both the defective and the nondefective. The genetically defective, for example, have a right not to be persecuted. This right holds even if the persecution they experience is partially caused by their having genetic defects. They could have existed without the persecution, though not without the defects. The property of "being persecuted" is detachable even though they would not be persecuted if they had not had their genetically defective traits.

The controllers are themselves partially responsible for the wrong acts generated by the defective traits they introduce into the world. They must refrain from violating the rights of future persons, and they can do this by not producing people with MDGT's. Since all persons have obligations to respect and protect the rights of others and since (in the world envisaged here) the controllers are persons, they also have such obligations. The recipients of respect and protection are, to be sure, future individuals as yet unconceived. But, whoever they will be, some such persons will exist and they will have human rights.[11] From the standpoint of genetic control, their rights may be violated by people acting many years prior to their birth and growth into adulthood. There is a complex, but definite, link between the acts and omissions of the genetic controllers and the acts generated by the MDGT's of those they produce.

III

I wish to provide further clarifications, implications, and responses to objections. First, I have used the word "obligation" somewhat more broadly than it is ordinarily used. In the sense that I mean, a person has an obligation to another not to violate a right because of a general moral duty, responsibility, or requirement of all persons not to violate the rights of others. Obligations are not limited to moral requirements arising out of promises, voluntary commitments and special relationships, offices, or positions. The rights and obligations involved here are quite general—roughly, what may be called "natural rights and duties."

It may be objected that there is great indefiniteness concerning the future persons to whom one has obligations. It is often said that such unspecified and unidentified persons cannot have rights against people living now. The import and relevance of this objection appears to be quite obscure. Planting a bomb now and setting it to explode in 100 years constitutes a clear violation of rights of (unspecified) persons injured or killed. There is surely no incoherence in the claim by a future person that his rights have been violated by actions of a member of a former generation. Consider an analogy with moral education. Suppose that a child's parents fail to attend to his moral education and that, as a consequence of this neglect, he treats his contemporaries meanly and unjustly Those whose rights to fair and humane treatment are violated can legitimately place blame on the parents of the immediate and direct violator. Why can we not conclude that since the parents are remote and indirect violators of such rights, they failed to fulfill obligations to the violated? Such judgments are similar to many that we often make and understand, and they are analogous to those in which the relevant bad qualities are genetic ones. The key requirement is that at time t an agent must be able reasonably to predict that, at (roughly) $t + 25$ years, there will exist persons whose rights will be immediately, directly violated by actions resulting from MDGT's that he can either prevent or insure. If, despite this level of understanding, he performs an act that brings those MDGT's into existence, then he is indirectly and remotely responsible for the rights violations occurring later.

We do not now possess the technical capacities to make predictions and to institute controls on the massive scale hypothetically envisaged. Some have suggested that we ought not to develop these capacities.[12] Whether we ought to develop genetic control technology, and whether we ought to use it if it is developed, partly depend upon whether we have a right to restrict human freedom to the extent required by the controls. After all, members of the present generation also have rights. Many believe that mandatory genetic screening, involuntary sterilization, and directed selective breeding would violate these rights. There is an intuitively persuasive prima facie case that these practices are morally impermissible. On the other hand, the failure to institute such controls — and many less serious ones, such as genetic counseling — may violate the rights of future persons. There are, then, several conflict-of-rights issues that must be resolved. I have not tried to settle them. I have argued, however, that there is a moral basis for genetic control of a certain type (vaguely, the "protection of rights" type) and that it is far from obvious that such conflicts must be resolved in favor of the present generation.

The references to "controllers" and "determiners" should not mislead. The notion of a genetic controller need not be understood on the model of the rulers in *Brave New World*. Limited genetic control techniques are available now to be exercised voluntarily by those who want to have children. One need not wait for further scientific developments in order to take seriously the moral questions concerning the rights of future generations. The arguments in section II suggest that persons with genetic defects must exercise care lest they have children whose possession of these qualities will result in wrong actions. Surely there is a serious moral question as to whether one should have a child who is very likely to violate, massively and repeatedly, the rights of others.

And it is also seriously questionable whether one should have a child whose rights will be systematically violated by others. Such acts are partly analogous, respectively, to teaching one's children to violate others' rights and to neglecting to help them protect their own rights.

I do not wish to de-emphasize the profound implications of restricting the reproductive freedom of human beings. There is something morally repugnant about limiting the right to bear children, the right to have one's own children, and the right to considerable liberty in the use of one's reproductive organs. But, however important these rights are, there are potentially serious conflicts between them and the rights of future persons. A large part of our present problem is that we do not know which rights will be violated by which future persons. And we do not know enough about definite links between certain traits and wrong actions. But suppose that we do come to know more of this. Suppose we know that any child born to prospective parents M and F will murder other people soon after his attainment of adulthood. He will have genetically based violent, murderous desires; and he will succeed in efforts to satisfy his desires. With that kind of knowledge and in that set of circumstances there would seem to be a powerful case for prohibiting M and F from having children. The rights of potential parents to have their own natural children appear less important than the rights to life of their child's contemporaries in a new generation. If they have a child despite such knowledge of his future acts, they would seem to be only somewhat less blameworthy than parents who have a child with the clear and settled intention of teaching him to become a murderer. In both kinds of cases present actions are partially, if remotely, responsible for the deaths of future persons.

There are other objections. As I have noted, many contend that there are serious dangers in genetic control.[13] Often arguments are made along two not always distinguished lines: (1) one cannot determine criteria for defective genetic traits, and (2) there would be abuse of power by those given the authority to determine whether people have children. Concerning the second objection, it is insisted that we cannot trust controllers to use their power within the moral limits set by finally established criteria. They will forbid, allow, or require the wrong individuals to have children, and they will produce children whose genetic traits are conducive to their own interests. It is difficult to assess such fears in the absence of the control technology and without a knowledge of the kind of political society in which it will be used. But it is only fair to admit that there almost certainly would be some abuse of power on the part of the controllers. It is also fair to say that it is not obvious that rights violated by such abuses would be more numerous or more serious than rights violated because of failure to have controls. Moreover, it is not obvious that the potential abuses are likely to be more widespread and more pernicious than those tolerated in presently functioning legal systems. The frequent abuses of power by law enforcers (from local policemen to chief executives) do not and should not deter human societies from instituting lawmaking authority to protect the rights of citizens. Here again is a partial analogy for future genetic control institutions.

What of the first objection? Many are sceptical about genetic control because they are sceptical about anyone's being able satisfactorily to determine criteria for desirable and defective traits. These doubts are akin to more general sceptical doubts about moral principles and moral values among those who ask such questions as who decides that a principle or value is morally right or good? and how can one determine that a principle or value is morally acceptable? Such rhetorical questions are often designated to generate the conclusion that it is wrong for anyone to decide such things and "impose" one's own values on others. To the extent that sceptical points about morally good genetic qualities are extensions of these generalized doubts, there is little that I can say here. It is important to note, however, that if there are no moral criteria and if no one can employ any proposed criteria, one cannot sensibly object *on these grounds* to genetic control. To do so would implicitly involve the use of some moral standards, and this would involve incoherence. To the extent that doubts about criteria for desirable genetic traits are not part of a general moral scepticism, there is also little to be said. I must reemphasize, however, that I have confined the discussion of undesirable genetic traits to *morally defective* qualities. The traits in question are limited to those that result in violations of human rights. I have not argued for genetic control on the grounds that valuable persons with especially estimable qualities should be produced or that intrinsic moral goodness should be maximized.[14] In any case, it is in principle no more difficult to determine criteria for genetically defective moral qualities than for nongenetically undesirable ones.

The basic point is that members of the present generation ought to respect the rights of members of future generations, and this is the basis for genetically related restrictions on reproductive freedom. The rights of future persons will be less often respected and protected if they do not have good genetic endowments. So there are strong obligations to limit production to persons whose rights will be respected by others and to persons who will respect the rights of others. A person with a poor genetic endowment may be treated very badly. Even though he does not have a right to have been given a better genetic constitution, or a right not to have been conceived, he does have rights that are threatened because of his endowment. He can reasonably complain about this threat even if it is due to the bad genetic constitutions of his contemporaries. Human beings have a fundamental right to live among persons who will respect their rights. If the members of a future generation have morally defective genetic traits, each can claim that they should not have been produced even though none can claim that his having been produced is a violation of his right.

NOTES

1. Among the more interesting discussions are those by Edwin Delattre, "Rights, Responsibilities, and Future Persons," *Ethics* 82 (1972), 254–58; M. P. Golding, "Ethical Issues in Biological Engineering," *U.C.L.A. Law Review* 15 (1968), 443–79 and

258   *Hardy Jones*

"Obligations to Future Generations," *The Monist* 56 (1972); 85–99; Jan Narveson, "Utilitarianism and New Generations," *Mind* 76 (1967), 62–72 and *Morality and Utility* (Baltimore: Johns Hopkins Press, 1967), 47–50; and John Rawls, *A Theory of Justice* (Cambridge: Harvard University Press, 1971), especially 284–93.

2. Perhaps the most famous of Muller's works is *Out of the Night* (New York: Vanguard Press, 1935). Articles such as "Our Load of Mutations," *American Journal of Human Genetics* 2 (1950), 111–76 and "The Guidance of Human Evolution," in *Evolution after Darwin* (Chicago: University of Chicago Press, 1960), 423–62 provide useful accounts of his basic position. See also the collections of articles *Man's Future Birthright and Studies in Genetics*. A similar view is taken by Julian Huxley in *Man Stands Alone* and *Evolutionary Ethics*.

3. Paul Ramsey's *Fabricated Man* (New Haven: Yale University Press, 1970) presents a useful survey of various positions and arguments. See also Gerald Leach, *The Biocrats* (New York: McGraw-Hill, 1970) especially chapters 4 and 5. A more popular discussion is provided in Frederick Ausubel, Jon Beckwith, and Kaaren Janssen, "The Politics of Genetic Engineering: Who Decides Who's Defective?" *Psychology Today* (June 1974).

4. Dwight Engle, *Who Should Have Children?* (New York: Bobbs-Merrill, 1973), 138.

5. Bentley Glass, "Science: Endless Horizons or Golden Age?" *Science* 171 (1971), 28. Glass has also written: "When I read in the bill of human rights of the United Nations that one incorrigible right of the individual is to reproduce, and that the right of every person to have a family is a basic human right that must not be infringed upon, I wonder whether this "right" is indeed to remain unrestricted. Is there not equally a right of every person to be born physically and mentally sound, capable of developing fully into a mature individual?" ("Human Heredity and Ethical Problems," *Perspectives in Biology and Medicine,* 15 (1972), 252.)

6. Derek Parfit has published several illuminating analyses of the paradox that "the same person" could *not* have been conceived at a different time, and thus cannot be said to be "better off" as a result of a decision by his parents to postpone conception. (See the references to Parfit in Part 2 of the bibliography to this anthology. See also Garrett Hardin's "Postscript," p. 275 below.)—ED.

7. In the works cited above, Narveson makes a point that appears to be somewhat similar to this one. But I cannot be sure that it is at all the same. He argues that utilitarianism does not require the production of new persons merely on the grounds that, if produced, they will be happy and therefore add to the store of world happiness. His point seems to be that one can have no duty to make a nonexistent person happy, or happier. Whether or not this point is similar to the one I have made, his idea is put forward in a very different context and for a very different purpose.

8. Muller notes that, "In time, children with genetic difficulties may even come to be resentful toward parents who had not used measures calculated to give them a better heritage." ("The Guidance of Human Evolution," 439). My point is that such feelings of resentment would not be reasonable.

9. See Rawls, *A Theory of Justice.*

10. See Engle, Glass, Huxley, and Muller in the above cited works. See also Golding, and Bernard Davis, "Prospects for Genetic Intervention in Man," *Science* 170 (1970), 1279–83, reprinted in Richard W. Wertz, ed., *Readings on Ethical and Social Issues in Biomedicine* (Englewood Cliffs: Prentice-Hall, 1973), 57–61. The following remark by Muller is most explicit: "Despite the carpings and quibblings of some

philosophers, the most generalized rational formulation of human aims that most persons concerned with the subject can agree upon is the promotion of the greatest over-all happiness." "The Guidance of Human Evolution," 440–41.

11. For a quite different view about possible rights of future persons, see Delattre.

12. See, for instance, Leon R. Kass, "The New Biology: What Price Relieving Man's Estate?" *Science* 174 (1971), 779–88. Reprinted in Wertz, 62–71.

13. See Kass and Ramsey.

14. See Glass, Huxley, and Muller.

Mary Anne Warren

Do Potential Persons Have Rights?

By a potential person I shall mean an entity which is not now a person but which is capable of developing into a person, given certain biologically and/or technologically possible conditions. This is admittedly a narrower sense than some would attach to the term "potential." After all, people of the twenty-fifth century, if such there will be, are in some sense potential people now, even though the specific biological entities from which they will develop, i.e., the particular gametes or concepti, do not yet exist. For there do exist, in the reproductive capacities of people now living and in the earth's resources, conditions adequate to produce these future people eventually, provided of course that various possible catastrophes are avoided. Indeed, in *some* sense of "potential" there have been countless billions of potential people from the beginning of time. But I am concerned not with such remote potentialities but with currently existing entities that are capable of developing into people. The question I want to ask is whether or not the fact that an entity is a potential person is, in itself, grounds for ascribing moral rights to that entity, in particular the right to be permitted or enabled to become a person.

It is worth noting that potential people need not be genetically human, though all those which we know of at present obviously are. If a serum were invented which would cause kitten embryos to develop into intelligent, self-aware, language-using beings, as in Michael Tooley's example,[1] then kitten embryos would have become potential people. True, the actualization of that potentiality would be dependent upon technological intervention in a way in which that of a normal human fetus is not, but it would not be a less genuine potentiality for that reason, any more than a human fetus which will survive only if its mother is given a drug to prevent miscarriage is therefore not a potential person. Potential personhood is the capacity to become a person, regardless of whether that capacity is likely to be realized. On the other hand,

This article is reprinted from the *Canadian Journal of Philosophy,* June 1977, with permission of the Canadian Association for Publishing in Philosophy and the author.

when I speak of *merely* potential people, I shall mean those which, though they have that capacity, will in fact never become people.

Because the concept of personhood is less than fully precise, and because that process through which a potential human person develops into an actual one is gradual rather than sudden, it is probably pointless to attempt to identify a precise moment at which the transition occurs. My own view is that a human being does not become a person until sometime after its birth,[2] but I will not need to assume here that this claim is true. If human beings become people sometime after conception but before birth, as many people believe, then my question is relevant to the moral status of abortion before but not after that time. The question is surely relevant to the moral status of abortion at *some* stages of pregnancy, since it is clear that a person is not present from the moment of conception; for the very least one must be able to say of a person is that it is a sentient being, which a conceptus in the first few weeks of its existence is not.

Almost as difficult as the question of when a potential person becomes a person is that of when it becomes appropriate to speak of there being even a potential person. There is at least a potential person from conception onward, but what about before conception? Is a male or female gamete a potential person? By itself, I think not, though it might be if we were able to reproduce parthenogenetically. But I see no reason why a viable sexually mixed *pair* of gametes should not be considered a potential person. For, as R. M. Hare points out, it does not seem to make a crucial conceptual difference that before conception the genetic material capable of becoming a person is in two locations, whereas afterwards it is in one.[3]

Hare has recently argued, in effect, that potential people do have a prima facie right to be permitted to become people, although he prefers to express this claim by saying that it is morally wrong, other things being equal, to prevent potential people from becoming actual.[4] He follows Tooley, and I will follow him, in calling this claim the potentiality principle. Because he believes that gametes are already potential people, and that fetuses are still only potential people, Hare concludes that the truth of the potentiality principle means that not just abortion, but contraception, and even the decision not to procreate at all, are all prima facie immoral (p. 212).

This sounds like a rather drastic conclusion; but Hare goes on to explain that it is less sweeping in its practical moral consequences than one might suppose, since the prima facie obligation to permit potential people to become actual can be overridden in any of a large number of ways. For example, he would accept as reasons adequate to justify abortion, that the pregnancy endangers the woman's health or fertility, that the abortion would permit the occurrence of another pregnancy with a better chance of resulting in a normal child, or that the parents already have as many children as they can adequately care for (p. 218). Hence, although the potentiality principle would imply that abortion, contraception and total abstinence are all "prima facie and in general wrong in default of sufficient countervailing reasons" (p. 221), it would not prevent them from being justified in a wide range of circumstances.

Consequently, one might suppose that in practice Hare's position in support of the potentiality principle is not strikingly different from the theoretically opposing position that potential people as such have no moral rights but that there are good independent reasons for having children and trying to avoid having abortions. And one might wonder why, if the right of a potential person to be permitted to become a person is so easily overridden, it matters whether or not there is such a right, I shall argue that not only is the potentiality principle false, but this fact has important moral consequences. It means, among other things, that in most cases no moral justification at all is required for the decision to remain celibate, use contraceptives, or have an abortion. This conclusion makes a difference to the way we ought to treat women seeking abortions, men or women seeking contraceptives or sterilization, and people who choose to remain permanently childless. Furthermore, the failure of the potentiality principle has an important bearing upon our long-term population policies. . . . Properly understood, however, it does not in any way lessen our moral obligations to future generations of human beings, whose rights, I shall argue, do not depend upon their present existence as potential people.

The argument that originally persuaded me that the potentiality principle is false is an intuitive one, and runs as follows. Imagine that you are approached by alien scientists who propose to create billions of replicas of you, that is billions of new people with your genetic code, by separating the cells of your body and using each to clone a new individual. Being moral, the aliens first ask your permission for this operation, assuring you that all these new people will be given the chance to lead reasonably happy lives on some distant planet where they will not contribute to the earth's overpopulation problems. My intuition is that you would have absolutely no moral obligation to agree to such a proposal at the cost of your own life; and indeed I think that you would not be obligated to agree even if they were to promise eventually to reconstitute you as good as new. Hence I think that any right to life which a potential person as such might have is at least billions of times as weak as that of an actual person.[5]

Unfortunately, arguments of this sort, which appeal to our intuitions regarding unusual or bizarre situations, are never conclusive. Proponents of the potentiality principle may well have intuitions different from my own, and even if they do not the case is still not closed, since our intuitions about such cases, while they may serve to clarify (the consequences of) our existing moral convictions, cannot establish what our moral convictions *ought* to be. The potentiality principle, like any specific moral claim, must ultimately be defended or refuted on the basis of some overall conception of the nature of morality.

In what follows I will try to explain why the potentiality principle cannot be true. In part 1, I will examine Hare's argument for the principle, which is based on his interpretation of the Golden Rule, but which I will argue rests upon a confusion. In parts 2 and 3, I will consider whether it is possible to argue for the potentiality principle in some way which does not involve this confusion, and present a very brief sketch of the type of moral theory which rules out such an argument. And, in part 4, I will explore a few of the moral consequences of the failure of the potentiality principle and warn against one apparent consequence that in fact does not follow.

1. The Argument from the Golden Rule

Hare argues that we can derive a proof of the potentiality principle, that it is wrong, other things being equal, to prevent a potential person from becoming an actual person, from a natural extension of one version of the Golden Rule, i.e., that we should do to others as we wish them to do to us. "It is," he says, "a logical extension of this form of argument to say that we should do to others what *we are glad was* done to us" (p. 212). As it happens, most of us are glad that the pregnancy which resulted in our own birth was not terminated by abortion. We are also, presumably, glad that our parents met, copulated, and conceived us in the first place. Hence, he concludes, it is a consequence of this extended Golden Rule that we have a prima facie obligation not to terminate any pregnancy which would otherwise result in the birth of a person who will be like us in being glad she or he was not aborted, and also a duty not to use contraceptives or to refrain entirely from procreating (p. 212).

I would argue, however, that even if we accept the Golden Rule as a sound moral principle, we cannot extend it to establish that we have even a very weak obligation to treat potential people in the way in which we are glad that the ones which eventually became ourselves were treated. For the extended Golden Rule, which prescribes that we behave toward others in ways in which we are glad that others once behaved toward us, is either irrelevant to the treatment of potential people, or—if it is so interpreted as to include them—incoherent.

As it stands, the principle that, other things being equal, we should treat others as we are glad that we were treated appears to be irrelevant to the treatment of potential people. For personal pronouns like "we" refer to people; we are essentially people if we are essentially anything at all. Therefore, if fetuses and gametes are not people, then we were never fetuses or gametes, though one might say that we emerged from them. The fetus which later *became* you was not *you* because you did not exist at that time. It was not you for the same reason that your dead body will not, or that your living body with the cognitive and perceptual centers of the brain permanently destroyed would not, be you, namely, that you are a particular *person,* not just a particular human organism regardless of its stage of development or degeneration. So if it had been aborted nothing whatever would have been done to *you,* since you would never have existed. You cannot coherently be glad that you were not aborted, since in order for there to be a you at all, you cannot possibly have been. And therefore the Golden Rule as Hare extends it does not proscribe abortion, much less contraception or celibacy.

But perhaps this is a problem which could be solved by a little rewording. Might not Hare just as well have extended the Golden Rule to cover what you are glad was done to the *potential person from which you emerged?* If the first extension is logical, might not this one be equally acceptable? I think not, at least not if the duties, obligations and wrongs associated with this principle are meant to be duties or obligations toward or wrongs done to potential people. For potential people, as such, are not the sort of entity toward which it is possible to have moral obligations. The very notion of acting wrongly toward a merely potential person, that is, one which will never become a person, is incoherent. For who is it that is being wronged when a potential person is prevented from becoming a person? Absolutely no one. To maintain otherwise is to misunderstand grotesquely what a merely potential person is.

Merely potential people, or rather the people they might have become, are not, just as possible worlds are not, things that exist alongside the actual world in, as it were, a super-space that includes not only the actual but the possible. Or at any rate we have absolutely no reason to think that they are. They are just things that might have existed, that is, that at some time were empirically possible, but which in fact do not, never did, and never will exist. And what does not exist and never will cannot be harmed or wronged or have its rights violated.

Why is this? Because harming someone, behaving wrongly towards someone, and violating someone's rights are all extensional rather than intentional concepts. I can think about Pegasus, but I cannot catch him, beat him, be unfair to him, or violate his rights. Mythical entities, which never did, do not now and never will exist, have no rights to be violated, and we have no duties or obligations toward such entities, simply because such entities cannot be acted upon in any way whatever, other than illusorily, through the intentional medium of thought.

Now Hare maintains that this sort of objection, i.e., any attempt to show that for one conceptual reason or another (he mentions the individuation problem) merely potential people cannot be the victims of moral wrongdoing, cannot be correct, because:

> It would be strange if there were an act whose very performance made it impossible for it to be wrong. But if the objection were correct, the act of aborting a possible person would be such an act; by preventing the existence of the object of the wrongdoing, it would remove its wrongness. This seems too easy a way of avoiding wrongdoing. (p. 219)

It is clear that the language in this passage is prejudicial, since if abortion is not prima facie wrong then it is inappropriate to speak of *removing* the wrongness. But more importantly, I think that there is a simple but fatal confusion behind the notion that one can act wrongly toward a merely potential person. Why does it tend to seem "too easy" to say that to abort a potential person cannot be to act wrongly toward someone *because it prevents the very existence of the person supposedly wronged?* I suggest it is because we tend to make an error not unlike the one which Bishop Berkeley made when he argued that it is impossible to conceive of an object existing without being conceived by anyone, since to (try to) conceive of such an object is still to conceive of an object which is conceived of by someone, viz. you.[6]

The error is that of illegitimately smuggling ourselves, the conceivers, into our conceptions of states of affairs which by definition exclude us. Berkeley's Hylas could not imagine a state of affairs consisting of there being an object of which no one conceives, because he could not imagine *himself* as not being part of the picture. He tried to conceive of an unconceived object, but succeeded only in conceiving of himself conceiving of an object, which then of course was not unconceived at all. Similarly, I think that when we try to imagine the state of affairs consisting of our never having existed at all, what we in fact tend to imagine is rather that we, the existing people that we are, are suddenly to have our very existence snatched away from us, as in the science fiction plot in which a time traveler "eliminates" someone by seeing to it that the person's parents never meet each other.

I will leave it to the reader to decide whether or not this science fiction scenario represents a logically possible occurrence. If it does, then no doubt this sort of total eradication of an actual person's past, present and future existence would be a terrible thing to inflict upon someone. But obviously nothing of the sort occurs in a normal case of abortion, which takes place without benefit of meddling time travelers. In the ordinary case nothing is inflicted upon anyone since there is no one for anything to be inflicted upon. If we find this hard to accept, it is because when we try to imagine our own non-existence our imaginations tend to falter. The same thing often happens when we try to imagine what it would be like to be dead. We tend to think that it would be like being shut up in a dark and silent room, with nothing there but ourselves, even though the reality of death is just the opposite: everything will go on much as before *except* ourselves.

Once this persistent confusion is eliminated, it becomes clear that it is neither meaningful nor coherent to claim, as Hare does, that God or our fathers would have done less than their moral best by us if they had not caused us to exist (p. 221). If a wrong is done when a potential person is prevented from becoming a person, it is not done to the person who might have been, since that person is a purely mythical being. And it is not done to the merely potential person, i.e., the non-sentient stuff which might have developed into a person, either, since non-sentient stuff cannot be wronged any more than non-existent people can. Hence the Golden Rule cannot be extended to prove that we have duties toward merely potential people.

2. The Quantity of Happiness Problem

However, we cannot yet conclude that it is not prima facie wrong to prevent a potential person that would otherwise have become a happy person from doing so. For it might be argued that even though no one's rights are violated when a potentially happy person is aborted, or never conceived, the action is still prima facie wrong because it constitutes a failure to produce a certain quantity of happiness which it is in the agent's capacity to produce, or at least not prevent. Certainly on any moral theory that counts happiness *per se* as a moral good, or that makes maximizing the *total quantity* of happiness a duty, we would have to say that other things being equal it is morally better to create a person who turns out to be happy than not to.

Another way to illustrate this possible defense of the potentiality principle is to consider the following question: Which world would God deserve more credit for creating, one containing fifty happy people, or one containing fifty million people who are no more and no less happy? Many people would be inclined to say that God would deserve more moral credit for creating the more populous world, even though in creating the less populous world (s)he would not have violated anyone's rights.

I think that the claim that, other things being equal, it is better to create happy people than to create no one, can be refuted. Creating happiness for people is morally good, but creating people for happiness is morally neutral. Granted, it is wrong to create people one knows will be unhappy, and worse than creating no one. But creating people one knows will be happy is not necessarily right; its moral status must be determined on the basis of the predictable effects that the existence of these new people will have on *other* people. To explain why I think that this is so will require an examination of some basic convictions about the nature of morality. Any extensive defense of these convictions would be beyond the scope of this paper. But at least we will be able to see that the rejection of the potentiality principle is required by a certain view of the proper function of morality, one which has a good deal of plausibility.

3. Sentience as the Basis of Moral Rights

The view to which I refer is simply that morality is or ought to be a system designed to promote the interests of sentient beings. Which sentient beings? Ideally, all there are and all there ever will be. Sentience is the ultimate source of all moral rights; a being that has experiences and that prefers experiences of some sorts to those of other sorts has on that basis alone a prima facie right that those preferences be respected by beings that have the intelligence to comprehend this fact. On the other hand, a being that lacks the capacity to have experiences, and/or to prefer some experiences to others, cannot coherently be said to have moral rights, because it has no interests to be respected.

It should not, but perhaps does, need to be pointed out that there is a difference between sentient beings and things that are only potentially capable of sentience. Francis Wade's is one of the most recent attempts to break down this distinction. Wade argues that a human fetus is in one significant sense already a personal being, already possessed of the capacities, including sentience, which are definitive of personhood, because "its whole natural thrust is to become a functioning person."[7] But however true this may be it is still one thing to be sentient now and quite another to be the sort of thing which may become sentient at a later time.

It is also crucial to distinguish between a purely potential capacity for sentience and a present but temporarily inoperative capacity, as in the case of a person who is asleep or unconscious. Some might argue that this distinction is untenable, and that to whatever degree a fetus is merely potentially sentient so too a person who is not conscious at the moment is only potentially sentient. Wade points out, correctly:

> The potentiality of the fetus . . . is an active natural potentiality or tendency, which is a guarantee of the future as far as the agent is concerned.[8]

And, it might be argued, this is as much as can be said about a person in a state of unconsciousness, however certain his or her eventual awakening may be. But it is a mistake to speak of an unconscious person as merely a potential sentient being. Such a person is an actual, developed sentient being who is in a temporary state of quiescence, just as an automobile which is out of gasoline is not a *potential* automobile but an actual one which just is not operating at the moment.

Thus, Tristram Engelhardt's remarks on the difference between the potential sentience of a fetus and that of an unconscious person, while correct, do not go far enough. He says:

> The potentiality of the sleeping person is concrete and real in the sense of being based upon the past development of a full-blown human person.[9]

But for this very reason it is more accurate to say that an unconscious person is not merely a being that is *potentially* capable of sentience, but one that has an actual and present capacity for sentience, even though this capacity is not and possibly cannot be exercised at present.

My claim, then, is that sentience is a necessary and sufficient condition for the possession of moral rights. It does not follow from this that all sentient beings deserve to have their interests given equal weight in moral considerations. All *people* have equal moral rights, but it is only people who have *full* moral rights. We need not value the lives of the bugs that bite us as highly as our own. Nevertheless, any degree of sentience entitles its bearer to some moral consideration. For instance, I would argue that the mere capacity to feel pain, which is one form or aspect of sentience, endows its possessor with the prima facie right not to have pain inflicted upon it. And to the extent that people have rights that other organisms do not it is because their sentience is, so to speak, of a higher order; that is, they not only have experiences, but know that they have them, think about them, use them in the formulation of theories, and so on. Needless to say, most human moral systems are designed to promote the interests of only a small subset of sentient beings; but this only shows that we have a long way to go in becoming completely moral.

That actions are right or wrong insofar as they promote or interfere with the interests of (at least certain) sentient beings is an insight which has been elaborated and defended in various teleological and contractualist moral theories. For instance, it is very much in the spirit of utilitarianism to say that the good is what promotes the interests of sentient beings. Most of the things identified as intrinsic moral goods by the different forms of utilitarianism, e.g., happiness, pleasure, the avoidance of unnecessary pain, and the satisfaction of rational and informed desires, are things that are usually, though not always, in the interest of the being that experiences them.

But utilitarians have often risked losing sight of this central insight by speaking loosely of "maximizing happiness" as the goal of morality, as though the point were to increase the number of "units" of happiness, without regard for how thinly or unevenly they might be distributed. This is a mistake. Maximizing the extent to which people's interests are promoted does not mean — though in some cases it may be achieved by — increasing the number of people that exist and have interests to be promoted. Rather, the prima facie aim of morality should be to maximize the extent to which each *actual* — present or future — person's interests are promoted. This means maximizing not just the *average* extent of interest-promotion, although that matters, but also the *equality* of the consideration given to each person. Each person's interests must be given prima facie equal weight; but it is only people and other sentient beings, that is those who do or will exist, who can possibly have interests to be weighed. For it is only they who care, or will care, or have reason for caring, what does or does not happen.

Morality, then, should be concerned with how happy each individual is or will be, not with how many individuals exist and are happy. (Being happy is not always quite the same thing as having what is in your interest, but it will do as an approximation for present purposes.) This means, for example, that other things being equal it is better to have one child who is very happy than two who are 51 percent as happy, even though in the latter case one might say that a greater quantity of happiness had been produced. It also means that a decision to have or not to have a child must be evaluated on the basis of its predictable effects upon people, and possibly other sentient beings, that do or will exist, given the outcome of the decision.

This is why failing to have a child, even when you could have had a happy one, is neither right nor wrong, so long as it is considered apart from its effects upon people other than the merely potential child. But the same cannot be said of *having* a child, since in this case the action results in the existence of a new person whose interests must be taken into account. Having a child under conditions that should enable one to predict that it will be very unhappy is morally objectionable, not because it violates the rights of a presently existing potential person, but because it results in the frustration of the interests of an actual person in the future. There is all the difference in the world between so acting as to cause needless misery to real but future people and refraining from bringing people into existence. In the first instance one creates unhappiness and frustration, thus violating the moral rights of real sentient beings who are no less worthy of our consideration just because they do not exist *yet*. In the second instance, no one is harmed, no one's interests are disregarded, and hence no moral wrong is done.[10]

4. Consequences

If I am right about this, then the use of contraceptives or abstinence to avoid parenthood are, insofar as they affect merely potential people, without moral significance. And the same is true of abortion, provided that unborn humans are only *potential* people. We have absolutely no obligation to our potential children to have them. However, once we do decide to have children then we are obligated to begin taking their interests into account, and this process may even lead to a reversal of that decision.

If this were more widely recognized it might prevent a good deal of suffering from unwarranted guilt feelings. Women who have abortions and people who perform or arrange for them often suffer from the persistent suspicion that they are wronging the potential people whose development they are bringing to an end. And people who deliberately remain childless often feel or are made to feel that this is a selfish decision on their part. Such feelings are misguided. It may be that at one time having children could have reasonably been regarded as a service to society as a whole; but *that* reason for having them is gone, probably forever, and indeed the reverse is probably the case now. Not only do we not have a duty to reproduce ourselves, we may even have a prima facie duty not to.

Another consequence of the failure of the potentiality principle is that we have no obligation to try to maximize the total number of human beings, a fact which makes a tremendous difference to what our long-term population policies ought to be. Granted, the earth is finite, and hence we will be forced to limit population growth at some point even if we do recognize such a prima facie obligation. However, if we believe that potential people have a right to life, even a very slight one, then we cannot avoid advocating a greater population expansion than we could otherwise justify. For if potential people have *no* right to life then it is clear that the expansion ought to be—or have been— halted or reversed as soon as it becomes the case that continued growth will have an overall negative impact upon people who do or will exist.

On the other hand, if potential people do have a right to life then we are morally obligated to tolerate some overall negative impact upon actual people in order to reach a just compromise between their rights and those of potential people. But this would be a serious moral error. If we populate the world to the point that our descendants will lead less satisfactory lives than they otherwise could have, then we *will* have done less than our best by them.

Furthermore, if we ever become capable of colonizing the habitable planets of other stars then our attitude toward the potentiality principle will make a difference to whether or not we make a point of doing so, and at what cost. If we believe that potential people have a right to life then we must conclude that we have a prima facie obligation to cover every humanly habitable planet with human inhabitants, as many as can be fitted in without undue crowding. Nor will we, in all probability, consider ourselves obligated to colonize only those planets that have no natives who object to our doing so. For the rights of natives will have to be weighed against those of the potential human beings who could live happily on their planet, and once again some compromise will have to be made.

This too would be an error. The decision whether to increase the total number of human beings by expanding into a new environment should be made on the basis of its effects upon all the sentient beings whose interests are involved. But the fact that the people thereby brought into existence will be happy cannot justify bringing them into existence at the expense of even a small overall negative effect upon the rest. To maintain otherwise is to condemn ourselves, our descendants, and all the sentient beings whose living space they will crowd, to a progressive erosion of the quality of life for the dubious purpose of creating more and more people who will be less and less happy. . . .

Finally, there is one apparent consequence of the failure of the potentiality principle that we have already touched upon, but which needs further elaboration. To say that merely potential people are not the sort of things which can possibly have moral rights is by no means to imply that we have no obligations toward people of future generations, or that they (will) have no rights that can be violated by things which we do now. We have many obligations toward the people who will exist after us, not least of which is the obligation not to overpopulate their world. If the human race were suddenly and deliberately to stop reproducing altogether no wrong would have been done to merely potential people, who cannot be wronged, or to people of future generations, since there would not be any. (Of course wrong would probably be done to those young or soon-to-be-born people who would be condemned to an old age devoid of younger companions; but that is another matter.) If, however, there are going to be people after us, then I think that morality requires that we respect their interests, insofar as this is possible, just as we should if they were our contemporaries.

This claim is in no way inconsistent with the claim that potential people *as such* have no moral rights. For there is a clear and crucial difference between actual but future people, i.e., those who do not yet but will exist, and present but merely potential people, i.e., things which could but will not become people in the future. The difference is that the former but not the latter will be sentient beings, with interests and desires, susceptible to pleasure and pain, and therefore possessed of moral rights. Our obligations to the people of future generations are in no way based upon the present existence of identifiable objects from which they will develop, or even on the present existence of conditions sufficient to guarantee their existence. For no reasonable person would maintain that these obligations would be eliminated if people were to cease developing from potential people and instead spring into existence fully formed and without biological parents. It would be just as objectionable to act deliberately so as to lower the quality of life for such spontaneously generated people as to do so for future people generated in the normal way.

Furthermore, if future generations owed their claim to moral consideration on the part of people in the present to the present existence of potential people from whom they will develop, then only the *next* generation would have such a claim, since the genetic material from which more remote generations will spring is not yet in existence. But it would be wrong to confine our consideration for the people of the future to those who will be born within the next third of a century or so, as wrong as it is to respect the rights of only some subclass of existing people. People have moral rights not because of such accidental properties as age, race, sex, or the historical period in which they exist, but because they are sentient, self-aware beings with needs and desires. If we are to protect the interests of all such beings then we cannot allow the unfortunate ambiguity in the phrase "potential people" to blind us to the morally relevant differences between the real people of the future, whose lives will be affected by what we do now, and the potential people of the present, which are not now, though they may later become, beings with moral rights.

NOTES

1. Michael Tooley, "Abortion and Infanticide," *The Rights and Wrongs of Abortion* (Princeton University Press, 1974), p. 75.

2. See my article "On the Moral and Legal Status of Abortion," *Monist,* 57 (January 1973), 43–62, for a defense of this view. In this paper I suggest that the following (actual, not merely potential) capacities are criteria of personhood: (a) "consciousness (of objects and events external and/or internal to the being), and in particular, the capacity to feel pain"; (b) "reasoning (the *developed* capacity to solve new and relatively complex problems)"; (c) "self-motivated activity . . ."; (d) the capacity to communicate, by whatever means, messages of an indefinite variety of types . . ."; (e) "the presence of self-concepts, and self-awareness . . ." (p. 55). These capacities may not be individually necessary conditions of personhood, but they are such that the constitutional absence of any of them casts at least some doubt on the personhood of the entity, and the absence of all of them is sufficient to preclude personhood.

3. R. M. Hare, "Abortion and the Golden Rule," *Philosophy and Public Affairs,* Vol. 4, No. 3 (Spring 1975), p. 212. All further page references not otherwise identified are to this article.

4. Hare objects to the use of the term "moral right" on the grounds that no philosopher has yet produced "a theory of rights which links the concept firmly to those of 'right', 'wrong', and 'ought'—concepts whose logic is even now a little better understood" (p. 213). I see no *especial* difficulty, however, in analyzing talk about rights, or translating it into talk about right and wrong and what we ought to do. As a rough first approximation it might be suggested that someone has a prima facie right to something if and only if other things being equal it would be wrong for anyone else to deprive that person of that thing. Insofar as one can't sensibly say that someone has been *deprived* of something unless that thing is something which the person wants or has reason to want, it is clear that rights and desires are closely connected, though the nature of the connection is difficult to state precisely. (See Tooley, pp. 60–64, for an exploration of this connection.)

5. Tooley uses the kitten example to present another intuitive argument against the potentiality principle. He argues that the "possibility of transforming kittens into persons will not make it any more wrong to kill newborn kittens than it is now" (*op. cit.,* p. 76), and that therefore potential personhood does not entail a right to life.

6. George Berkeley, "Three Dialogues Between Hylas and Philonous," *The Works of George Berkeley,* Vol. 2, edited by T. E. Jessop (London: Thomas Nelson and Sons, 1964), p. 200.

7. Francis C. Wade, "Potentiality in the Abortion Discussion," *The Review of Metaphysics,* Vol. 39, No. 2, December 1975, p. 255.

8. *Ibid.,* p. 245. (Wade is here using "agent" to mean anything which causes a change in itself or in something else, not necessarily a *conscious* agent.)

9. H. Tristram Engelhardt, "The Ontology of Abortion," *Ethics,* Vol. 84, No. 3 (April 1974), p. 220.

10. Professor Warren is here defending what has been called "the asymmetrist view" regarding "the right to be born" (of potentially happy persons), and "the right *not* to be born" (of potentially miserable persons). The asymmetrist, of course, *denies* the first "right" and affirms the second "right." Other papers in support of the asymmetrist view are by Narveson (1967, 1976, 1978), Feinberg (1976), and Partridge ("To Be . . ."). Among the "symmetrists" (i.e., those who affirm *both* rights) are Hare (1975 — see note 3, above), Sikora (1978), Sterba (1980) and Sumner (1978). Sprigge's (1968) criticism of Narveson's asymmetry is significant, though it is not an explicit endorsement of the symmetrist position. Anglin's (1978) criticism of asymmetry is directed specifically to this paper by Warren. (For full reference information for these sources, see part 2 of the bibliography to this anthology.) — ED.

Garrett Hardin

Of Being and Non-being: A Postscript

In the course of lecturing for several years on the subject [of abortion] I have repeatedly encountered several verbal stratagems used in the defense of prohibition. Some of the issues raised are profound, while others border on the ludicrous. Among the latter is the triumphant conclusion of a vituperative (and anonymous) letter sent to me following one of my lectures: "If your mother had had an abortion, where would *you* be today?"

I must confess, I don't know. This question (which has been put to me several times) raises the most fascinating problems of being and nonbeing. A philosopher would no doubt discuss the question in the jargon of ontology. As a biologist, I prefer a different approach. I am reminded of the beginning of Lawrence Sterne's novel *Tristram Shandy* wherein the hero is discussing the circumstances surrounding his conception. As the critical moment approached Mrs. Shandy said to Mr. Shandy, "Pray, my Dear, have you not forgot to wind up the clock?"—"Good G--!" replied Mr. Shandy, "Did ever woman, since the creation of the world, interrupt a man with such a silly question?" It was, as young Tristram pointed out, an "unseasonable question at least."

Whether Mr. Shandy stopped what he was doing and went downstairs to wind the clock, Tristram did not record. Perhaps Mr. Shandy merely paused and shifted his position. It does not matter. The result, we can be sure, was the same; of the three hundred million spermatozoa Mr. Shandy released somewhat later, a different one led the pack, a different one reached the egg first, and a different Tristram was engendered. Put another way, the Tristram (or the Nancy) who might have been had not Mrs. Shandy asked about the clock — this Tristram never was, not then or in any subsequent coming together of Mr. and Mrs. Shandy.

To reply to my correspondent, if my mother had had an abortion I almost certainly would not be here today. In fact, if my father had coughed at the crucial moment I would not be here today. . . . Perhaps he did cough. . . . Who am I, anyway?

From "The Semantic Aspects of Abortion," *ETC.*, 24 (1967), 263–281. The title above is by the editor, with the permission of Professor Hardin.

Richard and Val Routley

Nuclear Energy and Obligations to the Future

I. The Bus Example

Suppose we consider a bus, a bus which we hope is to make a very long journey. This bus, a third world bus, carries both passengers and freight. The bus sets down and picks up many different passengers in the course of its long journey and the drivers change many times, but because of the way the bus line is managed and the poor service on the route it is nearly always full to overcrowded, with passengers hanging off the back, and as in Afghanistan, passengers riding on the roof, and chickens and goats in the freight compartment.

In the bus's journey someone consigns on it, to a far distant destination, a package containing a highly toxic and explosive gas. This is packaged in a very thin container, which as the consigner well knows is unlikely to contain the gas for the full distance for which it is consigned, and certainly will not do so if the bus should encounter any trouble, for example if there is a breakdown and the interior of the bus becomes very hot, if the bus should strike a very large bump or pothole of the sort commonly found on some of the bad roads it has to traverse, or if some passenger should interfere deliberately or inadvertently with the cargo or perhaps try to steal some of the freight, as also frequently happens. *All* of these things, let us suppose, have happened on some of the bus's previous journeys. If the container should break, the resulting disaster would probably kill at least some of the people and animals on the bus, while others could be maimed or contract serious diseases.

There does not seem much doubt about what most of us would say about the morality of the consigner's action, and there is certainly no doubt about what the passengers would say. The consigner's action in putting the safety of the occupants of the bus at risk is appalling. What could excuse such an action, what sort of circumstances might justify it, and what sort of case could the consigner reasonably put up? The consigner might say that it is by no means

Reprinted from *Inquiry* (Universitetsforlaget, Oslo), 21 (Summer 1978), 133–79, with permission of the publisher and authors.

certain that the gas will escape; he himself is an optimist and therefore feels that such unfavourable possible outcomes should be ignored. In any case the bus might have an accident and the passengers be killed long before the container gets a chance to leak; or the passengers might change to another bus and leave the lethal parcel behind.

He might say that it is the responsibility of the passengers and the driver to ensure that the journey is a smooth one, and that if they fail to do so, the results are not his fault. He might say that the journey is such a long one that many of the passengers may have become mere mindless vegetables or degenerate wretches about whose fate no decent person need concern himself, or that they might not care about losing their lives or health or possessions anyway by that time.

Most of these excuses will seem little more than a bad joke, and certainly would not usually be reckoned any sort of justification. The main argument the consigner of the lethal parcel employs, however, is that his own pressing needs justify his actions. He has no option but to consign his potentially lethal parcel, he says, since the firm he owns, and which has produced the material as a by-product, is in bad financial straits and cannot afford to produce a better container or to stop the production of the gas. If the firm goes out of business, the consigner says, his wife will leave him, and he will lose his family happiness, the comfortable way of life to which he has become accustomed and sees now as a necessity; his employees will lose their jobs and have to look for others; not only will the firm's customers be inconvenienced but he, the consigner, will have to break some business contracts; the inhabitants of the local village through loss of spending and cancellation of the Multiplier Effect will suffer financial hardship, and, worst of all, the tiny flow of droplets that the poor of the village might receive (theoretically at any rate) as a result of the trickling down of these good things would dry up entirely. In short, some basic and some perhaps uncomfortable changes will be needed in the village.

Even if the consigner's story were accepted at face value — and it would be wise to look critically at his story — only someone whose moral sensibilities had been paralysed by the disease of galloping economism could see such a set of considerations, based on "needs," comfort, and the goal of local prosperity, as justifying the consigner's action.

One is not generally entitled to thus simply *transfer* the risks and costs arising from one's own life onto other uninvolved parties, to get oneself out of a hole of one's own making by creating harm or risk of harm to someone else who has had no share in creating the situation. To create serious risks and costs, especially risks to life or health for such others, simply to avoid having to make some changes to a comfortable life style, or even for a somewhat better reason, is usually thought deserving of moral condemnation, and sometimes considered a crime: for example, the action of a company in creating risks to the lives or health of its workers or customers to prevent itself from going bankrupt. What the consigner says may be an explanation of his behaviour, but it is not a justification.

The problem raised by nuclear waste disposal is by no means a perfect analogy to the bus case, since, for example, the passengers on the nuclear bus cannot get off the bus or easily throw out the lethal package. In many crucial moral respects, however, the nuclear waste storage problem as it affects future people, the passengers in the bus we are considering, resembles the consignment of the faultily packaged lethal gas. Not only are rather similar moral principles involved, but a rather similar set of arguments to the lamentable excuses the consigner presents have been seriously put up to justify nuclear development, the difference being that in the nuclear case these arguments have been widely accepted. There is also some parallel in the risks involved; there is no *known* safe way to package the highly toxic wastes generated by nuclear plants that will be spread around the world if large-scale nuclear development goes ahead.[1] The wastes problem will not be a slight one, with *each one* of the more than 2,000 reactors envisaged by the end of the century, producing on average *annual* wastes containing one thousand times the radioactivity of the Hiroshima bomb.[2] The wastes include not merely the spent fuels and their radioactive by-products, but also everything they contaminate, from fuel containers to the thousands of widely distributed decommissioned nuclear reactors which will have to be abandoned, still in a highly radioactive condition, after the expiry of their expected lifetimes of about thirty years, and which have been estimated to require perhaps one and a half million years to reach safe levels of radioactivity.[3] The wastes must be kept suitably isolated from the environment for their entire active lifetime; for fission products the required storage period averages a thousand years or so, and for the actinides (transuranic elements) which include plutonium, there is a half-million- to a million-year storage problem.[4]

Serious problems have arisen with both short-term and proposed long-term methods of storage, even with the comparatively small quantities of waste that have been produced over the last twenty years.[5] With present known short-term surface methods of storage there is a continued need for human intervention to keep the material isolated from the environment, while with proposed longer-term methods such as storage in salt mines or granite to the risk of human interference there are added the risks of leakage, e.g. through water seepage, and of disturbance, for example through climatic change, earth movements, etc. The risks are significant: no reasonable person with even a limited acquaintance with the history of human affairs over the last 3,000 years could be confident of safe storage by methods involving human intervention over the enormous time periods involved. No one with even a slight knowledge of the geological and climatic history of the earth over the last million years, a period which has seen a number of ice ages and great fluctuations in climate for example, could be confident that the waste material could be safely stored for the vast periods of time required. Much of this waste is highly toxic; for example, even a beachball-sized quantity of plutonium appropriately distributed is enough to give every person on the planet lung cancer — so that a leak of even a small part of this waste material could involve much loss of life, widespread disease and genetic damage, and contamination of large areas of land.[6]

Given the enormous costs which could be involved for the future, it is plainly grossly inadequate to merely speculate concerning untested, but possibly or even probably safe, methods for disposal of wastes. Yet none of the proposed methods has been properly tested, and they may prove to involve all sorts of unforeseen difficulties and risks when an attempt is made to put them into practice on a commercial scale. Only a method that could provide a rigorous guarantee of safety over the storage period, that placed safety beyond reasonable doubt, would be acceptable. It is difficult to see how such rigorous guarantees could be given concerning either the geological or future human factors. But even if an economically viable, rigorously safe long-term storage method *could* be devised, there is the problem of guaranteeing that it would be universally and invariably *used*. The assumption that it would be, especially if, as seems likely, such a method proved expensive economically and politically, seems to presuppose a level of efficiency, perfection, and concern for the future not previously encountered in human affairs, and certainly not conspicuous in the nuclear industry.[7] Again, unless we assume continuous and faultless guarding of long-term storage sites through perhaps a million years of possible future human activity, weapons-grade radioactive material will be accessible, over much of the million-year storage period, to any party who is in a position to retrieve it.

Our behaviour in creating this nightmare situation for the future is certainly no better than that of the consigner in the bus example. Industrialized countries, in order to get out of a mess of their own making — essentially the creation of economies dependent on an abundance of non-renewable energy in a situation where it is in fact in limited supply — opt for a "solution" which may enable them to avoid the making of uncomfortable changes during the lifetime of those now living, at the expense of passing heavy burdens on to the inhabitants of the earth at a future time — burdens in the shape of costs and risks which, just as in the bus case, may adversely affect the life and health of future people and their opportunity to lead a decent life.[8]

It is sometimes suggested that analogies like the bus example are defective; that morally they are crucially different from the nuclear case, since future people, unlike the passengers in the bus, will benefit directly from nuclear development, which will provide an abundance of energy for the indefinite future. But this is incorrect. Nuclear fission creates wastes which may remain toxic for a million years, but even with the breeder reactor it could be an energy source for perhaps only 150 years. It will do nothing for the energy problems of the people of the distant future whose lives could be seriously affected by the wastes. Thus perhaps 30,000 generations of future people could be forced to bear significant risks, without any corresponding benefits, in order to provide for the extravagant energy use of only five generations.

Nor is the risk of direct harm from the escape or misuse of radioactive materials the only burden the nuclear solution imposes on the future. Because the energy provided by nuclear fission is merely a stop-gap, it seems probable that in due course the same problem, that of making a transition to renewable sources of energy, will have to be faced again by a future population which will probably, again as a result of our actions, be very much worse placed to cope with it. For they may well have to face the change to renewable resources in a over-populated world not only burdened with the legacy of our nuclear wastes, but also in a world in which, if the nuclear proponents' dream of global indus-trialization is realized, more and more of the global population will have become dependent on high energy consumption and associated technology and heavy resource use, and will have lost or reduced its ability to survive without it. It will, moreover, probably be a world which is largely depleted of non-renewable resources, and in which such renewable resources as forests and soils as remain, resources which will have to form a very important part of the basis of life, are in a run-down condition. Such points tell against the idea that future people must be, if not direct beneficiaries of nuclear fission energy, at least indirect beneficiaries.

The "solution" then is to buy time for contemporary industrial society at a price which not only creates serious problems for future people but which reduces their ability to cope with those problems. Just as in the bus case, con-temporary industrial society proposes to get itself out of a hole of its own mak-ing by creating risk of harm, and by transferring costs and risks, to someone else who has had no part in producing the situation and who will obtain no clear benefit. It has clear alternatives to this action. That it does not take them is due essentially to its unwillingness to avoid changing wasteful patterns of consump-tion and to its desire to protect the interests of those who benefit from them.

If we apply to the nuclear situation the same standards of behaviour and moral principles that we acknowledge (in principle if perhaps often not in fact) in the contemporary world, it will not be easy to avoid the conclusion that the situation involves injustice with respect to future people on a grand scale. It seems to us that there are only two plausible moves that might enable the avoidance of such a conclusion. First, it might be argued that the moral prin-ciples and obligations which we acknowledge for the contemporary world and the immediate future do not apply because the recipients of our nuclear parcel are in the non-immediate future. Secondly, an attempt might be made to appeal to overriding circumstances; for to reject the consigner's action in the circum-stances outlined is not of course to say that there are *no* circumstances in which such an action might possibly be justifiable, or at least where the case is less clearcut. It is the same with the nuclear case. Just as in the case of the con-signer of the package there is a need to consider what these justifying circum-stances might be, and whether they apply in the present case. We turn now to the first of these possible escape routes for the proponent of nuclear develop-ment, to the philosophical question of our obligations to the future.

II. Obligations to the Distant Future

The area in which these philosophical problems arise is that of the distant (i.e. non-immediate) future, that is, the future with which people alive today will make no direct contact; the immediate future provides comparatively few problems for moral theories. The issues involved, although of far more than academic interest, have not received any great attention in recent philosophical literature, despite the fact that the question of obligations to future people presents tests which a number of ethical theories fail to pass, and also raises a number of questions in political philosophy concerning the adequacy of accepted institutions which leave out of account the interests of future people.

Moral philosophers have predictably differed on the issue. But contrary to the picture painted in a recent, widely read, and influential work discussing it, Passmore's *Man's Responsibility for Nature,* a good many philosophers who have explicitly considered the question have come down in favour of the same consideration being given to the rights and interests of future people as to those of contemporary or immediately future people. Other philosophers have tended to fall into three categories—those who acknowledge obligations to the future but who do not take them seriously or who assign them less weight, those who deny, or who are committed by their general moral position to denying, that there are moral obligations beyond the immediate future, and those like Passmore and Golding who come down, with admirable philosophical caution, on both sides of the issue, but with the weight of the argument favouring the view underlying prevailing economic and political institutions, that there are no moral obligations to the future beyond those to the next generation.

According to the most extreme of these positions against moral obligations to the future, our behaviour with respect to the future is morally unconstrained; there are no moral restrictions on acting or failing to act deriving from the effect of our actions on future people. Of those philosophers who say, or whose views imply, that we don't have obligations to the (non-immediate) future, i.e. those who have opted for the unconstrained position, many have based this view on accounts of moral obligation which are built on relations which presuppose some degree of temporal or spatial contiguity. Thus moral obligation is seen as grounded on or as presupposing various relations which could not hold between people widely separated in time (or sometimes in space). For example, obligation is seen as grounded in relations which are proximate or of short duration and also non-transitive. Among such suggested bases or grounds of moral obligation, or requirements for moral obligation, which would rule out obligations to the non-immediate future are these: First, there are those accounts which require that someone to whom a moral obligation is held be able to claim his rights or entitlement. People in the distant future will not be able to claim rights and entitlements as against us, and of course they can do nothing to enforce any claims they might have for their rights against us. Secondly, there are those accounts which base moral obligations on social or legal convention, for example a convention which would require punishment of offenders or at least some kind of social enforcement. But plainly these and other conventions will not hold invariantly over change in society and amendment of legal conventions and so will not be invariant over time. Also future people have no way of enforcing their interests or punishing offenders, and there could be no guarantee that any contemporary institution would do it for them.

Both the view that moral obligation requires the context of a moral community and the view that it is contractually based appear to rule out the distant future as a field of moral obligation, as they not only require a commonality, or some sort of common basis, which cannot be guaranteed in the case of the distant future, but also a possibility of interchange or reciprocity of action which cannot apply to the future. Where the basis of moral obligation is seen as mutual exchange, the interests of future people must be set aside because they cannot change the past and cannot be parties to any mutual contract. The exclusion of moral obligations to the distant future also follows from those views which attempt to ground moral obligations in non-transitive relations of short duration such as sympathy and love. There are some difficulties also about love and sympathy for (non-existent) people in the far distant future about whose personal qualities and characteristics one must know very little and who may well be committed to a life-style for which one has no sympathy. On the current showing in the case of nuclear energy it would be easy to conclude that contemporary society lacks both love and sympathy for future people; and it would appear to follow from this that contemporary people have no obligations to future people and can harm them as it suits them.

What all these views have in common is a naturalistic picture of obligation as something acquired, either individually or institutionally, something which is conditional on doing something or failing to do something (e.g. participating in the moral community, contracting), or having some characteristic one can fail to have (e.g. love, sympathy, empathy). Because obligation therefore becomes conditional, features usually thought to characterize it, such as universality of application and necessitation (i.e. the binding features), are lost, especially where there is a choice of whether or not to do the thing required to acquire the obligation, and so of whether to acquire it. The criteria for acquisition suggested are such as to exclude people in the distant future.

However, the view that there are no moral constraints with respect to future people, that one is free to act as one likes with respect to them, is a very difficult one to sustain. Consider the example of a scientific group which, for no particular reason other than to test a particular piece of technology, places in orbit a cobalt bomb which is to be set off by a triggering device designed to go off several hundred years from the time of its despatch. No presently living person and none of their immediate descendants would be affected, but the population of the earth in the distant future would be wiped out as a direct and predictable result of the action. The unconstrained position clearly implies that this is an acceptable moral enterprise, that whatever else we might legitimately criticize in the scientists' experiment, perhaps its being unduly expensive or badly designed, we cannot lodge a moral protest about the damage it will do to future people. The unconstrained position also endorses as morally acceptable the following sorts of examples: A firm discovers it can make a handsome profit from mining, processing, and manufacturing a new type of material which, although it causes no problems for present people or their immediate descendants, will over a period of hundreds of years decay into a substance which will cause an enormous epidemic of cancer among the inhabitants of the earth at that time. According to the unconstrained view the firm is free to act in its own interests, without any consideration for the harm it does to future people.

Such counterexamples to the unconstrained view might seem childishly obvious. Yet the unconstrained position concerning the future from which they follow is far from being a straw man; not only have a number of philosophers writing on the issue endorsed this position, but it is the clear implication of many currently popular views of the basis of moral obligation, as well as of economic theory. It does not appear, on the other hand, that those who opt for the unconstrained position have considered such examples and endorsed them as morally acceptable, despite their being clearly implied by their position. We suspect that when it is brought out that the unconstrained position admits such counterexamples, that being free to act implies among other things being free to inflict pointless harm, most of those who opted for the unconstrained position would want to assert that it was not what they intended. What those who have put forward the unconstrained position seem to have had in mind in denying moral obligation is rather that future people can look after themselves, that we are not responsible for their lives. The view that the future can take care of itself also seems to assume a future causally independent of the present. But it is not. It is not as if, in cases such as those discussed above and the nuclear case, the future is simply being left alone to take care of itself. Present people are influencing it, and in doing so must acquire many of the same sorts of moral responsibilities as they do in causally affecting the present and immediate future. The thesis seems thus to assume an incorrect model of an independent and unrelated future.

Also, to say that we are not responsible for the lives of future people does not amount to the same as saying that we are free to do as we like with respect to them, that there are no moral constraints on our action involving them. In just the same way, the fact that one does not have, or has not acquired, an obligation to some stranger with whom one has never been involved – that one has no responsibility for his life – does not imply that one is free to do what one likes with respect to him, for example to rob him or to pursue some course of action of advantage to oneself which could seriously harm him.

These difficulties for the unconstrained position arise in part from the failure to make an important distinction between, on the one hand, acquired or assumed obligations toward somebody, for which some act of acquisition or assumption is required as a qualifying condition, and on the other hand moral constraints, which require, for example, that one should not act so as to damage or harm someone, and for which no act of acquisition is required. There is a considerable difference in the level and kind of responsibility involved. In the first case one must do something or be something which one can fail to do or be, e.g. have loves, sympathy, be contracted. In the second case responsibility arises as a result of being a causal agent aware of the consequences or probable consequences of his action, and thus does not have to be especially acquired or assumed. Thus there is no problem about how the latter class, moral constraints, can apply to the distant future in cases where it may be difficult or impossible for acquisition or assumption conditions to be satisfied. They apply as a result of the ability to produce causal effects on the distant future of a reasonably predictable nature. Thus also moral constraints can apply to what does not (yet) exist, just as actions can cause results that do not (yet) exist. While it may be the case that there would need to be an acquired or assumed obligation in order for it to be claimed that contemporary people must make special sacrifices of an heroic kind for future people, or even to help them especially, only moral constraints are needed in order for us to be constrained from harming them. Thus, to return to the bus example, the consigner cannot argue in justification of his action that he has never assumed or acquired responsibility for the passengers, that he does not know them and therefore has no love or sympathy for them, and that they are not part of his moral community, in short that he has no special obligations to help them. All that one needs to argue in respect of both the bus and the nuclear case is that there are moral constraints against harming, not that there are specially acquired obligations to take responsibility for the lives of the people involved. . . .

III. Uncertainty and Indeterminacy Arguments

Although there are grave difficulties for the unconstrained position, qualification leads to a more defensible position. According to the *qualified position* we are not entirely unconstrained with respect to the distant future: there are obligations, but these are not so important as those to the present, and the interests of distant future people cannot weigh very much in the scale against those of the present and immediate future. The interests of future people then, except in unusual cases, count for very much less than the interests of present people. Hence such things as nuclear development and various exploitative activities which benefit present people should proceed, even if people of the distant future are disadvantaged by them.

The qualified position appears to be widely held and is implicit in most modern economic theories, where the position of a decrease in weight of future costs and benefits (and so of future interests) is obtained by application over time of an (opportunity cost) discount rate. The attempt to apply economics as a moral theory, something that is becoming increasingly common, can lead then to the qualified position. What is objectionable in such an approach is that economics must operate within the bounds of moral (deontic) constraints, just as in practice it operates within legal constraints, and cannot determine what those constraints are. There are, moreover, alternative economic theories and simply to adopt one which discounts the future is to beg all the questions at issue. The discounting move often has the same result as the unconstrained position; if, for instance, we consider the cancer example and consider costs as payable compensation, it is evident that, over a sufficiently long period of time, discounting at current prices would lead to the conclusion that there are no recoverable damages and so, in economic terms, no constraints. In short, even certain damage to future people could be written off. One way to achieve the bias against future people is by the application of discount rates which are set in accord with the current economic horizons of no more than about fifteen years,[9] and application of such rates *would* simply beg the question against the interests and rights of future people. Where there is certain future damage of a morally forbidden type the whole method of discounting is simply inapplicable, and its use would violate moral constraints.[10]

Another argument for the qualified position, which avoids the objections from cases of certain damage, comes from probability considerations. The distant future, it is argued, is much more uncertain than the present and immediate future, so that probabilities are consequently lower, perhaps even approaching or coinciding with zero for any hypothesis concerning the distant future.[11] But then if we take account of probabilities in the obvious way, by simply multiplying them against costs and benefits, it is evident that the interests of future people, except in cases where there is an unusually high degree of certainty, must count for (very much) less than those of present and neighbouring people where (much) higher probabilities obtain. So in the case of conflict between the present and the future where it is a question of weighing certain benefits to the people of the present and the immediate future against a much lower probability of indeterminate costs to an indeterminate number of distant future people, the issue would normally be decided in favour of the present, assuming that anything like similar costs and benefits were involved. But of course it can't be assumed that anything like similarly weighted costs and benefits are involved in the nuclear case, especially if it is a question of risking poisoning some of the earth for half a million or so years, with consequent risk of serious harm to thousands of generations of future people, in the shape of the opportunity to continue unnecessarily high energy use. And even if the costs and benefits were comparable or evenly weighted, such an argument would be defective, since an analogous argument would show that the consigner's action is acceptable provided the benefit, e.g. the profit he stood to gain from imposing significant risks on other people, was sufficiently large. Such a cost-benefit approach to moral and decision problems, with or without the probability frills, is quite inadequate where different parties are concerned, or for dealing with cases of conflict of interest or moral problems where deontic constraints are involved, and commonly yields counterintuitive results. For example, it would follow on such principles that it is *permissible* for a firm to injure, or very likely injure, some innocent party provided the firm stands to make a sufficiently large gain from it. But the costs and benefits involved are not transferable in any simple or general way from one party to another. Transfers of this kind, of costs and benefits involving different parties, commonly raise moral issues — e.g. is x entitled to benefit himself by imposing costs on y? — which are not susceptible to a simple cost-benefit approach of the sort adopted by some proponents of nuclear energy, who attempt to dismiss the costs to future people with the soothing remark that any development involves costs as well as benefits. The transfer point is enough to invalidate the comparison, heavily relied on by McCracken[12] in building a case for the acceptability of the nuclear risk, between nuclear risks and those from cigarette smoking. In the latter case those who supposedly benefit from the activity are also, to an overwhelming extent, those who bear the serious health costs and risks involved. In contrast the users and supposed beneficiaries of nuclear energy will be risking not only, or even primarily, their own lives and health, but also those of others who may be non-beneficiaries and who may be spatially or temporally removed, and these risks will not be in any direct way related to a person's extent of use.

The transfer objection is essentially the same as that to the utilitarian's happiness sums as a way of solving moral conflict between different parties, and the introduction of probability considerations does not change the principles involved but merely complicates analyses. One might further object to the probability argument that probabilities involving distant future situations are not always less than those concerning the immediate future in the way the argument supposes, and that the outcomes of some moral problems such as the bus example do not depend on a high level of probability anyway. In some sorts of cases it is enough, as the bus example reveals, that a significant risk is created; such cases do not depend critically on high probability assignments.

Uncertainty arguments in various forms are the most common and important ones used by philosophers and others to argue for the position that we cannot be expected to take serious account of the effects of our actions on the distant future. There are two strands to the uncertainty argument, capable of separation, but frequently entangled. Both arguments are mistaken, the first on *a priori* grounds, the second on *a posteriori* grounds. The first argument is a generalized uncertainty argument which runs as follows: In contrast to the exact information we can obtain about the present, the information we can obtain about the effects of our actions on the distant future is unreliable, woolly, and highly speculative. But we cannot base assessments of how we should act on information of this kind, especially when accurate information is obtainable about the present which would indicate different action. Therefore we must regretfully ignore the uncertain effects of our actions on the distant future. More formally and crudely: One only has obligations to the future if these obligations are based on reliable information; there is no reliable information at present as regards the distant future; therefore one has no obligations to the distant future.

The first argument is essentially a variation on a sceptical argument in epistemology concerning our knowledge of the future (formally, replace "obligations" by "knowledge" in the crude statement of the argument above). The main ploy is to considerably overestimate and overstate the degree of certainty available with respect to the present and immediate future, and the degree of certainty which is required as the basis for moral consideration both with respect to the present and with respect to the future. Associated with this is the attempt to suggest a sharp division as regards certainty between the present and immediate future on the one hand and distant future on the other. We shall not find, we suggest, that there is any such sharp or simple division between the distant future and the adjacent future and present, at least with respect to those things in the present which are normally subject to moral constraints. We can and constantly do act on the basis of such "unreliable" information as the sceptic as regards the future conveniently labels "uncertainty"; for sceptic-proof certainly is rarely, or never, available with respect to much of the present and immediate future. In moral situations in the present, action often takes account of risk and probability, even quite low probabilities. A good example is again the bus case. We do not need to know for certain that the container will break and the lethal gas escape. In fact it does not even have to be probable, in the relevant sense of more probable than not, in order for us to condemn the consigner's action. It is enough that there is a significant risk of harm in this sort of case. It does not matter if the decreased well-being of the consigner is certain and the prospects of the passengers quite uncertain; the resolution of the problem is still clearly in favour of the so-called "speculative" and "unreliable." But if we do not require certainty of action to apply moral constraints in contemporary affairs, why should we require a much higher standard of certainty in the future? Why should we require epistemic standards for the future which the more familiar sphere of moral action concerning the present and adjacent future does not need to meet? The insistence on certainty as a necessary condition before moral consideration can be given to the distant future, then, amounts to an epistemic double standard. But such an epistemic double standard, proposed in explaining the difference between the present and the future and to justify ignoring future peoples' interests, in fact cannot itself provide an explanation of the differences, since it already presupposes different standards of certainty appropriate to each class, which difference is in turn in need of justification.

The second uncertainty argument is a practical uncertainty argument, that whatever our *theoretical* obligations to the future, we cannot in practice take the interests of future people into account, because uncertainty about the distant future is so gross that we cannot determine what the likely consequences of actions upon it will be and therefore, however good our intentions to the people of the distant future, in practice we have no choice but to ignore their interests. Uncertainty is *gross* where certain incompatible hypotheses are as good as one another and there is no rational ground for choosing between them. The second uncertainty argument can also be put in this way: If moral principles are, like other principles, implications in form, that is of such forms as "if x has character h then x is wrong, for every (action) x," then what the argument claims is that we can never obtain the information about future actions which would enable us to detach the antecedent of the implication. So even if moral principles theoretically apply to future people, in practice they cannot be applied to obtain clear conclusions or directions concerning contemporary action of the "It is wrong to do x" type.

Many of the assumptions of the second argument have to be conceded. If the distant future really is so grossly uncertain that in every case it is impossible to determine in any way that is better than chance what the effects of present action will be, and whether any given action will help or hinder future people, then moral principles, although they may apply theoretically to the future, will not be applicable in practice for obtaining any clear conclusions about how to act. Hence the distant future will impose no practical moral constraints on action. However, the argument is factually incorrect in assuming that the future is always so grossly uncertain or indeterminate. Admittedly there is often a high degree of uncertainty concerning the distant future, but as a matter of (contingent) fact it is not always so gross or sweeping as the argument has to assume. There are some areas where uncertainty is not so great as to exclude constraints on action, especially when account is taken of the point, noticed in connection with the first argument, that complete certainty is commonly not required for moral constraints and that all that may be needed in some cases is the creation of a significant risk. Again there is considerable uncertainty about many factors which are not highly, or at all, morally relevant, but this does not extend to many factors which are of much greater importance to moral issues. For example, we may not have any idea what the fashions will be in a hundred years in girls' names or men's footwear, or what brands of ice cream people will be eating if any, but we do have excellent reason to believe, especially if we consider 3,000 years of history, that what people there are in a hundred years are likely to have material and psychic needs not entirely unlike our own, that they will need a healthy biosphere for a good life; that like us they will not be immune to radiation; that their welfare will not be enhanced by a high incidence of cancer or genetic defects, by the destruction of resources, or the elimination from the face of the earth of that wonderful variety of non-human life which at present makes it such a rich and interesting place. For this sort of reason, the second uncertainty argument should be rejected. While it is true that there are many areas in which the morally relevant information needed is uncertain or unavailable, and in which we cannot therefore determine satisfactorily how to act, there are certainly others in which uncertainty in morally relevant areas is not so great as to preclude moral constraints on action, where we ascertain if not absolute certainties at least probabilities of the same sort of order as are considered sufficient for the application of moral principles in parallel contemporary cases, especially where spatially remote people are involved. The case of nuclear waste storage, and of uncertainty of effects of it on future people, seems to be of the latter sort. Here there is no *gross* indeterminacy or uncertainty; it is simply not true that incompatible hypotheses about what may happen are as good as each other. It is plain that nuclear waste storage does impose significant risks of harm on future people, and, as we can see from the bus example, the significant risk of harm is enough in cases of this type to make moral constraints applicable.

In terms of the defects of the preceding uncertainty arguments, we can see the corresponding defects in a number of widely employed uncertainty arguments used to write off probable harm to future people as outside the scope of proper consideration. Most of these popular moves employ both of the uncertainty arguments as suits the case, switching from one to the other in a way that is again reminiscent of sceptical moves. For example, we may be told that we cannot really take account of future people because we cannot be sure that they will exist or that their tastes and wants will not be completely different from our own, to the point where they will not suffer from our exhaustion of resources or from the things that would affect us.[13] But this is to insist upon complete certainty of a sort beyond what is required for the present and immediate future, where there is also commonly no guarantee that some disaster will not overtake those we are morally committed to. Again we may be told that there is no guarantee that future people will be worthy of any efforts on our part, because they may be morons or forever plugged into enjoyment- or other machines.[14] Even if one is prepared to accept the elitist approach presupposed — according to which only those who meet certain properly civilized or intellectual standards are eligible for moral consideration — what we are being handed in such arguments as a serious defeating consideration is again a mere outside possibility — like the sceptic who says that the solid-looking desk in front of us is perhaps only a façade, not because he has any particular reason for doing so, but because he hasn't looked around the back, drilled holes in it, etc. Neither the contemporary nor the historical situation gives any positive reason for supposing that a lapse into universal moronity or universal pleasure-machine escapism is a serious possibility, as opposed to a logical possibility. We can contrast with these mere logical possibilities the very real historically supportable risks of escape of nuclear waste or decline of a civilization through destruction of its resource base.

The possibilities just considered in these uncertainty arguments of sceptical character are not real possibilities.[15] Another argument which may consider a real possibility, but still does not succeed in showing that it is acceptable to proceed with an action which would appear to be harmful to future people, is often introduced in the nuclear waste case. This is the argument that future people may discover a rigorously safe and permanent storage method for nuclear wastes before they are damaged by escaped waste material. Let us grant for the sake of the argument that this is a real possibility (though physical arguments may show that it is not). This still does not affect the fact that there is a significant risk of serious damage and that the creation of a significant risk is enough to rule out an action of this type as morally impermissible. In just the same way, future people may discover a cure for cancer, and the fact that this appears to be a real and not merely a logical possibility, does not make the action of the firm in the example discussed above, of producing a substance likely to cause cancer in future people, morally admissible. The fact that there was a real possibility of future people avoiding the harm would show that actions of these sorts were admissible only if what was required for inadmissibility was certainty of harm or a very high probability of it. In such cases, before such actions could be considered admissible, what would be required is far more than a possibility, real or not — it is at least the availability of an applicable, safe, and rigorously tested, not merely speculative, technique for achieving it, something that future people could reasonably be expected to apply to protect themselves.

The strategy of most of these uncertainty arguments is fairly clear then, and may be brought out by looking yet again at the bus example, where the consigner says that he cannot be expected to take account of the effect of his actions on the passengers because they may find an effective way to deal with his parcel or some lucky or unlucky accident may occur, e.g. the bus may break down and they may all change to a different bus leaving the parcel behind, or the bus may crash, killing all the passengers before the container gets a chance to leak. These are all possibilities of course, but there is no positive reason to believe that they are any more than that, that is they are not real possibilities. The strategy is to stress such outside possibilities in order to create the false impression that there is gross uncertainty about the future, that the real possibility that the container will break should be treated in the same way as these mere logical possibilities, that uncertainty about the future is so great as to preclude the consigner's taking account of the passengers' welfare and of the real possibility of harm from his parcel, and thereby excuse his action. A related strategy is to stress a real possibility, such as finding a cure for cancer, and thereby imply that this removes the case for applying moral constraints. This move implicitly makes the assumptions of the first argument, that certainty, or at least a very high probability, of harm is required before an action can be judged morally inadmissible, and the point of stressing the real possibility of avoidance of damage is to show that this allegedly required high degree of certainty or probability cannot be attained. That is, the strategy draws attention to some real uncertainty implying that this is sufficient to defeat the application of moral constraints. But, as we have seen, this is often not so.

An argument closely related to the uncertainty arguments is based on the non-existence and indeterminacy of the future.[16] An item is indeterminate in a given respect if its properties in that respect are, as a matter of logic, not settled (nor are they settlable in a non-arbitrary fashion). The respects in which future items are indeterminate are well enough known for a few examples to serve as reminders: all the following are indeterminate: the population of Australia at 2001, its distribution, its age structure, the preferences of its members for folk music, wilderness, etc., the size and shape of Wollongong, the average number of rooms in its houses and in its office blocks, and so on. Philosophical discussion of such indeterminacy is as old as Aristotle's sea battle and as modern as truth-value gaps and fuzzy logics, and many positions have been adopted on the existence and determinacy of future items. Nevertheless theories that there are obligations to the future are not sensitive to the metaphysical position adopted concerning the existence or non-existence of the future. Any theory which denied obligations to the future on the metaphysical grounds that the future did not exist, and did not have properties, so that the present could not be related to it, would be committed to denying such obvious facts as that the present could causally influence the future, that present people could be great-grandparents of purely future people, and so on, and hence would have to be rejected on independent grounds. . . .

. . . Future items *will* have properties even if they do not have them now, and that is enough to provide the basis for moral concern about the future. Thus the thesis of obligations to the future does not presuppose any special metaphysical position on the existence of the future.

If the non-existence of future items creates no special problems for obligations to the future, the same is not true of their indeterminacy, [which] . . . creates major difficulties for certain ethical theories and their treatment of the future.

The difficulties arise for theories which appear to require a high level of determinacy with respect to the number and character of future items, in particular calculus-type theories such as utilitarianism in its usual forms, where the calculations are critically dependent on such information as numbers, totals, and averages, information which so far as the future is concerned is generally indeterminate. The fact that this numerical information is typically indeterminate means that insofar as head-count utilitarianism requires determinate information on numbers, it is in a similar position to theories discussed earlier; it may apply theoretically to future people, but since the calculations cannot be applied to them their interests will be left out of account. And, in fact, utilitarianism for the most part does not, and perhaps cannot, take future creatures and their interests seriously. . . .

. . . We have yet another case of a theory of the sort that applies theoretically but in practice doesn't take the future seriously. But far from this showing that future people's interests should be left out of account, what these considerations show are deficiencies in these sorts of theories, which require excessive determinacy of information. This kind of information is commonly equally unavailable for the accepted areas of moral constraint, the present and immediate future; and the resolution of moral issues is often not heavily dependent on knowledge of such specific determinate features as numbers or other determinate features. For example, we do not need to know how many people there will be on the bus, how intelligent they are, what their preferences are or how badly they will be injured, in order to reach the conclusion that the consigner's action in despatching his parcel is a bad one. Furthermore, it is only the ability of moral considerations to continue to apply in the absence of determinate information about such things as numbers that makes it possible to take account of the possible effects of action, as the risks associated with action— something which is quite essential even for the present if moral considerations are to apply in the normal and accepted way. For it is essential in order to apply moral considerations in the accepted way that we consider alternative worlds, in order to take account of options, risks, and alternative outcomes; but these alternative or counterfactual worlds are not in so different a position from the future with respect to determinacy; for example, there is indeterminacy with respect to the number of people who may be harmed in the bus case or in a *possible* nuclear reactor melt-down. These alternative worlds, like the distant future, are indeterminate in some respects, but not totally indeterminate.

It might still be thought that the indeterminacy of the future, for example with respect to number and exact character, would at least prevent the interest of future people being taken into account where there is a conflict with the present. Since their numbers are indeterminate and their interests unknown, how can we weigh their competing claims against those of the present and immediate future where this information is available in a more or less accurate form? The question is raised particularly by problems of sharing fixed quantities of resources among present and future people, when the numbers of the latter are indeterminate. Such problems are indeed difficult, but they are not resolved by *ignoring* the claims of the future, any more than the problems raised by the need to take account in decision-making of factors difficult to quantify are resolved by ignoring such factors. Nor are such distributional problems as large and representative a class of moral problems concerning the future as the tendency to focus on them would suggest. It should be conceded then that there will be cases where the indeterminacy of aspects of the future will make conflicts very difficult or indeed impossible to resolve—a realistic ethical theory will not deliver a decision procedure—but there will equally be other conflict cases where the level of indeterminacy does not hinder resolution of the issue, e.g. the bus example which is a conflict case of a type. In particular, there will be many cases which are not solved by weighing numbers, numbers of interests, or whatever, cases for which one needs to know only the most general probable characteristics of future people. Moreover, even where numbers are relevant often only bounds will be required, exact numerical counts only being required where, for instance, margins are narrow; e.g. issues may be resolved as in parliament where a detailed vote (or division) is only required when the issue is close. It is certainly not necessary then to have complete determinacy to resolve all cases of conflict.

The question we must ask then is what features of future people could disqualify them from moral consideration or reduce their claims to it to below those of present people? The answer is: in principle, none. Prima facie moral principles are universalizable, and lawlike, in that they apply independently of position in space or in time, for example. But universalizability of principles is an outcome of those ethical theories which are capable of dealing satisfactorily with the present; in other words, a theory that did not allow properly for the future would be found to have defects as regards the present, to deal unjustly or unfairly with some present people, e.g. those remotely located, those outside some select subgroup such as (white-skinned) humans, etc. The only candidates for characteristics that would fairly rule out future people are the logical features we have been looking at, uncertainty and indeterminacy; what we have argued is that it would be far too sweeping to see these features as affecting the moral claims of future people in a general way. These special features only affect certain sorts of cases (e.g. the determination of best probable or practical course of action given only present information). In particular they do not affect cases of the sort being considered, the nuclear one, where highly determinate or certain information about the numbers and characteristics of the class likely to be harmed or certainty of damage are not required.

To establish obligations to the future a full universalizability principle is not needed: it is enough to require that the temporal position of a person cannot affect his entitlement to just and fair treatment, to full moral consideration;[17] inversely that it is without basis to discriminate morally against a person in virtue of his temporal position. As a result of this universalizability, *there is the same obligation to future people as to the present*; and thus there is the same obligation to take account of them and their interests in what we do, to be careful in our actions, to take account of the probability (and not just the certainty) of our actions' causing harm or damage, and to see, other things being equal, that we do not act so as to rob future people of what is necessary for the chance of a good life. Uncertainty and indeterminacy do not free us of these obligations. If, in a closely comparable case concerning the present, the creation of a significant risk is enough to rule out an action as immoral, and there are no independent grounds for requiring greater certainty of harm in the future case under consideration, then futurity alone will not provide adequate grounds for proceeding with the action, thus discriminating against future people. Accordingly we cannot escape, through appeal to futurity, the conclusion tentatively reached in our first section, that proposals for nuclear development in the present state of technology for future waste disposal are immoral.

IV. Overriding Consideration Arguments

In the first part we noticed that the consigner's action could not be justified by purely economistic arguments, such as that his profits would rise, the firm or the village would be more prosperous, or by appealing to the fact that some possibly uncomfortable changes would otherwise be needed. We also observed that the principle on which this assessment was based, that one was not usually entitled to create a serious risk to others for these sorts of reasons, applied more generally and, in particular, applied to the nuclear case. For this reason the economistic arguments which are thus most commonly advanced to promote nuclear development — e.g. cheapness, efficiency, profitability for electricity utilities, and the need otherwise for uncomfortable changes such as restructuring of employment, investment, and consumption — do not even *begin* to show that the nuclear alternative is an acceptable one. Even if these economistic assumptions about benefits to present people were correct (and there is reason to doubt that most of them are),[18] the arguments would fail because economics must operate within the framework of moral constraints, and not vice versa.

What one does have to consider, however, are moral conflict arguments, that is, arguments to the effect that, unless the prima facie unacceptable alternative is taken, some even more unacceptable alternative is the only possible outcome, and will ensue. For example, in the bus case, the consigner may argue that his action is justified because unless it is taken the village will starve.

It is by no means clear that even such a justification as this would be sufficient, especially where the risk to the passengers is high, as the case seems to become one of transfer of costs and risks onto others; but such a moral situation would no longer be so clearcut, and one would perhaps hesitate to condemn any action taken in such circumstances.

Some of the arguments advanced to show moral conflict are based on competing duties to present people, and others on competing obligations to future people, both of which are taken to override the obligations not to impose on the future significant risk of serious harm. The structure of such moral conflict arguments is based crucially on the presentation of a genuine and exhaustive set of alternatives (or at least practical alternatives), and upon showing that the only alternatives to admittedly morally undesirable actions are even more undesirable ones. If some practical alternative which is not morally worse than the action to be justified is overlooked, suppressed, or neglected in the argument—for example, if in the bus case it turns out that the villagers have another option to starving or to the sending off of the parcel, namely, earning a living in some other way—then the argument is defective and cannot readily be patched. We want to argue that suppression of practicable alternatives has occurred in the argument, designed to show that the alternatives to the nuclear option are even worse than the option itself, and that there are other factual defects in these arguments as well. In short, the arguments depend essentially on the presentation of false dichotomies.

The first argument, the *poverty argument,* is that there is an overriding obligation to the poor, both the poor of the third world and the poor of industrialized countries. Failure to develop nuclear energy, it is often claimed, would amount to denying them the opportunity to reach the standard of affluence we currently enjoy and would create unemployment and poverty in the industrialized nations.

The unemployment and poverty argument does not stand up to examination either for the poor of the industrial countries or for those of the third world. There is good evidence that large-scale nuclear energy will help to increase unemployment and poverty in the industrial world, through the diversion of great amounts of available capital into an industry which is not only an exceptionally poor provider of direct employment, but also helps to reduce available jobs through encouraging substitution of energy use for labour use.[19] The argument that nuclear energy is needed for the third world is even less convincing. Nuclear energy is both politically and economically inappropriate for the third world, since it requires massive amounts of capital, requires numbers of imported scientists and engineers, and creates negligible employment, while politically it increases foreign dependence, adds to centralized entrenched power and reduces the chance for change in the oppressive political structures which are a large part of the problem.[20] The fact that nuclear energy is not in the interests of people of the third world does not, of course, mean that it is not in the interests of, and wanted by, their rulers, the westernized and often military elites in whose interests the economies of these countries are usually organized; but it is not paternalistic to examine critically the demands these ruling elites may make in the name of the poor.

The poverty argument then is a fraud. Nuclear energy will not be used to help the poor.[21] Both for the third world and for the industrialized countries there are well-known energy-conserving alternatives and the practical option of developing other energy sources,[22] alternatives which are morally acceptable and socially preferable to nuclear development, and which have far better prospects for helping the poor.[23]

The second major argument advanced to show moral conflict appeals to a set of supposedly overriding and competing obligations to future people. We have, it is said, a duty to pass on the immensely valuable things and institutions which our culture has developed. Unless our high-technological, high-energy industrial society is continued and fostered, our valuable institutions and traditions will fall into decay or be swept away. The argument is essentially that without nuclear power, without the continued level of material wealth it alone is assumed to make possible, the lights of our civilization will go out.[24]

The *lights-going-out argument* raises rather sharply questions as to what is valuable in our society, and of what characteristics are necessary for a good society. These are questions which deserve much fuller treatment than we can allot them here, but a few brief points should be made.

The argument adopts an extremely uncritical position with respect to existing high-technology societies, apparently assuming that they are uniformly and uniquely valuable; it also assumes that technological society is unmodifiable, that it can't be changed in the direction of energy conservation or alternative energy sources without collapse. Such a society has to be accepted and assessed as a whole, and virtually unlimited supplies of energy are essential to maintain this whole.

These assumptions are hard to accept. The assumption that technological society's energy patterns are unmodifiable is especially so — after all, it has survived events such as world wars which have required major social and technological restructuring and consumption modification. If western society's demands for energy are totally unmodifiable without collapse, not only would it be committed to a programme of increasing destruction, but one might ask what use its culture could be to future people who would very likely, as a consequence of this destruction, lack the resource base which the argument assumes to be essential in the case of contemporary society.

There is also difficulty with the assumption of uniform valuableness; but if this is rejected the question becomes not: what is necessary to maintain *existing* high-technological society and its political institutions? but rather: what is necessary to maintain what is *valuable* in that society and the political institutions which are needed to maintain those valuable things? While it may be easy to argue that high energy consumption is necessary to maintain the political and economic *status quo,* it is not so easy to argue that it is essential to maintain what is *valuable,* and it is what is valuable, presumably, that we have a duty to pass on to the future.

The evidence, e.g. from history, is that no very high level of material affluence or energy consumption is needed to maintain what is valuable. There is good reason in fact to believe that a society with much lower energy and resource consumption would better foster what is valuable than our own. But even if a radical change in these directions in independently desirable, as we believe it is, it is not necessary to presuppose such a change, in the short term at least, in order to see that the assumptions of the lights-going-out argument are wrong. No enormous reduction of well-being is required to consume less energy than at present, and certainly far less than the large increase over present levels of consumption which is assumed in the usual economic case for nuclear energy.[25] What the nuclear strategy is really designed to do then is not to prevent the lights going out in western civilization, but to enable the lights to go on burning all the time—to maintain and even increase the wattage output of the Energy Extravaganza.

In fact there is good reason to think that, far from the high energy consumption society fostering what is valuable, it will, especially if energy is obtained by nuclear-fission means, be positively inimical to it. A society which has become heavily dependent upon an extremely high centralized, controlled, and garrisoned, capital- and expertise-intensive energy source, must be one which is highly susceptible to entrenchment of power, and one in which the forces which control this energy source, whether capitalist or bureaucratic, can exert enormous power over the political system and over people's lives, even more than they do at present. Very persuasive arguments have been advanced by civil liberties groups and others in a number of countries to suggest that such a society would tend to become authoritarian, if only as an outcome of its response to the threat posed by dissident groups in the nuclear situation.[26]

There are reasons to believe then that with nuclear development what we would be passing on to future generations would be some of the worst aspects of our society (e.g. the consumerism, growing concentration of power, destruction of the natural environment, and latent authoritarianism), while certain valuable aspects would be lost or threatened. Political freedom is a high price to pay for consumerism and energy extravagance.

Again, as in the case of the poverty arguments, clear alternatives which do not involve such unacceptable consequences are available. The alternative to the high-technology-nuclear option is not a return to the cave, the loss of all that is valuable, but the development of alternative technologies and life-styles which offer far greater scope for the maintenance and further development of what is valuable in our society than the highly centralized nuclear option.[27] The lights-going-out argument, as a moral conflict argument, accordingly fails, because it is also based on a false dichotomy. Thus both the escape routes, the appeal to moral conflict and the appeal to futurity, are closed.

If then we apply the same standards of morality to the future as we acknowledge for the present—as we have argued we should—the conclusion that the proposal to develop nuclear energy on a large scale is a crime against the future is inevitable, since both the escape routes are closed. There are, of course, also many other grounds for ruling it out as morally unacceptable, for saying that it is not only a crime against the distant future but also a crime against the present and immediate future. These other grounds for moral concern about nuclear energy, as it affects the present and immediate future, include problems arising from the possibility of catastrophic releases of radioactive fuel into the environment or of waste material following an accident such as reactor melt-down, of unscheduled discharges of radiation into the environment from a plant fault, of proliferation of nuclear weapons, and of deliberate release or threat of release of radioactive materials as a measure of terrorism or of extortion. All these are important issues, of much moral interest. What we want to claim, however, is that on the basis of its effects on the future *alone,* the nuclear option is morally unacceptable.[28]

NOTES

The following is a revised and abbreviated version of the Routleys' extensive and well-documented collection of supporting citations and notes. It has been revised to conform with the format of this anthology and abbreviated to meet space constraints. The reader who wishes to look further into the moral implications of nuclear technology is well-advised to examine the original article in *Inquiry* (Summer 1978). The complete article also contains careful and insightful criticisms of John Passmore's and John Rawls's view concerning the duty to future generations. — ED.

1. Thus according to the Fox Report:

> There is at present no generally accepted means by which high level waste can be permanently isolated from the environment and remain safe for very long periods. . . . Permanent disposal of high-level solid wastes in stable geological formations is regarded as the most likely solution, but has yet to be demonstrated as feasible. It is not certain that such methods and disposal sites will entirely prevent radioactive releases following disturbances caused by natural processes or human activity.

Ranger Uranium Environmental Inquiry First Report (Australian Government Publishing Service, Canberra, 1977), p. 110.

2. See A. Roberts, "The Politics of Nuclear Power," *Arena,* No. 41 (1976), pp. 24–5.

3. On all these points, see R. Nader and J. Abbotts, *The Menace of Atomic Energy* (Outback Press, Melbourne, 1977), esp. p. 141. According to the Fox Report (note 1, above), p. 110:

> Parts of the reactor structure will be highly radioactive and their disposal could be very difficult. There is at present no experience of dismantling a full-size reactor.

4. See, in particular, The Union of Concerned Scientists, *The Nuclear Fuel Cycle* (Friends of the Earth Energy Paper, San Francisco, 1973), p. 47; also, A. M. Weinberg, "Social Institutions and Nuclear Energy," *Science,* Vol. 177 (July 1972), p. 32, and Nader and Abbotts (see note 3, above), p. 149.

5. As the discussion in Nader and Abbotts (note 3, above), pp. 153–7, explains.

6. Cf. A. B. Lovins and J. H. Price, *Non-Nuclear Futures: The Case for an Ethical Energy Strategy* (Friends of the Earth International, San Francisco, 1975), pp. 35–6.

For much detail, see J. R. Goffman and A. R. Tamplin, *Poisoned Power* (Rondale Press, Emmaus, Pa., 1971).

7. On the pollution and waste disposal record of the infant nuclear industry, see Nader and Abbotts (note 3, above) and Lovins and Price (note 6, above).

The record of many countries on pollution control, where in many cases available technologies for reducing or removing pollution are not applied because they are considered too expensive or because they adversely affect the interests of some powerful group, provides clear historical evidence that the problem of nuclear waste disposal would not end simply with the devising of a "safe" technology for disposal, even if one could be devised which provided a sufficient guarantee of safety and was commercially feasible. . .

It must be stressed then that the problem is not merely one of disposal technique. Historical and other evidence points to the conclusion that many of the most important risks associated with nuclear waste disposal are not of the kind which might be amenable to technical solutions in the laboratory. A realistic assessment of potential costs to the future from nuclear development cannot overlook these important non-technical risk factors.

8. Of course, the effect on people is not the only factor that has to be taken into consideration in arriving at a moral judgment. Nuclear radiation, unlike most ethical theories, does not confine its scope to human life. But since the harm nuclear development is likely to cause to nonhuman life can hardly *improve* its case, it suffices if the case against it can be made out solely in terms of its effects on human life in the conventional way.

9. Discount, or bank, rates in the economists' sense are usually set to follow the market; cf. P. A. Samuelson, *Economics,* 7th ed. (McGraw Hill, New York, 1967), p. 351. Thus the rates have little moral relevance.

10. Cf. Rawls, *A Theory of Justice* (Harvard University Press, Cambridge, Mass, 1971), p. 287. "From a moral point of view there are no grounds for discounting future well-being on the basis of pure time preference."

11. What the probabilities would be depends on the theory of probability adopted: a Carnapian theory, e.g., would lead back to the unconstrained position.

12. S. McCracken, "The War Against the Atom," *Commentary,* September, 1977, pp. 33–47.

13. Cf. Passmore, *Man's Responsibility for Nature* (Duckworth, London, 1974, and Scribner's, New York, 1974).

14. Cf. Golding, "Obligations to Future Generations," *Monist,* Vol. 56 (1972), pp. 85–99, also this collection.

15. A real possibility is one which there is evidence for believing could eventuate. A real possibility requires producible evidence for its consideration. The contrast is with mere logical possibility.

16. Thus, to take a simple special case, economists discuss distant future people from their assessments of utility, welfare, etc., on the basis of their non-existence; cf. Ng ("the utility of a non-existent person is zero") and Harsanyi ("only existing people [not even "non-existing potential individuals"] can have real utility levels since they are not the only ones able to enjoy objects with a positive utility, suffer from objects with a negative utility, and feel indifferent to objects with zero utility") (see Appendix B of Y. K. Ng, "Preference, Welfare, and Social Welfare," paper presented at the *Colloquium on Preference, Choice and Value Theory,* RSSS (Australian National University, August 1977), pp. 24, 26–7). Non-existent people have no experiences, no preferences;

300 *Richard Routley and Val Routley*

distant future people do not exist; therefore distant future people have no utility assignments—so the sorites goes. But future people at least will have wants, preferences, and so on, and these have to be taken into account in adequate utility assessments (which should be assessed over a future time horizon), no matter how much it may complicate or defeat calculations.

17. Such a principle is explicit both in classical utilitarianism (e.g., Sidgwick, *The Methods of Ethics* (Macmillan, London 1962, reissue), p. 414), and in a range of contract and other theories from Kant and Rousseau to Rawls (see note 9, above). How the principle is argued for will depend heavily, however, on the underlying theory; and we do not want to make our use depend heavily on particular ethical theories.

18. See esp. R. Lanoue, *Nuclear Plants: The More They Build, The More You Pay* (Center for Study of Responsive Law, Washington, DC, 1976); also see Nader and Abbotts (note 3, above).

19. On all these points see R. Grossman and G. Daneker, *Guide to Jobs and Energy* (Environmentalists for Full Employment, Washington, DC, 1977), pp. 1-7, and also the details supplied in substantiating the interesting case of B. Commoner, *The Poverty of Power* (Knopf, New York, 1976). On the absorption of available capital by the nuclear industry, see as well Roberts (note 2, above), p. 23. On the employment issues, see too H. E. Daley in B. Commoner, H. Boksenbaum and M. Corr (eds.), *Energy and Human Welfare—A Critical Analysis,* Vol. III (Macmillan, New York, 1975), p. 149. A more fundamental challenge to the poverty argument appears in I. Illich, *Energy and Equality* (Calder & Boyars, London, 1974), where it is argued that the sort of development nuclear energy represents is exactly the opposite of what the poor need.

20. For much more detail on the inappropriateness see E. F. Schumacher, *Small is Beautiful* (Blond & Briggs, London, 1973). As to the capital and other requirements, see the Fox Report (cited note 1, above), p. 48, and also Commoner's *The Poverty of Power,* and Commoner, Boksenbaum and Corr (eds.), *Energy and Human Welfare . . .* (both cited in note 17, above).

21. This fact is implicitly recognized in the Fox Report (note 1, above) p. 56.

22. A useful survey is given in A. Lovins, *Energy Strategy: The Road Not Taken* (Friends of the Earth, Australia, 1977); reprinted from *Foreign Affairs,* October 1976). See also Lovins and Price (note 6, above), Commoner (note 17, above), Nader and Abbotts (note 3, above), and Schumacher (note 18, above).

23. This is also explained in the Fox Report (note 1, above), p. 56.

24. An argument like this is suggested in Passmore (note 11, above), Chs. 4 and 7, with respect to the question of saving resources. In Passmore this argument for the overriding importance of passing on contemporary culture is underpinned by what appears to be a future-directed ethical version of the Hidden Hand argument of economics—that, by a coincidence which if correct would indeed be fortunate, the best way to take care of the future (and perhaps even the only way to do so, since do-good intervention is almost certain to go wrong) is to take proper care of the present and immediate future. The argument has all the defects of the related Chain Argument discussed above and others.

25. See Nader and Abbotts (note 3, above), p. 66, p. 191, and also Commoner (note 17, above).

26. For such arguments see esp. M. Flood and R. Grove-White, *Nuclear Prospects: A Comment on the Individual, the State and Nuclear Power* (Friends of the Earth, Council for the Protection of Rural England and National Council for Civil Liberties, London, 1976).

27. For a recent sketch of one such alternative which is outside the framework of the conventional option of centralized bureaucratic socialism, see E. Callenbach's novel, *Ecotopia* (Banyan Tree Books, Berkeley, Calif., 1975). For the outline of a liberation socialist alternative see *Radical Technology,* ed. by G. Boyle and P. Harper (Undercurrents Limited, London, 1976), and references therein.

28. We have benefited from discussion with Ian Hughes and Frank Muller and useful comments on the paper from Brian Martin and Derek Browne.

AFTERWORD

Nicolai Hartmann

Love of the Remote

All ethically active life is prospective, a living in the future and for the future. This inheres in the nature of activity. Only the future belongs to striving. This will has no power over what has already transpired, once it exists. The great gift of foresight and predetermination (teleology), which is peculiar to man, imposes a profound obligation. It loads him with responsibility for the future, in so far as the future is in his power. How far it is so, cannot of course be estimated beforehand. But no absolute limits can here be set. Man's power of intervening in the cosmic process and determining its course extends just so far as he knows how to expand his capacity by his own energies. The fact that his will goes beyond his capacity is here irrelevant. . . .

To combine a life, viewed in the light of ideals, with a cool eye for the actual and the possible, requires an ethos considerably above the average. Such a synthesis gives to the bearer of it a certain dignity, which grows with the greatness of the ends he pursues and with the practical effect. In such a life is fulfilled something of man's destiny, which is to become a participant in the creation of the world. But just here it is seen that the perspective of any one individual's life is too small for the actualization of human ideals. One individual can advance a few steps upon such a path. And also in the work which he accomplishes he can go far; he can draw a group of men into the circle of his own idea, and under favourable circumstances he may evoke a total transformation of historical importance. But what will that signify, if his life-work dies with him, or soon after? It is just such work that requires permanence, continuation, a living energy of its own. It inheres in the nature of all effort that looks to an objective value, to go on beyond the life and enterprise of the individual, into a future which he no longer can enjoy. It is not only the fate but is also the pride of a creative mind and is inseparable from his task, that his work survives

Reprinted from Nicolai Hartmann, *Ethics,* vol. 2, 1932, pp. 311–331, with permission of the publishers: George Allen and Unwin, Ltd. (London), and the Humanities Press, Inc. (Atlantic Highlands, N.J.).

him, and therefore passes from him to others, in whose life he has no part. . . .

. . . Animal nature, in that it reproduces itself, survives in what it brings forth. Its care for its young, its capacity to die for them, the fixed attachment to the future life of the species, is symbolical. It is an immortality in the mortal. But besides physical procreation, man knows another kind, spiritual procreation, whereby he passes into the imperishable. His work survives him, he participates in the eternal through immortal virtue. He too can live and die for his offspring.

The Platonic *eros**— when we strip it of everything else and attend only to its ethical substance — is deeper absorption in the Idea, great passion for it, personal commitment to it. This passion brings it about that a man is transported beyond himself and beyond his environment. It is a man's losing of himself in his work, his inward life in what is not yet, in what is "still on the way from Non-being to Being"; it is the abandonment of the present for what is future, uncertain; the sacrifice of his life for another life, for one more valuable, but one that is not his own.

There is a potency *sui generis* in man, which here emerges, a germinal capacity with a distant aim, a generative energy of the ethos. Plato called it a pregnancy and a bringing to the birth. The driving force is the Idea. The creative worker is carried with it. It is the generating power of values in man, for instance, of his ideals which are laden with values. Through them he outgrows himself. He transcends himself. But the direction and the extent of the transcendence are not the same as in the case of brotherly love and of everything akin to it. It lies in another dimension of life; it does not tend to fellowship with individuals nor even to union with the community, but is prospective towards some future time which is still asleep in the non-existent. The trend of its intention has exchanged the breadth of simultaneity for the depth of succession. Herein the transcendence advances not only in degree but in quality: it goes beyond the boundary of the actual and present and plunges into the unreal, which can be discerned only in the Idea, in order to actualize it. . . .

In every cultural relationship each one sees himself in the setting of another community, that of the following generation, which teaches him that he himself is but a link in a chain. The responsibility which arises therefrom signifies a solidarity of a newer and greater kind than that of justice, brotherly love and faith. Like these it is a bond, a fellowship, a pledge, a joint responsibility of person for person. And still it is altogether different. In it the man of today feels himself one with the man of the far-away future, though the latter will have forgotten him and cannot be of help to him. The temporal direction of cause and effect is not reversible. The influence of man on man, solidarity itself, is only one-sided. Only he who lived previously can be of service to him who lives afterwards. The successor bears no retrospective obligation. Instead,

---

* I.e., "desire," "striving."—ED.

there falls to him a new obligation towards the generations coming after him. Solidarity is directed forward only; its form is progress, not co-existence. Still it is a bond which is great not only in extent but great in the quality of its task.

That it is a bond of a more fragile kind, that it is taken so much less earnestly by the living than is the solidarity of justice or love, this is not due to its own nature. It is due to the moral immaturity of the living, to their not having wakened to their greatest task. It is their lack of thorough self-conquest, which transcends the sphere of the Now and the Near.

There is an ethos which brings about this new transcendence with the emotional strength of the Platonic *eros*. It is an ethos of love, but of another love than that for one's neighbour, a love for the man who is to be, as he is conceivable in Idea by the living. It is a love which knows no return of love, which radiates only, gives only, devotes, overcomes, sacrifices, which lives in the high yearning that cannot be fulfilled for the one who loves, but which knows that there is always a future and that indifference to it is a sin. Such love is "Fernstenliebe" (Love of the remotest). . . .

The content of a fruitful ideal necessarily lies beyond the momentarily actual. And because it reaches beyond the limits of an individual life, it naturally reduces the individual to a link in the chain of life, which connects the past with the future. Man sees himself caught up into a larger providence, which looks beyond him and yet is his own.

Such an ideal, as a value, manifests itself in life as a really creative power. It is the form in which values become driving energies in personal life and in history. It attracts the faith of the strong to itself, like a magnet. And with this power of faith it transforms man and his human world. For in content it is objective, it is never the possession of one man, even if he be the only one who discern it. It draws others after it, binds together all who are able to grasp it. At first it separates the few, the seeing and believing, the noble and self-sacrificing, and forms them into a group. And this closed group moves forward in the process. . . .

The ideals we are considering are human ideals, but they are by no means merely ethical. They embrace all sides of humanity. . . . The Idea of man requires the rounding out of his whole nature, physical as well as spiritual, of all capacities and all the splendid possessions which are within his power. The great yearning of the creative spirit is for a humanity which is altogether more nearly perfect, more abounding in life and richer than mankind is at present. Out of the abundance which his prophetic sense discerns, the creative spirit gives to the ideal a vastness which it does not find in itself nor in its environment and which it is not able to actualize. And it is unable, because to actualize it is not the work of one man but of generations.

. . . Who would take it upon himself . . . to abandon the *eros* which reaches out towards the future! That would be a moral scepticism, a flaccid pessimism, a renunciation of the higher meaning and value of life. In spite of everything, responsibility for the future is of a provident nature and is capable of actively determining beforehand. No scepticism can free us from that responsibility.

This difficulty inherent in love of the remotest is easily solved, provided its moral value is independent of its success or failure, of whether it attains or misses its objective goal, indeed provided it is also independent of the valuational height of what it aims at. However much man may err and fail in his intended object, the moral quality of his intention can nevertheless be right and possess the higher value. Indeed, it is a distinctive moral quality, in which love of the remotest on this account excels brotherly love and every other virtue: greatness of moral spirit, intensity of spiritual energy, which is required in the taking upon oneself of what is inherently uncertain. The venture is great. Only a deep and mighty faith, permeating a person's whole being, is equal to it. It is a faith of a unique kind, different from trust between man and man; a faith which reaches out to the whole of things and can do no other than stake all it has. It is faith on the grand scale, faith in a higher order, which determines the cosmic meaning of man. When it becomes active and carries out its schemes, its work is of historic import. In a pre-eminent sense the expression "Remove mountains" may apply to it. And this energy is harmonious with a similar feeling—hope, when it is raised to its highest power, the basic feeling of ethical idealism, which bears all things and gladly suffers for an Idea, never despairing: hope, the peculiar assurance which takes hold on one who risks all on a single issue. . . .

BIBLIOGRAPHY

The topic of this anthology might briefly be summarized as follows: What are the moral obligations and responsibilities of those now living to future persons *who may be assumed to exist in the future?* Thus formulated, the issue can be conceptually detached from another issue that is at present attracting considerable attention among moral philosophers: Under what circumstances, and according to what principles, are we obliged and permitted willfully to produce, or refrain from producing, future persons? The first question might simply be called "the issue of the duty to posterity," and the second "the population policy question." Though the issues can be conceptually distinguished with little difficulty, a moment's reflection will indicate that they cannot be easily separated in a careful and perceptive philosophical examination of one or the other topic. On the one hand, persons who "will exist in any case" will surely be affected by the reproductive decision of the present generation. On the other hand, procreative decisions must be based, in part, upon anticipation of conditions in the future "apart from" these decisions. But though the issues are thus combined, philosophical writings on these topics can be distinguished by their *emphases* upon one question or the other. Indeed, such a division must be attempted in order to confine to a manageable space the scope of a paper, or even, as in this case, of an anthology.

This anthology is apparently the only collection in print that contains philosophical papers directed especially and exclusively to the issue of the duty to posterity. (Another collection, tentatively titled *Energy Policy and Obligations to Future Generations* and sponsored by the Center for Philosophy and Public Policy at the University of Maryland, may be published in the near future.) Several papers dealing with the duty to posterity appear in R. I. Sikora's and Brian Barry's anthology *Obligations to Future Generations* (Temple University Press, 1978), although the larger portion of that collection is directed to the issue of population policy. Michael Bayles's anthology *Ethics and Population* (Schenkman, 1976) is also primarily directed to population policy.

The following bibliography is divided according to the two issues as defined above. Of the two, the first list, "The Duty to Posterity," is by far the most complete. These references have been gathered through a careful search of all twelve annual volumes of *The Philosopher's Index,* an examination of the references *within* these and other papers, books and bibliographies, published and unpublished, consultations with professional friends and colleagues, and some degree of good luck. Surely some worthy candidates for this list have evaded my attention, but I venture to guess that there are not very many maverick references. The reader will be interested to note that all but two of these papers were published within the past decade and that the frequency of publication increases as the decade moves toward its close.

The second list, "Population Policy," is selective and contains what I believe to be the most significant recent discussions of the issue. (I suspect that the amount of material written and published on this second topic is somewhat greater than the amount of material dealing primarily with the posterity issue.) The reader who wishes to examine the population question and its literature more closely is advised to look at the essays in Sikora's and Barry's anthology, especially the notes to these essays (unfortunately, the anthology contains no general bibliography), and Bayles's anthology. The number of references increases substantially if one includes papers and books that deal indirectly with population policy by way of the related, and highly controversial, moral issues of abortion and genetic engineering.

I. The Duty to Posterity

Ashby, Eric. "The Search for an Environmental Ethic." In *The Tanner Lectures on Human Values: 1980.* Salt Lake City: University of Utah Press, 1980.

Bandman, Bertram. "Can Future Generations Be Said to Have the Right to Breathe Clean Air?" Eastern Division, American Philosophical Association Symposium, Atlanta, Georgia. 28 December 1973.

Barry, Brian. "As Much and As Good." In *Energy Policy and Future Generations.* Ed. Peter Brown and Douglas MacLean. Tottowa, N.J.: Rowman and Littlefield, forthcoming.

———. "Circumstances of Justice and Future Generations." In *Obligations to Future Generations.* Ed. Brian Barry and R. I. Sikora. Philadelphia: Temple University Press, 1978.

———. "Justice Between Generations." In *Law, Morality and Society.* Ed. P. M. S. Hacker and J. Raz. Oxford: Oxford University Press, 1977.

Barton, Marthalee, and Dwight W. Stevenson, eds. *Technology and Pessimism.* Special issue of *Alternative Futures,* 3:2 (Spring 1980).

Bayles, Michael D. "Contractarian and Population Policies." Unpublished.

———. *Ethics and Population.* Cambridge, Mass.: Schenkman, 1976.

Braaten, Carl E. "Caring for the Future: Where Ethics and Ecology Meet." *Zygon,* 9:4 (December 1974), 311–22.

Brewster, Leonard. "Where Future Generations May Correctly Be Said to Have Rights." Eastern Division, American Philosophical Association Symposium, Atlanta, Ga. 28 December 1973.

Brown, Peter, and Douglas MacLean, eds. *Energy Policy and Future Generations.* Tottowa, N.J.: Rowman and Littlefield, forthcoming.

Cunningham, Robert L. "Ethics, Ecology and the Rights of Future Generations." *Modern Age* (Summer 1975), 260.

Delattre, Edwin. "Rights, Responsibilities, and Future Persons." *Ethics,* 82:2 (April 1972), 254–58.

Doeleman, J. A. "On the Social Rate of Discount." *Environmental Ethics,* 2:1 (Spring 1980), 45–58.

Eckstein, Otto. "Investment Criteria for Economic Development and the Theory of Intertemporal Welfare Economics." *Quarterly Journal of Economics* (February 1957).

Ehrman, Lee. "Genetics and the Right to Plan Future Generations." In *Bioethics and Human Rights: A Reader for Health Professionals.* Ed. Elsie L. Bandman and Bertram Bandman. Boston: Little, Brown, 1978.

Engelhardt, H. Tristram, Jr. "Individuals and Communities, Present and Future: Toward a Morality in a Time of Famine." In *Lifeboat Ethics: The Moral Dilemmas of World Hunger.* Ed. George R. Lucas and Thomas W. Ogletree. New York: Harper and Row, 1976.

English, Jane. "Justice Between Generations." *Philosophical Studies,* 31 (1977), 91–104.

Glover, Jonathan. "How Should We Decide What Sort of World Is Best?" In *Ethics and Problems of the 21st Century.* Ed. K. E. Goodpaster and K. M. Sayre. Notre Dame, Ind.: University of Notre Dame Press, 1979.

Golding, Martin P. "Ethical Issues in Biological Engineering." *UCLA Law Review,* 15:267 (1968), 443–79.

____. "Future Generations, Obligations to." *Encyclopedia of Bioethics,* vol. 2. New York: Macmillan and Free Press, 1978.

Golding, M. P., and N. H. Golding. "Why Preserve Landmarks? A Preliminary Inquiry." In *Ethics and Problems of the 21st Century.* Ed. K. E. Goodpaster and K. M. Sayre. Notre Dame, Ind.: University of Notre Dame Press, 1979.

Goodin, Robert, and Lewis Perelman. "Symposium on Choices in Energy Policy." *Ethics,* 90:3 (April 1980), 391–449.

Goodpaster, K. E., and K. M. Sayre, eds. *Ethics and Problems of the 21st Century.* Notre Dame, Ind.: University of Notre Dame Press, 1979.

Govier, Trudy. "What Should We Do About Future People?" *American Philosophical Quarterly,* 16:2 (April 1979), 105–13.

Green, Ronald M. *Population Growth and Justice: An Examination of Moral Issues Raised by Rapid Population Growth.* Missoula, Mont.: Scholars Press, 1976.

Hare, R. M. "Contrasting Methods of Environmental Planning." In *Ethics and Problems of the 21st Century.* Ed. K. E. Goodpaster and K. M. Sayre. Notre Dame, Ind.: University of Notre Dame Press, 1979.

Hocutt, Claude R. "Whither Our Energy Heritage?" In *Ethics, Free Enterprise, and Public Policy.* Ed. Richard T. De George and Joseph A. Pichler. New York: Oxford University Press, 1978.

Hubin, D. Clayton. "Justice and Future Generations." *Philosophy and Public Affairs,* 6:1 (Fall 1976), 70–83.

———. "The Scope of Justice." *Philosophy and Public Affairs,* 9:1 (Fall 1979), 3–24.

Jonas, Hans. "The Concept of Responsibility: An Inquiry into the Foundations of an Ethics for Our Age." In *Knowledge, Value and Belief.* Ed. H. Tristram Engelhardt, Jr., and Daniel Callahan. Hastings-on-Hudson, N.Y.: Hastings Center, 1977.

———. "Responsibility Today: The Ethics of an Endangered Future." *Social Research,* 43:1 (Spring 1976), 77–97.

Kavka, Gregory. "The Future Individuals Paradox." *Philosophy and Public Affairs* (to appear).

Lappé, Marc. "Genetics and Our Obligations to the Future." In *Bioethics and Human Rights.* Ed. Elsie L. Bandman and Bertram Bandman. Boston: Little, Brown, 1978.

Laslett, Peter. "The Conversation Between the Generations." In *The Proper Study.* Ed. Peter Laslett. Royal Institute of Philosophy Lectures, vol. 4. New York: Macmillan, 1971.

Lee, Donald C. "Some Ethical Decision Criteria with Regard to Procreation." *Environmental Ethics,* 1:1 (Spring 1979), 65–69.

MacIntyre, Alasdair. "Seven Traits for the Future." *Hastings Center Report* (February 1979), 5–7.

MacLean, Douglas. "Do the Unborn Have Rights?" Unpublished.

———. "Energy Policy and Our Obligations to Future Generations." Unpublished. Released through the Center for Philosophy and Public Policy, University of Maryland, April 4, 1979.

———. "A Moral Requirement Regarding the Future." In *Energy Policy and Future Generations.* Ed. Peter Brown and Douglas MacLean. Tottowa, N.J.: Rowman and Littlefield, forthcoming.

Marglin, Stephen. "The Social Rate of Discount and the Optimal Rate of Investment." *Quarterly Journal of Economics* (February 1963), 95–111.

Mishan, E. J. "Economic Criteria for Intergenerational Comparisons." *Futures* (October 1977), 383–403.

Mueller, Dennis C. "Intergenerational Justice and the Social Discount Rate." *Theory and Decision,* 5 (1974), 263–73.

Nagel, Ernest. "Comments on the Presentations of Drs. Ehrman and Lappé." In *Bioethics and Human Rights.* Ed. Elsie L. Bandman and Bertram Bandman. Boston: Little, Brown, 1978.

Namkoong, Gene. "Genetic Resources for Future Generations." Conference on Obligations to Future Generations, University of Delaware. 2–3 December 1977.

Nielsen, Kai. "The Enforcement of Morality and Future Generations." *Philosophia* (Israel), 3:4 (October 1973), 443–48.

Oelschlaeger, Max. "The Entropy Ethic and Responsibility to Future Generations." Unpublished.

Page, Talbot. "Intertemporal Equity (Part 3)" In *Conservation and Economic Efficiency.* Johns Hopkins University Press for Resources for the Future, 1977, pp. 145–215.

Parfit, Derek. "Energy Policy and the Further Future." In *Energy Policy and Future Generations.* Ed. Peter Brown and Douglas MacLean. Tottowa, N.J.: Rowman and Littlefield, forthcoming.

Partridge, Ernest. "Posterity: A Neglected Dimension of Educational Philosophy." *Proceedings of the Philosophy of Education Society,* Thirty-Second Annual Meeting, Vancouver, British Columbia. 10–13 April 1976. Published for the Society by *Educational Theory.* Urbana, Ill.: University of Illinois, 1976.

———. "Rawls and the Duty to Posterity." Ph.D. Dissertation, University of Utah, 1976.

———. "The Rights of Future Generations." Unpublished.

Polak. Fred L. "Responsibility for the Future and the Far Away." *Philosophy Today,* 2 (Spring 1958), 22–28.

———. "Responsibility for the Future." In *Images of the Future: The Twenty-First Century and Beyond.* Ed. Robert Bundy. Buffalo, N.Y.: Prometheus, 1976.

Rawls, John. "Justice Between Generations." Section 44 of *A Theory of Justice.* Cambridge, Mass.: Harvard University Press, 1971.

Richards, David A. J. "Contractarian Theory, Intergenerational Justice, and Energy Policy." In *Energy Policy and Future Generations.* Ed. Peter Brown and Douglas MacLean. Tottowa, N.J.: Rowman and Littlefield, forthcoming.

Rosenbaum, Stuart. "Do Future Generations Have Rights?" Eastern Division, American Philosophical Association Symposium, Atlanta, Ga. 28 December 1973.

Sartorius, Rolf. "Nuclear Fission Power and the Rights of Members of Future Genera-tions." In *Energy Policy and Future Generations*. Ed. Peter Brown and Douglas MacLean. Tottowa, N.J.: Rowman and Littlefield, forthcoming.

―――. "Governmental Regulation and Intergenerational Justice." In *Regulation or Deregulation*. Ed. Tibor R. Machan and M. Bruce Johnson. Urbana, Ill.: University of Illinois Press, forthcoming.

Schwartz, Thomas. "Obligations to Posterity." In *Obligations to Future Generations*. Ed. Brian Barry and R. I. Sikora. Philadelphia: Temple University Press, 1978.

Selk, Eugene E. "Toward an Environmental Ethic: Royce's Theory of Community and Obligation to Future Generations." *Transactions of the C. S. Peirce Society,* 13:4 (Fall 1977), 253–76.

Sikora, R. I., and Brian Barry, eds. "Introduction." *Obligations to Future Generations*. Philadelphia: Temple University Press, 1978.

Skinner, B. F. "The Evolution of a Culture." *Beyond Freedom and Dignity*. New York: Knopf, 1971, chapter 7.

Soble, Alan. "Comments on 'Why Should We Conserve Energy?'" Colloquium Re-sponse, Pacific Division, American Philosophical Association, San Diego, Calif. 23 March 1979.

Steiner, Hillel. "The Rights of Future Generations." In *Energy Policy and Future Gen-erations*. Ed. Peter Brown and Douglas MacLean. Tottowa, N.J.: Rowman and Littlefield, forthcoming.

Sterba, James. "Abortion and Future Generations." *Journal of Philosophy,* 77:7 (July 1980), 424.

Surber, Jere Paul. "History and the Responsibility to Future Generations." *Philosophic Research and Analysis,* 6:12 (Late Winter 1978), 14–20.

―――. "Obligations to Future Generations: Explorations and Problemata." *Journal of Value Inquiry,* 11 (Summer 1977), 104–16.

Williams, Mary B. "Discounting Versus Maximum Sustainable Yield." In *Obligations to Future Generations*. Ed. Brian Barry and R. I. Sikora. Philadelphia: Temple University Press, 1978.

Yanal, Robert J. "Queue-Line Earth." *Metaphilosophy* (to appear).

―――. "Why Should We Conserve Energy?" Pacific Division, American Philosophical Association, San Diego, Calif. 23 March 1979.

II. Population Policy

Anglin, William. "In Defense of the Potentiality Principle." In *Obligations to Future Generations*. Ed. Brian Barry and R. I. Sikora. Philadelphia: Temple University Press, 1978.

―――. "The Repugnant Conclusion." *Canadian Journal of Philosophy,* 7:4 (1977), 745–54.

Bayles, Michael D. "Harm to the Unconceived." *Philosophy and Public Affairs,* 5:3 (Spring 1976), 292–304.

―――. "Limits to a Right to Procreate." In *Ethics and Population*. Ed. Michael D. Bayles. Cambridge, Mass.: Schenkman, 1976.

―――. "Moral Philosophy and Population Issues." In *Ethics and Population*. Ed. Michael D. Bayles. Cambridge, Mass.: Schenkman, 1976.

Bennett, Jonathan. "On Maximizing Happiness." In *Obligations to Future Generations*. Ed. Brian Barry and R. I. Sikora. Philadelphia: Temple University Press, 1978.

Callahan, Daniel. "Population and Human Survival." In *The Population Crisis and Moral Responsibility.* Ed. J. Philip Wogaman. Washington, D.C.: Public Affairs Press, 1973.

Dyck, Arthur J. "Alternative Views of Moral Principles in Population Policy." *BioScience,* 27:4 (April 1977), 272–76.

———. "Population Policies and Ethical Acceptability." In *The American Population Debate.* Ed. Daniel Callahan. New York: Doubleday, 1971.

Feinberg, Joel. "Is There a Right to Be Born?" In *Understanding Moral Philosophy.* Ed. James Rachels. Encino, Calif.: Dickenson, 1976.

Golding, Martin P., and Naomi H. Golding. "Ethical and Value Issues in Population Limitation and Distribution in the United States." *Vanderbilt Law Review,* 24 (1971), 495–523.

Hare, R. M. "Abortion and the Golden Rule." *Philosophy and Public Affairs,* 4:3 (Spring 1975), 201–22.

Kavka, Gregory S. "Rawls on Average and Total Utility." *Philosophical Studies,* 27 (1975), 237–253.

Miller, Frank, and Rolf Sartorius. "Population Policy and Public Goods." *Philosophy and Public Affairs,* 8:2 (Winter 1979), 148–174.

Narveson, Jan. "Future People and Us." In *Obligations to Future Generations.* Ed. Brian Barry and R. I. Sikora. Philadelphia: Temple University Press, 1978.

———. "Moral Problems of Population." In *Ethics and Population.* Ed. Michael D. Bayles. Cambridge, Mass.: Schenkman, 1976.

———. "Semantics, Future Generations, and the Abortion Problem: Comments on a Fallacious Case Against the Morality of Abortion." *Social Theory and Practice,* 3:4 (Fall 1974), 461–85.

———. "Utilitarianism and New Generations." *Mind,* 76 (1967), 62–72.

Parfit, Derek. "On Doing the Best for Our Children." In *Ethics and Population.* Ed. Michael D. Bayles. Cambridge, Mass.: Schenkman, 1976.

———. "Rights, Interests and Possible People." In *Moral Problems in Medicine.* Ed. Samuel Gorovitz, et al. Englewood Cliffs, N.J.: Prentice-Hall, 1976.

Partridge, Ernest. "To Be or Not to Be: That is the Paradox." Western Division, American Philosophical Association, Detroit, Mich., April 1980.

Scott, Robert, Jr. "Environmental Ethics and Obligations to Future Generations." In *Obligations to Future Generations.* Ed. Brian Barry and R. I. Sikora. Philadelphia: Temple University Press, 1978.

Sikora, R. I. "Is It Wrong to Prevent the Existence of Future Generations." In *Obligations to Future Generations.* Ed. Brian Barry and R. I. Sikora. Philadelphia: Temple University Press, 1978.

———. "Utilitarianism, Supererogation and Future Generations." *Canadian Journal of Philosophy,* 9:3 (September 1979), 461–66.

Sikora, R. I., and Brian Barry, eds. *Obligations to Future Generations.* Philadelphia: Temple University Press, 1978.

Singer, Peter. "Anglin on the Obligation to Create Extra People." *Canadian Journal of Philosophy,* 7:3 (September 1978), 583–85.

———. "A Utilitarian Population Principle." In *Ethics and Population.* Ed. Michael D. Bayles. Cambridge, Mass.: Schenkman, 1976.

Sprigge, Timothy L. S. "Professor Narveson's Utilitarianism." *Inquiry,* 11 (Autumn 1968), 332–48.

Stearns, J. Brenton. "Ecology and the Indefinite Unborn." *Monist,* 56:4 (October 1972), 612–25.

Sterba, James P. "Abortion and Future Generations." *Journal of Philosophy,* 77:7 (July 1980), 424–40.

Sumner, L. W. "Classical Utilitarianism and the Population Optimum." In *Obligations to Future Generations.* Ed. Brian Barry and R. I. Sikora. Philadelphia: Temple University Press, 1978.

Wogaman, J. Philip, ed. *The Population Crisis and Moral Responsibility.* Washington, D.C.: Public Affairs Press, 1973.

CONTRIBUTORS

ANNETTE BAIER, who was born in New Zealand, is a graduate of Otago and Oxford universities. She has taught philosophy at Aberdeen, Auckland, Sydney, and Carnegie-Mellon universities and is currently professor of philosophy at the University of Pittsburgh. Her work is mainly in the philosophy of mind and in Hume's philosophy of mind and society.

MICHAEL D. BAYLES is director of the Westminster Institute for Ethics and Human Values in London and Canada. Among his publications are *Ethics and Population,* which he edited (1976), and *Morality and Population Policy* (forthcoming).

DANIEL CALLAHAN is the founder and director of the Hastings Institute of Society, Ethics and the Life Sciences, Hastings-on-Hudson, New York. He received his Ph.D. in philosophy from Harvard. He is the author or editor of nineteen books and over 250 articles. His most recent book is the *Tyranny of Survival.*

RICHARD T. DE GEORGE is University Distinguished Professor of Philosophy and co-director of the Center for Humanistic Studies at the University of Kansas. He is author or editor of eleven books, including *Ethics, Free Enterprise and Public Policy.*

THOMAS SIEGER DERR is professor of religion at Smith College and consultant to the Department on Church and Society and the Commission on Faith and Order of the World Council of Churches. He received his M.Div. from Union Theological Seminary and his Ph.D. from Columbia University.

JOEL FEINBERG is professor of philosophy at the University of Arizona. He holds a Ph.D. from the University of Michigan and has taught at Brown, Princeton, UCLA, and Rockefeller universities. He is the author of *Doing and*

317

Deserving (1970), *Social Philosophy* (1973), and numerous significant papers in moral, social, and legal philosophy.

MARTIN P. GOLDING, a graduate of UCLA, received his doctorate from Columbia University. He taught at Columbia and John Jay College of Criminal Justice and is now professor of philosophy at Duke University. He is the author of *Philosophy of Law* and articles in legal and philosophical journals.

RONALD M. GREEN is associate professor in the Department of Religion at Dartmouth College. He received his Ph.D. from Harvard and is the author of a number of articles and two books, *Population Growth and Justice* (1975) and *Religious Reason* (1978).

GARRETT HARDIN is professor emeritus of human ecology at the University of California, Santa Barbara. He is the author of numerous articles and books, including *Nature and Man's Fate, Exploring New Ethics for Survival,* and *Stalking the Wild Taboo.* His paper "The Tragedy of the Commons" (1968) has been widely reprinted.

NICOLAI HARTMANN (1882–1950) was a prominent German realist philosopher. Born in Riga, Latvia, he taught at Marburg, Cologne, Berlin, and Göttingen. He published works in epistemology, metaphysics, and ethics. His three-volume work, *Ethics,* was published in 1926 (English edition, 1932).

CHARLES HARTSHORNE is emeritus professor at the University of Texas, Austin. Born in 1897, he was educated at Haverford, Harvard (Ph.D.), and two German universities and taught philosophy at Harvard, Chicago, Frankfurt, Melbourne, Emory, Washington, Kyoto, Banaras, Louvain, and Colorado College. He is the author of many books in philosophy and one in ornithology.

ROBERT L. HEILBRONER is the author of many well-known books on economics, beginning with *The Worldly Philosophers* and including his most recent book, *Marxism: For and Against.* He is chairman and Norman Thomas Professor of Economics of the Graduate Faculty's Department of Economics, New School for Social Research, and has lectured widely in many universities.

HANS JONAS is professor emeritus of philosophy at the New School for Social Research. He has taught at several universities, including Princeton, Harvard, Columbia, and the University of California, Riverside. He is the author of numerous papers and books in English and German.

HARDY JONES is associate professor of philosophy at the University of Nebraska–Lincoln. He is a Texan who has studied at Baylor University and the University of Wisconsin. He has published *Kant's Principle of Personality* and several philosophical papers on moral and social topics.

GREGORY KAVKA received his Ph.D. from the University of Michigan and is currently associate professor of philosophy at the University of California, Irvine, where he teaches political philosophy and ethics.

RUTH MACKLIN is associate for behavioral studies at the Hastings Center and is also associate clinical professor of community health at Albert Einstein College of Medicine. She works mainly in the area of applied ethics and has contributed to professional journals in philosophy, psychiatry, and law.

ERNEST PARTRIDGE is a visiting associate professor of environmental studies at the University of California, Santa Barbara, and has taught philosophy at Hunter College and Weber State College. He received his Ph.D. from the University of Utah and is now at work on a text in environmental ethics and an original work dealing with the posterity issue.

JOHN PASSMORE is professor of philosophy, Research School of Social Sciences, Australian National University. He is the author of many articles and books, including *A Hundred Years of Philosophy* (1968), *Man's Responsibility for Nature* (1974), and *Science and Its Critics* (1978).

GALEN K. PLETCHER is associate professor of philosophical studies, Southern Illinois University at Edwardsville. His Ph.D. is from the University of Michigan, and he has publications on such topics as ethics, philosophy of religion, and mystical experience.

HOLMES ROLSTON III is professor of philosophy at Colorado State University, where he teaches environmental ethics. His research interests and publications are concentrated on philosophical, religious, and scientific concepts of nature. He is associate editor of *Environmental Ethics*.

RICHARD ROUTLEY is senior fellow in philosophy at the Australian National University and works academically mainly in logic and metaphysics but has a long-standing concern with ethics. Over the past several years a good deal of his spare time has been taken up with work on practical conservation issues, alternative life-styles, and social theory.

VAL ROUTLEY is active in environmental affairs and field biology and frequently cooperates on philosophical papers with Richard Routley.

THOMAS H. THOMPSON is professor of philosophy and head of the Department of Philosophy and Religion at the University of Northern Iowa in Cedar Falls. His reviews and articles have appeared in the *North American Review* and *Alternative Futures*.

MARY ANNE WARREN received her Ph.D. in philosophy from the University of California at Berkeley in 1974 and currently teaches philosophy at San Francisco State University. She has published several papers in the field of moral philosophy.

"While our ability to affect the future is immense, our ability to foresee the results of our environmental interventions is not. But we are not totally blind to the consequences of the technical ventures now at work or contemplated. Our age has witnessed not only a revolution in power but also a revolution in communications and information processing. From satellites and worldwide recording and transmitting stations, we monitor the pulse of the planetary machine: the solar input, the hydrological and nutrient cycles, the climatic changes, the patterns of land use, and so on. We know what is happening; and, with new developments in computer modeling of complex integrated functions, we may be able to discover the graver hazards that lie in the paths ahead, both for us and for our posterity. Furthermore, the very enormity of the changes that are projected or imminent may render a finely tuned science of forecasting somewhat irrelevant. For whatever their tastes in music and poetry, or whatever their preferences in sports and other amusements, our descendants will need croplands and watersheds to supply their food and water, and they will need to be free of ultraviolet and nuclear radiation. And it is **these** necessities of future life and welfare that are in grave jeopardy **now,** and we know this **now.**" (from the Introduction)